_____

*How to Make Your Shrinking Salary
Support You in Style for the
Rest of Your Life*

How to Make Your Shrinking Salary Support You in Style

— *for* —

the Rest of Your Life

MICHAEL K. EVANS

Random House New York

Grateful acknowledgment is made to *The Wall Street Journal* for permission to reprint
excerpts from "Here's a Guarantee You Can't 'Always' Take to the Bank" by Randall
Smith from the March 17, 1989, issue of *The Wall Street Journal*. Copyright © 1989
Dow Jones & Company, Inc. All rights reserved worldwide. Reprinted by permission
of *The Wall Street Journal*.

Library of Congress Cataloging-in-Publication Data
Evans, Michael K.
How to make your shrinking salary support you in style for the
rest of your life / by Michael K. Evans.
p.   cm.
Includes index.
ISBN 0-394-58263-2
1. Finance, Personal.   2. Investments.   I. Title.
HG179.E88   1991   332.024—dc20   90-52929

Manufactured in the United States of America
24689753
First Edition

To my finest investments:
Ellen, David, and Rebecca

Preface

The 1980s brought forth a surfeit of money-management and investment-advice books suggesting that becoming wealthy was very simple: all you had to do was Think Positive and Follow a Few Simple Rules—which were conveniently contained in the book you were about to purchase.

Of course it was never that simple, and the end of the 1980s showed just how bankrupt such theories really are. Only one out of every thousand people really have enough money to enjoy life in the style they want—but the vast majority of the other 999 would like to be in that position. If so many people would like to accomplish this goal but so few actually do, it must be difficult.

That is the real message of this book: becoming wealthy is hard, not easy. However, it can be done. In the following pages, I'll offer you some of the recipes for success that have worked well for me. These rules are not carved in stone, because the financial world is constantly changing over time. But to become wealthy, certain factors are invariant. You must save early and often, minimize your taxes, avoid scams, and fine-tune your investment philosophy in line with upheavals in world financial markets.

If you're looking for a panacea—how to become wealthy by following a few simple rules without taking any risks—you won't find it here. But if you realize the road to wealth is paved with intelligent financial planning, the following pages should provide enough valuable hints to move you from the ranks of the 99.9% who are struggling to the 0.1% at the top of the financial pyramid.

Acknowledgments

First and foremost, I would like to thank Art Cooper, editor-in-chief of *GQ* magazine, for suggesting this book over one of our occasional lunches at the Four Seasons. If he had not invited me to write the Money column for *GQ*, this book would never have reached fruition. Editors Martin Beiser and Eliot Kaplan worked with me on those columns, and provided numerous helpful and timely suggestions, many of which are incorporated in this book.

Susan Carroll, as always, proved essential in preparing this manuscript on a timely basis; without her usual bravura performance of administrative talent, this book would not have been completed.

I would also like to thank senior editor Becky Saletan and the capable staff at Random House for shepherding this manuscript into its final form; their helpful comments, pleasant demeanor, and forbearance are all appreciated.

Finally, to my colleagues at Evans Economics and Evans Investment Advisors who assisted me with the collection of this material, my heartfelt appreciation.

Contents

Introduction

How would you like to make a million dollars a year?

Visions of stately mansions, yachts, five-star vacations, and luxurious retirement years dangle before your eyes. But of course it all depends on what that million dollars will buy.

If you are 25 now, by the time your children retire they will be earning an average of more than $1 million per year. But in fact they will be worse off than you are right now, with the average annual salary at $26,500. Higher inflation and taxes will gobble up that entire gain—and more.

Does all this sound farfetched?

Just consider that 75 years ago, the annual average wage was $633 a year. That's right, per year. Sixty years ago it was $1,400 a year, and 45 years ago, right after World War II ended, it was $2,189 a year. Most of the gains made since then have been due to inflation.

Furthermore, the tax bite is much larger now. The government—federal, state, and local—now takes 36 cents out of every dollar that the average person earns. Some of this is hidden; you don't see it. But you do pay it. Social Security taxes account for 15 cents of every dollar: You pay half, and your employer pays half, but it's all really coming out of your pocket. Income taxes take another 13 cents, sales taxes 5 cents, and real estate taxes 3 cents out of every dollar. Before World War II, taxes took only about 10 cents per dollar.

So if you've been feeling poorer lately in spite of a paycheck that increases steadily every year, welcome to the party.

This trend can only accelerate in the future. Inflation has averaged 5 percent per year ever since 1945. Some Pollyannas think we've come up with a cure just because the rise halted temporarily during the 1980s. But it took the worst recession in 50 years and a once-in-a-lifetime 50 percent drop in oil prices to accomplish that. Under normal circumstances, the rate of inflation will just keep inching higher.

The federal budget deficit for fiscal year 1990 was almost $200 billion—after our elected representatives passed a bill four years earlier saying it would decrease to $36 billion. And how did the best and the brightest minds propose to narrow that gap? Why, by raising taxes. Many were disgusted, but few were shocked.

In addition, the gains in productivity and the standard of living that fueled growth from 1945 to 1973 have come to a standstill. Since then, the average wage rate, adjusted for inflation, has fallen 10 percent. If you're better off, it's because you switched jobs or got a big promotion—or because your spouse went to work. This trend isn't about to change. Our country spends so much of its income paying back past debts that there isn't enough money left for new investments that would raise productivity.

What does all this mean for you?

First, you can no longer get rich just by working hard. No matter how much your salary rises, inflation and taxes will negate all your hard-earned gains. By the time wages rise to $1 million a year, inflation will have increased 40-fold.

Second, in order to become wealthy, you must save early and often. If you don't start young, you'll make it much harder on yourself.

Third, although inflation will rob your savings of their earning power if you leave them in the bank, you can make inflation work in your favor by buying assets that appreciate faster than inflation. If you can leverage them, so much the better.

Fourth, although tax rates will continue to increase in future generations, you can use the remaining advantages of the tax law to shelter your earnings. In fact, unless you use tax-sheltered investments, it will be almost impossible to become wealthy.

Fifth, the road to riches usually means earning an above-average rate of return on your assets. That means avoiding money market funds and bonds, and investing in stocks and real estate.

Higher inflation and higher taxes are inevitable. Allowing them to reduce your standard of living and accumulation of wealth isn't. I'll show you how to overcome these handicaps and accumulate at least $10 million by the time you retire. To accomplish that goal, here's what you need to do:

1. Start saving 10 percent of your after-tax income right now, and don't backtrack.
2. Use the current tax laws to their best advantage.
3. Earn 12 percent per year on your money—the average rate of return for stocks over the past 50 years.

Of course, even $10 million in 40 years won't be worth what it's worth today. But you will have enjoyed an enviable lifestyle, your retirement years will be golden, and your heirs will always be well provided for. Just follow those three simple rules. In this book, I'll explain how to accomplish that.

BASIC INVESTMENT

CONCEPTS

Chapter 1

Working Hard
Is Not Enough

You can no longer get rich just by working hard.

From the end of World War II until 1973, the standard of living increased fairly steadily, rising 2 percent to 3 percent per year. As a result, each generation was roughly twice as well off as the previous one had been. Young adults could rely on the fact that they would be better off than their parents, and their children would in turn be better off than they were. That permitted planning for upward mobility—a college education for the kids, a better place to live, more frequent vacations, and a second home. Furthermore, some of the extra income could be set aside and invested, leading to retirement in comfort and dignity. Prices were rising, but incomes were rising faster.

THE SHRINKING STANDARD OF LIVING

All that changed after 1973. For a while, people blamed the energy crises and double-digit inflation, but during the 1980s, energy prices declined and inflation returned to normal—but the standard of living continued to decline. During the 1970s, bracket creep pushed workers into higher tax brackets whenever they got a raise, making the government the big winner from inflation. But starting in 1985, indexation of the tax schedule terminated the government's ill-gotten gains from higher inflation. Yet even during the Reagan administration, when 17 million new jobs were created and the economy returned to full employment, the real value of the average paycheck continued to shrink. Wages routinely rose more slowly than did prices, a trend that shows every sign of continuing through the 1990s.

Many families managed to sidestep this reduction in real wages by adding a second breadwinner. In 1989, 74 percent of all women between 25 and 54 were part of the labor force, compared with only 43 percent in 1962. But that's a one-time solution, and doesn't offset the continuing drumbeat of higher inflation.

The only way to beat the long-term decline in the value of your paycheck is to save, invest, and let your assets grow. Unless you have some unique talent or skill, labor income alone will no longer provide financial stability and security. Furthermore, you won't be able to continue your current standard of living in the years ahead unless you begin saving now, because your paycheck will keep buying less in the future.

Prices of Luxury Items Rise Even Faster than Inflation

Not only is inflation rising faster than wages, but the prices of those desirable expensive items are rising even faster than the overall rate of inflation. Food prices rise at about the same rate as inflation, but restaurant meals—particularly at four-star establishments—rise faster. The cost of those humdrum vacations by car won't rise faster than inflation, but if you haven't recently flown first-class to a deluxe resort, the bill may send you into shock. The cost of Mercedeses and BMWs rises much faster than that of Fords, and not just because the German mark is stronger than the dollar. Try pricing top-of-the-line Jaguars: $4,000 in 1948, $65,000 now, even though the British pound is worth less than half as many dollars now as it was in 1948.

Housing prices generally outpace inflation in any case, but prices in desirable areas rise much faster. Houses in Georgetown (Washington, D.C.) that sold for less than $10,000 shortly before World War II now routinely sell for more than $1 million. Does that mean that in another 50 years these same houses will be selling for $100 million? Hardly, since 50 years ago the economy was still in a depression, Washington was a small town, and Georgetown, if not a slum, certainly wasn't the high-rent district. But it isn't only Washington, D.C., prices that have exploded. Check the prices of Park Avenue condos in Manhattan or of Beverly Hills mansions, and you'll find that at their recent peak, these prices had also appreciated 100-fold since the end of World War II. And while this phenomenal rate of increase has taken a breather, over the long run those prices will continue to outpace the overall rate of inflation.

The most daunting challenge many families face is how to pay for their children's college education, particularly at those exclusive—or is it just overpriced—Ivy League schools, where costs continue to rise *twice* as fast as inflation. When I graduated from Brown University in 1960, the total bill for the year was $2,000. My son graduated in 1989, and the bill for his last year was $20,000. That's a 10-fold increase over a 29-year period, or more than 8 percent per year during a time when the inflation rate averaged 5 percent per year.

Even worse, college costs kept rising 8 percent per year during the 1980s, even when inflation declined to 4 percent. If the same rate of increase continues, in 2021 the bill will be a neck-snapping $250,000 per year—a cool $1 million for that prestigious education. Of course that will be in 2021 dollars, which won't be worth as much, but even after adjusting for inflation, the sums are prodigious. In today's dollars, the tab will be $40,000 per year—not something that most families can handle out of their annual income, especially with two or more children.

So if you're just embarking on your career now, remember that in 30 years, the house you want, the prestigious college education for your children, and the vacations you plan to enjoy will all cost roughly twice as much in inflation-adjusted dollars as they do today. Unless you begin saving now, you'll be priced out of the market. The luxury goods and services will be snapped up by those wealthy individuals who were either born with a silver spoon in their mouths, won the lottery—or got their act together and saved enough to enjoy life instead of watching it drift away from them.

HOW MUCH SHOULD YOU SAVE?

Most people worry about eating, paying the rent, and putting some clothes on their backs before they even begin to think about saving. However, as soon as you can procure the basic necessities of life and have a little something left over, it's time to plan ahead and accumulate enough money for a comfortable house in a desirable location, a college education for the children, and a retirement income that will allow you to enjoy the same lifestyle.

Throughout this book, I'll assume that you can begin to think seriously about saving when your household income reaches $50,000 per year and you can save 10 percent of your after-tax income, which at $50,000 per year is approximately $300 a month.

Of course, $50,000 doesn't mean the same thing to everyone. It buys a lot more house in Louisville than it does in San Francisco, and it goes a lot farther for just one person than for husband, wife, and three children. For that matter, very few families have precisely the same income stream or expense requirements.

That's why many money-management books suggest that you sit down with a work sheet, figure out all your regular weekly or monthly expenses, estimate what you will probably need for emergencies, the down payment and mortgage for your house, college education for the children, and retirement. Then calculate how much you should save.

Designing a coherent financial plan isn't a bad idea, of course, but my experience with that approach is that somehow, there are always "unexpected" expenses that materialize out of the blue, and the saving usually gets postponed indefinitely. That's one reason there aren't more millionaires. So I recommend a different approach. Save 10 percent of your after-tax income—and write that check first, not last. Start the saving habit right now, and stick to it.

Unlimited Wants, Limited Means

Of course, emergencies will surface. Many people complain that they can't save any of their income—that it's hard enough just to make ends meet. Then there's always some emergency: the car transmission sounds like a meat grinder, Kevin needs orthodontia, the roof leaks like a sieve, insurance rates just rose 25 percent.

I'll concede that most Americans don't save anything except the equity buildup in their houses and their company-sponsored pension plans. Then again, most Americans aren't rich. However, the percentage of income that individuals and families save has *no relationship* to their average level of income. Some relatively poor people manage to put money aside every year, while some millionaires not only fail to increase their assets but deplete sizable inheritances as well. Just remember that for all those reasons why you can't save, there are many people in this country with the same income, the same number of dependents, and the same expenses who manage to save and increase their wealth every year. Of course it's easier to save on a $500,000 annual income than on a $50,000 one. But if you don't start now, you'll be mired in the middle-class rut for the rest of your life. And with prices rising faster than wages, that rut can only get deeper and deeper.

When the inevitable emergencies do arise, borrow from yourself, so to speak. Act as if you borrowed the money from some financial institution, and pay it back on a regular schedule. There will be times when it would be more fun to splurge, and I'm not suggesting that everyone is perfect all the time. However, if you can't commit yourself to saving 10 percent of your after-tax income on a regular basis, you probably won't save much at all.

You can buy a new Ford Escort every four years on installment payments, or you can drive a used car for a few years and a Mercedes ever after. You can take an inexpensive vacation now and sail the Riviera later. If you're in your twenties or even early thirties, it's all too easy to claim that you're still building up your stock of household assets and will begin to save later, when there aren't so many pressing needs for your cash. "Later" usually turns out to be about ten years before retirement, and by that time even a genius couldn't make you rich.

With an income of $50,000, you pay an average of about $6,000 per year in federal income taxes; of course, the precise amount depends on the size of your deductions and exemptions. The part of Social Security you pay takes about another $4,000, and state and local taxes (including sales and property taxes) will take about another $4,000; obviously this item varies greatly according to locality. In other words, about $14,000 of your $50,000 income is extracted by the various tax authorities before you get your hands on it, leaving an after-tax income of $36,000, or $3,000 per month. You should save 10 percent of that. And it should definitely be placed in a tax-deferred investment so you don't have to pay taxes on the gains every year.

Some of you may object that you can't put $3,600 per year into a tax-deferred investment since the government chopped IRAs off at the knees. Not so. There are many different ways to get around this, and they'll be discussed in detail later. These loopholes include a company-sponsored pension plan, real estate, or variable life insurance. In almost all cases, finding a suitable tax-deferred investment plan will be the least of your worries. Finding the money to save in the first place will be much more difficult.

NO FREE LUNCH . . . AND
NO WEALTH WITHOUT RISK

Putting aside money for saving is certainly necessary if you want to accumulate wealth, but it's just the first step. Putting your funds in the bank or money market fund simply won't do the trick. After inflation and taxes take their share, the real value of your investment won't increase at all. From 1983 through 1989, inflation averaged about 4 percent per year. Over that same period, the average rate paid on a CD or money market fund was about 7 percent. The federal government takes about 33 percent of the interest income, and the state and local governments generally take another 5 percent or so, depending on where you live. That means that for every 7 cents earned per dollar of investment, the government ends up with almost 3 cents. Inflation takes another 4 cents, which doesn't leave you, the investor, much to write home about.

All other forms of investment involve some risk of principal. Nobody except the banker ever got rich by leaving his money in the bank. You have to decide what you want out of life—and whether you're willing to accept the inevitable fact that some of your investment decisions will be wrong in order to amass substantial wealth.

Some investment gurus will try to convince you that they accumulated great wealth by making the right decisions all the time. That's garbage. Let me give you one example. Any investor who only knew the *direction* in which the stock market would move each month—without having any idea of which stocks to buy—could earn an average of 60 percent per year on his money. Over a 40-year period, a $1,000 investment would grow to $150 *billion*. Not even the fabled oil sheikhs have anywhere near that amount of money. Sultan Haji Hassan al-Bolkiah, ruler of Brunei, is worth "only" $25 billion. The richest American, Sam Walton, together with his family, is listed at a paltry $9 billion. Obviously no one can predict the direction of the market all the time, let alone which stocks will rise the most.

Even the best investment managers make mistakes, and the better they are, the more willing they are to admit it. But they don't get maudlin about it; they learn from their mistakes and move on to more profitable investments the next time. You should, too.

However, not everyone can tolerate the same amount of risk.

Risk and Reward—Always a Trade-off

Some people can drop $10,000 on a turn of the futures market as non-chalantly as they go shopping at the supermarket. Others spend days worrying about what they did wrong if the price of their 100 shares of Associated Xygots drops from 26¾ to 24½. Some people feel at ease buying on margin; others can't sleep at night. Some feel that a steady 12 percent gain, year in and year out, in the stock market is acceptable; others sneer at anything less than 20 percent.

I'm not going to try and talk you into accepting the kind of risk that's beyond your comfort level. However—and this is important—*there is always a trade-off between risk and return*. Anyone who is determined to play it safe must realize that he or she will receive a lower rate of return than someone who's willing to take greater risks. Pretending it's possible to accumulate wealth without risk may make certain authors and publishers rich, but it will only leave you poorer.

That doesn't mean you should take foolish risks, or take risks where the odds are against you. But earning a high enough rate of return to become wealthy does mean choosing a variety of investments and switching among them as the economic climate changes.

Of course you have to put aside money for the groceries, the car payments, and the mortgage. Anyone who risks that money needs to turn himself in to Gamblers Anonymous. But once your income has reached the point where you can save $300 per month, you should apportion your investment among the various types of investments, rated by risk, to balance the higher rate of return with the highest risk level you can comfortably tolerate. I've grouped the broad panoply of investments into four major classifications, each with its own risk characteristics.

1. Absolute security of principal. This means bank accounts insured by the federal government, Treasury bills, and money market funds that invest in insured CDs. You can't lose a penny of your original investment—in nominal terms. The trouble is that after inflation and taxes, you don't make a penny in real terms. An absolute guarantee on your principal provides no protection at all against inflation.

Some people put Treasury bonds in the no-risk category, but be careful. While you will always get all your money back when the bond matures, higher interest rates could reduce the value of that bond by as much as 30 to 40 percent in the interim years. It happened during the early 1980s. If you needed the money or wanted to switch to another type of investment, you faced a staggering loss.

2. Your house. Unless you plan to spend the rest of your life changing locations every three years or less, owning your own home should be the cornerstone of your investment philosophy. It is possible to lose money on a house—some people who bought Houston real estate in 1981 will be glad to tell you about it—but if you hold it for five years or more, losses occur less than 1 percent of the time. You already know to buy in appreciating neighborhoods, but not the most expensive house on the block. As long as you keep your eyes open and pay fair market value, your home will be a high-quality investment over the long run.

3. The stock market. The market has returned an average of 12 percent per year—capital gains plus dividends—over the past 45 years. Obviously this doesn't mean that it returns 12 percent *every* year. The stock market fell over 20 percent on October 19, 1987, and many so-called growth stocks plunged a lot more. But on the other hand, long-term traders weren't hurt at all. Suppose you had bought stocks on January 1, 1987, when the Dow Jones Industrial Average (Dow) was at 1900, gone to sleep for two years, and woken up on December 31, 1988, when the Dow was at 2200. Your capital would have increased 16 percent—plus an extra 8 percent from dividends—during a period when some financial gurus were claiming that the world was absolutely, positively coming to an end.

The stock market is certainly not the only place to invest your money. Often it isn't even the right place. The best way to accumulate wealth is *not* through a buy-and-hold strategy. However, if you purchase stocks with cash (not on margin), stick with high-quality issues, and don't get discouraged and sell out at the bottom, the long-term rate of return will indeed be much higher than it is on riskless assets. Buying stocks isn't a risky strategy in the long run, in spite of an occasional Black Monday. But it does require moving your money out of the market every so often.

If you want to read "How to Survive the Coming Financial Holocaust" or other such doomsday titles because you enjoy comedy, that's fine. But as serious investment guides, they're less than useless. Ask anyone who bought gold in 1980 at $800 an ounce and now finds that it's worth only half as much, while the stock market tripled over the same period.

4. Speculative investments. This is where astute investors make above-average returns—but with higher risks to match. These investments can be grouped into three major subgroups. First, *riskier stock market strategies*: secondary issues, warrants, buying on margin, and market timing. Second, *options and futures* in different markets. Third, *starting your own business*.

The first two are generally on everyone's risky investment list, but not the third. Yet starting your own business is both very risky and potentially very rewarding, and you have more control than you would in the financial markets. No mean-spirited broker will ever give you a margin call on your own business, although if you've borrowed money, a banker might.

Four out of five original ventures don't make it past the first few years, so it's no bed of roses. On the other hand, many of the truly great fortunes in America were built by entrepreneurs who had the vision to start their own companies. Starting my own company in 1970 and selling it to the

Chase Manhattan Bank for $2.5 million in 1979 was clearly the best investment I ever made—even taking into account all the other companies I started that never got off the ground.

Some investment advisers will tell you to shun risky investments; if you want to gamble, go to the track. Certainly, plunking your money down where the odds are known to be against the investor from the start makes no sense at all. However, some of these risky ventures have very high expected rates of return to accompany that high risk. Just remember, the capital markets are large enough that you, the individual investor, aren't going to discover some high-yielding asset that doesn't involve greater risk.

There's always some trade-off between risk and return. The lower the risk, the lower the return. The higher the risk, the higher the return *on average*—but your investment might turn out to be below average.

Assessing Your Own Level of Risk: The One-Sentence Test

That's why you have to know yourself and determine ahead of time how much your stomach churns when your investment drops 50 percent in value, or even gets wiped out completely. Only one out of five players in risky investments ever makes any money—about the same odds, it turns out, for starting your own business—but many who win become millionaires many times over.

Ask yourself the following question. Suppose you have the chance to invest $10,000. A year later, there is a 20 percent chance you'll have $100,000 and an 80 percent chance you'll have nothing. Will you take the risk? If the answer is no, stick to low-risk investments.

I'll assume that since you're reading this book, you want something more out of life than leaving your money in the bank and earning 0 percent after inflation and taxes. In later chapters, I'll present a menu of alternative investments, showing how much you can earn per year and during your productive lifetime by choosing various alternatives. Then I'll discuss various investment strategies for different financial objectives and different degrees of risk. Just remember, accumulating and preserving wealth isn't easy. If it were, more people would succeed at it.

Chapter 2

The Miracle of
Compound Interest

How do people get to be billionaires?

Some Discover Oil in their backyards. Or receive Inside Information on the stock market (before they started shipping those types off to the hoosegow). Or Win the Lottery on a 10-million-to-1 shot. Yet even if these kinds of events really did occur as often as the news suggests, such windfalls would represent only a tiny proportion of the Very Rich in this country. While some of the centimillionaires started life with a fairly decent nest egg, most of them made their money by saving and investing it at above-average rates of return. They let the Miracle of Compound Interest do most of the work for them.

Here's my pitch. Just set aside $300 a month starting at age 25, earn 25 percent on your investment every year, and by the time you're 75, you'll have more than a billion dollars—$1.26 billion, to be exact, but I'm allowing for a bad month every now and then.

That's right. Set aside a grand total of $180,000 in savings over your lifetime, and you end up with $1,260,000,000—7,000 times your original investment. This is not a wild exaggeration. Neither is it a pie-in-the-sky promise. It is plain, simple arithmetic. But it still seems hard to believe. After all, we all know lots of people who set aside $300, $3,000, or maybe even $30,000 to invest—but virtually none of them turn out to be billionaires.

Of course, there is a tremendous difference between saving $300 each and every month and saving $300 every once in a while.

Furthermore, you should start early. Those who start at age 40 instead of at age 25 will only end up with $35.5 million—although that's not peanuts either.

Third, a 25 percent annual rate of return, achieved year in and year out, is a tremendous accomplishment. It's possible to do even better; some people become billionaires before they reach 75. But the average investor, or investment manager, earns less than half that rate.

SAVE EARLY AND OFTEN

These, then, are my secrets to success: Save often. Start early. And earn an above-average rate of return.

Maybe this sounds like a parody of the oldest chestnut of them all: Buy Low, Sell High. On the other hand, you certainly won't get rich if you don't follow these three simple rules.

Remember: Because of inflation and the shrinking purchasing power of the dollar, a million dollars no longer buys what it used to. One million dollars in assets isn't rich anymore. Here's my scale:

$3 million will provide you with whatever you need to live in comfort,

$5 million provides the margin for an occasional true luxury, and

$10 million means you're rich—the equivalent of the old "millionaire" before inflation and taxes emasculated the meaning of a million dollars.

In 1989, over 1 million adult individuals and families—approximately 1 percent of the total number of taxpayers—had total assets of over $1 million, including the equity in their homes and their pension plans. How did they do it?

Some inherited their wealth. Others benefited from some major windfall. In a few cases, incomes are stratospherically high because of unique talents in sports, as authors, or in the performing arts.

In most cases, though, incomes and assets at the top of the scale do not represent labor income but the income from capital. The vast majority of the wealthy people in this country reached that exalted status by saving early and often.

Even if a 25 percent annual rate of return seems out of reach, you can still become rich by earning more modest rates of return. For example, suppose you start saving at age 25, and put $300 a month into blue chip stocks, which will probably earn an average rate of return of 12 percent per year. Over the past 45 years, through good times and bad, that has been the historical record: The S&P 500 has appreciated at an annual rate of 7.8 percent and has paid an average dividend yield of 4.2 percent. Assuming that you managed to accumulate the funds in a tax-deferred account, you would indeed have accumulated $3 million over a 40-year period. Not too shabby for a buy-and-hold strategy based on a random selection of stocks.

Now let's assume you were able to pick stocks that appreciated an average of 1 percent per year more than the overall market. Perhaps that doesn't sound like much of a difference. Yet by age 65, your total accumulated wealth would be $4.2 million instead of $3.1 million. That "insignificant" difference between 12 percent and 13 percent per year is worth $1.1 million over a 40-year period. If you manage to get the rate of return up to 16 percent per year by avoiding the stock market during major declines, your nest egg will total $10 million even if you stop saving at age 65. Now we're talking real money.

Just to round out the arithmetic, if you could somehow manage to earn 25 percent per year for 40 years, the total would be an eye-popping $135 million. Admittedly, all these figures have to be adjusted for inflation. Yet even—or especially—with inflation, the same principal guideline applies: It is better to start saving early.

MONEY IS TIME

It may seem hard to believe, but most of the accumulated wealth in the examples above is earned from the savings of the first few years.

If you could earn 25 percent per year over a 40-year period, you would end up with *more* money by saving $300 a month at ages 25, 26, and 27 than if you had started saving $300 a month at age 28 and kept saving that amount *every year* until you were 65. Each additional year that savings earn a high rate of return makes a tremendous difference in the long run.

If 25 percent per year seems out of sight, let's try the same calculation for a 15 percent rate. As it turns out, the results are almost identical. Over a 40-year period, you would end up with more money by saving $300 a month for the first five years than by saving that amount in each of the remaining 35 years. So while high rates of return do indeed generate impressive results, starting to save early is even more important than earning those impressive rates of return.

Starting early also means that if you need to use some of those funds for your children's college education, a bigger house in a tonier neighborhood, or some other major expense, you'll still have done most of the saving needed to accumulate a substantial amount of wealth by retirement age.

THE RULE OF 72

The examples given above, and many more similar ones that depend on the miracle of compound interest, can be summarized by a simple rule of thumb known as the *Rule of 72*. The figure 72 represents the number of years it takes to double your money, divided by the interest rate.

For example, at an annual rate of 6 percent, it takes 12 years to double your money. If you earn 9 percent per year, it doubles every 8 years, and at a 12 percent rate of return, which is the long-term historical stock market average, it doubles every 6 years. That means your original sum rises 4 times in 12 years, 8 times in 18 years, 16 times in 24 years, and so on. By the time you reach the 50-year time horizon, each individual dollar invested at 12 percent has risen more than 300 times. That's why it's so important to start saving early.

An annual rate of return of 25 percent per year means your investment would double in value within less than three years—and increase almost 10-fold every decade. Over a period of four decades, the original sum would increase by a factor of almost 10,000. That's how it's possible to accumulate what seems like a fantastic amount of money over a 40-year earning span.

Let me repeat. At 25 percent per year, every $1,000 invested is worth $10 million 40 years later. That's the true miracle of compound interest.

Table 1A shows how your money accumulates at rates of 0, 7, 10, 12, 15, 20, and 25 percent per year, assuming that you put aside $3,600 every year ($300 a month). The 7 percent figure is the average return earned in a money market account, while 12 percent is the average rate of return on high-quality stocks. Naturally the total accumulation is greater if the rate of return is higher, but note how important it is to get started early, even with relatively moderate rates of return in the 10 to 15 percent range. Starting to save at age 25 and earning an average 12 percent rate of return nets you twice as much at age 65 as would the rarefied 25 percent rate of return if you started at age 45.

These figures are overstated because they do not take into account the rate of inflation, which I think will average 5 percent per year in the future.

Table 1
Amount Accumulated by Investing $3,600 per Year

A: In Current Dollars

Years of saving for retirement	Bank		Stock				
	0%	7%	10%	12%	15%	20%	25%
10	36,000	53,221	63,129	70,775	84,079	112,171	149,677
20	72,000	157,915	226,868	290,592	424,227	806,702	1,543,653
30	108,000	363,958	651,566	973,307	1,800,314	5,107,059	14,526,070
40	144,000	769,195	1,753,123	3,093,719	7,367,354	31,733,737	135,434,249
50	180,000	1,566,358	4,610,279	9,679,396	29,889,136	196,599,106	1,261,479,409

B: Adjusted for 5% Inflation (Constant Dollars)*

Years	0%	7%	10%	12%	15%	20%	25%
10	32,673	47,823	55,124	60,720	70,379	90,533	112,746
20	59,516	110,258	147,442	180,815	248,989	436,939	731,664
30	84,190	196,562	306,785	423,310	707,999	1,772,962	4,634,939
40	109,232	313,954	575,498	901,990	1,866,610	6,874,710	26,670,604
50	136,557	471,625	1,021,444	1,834,383	4,766,633	26,295,562	152,693,082

* Assuming your income grows with inflation

Thus Table 1B adjusts those figures down to show what your money would be worth in today's dollars; they also reflect the fact that your income rises because of inflation. Seen in this light, the $3 million after 40 years at a 12 percent interest shrinks to $900,000. Nonetheless, that's still enough to allow you to live happily ever after. The same guiding principles also hold in an inflationary atmosphere.

Remember, let your money work for you right from the beginning, not just during the last 10 or 20 years of your active career. If you're over 25, that doesn't mean the chances for great wealth have passed you by permanently. The arithmetic is still compelling if you're 30, 35, or even 40. But regardless of your age, if you haven't yet started a regular savings plan, do so immediately if not sooner. You certainly can't hope to become rich by spending all your money.

How Earnings Grow Over 40 Years

Let's review the highlights of these numbers once more.

Suppose at age 25 you start to save $300 a month, which would be approximately 10 percent of your after-tax income on a salary of $50,000 per year. At age 65, assuming your income remained constant, you would have set aside a grand total of $144,000. Since that money would be earning interest or otherwise appreciating, you would have accumulated the following amounts based on various alternative investment strategies:

- If you left it in liquid assets and earned an average rate of 7 percent per year, the sum would grow to $769,000.
- If you invested it in the stock market and earned an average rate of 12 percent per year, which includes both interest and dividends, it would grow to $3.09 million.
- If you enhanced your performance by buying stocks during boom periods and switching your funds into the money market during declines, you could earn an average of 25 percent per year, and your savings would grow to $135.4 million.
- If you started your own business and earned 40 percent per year, as a few very wealthy Americans have done, you would have $8.82 billion by age 65.

And just for fun, if you were able to earn 50 percent per year, the amount would soar to $119.4 billion in 40 years. This is on a total investment of $3,600 per year. I haven't included that in Table 1 because no one in the history of the world—King Croesus, John D. Rockefeller, or anyone else—has ever accumulated that much wealth, even adjusted for inflation over the ages. Even the authentic financial wizards top out at around 40 percent per year. And there's a lesson in that.

25 PERCENT PER YEAR—
THE PINNACLE OF SUCCESS

Of the millions of money managers and investors, only a handful have consistently managed to earn 25 percent per year over an extended period of time. My ideas of how to accomplish this goal are sprinkled throughout this book. But before you turn to them, please keep one sobering thought in mind: The best minds in the business—the towering geniuses of finance—consider themselves fortunate to earn 25 percent per year on a long-term basis.

So anytime that friendly snake-oil salesman sidles up to you and claims his unique offering will guarantee you 40 to 50 percent or more per year and that he has the documented track record to prove it, just look him straight in the eye and remember the odds are roughly the same as discovering the cure for cancer in your basement. Just ask yourself: If someone can consistently earn 100 percent per year—which means $1,000 becomes $1 million in 10 years and $1 billion in 20 years—why on earth is he wasting his time soliciting *your* money instead of enjoying all the good things life has to offer?

In fact, it invariably turns out that those who are seduced by a 40 percent or better rate of return eventually find out that the return is closer to *minus* 100 percent. Most of these packages are nothing more or less than a giant Ponzi scheme, where the funds you "invest" are used to pay those enormous rates of return to the next investor in line. Suddenly all your money will be gone, and you can't expect to get much of it back when the erstwhile financial genius is either in Rio or in one of those country-club prisons earning the maximum rate of 11 cents an hour.

A 25 percent annual rate of return represents the pinnacle of success and, if followed over a lifetime, will make you wealthy beyond your current dreams. The few people who have ever been able to do better than that on a consistent, long-term basis are enshrined in the *Forbes* 400 and similar lists.

Sam Walton, owner of the Wal-Mart stores, built his stake from $10,000 to $9 billion over 45 years by earning 37 percent a year. Warren Buffett, investor extraordinaire, built $100,000 into $5 billion in 33 years—a 39 percent annual rate of return. These are the two richest men in the United

States; their successes have often been chronicled and feted, and deservedly so. Mere mortals can't be expected to match these rates over the long run, and I'm not about to suggest that I can do it either. A 25 percent rate is accomplishment enough. Get-rich-quick schemes only benefit the flimflam artist, not the bemused investor.

Steps to a 25 Percent Annual Rate of Return

To have a reasonable chance of earning 25 percent per year on your assets over the long run, you need both a *long-term* and a *cyclical* investment strategy.

Long-term: Assets that keep pace with inflation and provide a positive yield always do better than assets that are fixed in dollar terms and provide an apparently generous yield but no capital gains. That means in the long run, stocks and real estate always do better than bonds and liquid assets. The latter are only for those who have no further desire for capital accumulation but merely want current income. However, choosing the right assets alone won't get you anywhere near the 25 percent goal. Since gold and silver provide no yield, they are not recommended for long-term investment either.

Cyclical: Lots of assets earn 25 percent per year for a few years at a time, but virtually no asset earns 25 percent per year indefinitely. You have to be flexible. Sometimes it's best to be in stocks, other times in real estate, other times in gold and silver, and once in a while—when the economy is heading into a major recession and inflation is declining—in bonds and liquid assets.

Since no type of investment has ever provided an annual rate of return of 25 percent per year over an extended period of time, does that mean this rate of return is an impossible target? Not at all. Several different types of investments have appreciated 25 percent per year for up to five years in a row—and not all of them are exotic investments, like Ming vases or paintings of flowers by Dutch masters who were missing an ear or two. The key to success is to identify major investment opportunities when they arise, but not to overstay your welcome.

Using Tax-Deferred Dollars

Successfully earning 25 percent per year is like climbing Mt. Everest. It can be done, but it's a stupendous feat. And that's assuming this return is in pretax dollars. Duplicating that performance with after-tax dollars would be like climbing Mt. Everest in the middle of winter in a bathing suit and without Sherpas; it can't be done at all. You must choose forms of investment where the tax code works for you, not against you. Since the Tax Reform Act of 1986, this has become more difficult, but it is by no means impossible. No matter how much of a wizard you are at investment strategy, amassing wealth is almost impossible if, every time you make a dollar, you have to give at least one-third of it back to the government.

Several legitimate ways to avoid the tax trap still exist. IRAs, 401(k)s, Keoghs, and SEPs (simplified employee pension plans) represent one set of options. Investing in real estate is another; the annual gains on your house or building aren't taxed as they accumulate. The gains in stocks aren't taxed until you sell either, but there is no tax-free rollover into other stocks, as is usually the case with real estate. Starting your own business is a third method, and can be a very powerful one if you're willing to take that risk.

The tax code still contains a few "gimmicks" to avoid taxes, but nowadays they tend to disappear as soon as Congress discovers that they're being used for tax avoidance. Use the tax code wisely. While that means not paying any more taxes than are required by law, don't try to outsmart the IRS—even legally—unless you enjoy watching those legal bills pile up when you get audited. For practical purposes, the IRS killed tax shelters in 1986. I know some salesmen will still try to push them—but you shouldn't be buying.

A 25 percent rate of return isn't something that should be attempted by everyone, since it does involve substantial risk. Having said that, I claim it's a pretty safe bet that over the coming decades, (a) the economy won't fall apart, (b) inflation will remain near recent levels over the long run, and (c) stock prices will keep pace with the economy. Of course recessions will occur from time to time, as they did in 1990—but the recessions that do occur will be brief and of modest duration: no more depressions.

Under those eminently reasonable assumptions, the stock market will continue to provide an average return of 12 percent per year. With a few simple rules of thumb, which will enable you to exclude the cats and dogs, you can raise that to 15 percent per year. For many sobersided citizens and would-be investors, that will be sufficient. On the other hand, for those with more expansive aspirations, I'll explain later how to augment that 15 percent rate to a 25 percent figure by taking somewhat greater, but not undue, risks. First, though, let's have a look at how inflation affects your income, assets, and the accumulation and preservation of wealth.

Chapter 3

Inflation Is Forever

You've seen how relatively small amounts of money, invested wisely over many years, can turn into a fortune. That's the good news. The bad news is that the Miracle of Compound Interest also works for inflation, which reduces what those millions of dollars will buy in years to come. To a certain extent, this represents two sides of the same coin. The money market fund earns 7 percent instead of 2 percent because inflation is 5 percent. Similarly, if the inflation rate were zero, over the long run stocks would provide an average yield of 7 percent rather than 12 percent.

The effect of what has come to be considered a fairly modest inflation rate of 5 percent can be dramatic over a lifetime. If the rate of inflation averages 5 percent over the next 40 years, each dollar will then buy only one-seventh of what it can purchase now. So that $10 million fortune, while still substantial, would be worth less than $1.5 million in today's dollars. And over an entire lifetime of 75 years, a 5 percent annual rate of inflation works out to a 39-fold increase in the price level. Each dollar you had as a toddler buys only about 2.6 cents worth of goods by the time you reach the end of your life span.

If this sounds ridiculous, consider that in 1915, the average annual wage was $633 per year. Today it is $26,500, or a 42-fold increase—an increase just slightly in excess of 5 percent per year. If the inflation rate averages 5 percent per year in the future, the average wage will rise 6 to 7 percent per year. If inflation rises 6 percent per year, the average wage will reach

$1 million in 2052. If inflation grows 7 percent, that milestone will be reached in 2044. However, with higher taxes, housing, and medical-care costs, that million dollars won't buy any more than $26,500 buys today— and it will probably buy less. To outpace the steady increase in inflation, you must earn an above-average rate of return on your assets.

PRICES OF KEY ITEMS THAT RISE
FASTER THAN INFLATION

Over the past 40 years, the rate of inflation has averaged just under 4.3 percent per year. In round numbers, that means things cost 5 times as much now as they did in 1950. Of course, not everything costs exactly 5 times as much. Long-distance calls, for example, are cheaper. Black-and-white TV sets are cheaper; for that matter, many people didn't even know what TV was back then.

More disturbing, however, is that some major items cost much more than 5 times what they did back then, especially the "big three": housing, private education, and medical care. A house now costs 13 times as much as it did in 1950; a college education at a private university 17 times as much; and a day in the hospital, believe it or not, costs 68 times as much as it did in 1950. This last figure sounds absurd, yet it is indeed the case that the average cost per day of a hospital stay has risen from $11 in 1950 to $753 in 1990.

The price of most goods and services will rise at approximately the same rate as inflation, but if historical trends are any guide to the future, these three big budget-busters—housing, college education, and medical care— will not only rise faster than inflation, but faster than your salary.

This may seem illogical. If the items on which consumers spend almost half their income rise much faster than the average, and the only items that rise less than the average are a few relatively inconsequential items such as long-distance phone calls and household appliances, then by definition inflation itself should rise faster, which in turn will cause wage rates to rise faster as workers keep pace with inflation.

Don't believe it. The consumer price index (CPI), which is the official arbiter of the rate of inflation, actually understates true inflation—particularly for upper-income consumers.

The case is particularly severe for medical-care costs. In the olden days, when you checked into the hospital for pneumonia, the staff didn't run a whole battery of tests to see if you had a broken leg. But nowadays the vast majority of patients who go into the hospital undergo an extensive battery of tests that have little or nothing to do with the illness at hand. The results are skyrocketing hospital costs. But this isn't counted in inflation, because you're getting "better," or at least "more," medical care than you would have gotten in the past.

In 1990, the average cost per day for a hospital stay—the basic room rate plus all the tests for which the hospital billed you—was $753 a day; for Medicare patients, the cost was over $1,000 a day, compared with $11 a day in 1950. Yes, they ran fewer tests then. Most people would probably say the difference isn't worth it—if they were paying for it directly. But most people have their medical bills paid by a company health-insurance plan, or the government, so they don't even know what the costs are. However, to the extent that businesses have to pay more in health-care costs, either they will grant smaller wage gains or inflation will accelerate, cutting the real value of the paycheck. Either way, spiraling medical-care costs reduce the standard of living, whether they're reflected in the CPI or not.

This increase is also supported by the aggregate figures. In 1950, the total amount spent on hospital stays was $2.1 billion. In 1990, the figure was $224 billion—more than a 100-fold increase (the difference between that and 70 times is due to population growth, especially among the elderly). Total medical-care services costs, which represented only 3.3 percent of total disposable income in 1950, rose to 12.7 percent in 1990. That's almost 10 percent more of your paycheck spent on medical care—which means 10 percent less spent on everything else. And there's no sign that this trend is about to abate.

Over the past 40 years, the average annual increase in hospital costs has been 11 percent. Suppose that same rate of increase was maintained for the next 40 years. That would come out to a nifty—are you ready—$50,000 per day. And if you don't pay that directly, you'll pay it indirectly through higher taxes.

Besides medical costs, there are other factors that make the true rate of inflation—what your after-tax paycheck will buy—considerably higher than the published rates of inflation.

Housing prices exceed the published rate of inflation by 2 to 3 percent per year. Yet these prices were dropped from the CPI in 1983.

New car prices also rise faster than the rate of inflation, although the official statistics show that they're growing slower. The difference is all the safety and emissions-control equipment now required in each car. In

1973, the Nixon administration directed the Bureau of Labor Statistics (BLS), which compiles the CPI, to exclude all additional costs caused by government regulations. So while you're paying more, the government says the price hasn't increased—just the quality.

The percentage of total consumption spent on a college education is also far understated by BLS for those families who send their children to a four-year private college or university. They don't understate the inflation in tuition costs; they just give it far too little weight. For example, if you make $100,000 per year and send two children to an Ivy League school, that tuition will represent about 6 percent of your total after-tax income over your working career. But *total* private-college tuition costs represent only ½ percent of the nation's total consumption, and that is the weight it gets in the CPI.

Finally, when income or Social Security taxes (including Medicare premiums) rise, that's not considered inflationary, because these higher taxes don't directly boost the price level. However, your income declines. As a result, you have less to spend even if prices didn't change at all.

THE MILLION-DOLLAR WAGE: LESS THAN YOU MAKE NOW AFTER INFLATION AND TAXES

The million-dollar wage may sound great in theory. But in fact, the real value of the average take-home pay stopped rising after 1973, and I don't expect it to increase again in your lifetime.

To get a flavor of what things will cost under the million-dollar wage, Table 2 shows what a few major goods and services cost in 1915, 1950, 1970, and today. Then, assuming the same average growth rates, these figures are extrapolated into the future. I realize that not many of you who are reading this will be around 75 years from now; the figures for 2065 are included just to provide a panoramic view of how inflation works. But the figures for 20 and 40 years from now are realistic, if scary. Besides the $50,000-a-day hospital room, we have the $335,000 annual fee for an education at a private university—$1.34 million for four years; Ivy League costs will be about 40 percent higher than that. Then there's $1.8 million for the average home.

Reading Your $5 Newspaper on the $20 Subway Ride

On a humbler level, how many will ride the subway when the fare is a $20 bill—and will New York City still insist on exact change? And we

Table 2
The Million-Dollar Wage

	1915	% chg avg. 1915–50	1950	% chg avg. 1950–70	1970	% chg avg. 1970–90	1990	% chg avg. future	2010	2030	2065	2065 in 1990 dollars
Average annual wage, $/year	633	4.6	3,030	4.8	7,750	6.3	26,500	{7 / 6	102,547 / 85,000	396,800 / 272,570	4,237,000 / 2,095,000	109,114 / 53,842
Taxes as % of income	8.7		22.5		30.5		35		40	45	50	
Take-home pay, $/year	578		2,348		5,386		17,225		42,187	102,575	514,500	
CPI (1982–84=100)	10.8	2.3	24.1	2.4	38.8	6.2	128.3	5.0	340.4	903.2	4,982	
Real take-home pay, $/yr	5,351	1.7	9,743	1.8	13,881	–0.2	13,423	–0.4	12,393	11,357	10,327	
Monthly benefit Soc. Security, $ (beg. of year)	0		41	8.2	199	8.4	1,002	5	2,657	7,054	38,910	
Avg. home price, $	2,750	3.6	9,400	5.2	25,700	8.1	122,800	7	475,000	1,839,000	19,633,000	504,000
Ratio of home price to avg. annual wage	4.3		3.1		3.3		4.6					
Monthly payment on home, $	11		31		145		839		3,167	12,260	130,800	3,360
New car, $	889	2.0	1,759	2.8	3,067	7.8	13,867	6	44,470	142,600	1,096,282	28,166
Monthly payment on car, $	n/a		54		87		332		1,064	3,412	26,231	673
Hospital room, per day, $	n/a		11	10.0	74	12.3	753	11	6,070	48,950	1,888,000	48,600
College education, annual, $			906	6.0	2,920	8.7	15,463	8	72,000	335,900	4,970,000	128,000

can hardly wait for the $19.95 hamburger at McDonald's, or the $25 hot dog to go along with the $100 baseball ticket and the $15 scorecard. If you want to keep up with these figures, you'll be able to read all about them in your *New York Times* or *Wall Street Journal* at $5 a copy, or tune in FNN on cable TV—only $200 a month for your basic service. And if you're in the mood, you can stay at one of those newly decorated rooms at the Plaza Hotel for $10,000 per night, and enjoy your continental breakfast the next morning for only $150–$250 with bacon and eggs.

Maybe some of these price increases won't really come true. As educational and medical costs rise disproportionately, demand might be cut back so far that suppliers will be forced to trim their price hikes. However, that's what I thought in 1970, yet over the past 20 years those cost increases actually accelerated. Besides, even if these figures turn out to be somewhat exaggerated, most people won't be able to pay more out of their current income—especially if the federal, state, and local governments end up taking almost half their paychecks.

Tax Rates: Already Heading Up Again

During the 1980s, taxes paid by individuals—income tax; sales, property, and other excise taxes; and Social Security taxes paid by both employee and employer—almost leveled off as a percentage of personal income, rising only from 34.2 to 34.8 percent. As the 1990s began, however, politicians of virtually all stripes decided to go for higher taxes. George Bush's flip-flop was the most notable, but tax increases were also passed in most major states—not only the liberal bastions of Massachusetts, New York, and New Jersey but California, Texas, and Florida as well. In many cases these tax hikes were labeled "temporary" because of "unforeseen" revenue shortfalls. Sure they are.

I don't think the average tax rate will increase as fast as it did from 1950 to 1980, when it rose from 22.5 to 34.2 percent of your income. However, further tax hikes will probably take the form of (a) higher "sin" taxes on alcohol, gasoline, tobacco, and expensive "luxuries," (b) higher Medicare premiums as part of the Social Security tax, and (c) higher taxes of all kinds, particularly property taxes, at the state and local levels. All three of these cut into real disposable income even if the federal income-tax schedule is left unchanged.

In case the prices in 2065 dollars seem bizarre to those who are unaccustomed to working with compound interest tables, I've also listed them in today's dollars. Even these make pretty unnerving reading, however. The $122,800 average price for a house in 1990 is over $500,000 in 2065—in today's deflated dollars. The cost of a new car will more than double, from just under $14,000 to over $28,000. It will be a fancier car in the sense that it will have more computer gadgetry and spew out fewer emissions, but it will take a bigger hunk of your paycheck. Then there's the $48,600 *daily* hospital stay—in today's dollars—and the $128,000 annual bill for college education. Maybe these figures are "impossible," but they represent nothing more than simple extrapolation of inflation rates over the past 40 years.

If you're being squeezed by higher medical-care costs, higher housing costs, higher education costs, and higher taxes, something has to give. And what gives is your real income: Without investing your money wisely, you will unquestionably be poorer in the years ahead.

Why the Real Wage Is Declining

The decline in the real wage and the standard of living started after 1973. From 1915 to 1950, the average annual wage rose 4.6 percent per year, while inflation rose only 2.3 percent. Even with the higher tax bite, real take-home pay rose 1.7 percent per year. From 1950 to 1970, ditto: Real take-home pay rose 1.8 percent. But in 1973, when the first energy crisis erupted, the good times came to an end. Since then, the average take-home pay has fallen an average of 0.2 percent per year. As I said earlier, if you feel poorer, that's why.

Furthermore, the same factors that diminished the real standard of living from 1973 to the present are still very much with us. That's one of the reasons the fight against higher taxes has become so much more bitter recently; yet on an overall basis rates keep rising. The long-term outlook for the standard of living calls for a continuing decline that will reduce your real take-home pay by about 10 percent over your working lifetime— even if those paychecks keep pace with the published rate of inflation. Unless you're able to find a job with wage increases that far outstrip inflation, your only other choice for financial security is to make your investments work hard for you.

The figures presented in Table 2 also suggest that higher inflation reduces real wages and salaries. When inflation has risen less than 4 percent per year, the average *real* wage rate has risen by about 2 percent per year. When inflation has exceeded 4 percent per year, the average real wage has *declined* almost 1 percent per year. Wages only partially keep up with inflation, and they never recovered from the jump in the average inflation rate from 2.3 percent between 1951 and 1972 to 6.6 percent after that.

Inflation Helps the Rich Get Richer

Higher inflation doesn't hurt everyone. By definition, if inflation makes some people poorer, it must make other people richer. After all, the extra money that's being charged for these goods and services doesn't disappear into a black hole—it ends up in someone's pocket.

Sometimes those who benefit are Texas oil men and Arab sheikhs; sometimes they are farmers, real estate moguls, or Wall Street whiz kids. The point is, it's never the average wage or salary earner. And as these people benefit more from higher inflation, they drive up the price of items that are most desirable.

In particular, inflation boosts the price of luxury goods the most. To understand this, consider two families, each of which has $50,000 before the latest burst of inflation, which is caused by a rise in oil prices. Assume that the real income of Family A, who owns oil wells, doubles, while the real income of Family B, which works in Detroit, is cut in half.

Now see what happens to the price of necessities, and to the price of luxuries—to take a specific example, the price of hamburger and the price of caviar. Family A won't eat any more hamburger—in fact, they might eat slightly less—but Family B won't eat any less hamburger either. The demand for hamburger therefore stays about the same, and so does its relative price. Family A joins the nouveau riche and develops a taste for caviar. Family B, which never ate the stuff before, certainly won't pick up the habit now, so their demand stays the same—namely, zero. Since the total demand for caviar has risen, its relative price increases, while the price of hamburger stays the same.

The same general argument can be made for any type of luxury goods, whether it's Mercedes-Benz 560 SELs, dinner at four-star hotels, flawless diamonds, sable coats, mansions in tony neighborhoods, or Ivy League educations. The upper-income folks always want more of the best. Thus as inflation rises, income redistribution raises the price of luxury goods the most. The biggest swings usually occur in home prices, since the quantity of land in desirable locations is fixed and can't be increased no matter how much the demand rises. Luxury items of this sort are invariably excluded from any measure of consumer prices. So when inflation increases, the price index for luxury goods rises even faster, and you are actually poorer—even if your salary keeps pace with the published rate of inflation.

Thus inflation diminishes your standard of living if wages and salaries represent almost all of your income because:

1. When inflation accelerates, wages and salaries usually don't keep pace.
2. Government spending accelerates along with inflation, mainly because interest costs rise. Eventually taxes go up, reducing your disposable income. Even if they don't, interest rates rise, penalizing those who are net debtors—those with relatively few assets.
3. Items that are measured incorrectly in the CPI—such as medical care, housing, new cars, and college education—rise much faster than inflation.
4. Inflation boosts the price of luxury goods and services at an increasing rate because the newly rich buy more of them.

There is virtually nothing you, as an individual, can do to stop inflation. Oh, you could vote for someone who promises to reduce inflation when he or she gets to Washington, but we all know how that turns out. The most conservative president in the past 50 years presided over the biggest increase in real government spending, the biggest increase in the deficit, and the biggest increase in both the national and the international debt ever in peacetime. Inflation is here to stay—just as it has been every year since 1955. Furthermore, all the evidence I can muster suggests that this trend in the rate of inflation will not only continue but increase during the years ahead.

WHY INFLATION WILL RISE DURING THE 1990s

Since 1940, the inflation rate has averaged 4.5 percent per year. It has, however, deviated from that level for fairly long periods of time. From 1952 through 1965, the inflation rate averaged only 1.3 percent per year. By comparison, from 1973 through 1981, it averaged 9.3 percent per year. The major swings in inflation since 1940 are:

1941–47	7.6%	World War II
1948–49	0.4%	Postwar normalcy
1950–51	6.0%	Korean War speculation
1952–65	1.3%	Stable growth
1966–70	4.6%	Vietnam War
1971–72	3.3%	Price controls
1973–81	9.3%	Energy crises
1982–86	3.1%	Energy prices decline
1987–89	4.5%	Postenergy normalcy

This list might suggest that except for wars and energy crises, the inflation rate hasn't exceeded 4½ percent. That's true, but it ignores a much more insidious development.

Before 1940, inflation always surged during wartime, but the price level itself—not just the rate of inflation—usually returned to its previous level. Indeed, from 1790 to 1940, the overall rate of inflation averaged less than 1 percent per year, wars and all.

Not any more. Since 1940, the inflation rate during noncrisis periods has risen consistently—from 0.4 to 1.3 to 3.3 to 4.5 percent. Even before the 1990 oil shock, inflation had headed back above 5 percent. Creeping inflation is alive and well.

Many economists and politicians pretend they don't know what causes inflation. They claim it's like hurricanes and earthquakes—an unpleasant event, but not preventable.

Of course, this is pure moonshine. Except for outside shocks—famines, wars, or energy crises—inflation is the handmaiden of the government. In the long run, it's fiscal and monetary policy that determines the inflation rate for each country. That's why, although all countries are subject to the same major worldwide shocks, the inflation rate in Germany and Japan is invariably much lower than it is in the United States, while in the United Kingdom and Italy it's much higher. Government policy also explains why the rate of inflation is 100,000 percent in Brazil one year and zero the next.

How the Government Affects the Inflation Rate

Government policy affects the rate of inflation in several ways.

1. It helps determine the growth rate of productivity. Anemic growth in productivity boosts inflation. Also, if productivity slumps, the United States cannot compete as well abroad: The value of the currency declines, imports and import substitutes cost more, and inflation accelerates.

2. The larger the size of the government sector—in terms of both expenditures and taxes—the less resources are available to boost productivity in the private sector, and hence the higher the rate of inflation will be. Even an increase in government expenditures and taxes that leaves the budget balanced can be inflationary. More often, though, higher expenditures are accompanied by a larger deficit.

3. An increase in the budget deficit is always inflationary, but the timing of the rise in prices depends on the reaction of the monetary

authorities. They can accommodate the deficit by holding interest rates constant, which raises inflation in the short run. Or they can boost interest rates, which holds inflation steady in the short run but raises it in the long run, because higher interest rates reduce investment, which in turn reduces productivity and boosts inflation. The choice made by the monetary authorities is critical in determining what happens to inflation in the short run. (This will be explained in the next chapter.)

4. Interference with market forces raises inflation. This could take the form of anticompetitive measures, excessive regulations, quotas in the labor force, or regulations for pollution control and abatement. Many people claim that the benefits from these regulations are worth the higher inflation rate. I don't debate this point, but merely point out that such programs do raise inflation.

5. Removing pricing decisions from the marketplace also boosts inflation. The major example of this is Medicare, which was instituted in 1966. Before then, the price index for medical-care services rose at approximately the same rate as other services; now it rises 3 percent per year faster.

6. The breakdown of society, in terms of the collapse of inner-city school education and burgeoning crime and drug problems, also reduces productivity and raises inflation. More resources are used to fight crime and incarcerate criminals, leaving less money for productive activities. The vast majority of drug users also performs at a lower level of activity.

The monetary authorities have often inflamed inflationary trends in the short run by failing to tighten when the economy shows signs of overheating. Also, autonomous shocks such as the energy crises temporarily boost inflation. However, these aberrations cannot explain why the long-term rate of inflation in the United States moved steadily upward for the past 40 years. This trend is due to an increasing government sector and to lower productivity growth—trends that will continue indefinitely.

I expect the inflation rate to average at least 5 percent during the 1990s, with occasional forays to 6 percent. Most people are comfortable with this rate of inflation, so they don't want to rock the boat by imposing drastic solutions. They're willing to pay an extra 1 to 2 percent in higher inflation rates in return for a healthier environment and what they perceive as more equal justice in the workplace.

Even under Ronald Reagan, the ratio of government spending to GNP (gross national product) continued to rise, and it has grown even faster under George Bush. New legislation to purify the environment and improve access for the handicapped is also inflationary. In addition, noth-

ing is being done to reduce the budget deficit. After declining as a percentage of GNP from 1987 through 1989, the deficit rose again in 1990
and 1991. The appreciation of the dollar from 1981 to 1985, which
reduced inflation slightly, has been reversed, and the greenback is likely
to decline further in the years and decades ahead.

It's the voters who ultimately decide on the rate of inflation because in
a democracy, people get the kind of government they vote for. Since most
people in the United States prefer moderate inflation, that's what occurs.
Some other countries have a much lower rate of inflation. From 1982
through 1989, the average annual rates of inflation in Japan and West
Germany were only 1.5 and 1.7 percent per year, compared with 3.6
percent per year in this country. People in those countries chose lower
inflation by voting for smaller or no deficits, tax laws that favor investment
instead of consumption, and a strong currency. In the United Kingdom
and Italy, by comparison, inflation averaged 5.1 and 8.0 percent per year
from 1982 through 1989; their citizens voted for more inflation.

Most people, if asked a direct question, naturally say they favor lower
inflation, lower deficits, higher productivity, and a strong currency. In
actual practice, however, they favor no such thing.

From time to time in my speeches, I ask how many in the audience
would like to see the deficit reduced. Since these groups usually consist
of either investors or business executives, no one disagrees. Then I add:

How many would like to see Social Security benefits reduced? Stony
silence.

How many would like to have their mortgage deduction axed? A smat-
tering of boos.

And how many would like a 50¢ a gallon tax on gasoline? (My own
personal favorite.) A few snarls—also, a few laughs from those who figure
I'm not really serious. But no cheers.

In every election it turns out that the majority of voters want to see
government services increased over time, but they don't want to pay for
it. Inflation may creep up gradually from 5 percent over this decade. But
even if it holds at 5 percent, it's a lead-pipe cinch it won't go any lower.

INFLATION AND RETIREMENT

So I've convinced you that inflation will continue. Good. On to the next
step.

As long as you're working, your paycheck will probably keep pace with inflation, even if it doesn't exceed it. When you retire, though, inflation will continue to eat away at your assets at a rate of at least 5 percent per year. If, for example, you have an annual income of $100,000 at age 65, it will be worth only $37,700 at age 85. In calculating your retirement needs, therefore, you need to have enough assets that (a) your spendable annual retirement income will be the same as the year before you retired, (b) your income will keep pace with inflation until you or your spouse dies, and (c) you will be able to bequeath to your heirs an estate that, in real terms, is the same size it was the year you retired. That's one of the main objectives of this book—to help you accomplish these goals.

Retiring with Your Living Standard Intact

The ground rules are as follows:

1. You save 10 percent of your after-tax income during your working years, as discussed in Chapter 1.
2. Your real income increases at an average rate of about 2 percent per year over your working lifetime. This reflects promotions you will receive or transfers to better-paying positions. If you stay in the same job all your life, your real income will hardly rise at all.

   The 2 percent annual gain generally isn't a perfectly smooth progression. Your real income will probably rise more than 2 percent per year during the first 20 years of your working life, as you're promoted or take advantage of better opportunities elsewhere, and less than 2 percent during your latter 20 years. However, I've assumed a steady growth rate in order to simplify the arithmetic. If in fact your real income grows more rapidly early in your career, you'll end up with slightly more money than is shown in Table 3. In this case, the required rate of return would be slightly lower than I have calculated.
3. While you want to retire with your living standard intact, your income can be substantially lower than your last year's salary for several reasons. Your mortgage has been paid down to zero, you don't have to put 10 percent of your after-tax income aside for saving, your medical-care premiums will decline sharply because of Medicare, your children are finished with their college education, and you won't have to pay Social Security taxes on your investment income, although of course you'll still have to pay income tax. Also, you'll receive Social Security benefits. All of these adjustments for various levels of income are shown in Table 3. The higher your salary, the less important will be the adjustments for Social Security, medical care, and education.

Table 3
Assets Required for Alternative Levels of Retirement Income*

Pretax salary level	100	200	300	400	500
Federal income tax	12	33	54	74	94
State/local taxes	4	9	14	19	24
Soc. Security tax†	8	8	8	8	8
After-tax income	76	150	223	299	374
Mortgage	20	40	60	80	100
10% saving of after-tax income	8	15	22	30	37
Spendable income	48	95	141	189	237
Medical-care premium	4	4	4	4	4
College education	4	4	4	4	4
Discretionary income	40	87	133	181	229
Less: Soc. Security payments	12	12	12	12	12
Additional income needed to maintain living standard	28	75	121	169	217
Pretax equivalent basis‡	35	108	185	251	318
Assets required at retirement age	500	1,543	2,643	3,586	4,543

* All figures in thousands of dollars.

† Including employer's contribution.

‡ Assuming no state or local income taxes, but Social Security benefits are included in taxable income above $32,000.

4. The rate of inflation remains at 5 percent during both your working and retirement years. However, if it increases to a higher rate and remains there, the analysis basically stands, unless you're holding bonds or liquid assets. The nominal rate of return on other investments will rise proportionately with inflation, while the real rate will remain the same.

5. Since you want to maintain the same real standard of living for the rest of your life, and pass along to your heirs the same amount of money in real terms that you had when you retired, I assume your money is invested in the stock market earning 12 percent per year. You spend 7 percent; the other 5 percent is used to keep pace with inflation.

If your last pretax salary was $100,000 per year, you will need an annual income of only $40,000 to maintain that standard of living with all the adjustments mentioned in (3). That would require assets of $571,000. For a salary of $200,000, you'll need assets of $1.54 million; the figure rises more than proportionately because the effective tax rate rises. Table 3 gives figures for $100,000 increments up to $500,000, after which the results are almost proportional.

If you save 10 percent of your pretax income, what annual rate of return must you earn over your working life in order to achieve this goal of financial independence? Obviously the answer to this question depends on when you start saving. Based on the comments I made in the previous chapter, the earlier you start saving, the lower will be the required rate of return. Starting at age 25, you can reach this goal by earning 12 percent per year, the average rate of return for the stock market. If you start at age 35, the required rate of return rises to 15 percent, at age 45 it rises to 19 percent, and at age 55—forget it.

All the figures in Table 4 have been adjusted for inflation. In other words, a salary of $100,000 in that table means an income sufficient to purchase $100,000 worth of goods and services at today's prices when you retire, which might be $200,000 or $300,000 then. The inflation rate for both income and the value of your assets has been built into these calculations.

For example, suppose you're 30 years old now and your annual salary is $100,000. It will rise to approximately $200,000 per year *in real terms* at age 65, assuming it grows 2 percent per year faster than inflation. According to Table 4, then, you would have to earn an average annual rate of return of 13 percent in order to meet these retirement goals, which are 35 years away. If you have only 20 years until retirement with a current income of $100,000, your final year's salary would be $148,000 in real terms.

The results of Table 4 again emphasize that if you start saving early enough, you can reach your retirement goals with a rate of return that is no higher than the average gain in the stock market. If you wait until age 55, however, you'll need an annual rate of return of over 50 percent each year. Lots of luck.

Don't Let Inflation Diminish Your Retirement Income

As I mentioned above, your income will probably outpace the reported rate of inflation during your working years. After retirement, though, it's a completely different story. Suppose you invested $500,000 in bonds

Table 4
Rate of Return Required to Maintain Living Standard for Various Income Levels and Years of Saving*

Number of years before retirement	Pretax income level last year before retirement 100,000	200,000	300,000 or more
10	43.5	51.8	54.9
11	38.4	45.7	48.4
12	34.3	40.9	43.3
13	31.0	37.0	39.1
14	28.2	33.8	35.7
15	26.0	31.1	32.9
16	24.0	28.8	30.5
17	22.4	26.8	28.4
18	20.9	25.1	26.6
19	19.7	23.7	25.1
20	18.6	22.4	23.7
21	17.6	21.2	22.5
22	16.8	20.2	21.4
23	16.0	19.3	20.4
24	15.3	18.5	19.6
25	14.7	17.7	18.8
26	14.1	17.0	18.1
27	13.6	16.4	17.4
28	13.1	15.9	16.8
29	12.7	15.3	16.3
30	12.3	14.9	15.8
31	11.9	14.4	15.3
32	11.6	14.0	14.9
33	11.3	13.7	14.5
34	11.0	13.3	14.1
35	10.7	13.0	13.8
36	10.5	12.7	13.4
37	10.2	12.4	13.1
38	10.0	12.1	12.8
39	9.8	11.9	12.6
40	9.6	11.6	12.3

* All rates of return are based on saving 10% of your after-tax income.

earning $40,000 per year. Twenty years later, assuming the inflation rate averages 5 percent, the real value of that income would decline to $15,000.

If you leave your money in bonds, that's precisely what will happen—and that's what you deserve. Investing in bonds is clearly the wrong move, unless you plan to consume your capital and leave nothing to your heirs. Investing your money in some asset that keeps pace with inflation over the long run, such as stocks, means you can spend some of the earnings and plow the rest back into the market. This way, your capital keeps pace with inflation and provides the same real income in future years. That's my suggestion, and all the required asset figures given in Table 3 include this assumption.

Let Stocks Appreciate During Your Retirement Years

Suppose you have $500,000 invested in stocks, with an average dividend yield of 4 percent and an annual appreciation of 8 percent for a total yield of 12 percent. Use 7 percent of that yield, or $35,000, for current consumption, with the other 5 percent for capital appreciation. That would boost the value of your portfolio to $525,000 next year. You can then spend 7 percent of that—in other words, your spendable income has risen by the amount of inflation—and achieve an additional 5 percent appreciation during the following year. Over the long run, your spendable income will remain at $35,000 in constant prices, and the nominal value of the portfolio will continue to appreciate enough to remain at $500,000 in real terms. As long as the stock market grows at the same rate as GNP, the real value of your portfolio and your annual income will keep pace with inflation.

Suppose the inflation rate were zero. Instead of earning 8 percent, bonds would earn only 3 percent; and instead of earning 12 percent, stocks would earn only 7 percent—which in this case would consist of a 4 percent dividend yield and a 3 percent annual appreciation, representing the rate of real growth. But the real value of your income would be precisely the same. Your stock portfolio would provide income of $35,000 each year, which represents the dividends plus all the capital gains. Because none of the income would be reinvested, the portfolio wouldn't appreciate in value, but with no increase in inflation, its real value wouldn't diminish. You would continue to receive the same $35,000 every year, and its purchasing power would remain fixed.

Now back to the real world. If inflation rises, the rate of return would increase proportionately in the long run to adjust for inflation. But there's the rub. *In the long run.* Because in the short run, the rate of return on stocks and bonds doesn't mirror the inflation rate at all. In fact, it's inversely related. Thus in order to generate above-average rates of return in your portfolio, it's critical to adjust your asset mix as the rate of inflation changes. This important concept is discussed in the next two chapters.

Chapter 4

Cyclical Investment

STOP THE MUSIC

From 1949 through 1965, the rate of return on the S&P 500—capital gains plus dividends—averaged 16.3 percent per year, for a total return of $13 for every dollar invested. Stockbrokers extolled the strategy of buying common stock as the surest path to riches. Then, suddenly, the music stopped. For the next nine years, through 1974, the average rate of return per year was *zero*. That's 0.0 percent. Many stockbrokers went out of business, and the ones who were left ate sandwiches at their desks. But then the music started again—and from 1975 to the middle of 1990, the average rate of return once again soared to 16.6 percent, or a total return of $10 for every dollar invested. Sure, there were dips in the market—including the saber-rattling crash on October 16, 1987—but the overall trend was still up.

Then the music stopped again in mid–1990, as Iraq invaded Kuwait and the economy headed into a recession. Most investment wizards were surprised. They shouldn't have been, though. For one thing, the economy had been heading toward a recession ever since early 1989—while at the same time, inflation was accelerating. Even more important, though, it's foolish to believe that the stock market will continue to outpace the economy indefinitely.

Indeed, one of the key rules of investing is that no single type of asset is the best choice all the time. To maximize your return, you must adjust your asset mix during various phases of the business cycle.

Table 5 shows the average annual rates of return since 1950 for 18 major types of assets, calculated by five-year intervals. This table, if used correctly, should debunk 90 percent of what your investment adviser tells you when he or she is trying to push some particular type of high-commission merchandise. No single type of asset is consistently at the top of the list.

In fact, assets that perform best in any given five-year cycle are likely to perform worst during the next five-year cycle. This is clearly illustrated in Table 6. For example, bonds were the best investment for the 1980–85 period, but they had been dead last during the previous five-year cycle. During that period, smaller stocks were the best, but they in turn had been the worst for the 1970–75 period.

Gold was the star performer from 1970 to 1975. But during the 1980–85 period, its rate of return ranked a distant 16th out of 18 assets. Only diamonds and silver were worse—and silver had been second in the previous period.

The Tokyo stock market has made some investors very rich. But from 1960 to 1965, its rate of return was 14th out of 15. And just when some people were beginning to think Japanese stocks were impervious to decline, the Nikkei fell 39 percent during 1990.

The skyrocketing price of Impressionist paintings made them the number one category for 1985–90. But those same paintings came in an unimpressive 11th during the 1970s, and I'm willing to bet this recent stellar performance will be reversed during the 1990–95 period.

On a five-year basis, residential real estate is the most stable performer and, if you leverage it by buying your home with 20 percent down, the best long-term investment as well. The declines in home prices that occurred in major metropolitan areas in 1989 and 1990 were only temporary. However, from 1980 to 1985, housing prices failed to outpace inflation, so even housing isn't a sure road to riches—although it is the most reliable.

I'm certainly not suggesting you change your asset portfolio mix every month or quarter. However, it's just common sense to invest in different types of investments when inflation is accelerating and the economy is booming than when inflation is declining and the economy is in a recession. That's the main idea behind *cyclical investing*.

We live in inflationary times, so in the long run, fixed-income assets will always underperform assets that are tied to inflation. It's useful to

Table 5

Major Assets: Average Annual Rate of Change by Five-Year Intervals

	50–55	55–60	60–65	65–70	70–75	75–80	80–85	85–90‡	50–70	70–90
Inflation	2.1	2.0	1.3	4.3	6.8	8.9	5.5	3.8	2.4	6.2
Large stocks	23.9*	8.9	13.2	3.3	3.2	13.9	14.7	15.0	10.9	11.6
Small stocks	15.0	10.6	20.3*	7.5	0.6	37.4*	4.8	5.8	14.6	11.3
Treasury bonds	1.2	1.2	2.6	0.0	6.2	1.7	16.8*	9.4	1.2	8.4
Liquid assets	2.2	3.5	3.7	6.4	6.8	8.4	10.9	7.6	3.9	8.4
Single-family home										
Leveraged	16.6	14.0	12.1	21.3*	24.5	34.1	14.2	18.1	15.3	20.8
Unleveraged	5.4	4.4	3.7	7.3	8.7	13.3	4.5	6.0	5.2	8.1
Farmland	5.6	6.0	5.0	5.8	12.5	14.1	-2.4	-1.4	5.6	5.4
DMark	0.0	0.0	1.0	1.8	6.9	6.2	-9.1	10.9	0.7	3.4
German stocks	18.6	32.2*	-2.1	6.8	16.1	6.6	5.6	22.7	14.3	12.5
Yen	0.0	0.0	0.0	0.0	3.4	8.5	0.2	6.0	0.0	4.5
Japanese stocks	23.4	24.1	-1.3	12.3	17.7	17.9	16.2	23.9	14.0	18.9
Gold	0.0	0.0	0.0	2.4	30.1*	33.3	-10.9	-3.5	0.6	10.5
Silver	2.1	0.8	7.2	6.5	20.1	36.1	-21.5	-4.0	4.0	5.4
Oil	2.0	0.8	0.0	2.1	26.7	15.8	2.2	-5.6	1.2	15.0
Diamonds†	6	6	6	6	28.0	31.8	-20.6	8.2	6.0	9.7
Coins	11.6	14.5	19.0	6.9	28.3	23.2	0.0	15.0	17.0	16.1
Stamps	1.3	4.5	6.2	12.1	17.3	26.4	-9.8	1.0	6.0	6.8
Old masters†	12	12	12	12	6.1	20.6	1.8	23.9	12.0	12.7
Impressionists†	13	13	13	13	10.4	15.6	11.3	39.8*	13.0	18.7

* Leader for that five-year period.

† Approximate values only for 1950 through 1970.
Surge in German stock market in 1955–60 period due to a 4.4-fold increase in stock prices starting with the formation of the Common Market in 1958.

‡ Some figures for 1990 are approximate.

Table 6
Ranking of Major Assets by Five-Year Intervals

	50–55	55–60	60–65	65–70	70–75	75–80	80–85	85–90	70–90*
Large stocks	1	6	3	10	17	13	3	6	7
Small stocks	5	5	1	4	18	1	8	13	6
Treasury bonds	12	10	9	14	14	18	1	9	16
Liquid assets	8	9	8	8	13	15	6	11	11
Lev. real estate	4	4	4	1	5	2	4	5	1
Farmland	7	7	7	9	10	12	13	15	12
DMark	13	13	10	13	12	17	14	8	18
German stocks	3	1	15	6	9	16	7	4	5
Yen	13	13	11	14	16	14	11	12	17
Japanese stocks	2	2	14	2	7	9	2	2	2
Gold	11	13	11	11	1	4	16	16	13
Silver	9	11	5	7	6	2	18	17	15
Oil	10	11	11	12	4	10	9	18	14
Diamonds	na	na	na	na	3	5	17	10	9
Coins	6	3	2	5	2	7	12	7	5
Stamps	11	8	6	3	8	6	15	14	10
Old masters	na	na	na	na	15	8	10	3	8
Impressionists	na	na	na	na	11	11	5	1	3

* This column is adjusted for buying and selling costs; five-year figures are not adjusted, except for real estate.

keep these long-term rankings in mind when you make these cyclical investment decisions. If you do choose some asset with a below-average long-term rate of return in a certain phase of the cycle, you'll want to jettison it as soon as economic conditions change. So let's first turn to the long-term performance record of asset classes, grouped by their sensitivity to inflation.

ASSET PERFORMANCE AND INFLATION

Assets can be grouped into three major classifications, based on their relationship with inflation. *Fixed-income assets*, like money market funds and bonds, by definition cannot appreciate in price over time. Your total yield is the interest. Obviously these assets are hurt by inflation. Even if the rate of interest increases, the real value of your capital erodes over time. In real terms, the long-term rate of return from fixed assets will never be more than 2 to 3 percent.

Equities keep pace with GNP and corporate profits in the long run but are also affected by changes in interest rates. Equities are often recommended as a hedge against inflation, but that's not true over the course of the business cycle. They keep up with inflation in the long run, but in the short run, higher inflation usually depresses stock prices.

Tangible assets—real estate, precious metals and gemstones, natural resources, and collectibles—generally rise faster than the rate of inflation when it is accelerating and slower than the rate of inflation when it is declining.

Within this group, however, the long-term rates of return vary considerably. Real estate generally outperforms inflation by about 2 percent per year. Precious metals and gemstones, although they are favored by many investors, do *not* outperform the rate of inflation at all in the long run. Natural resources follow no set pattern: Oil prices rise faster than inflation; farmland rises more slowly. The published indexes of high-quality collectibles substantially outpace the rate of inflation, but you must be knowledgeable. The rate of return is diminished by the costs of storage and insurance, and by hefty buying and selling commissions. Also, the indexes overstate the average gain in collectible prices by chronicling the successes but omitting the failures.

Inflation Is the Key Economic Variable

Many economic factors affect your investment, but the key factor is inflation. Almost by definition, when inflation rises, bond prices decline, offsetting any gain in yield. Thus if inflation is increasing, bonds are always a bad investment, because their prices will always decline until they reach maturity.

Short-term liquid assets, on the other hand, might still be a reasonable investment during periods of high inflation, because interest rates usually keep pace with higher inflation. When inflation is high but no longer rising, liquid assets are usually the best investment.

Most of the time stock prices are hurt by higher inflation, but not always. The key is whether profits rise faster than bond yields. Since a rise in interest rates generally dampens economic growth, profits are often depressed when inflation rises, so most of the time an increase in the inflation rate will depress the stock market.

You should never make an investment decision without first considering how the rate of inflation is likely to change within the next few years. In Chapter 5, I'll explain how to tell where inflation is heading. However, as important as inflation is in determining short-term cyclical performance, you shouldn't lose track of the long-term record of these investments either. It's always a mistake to choose an asset with a below-average rate of return for more than brief cyclical interludes.

Long-Term Real Rates of Return

During the period from 1950 to 1980, inflation generally trended upward except during and shortly after recessions. Inflation then plunged in 1981 and 1982, and remained fairly stable for the rest of the decade, although it started to increase again in 1987. Thus the 40-year period summarized in Table 7 is generally one of rising inflation; I think that will continue, so these long-term comparisons are probably a fairly reliable guide for what to expect in the future. Over the past 40 years:

1. The rate of return on liquid assets and bonds in nonrecession years is equal to the rate of inflation plus 2 to 3 percent. If the yield on bonds is much higher than on liquid assets, it's because investors expect the inflation rate to increase soon. A large budget deficit usually widens the spread between bond yields and liquid assets because investors perceive that big deficits are inflationary.
2. Residential real estate prices rise at the same rate as family income

in the long run, which is also inflation plus 2 to 3 percent. On the average, real estate prices do *not* grow faster than income. If they do, eventually most families would not be able to afford a home. The reason real estate is such a superb long-term investment is the combination of leverage—20 percent down—and inflation.

3. Stock prices rise at the same rate as corporate profits in the long run, or the same rate that GNP grows. Again, that is inflation plus 2 to 3 percent. In addition, the dividend yield averages 3 to 4 percent per year. If profits and GNP in a particular foreign country rise faster than they do in the United States, and the currency of that country is stable or appreciates relative to the dollar, those stocks will provide a higher rate of return than Wall Street.

4. The prices of gold, silver, other precious metals, diamonds, and other gemstones rise only at the rate of inflation. This makes them a very poor long-term investment, except for people with income to hide.

5. High-quality collectibles generally rise about 3 percent per year faster than inflation after taking buying and selling costs into account. However, to realize this rate of return, you must be quite knowledgeable about the collectibles being purchased.

These are the basic rules. Now let's look at each of the major classifications of assets. I'll start at the bottom of the list, so the turkeys can be discarded first.

ASSETS THAT PERFORM WORSE THAN BANK ACCOUNTS

Don't Invest in Used Kleenex

Over the long run, some assets consistently underperform the average rate of return. Presumably you wouldn't want to invest in used Kleenex under any circumstances, even if there was a temporary tissue shortage. Table 7 provides a bird's-eye view of the rankings over the past 20 and 40 years. Some types of assets never make the top of the list and are usually anchored near the bottom. I'd avoid these almost all the time.

The simplest no-risk investment you can make is to put your funds into an insured bank account, such as a CD; these are known as *liquid assets*. That is the rock-bottom rate of return you should be willing to accept. If a particular asset has a long-term rate of return even worse than what you

Table 7
Major Assets Ranked Over
20- and 40-Year Rates of Return

40 Years		20 Years	
Leveraged real estate	18.0†	Leveraged real estate	20.8†
Japanese stocks	16.4	Japanese stocks	18.9
Impressionist paintings	15.1*	Impressionist paintings	17.4*
Coins	13.8*	Oil	15.0
German stocks	13.4	Coins	14.8*
Small stocks	12.2	German stocks	12.5
Large stocks	11.9	Large stocks	11.6
Old masters	11.8*	Old masters	11.4*
		Small stocks	11.3
Diamonds	7.2*		
Cash real estate	6.3†	Gold	10.5
Stamps	6.3	Diamonds	8.5
Liquid assets	6.2	Liquid assets	8.4
Farmland	5.5	Bonds	8.4
Gold	5.4	Cash real estate	6.9†
Oil	5.1		
Silver	4.7	Inflation	6.2
Bonds	4.7		
		Stamps	5.6*
Inflation	4.4	Silver	5.4
		Farmland	5.4
Yen	2.2	Yen	4.5
DMark	2.1	DMark	3.4

* Adjusted for 10% buying and selling commission.
† Adjusted for 6% buying and selling commission.

would earn by leaving your money in the bank, the decision is very simple: Forget it.

Foreign Exchange: The Worst Investment

The worst investment on a long-term basis is foreign exchange. The value of the dollar has declined somewhat over the past 20 years, but only by an average of about 1 percent per year—although of course the annual swings have been much greater. Investing in foreign stocks or foreign real estate is often a profitable move, but that's because of the intrinsic value of the investment, not because it happens to be denominated in something other than dollars.

Betting against the dollar in the long run provides an extremely anemic rate of return, and one that probably won't change much over the next decade. In one big global marketplace with the dollar one of the key currencies, it can't drift steadily lower without disrupting trade patterns and capital flows with other currencies. Furthermore, even in years when the dollar was depreciating rapidly, its decline was due either to falling interest rates or accelerating inflation. In that case you're *still* better off investing in some other type of asset.

Farmland: Will Rogers Was Wrong

Farmland is another very poor investment. Over the past 20 years, it has even failed to keep up with inflation. Will Rogers is often quoted as saying that he favored investing in land "because they aren't making any more of it." Will should have stuck to being a comedian instead of turning investment adviser, although I'll admit some people think there isn't any difference.

Manufacturers aren't making too many buggy whips or vacuum tubes these days either, but that doesn't mean these would have been good investments. Demand matters as well as supply. Raw land isn't a good investment unless the demand for that type of property promises to rise in the future. But if that's the case, it makes more sense to put a building on it and earn the rent as well as benefit from the capital appreciation of the land.

Gold, Silver, and Diamonds: Only in Special Situations

Gold and silver are trickier. The most important thing to remember is that over the long run, the prices of gold and silver—as well as other precious metals, diamonds, and other gemstones—rise only at the rate of inflation. Since they don't provide any yield, the overall rate of return is puny.

If you happen to live in a country in which inflation is endemic, government stability is a sometime thing, the banking system is unsafe, and citizens aren't legally allowed to move their money out of the country, then gold, silver, and diamonds are probably your best long-term investment. If you honestly think the above sentence accurately describes the

United States, then go buy gold, silver, and diamonds. But that's certainly not my choice.

Admittedly, the late 1970s were a time of spectacular gains for gold, silver, and diamond prices. Gold prices rose from $100 to over $800 an ounce. Silver rose from $4 to over $50 an ounce. And highest-quality diamonds—internally and externally flawless, round brilliant cut, D color—rose from $6,000 to a peak of $60,000 per carat. These spectacular increases hoodwinked many investors into thinking that these price increases would continue indefinitely.

Of course that wasn't true. As this book went to press, gold was about $400 an ounce, silver had fallen to $5 an ounce, and flawless diamond prices were down to $18,000 per carat. So over the past 15 years the annual rates of return were a very unimpressive 7.3 percent for gold, 1.5 percent for silver, and 7.6 percent for diamonds. You would have done better to have left your money in the bank. That's right—in the bank, earning an average interest rate of 8.4 percent.

Nonetheless, if you had invested in these assets during the right five years—from 1975 to 1980—the annual rates of return would have been 51 percent for gold, 66 percent for silver, and 58 percent for diamonds. And that's only if you had bought them strictly for cash. If you had leveraged your position, the returns would have been even more spectacular.

Will gold, silver, and diamond prices ever again approach anything like these fantastic rates of return? I say no, because the spectacular gains of the late 1970s were accompanied by four unusual, if not unique, events.

1. The price of crude oil increased more than 10-fold, rising from about $3 to $34 a barrel. While oil prices will outpace inflation in the long run, as discussed below, it's highly unlikely that they'll ever again increase 10-fold in the space of six years, or an average rate of 50 percent per year. This is just about the same as those spectacular gains for gold, silver, and diamonds.
2. Gold and silver prices had been set by government fiat for many years, with silver at $1.29 an ounce and gold at $35 an ounce. Once these ceiling prices were removed, prices quickly moved up toward equilibrium levels. Some of this catch-up occurred in 1973 and 1974, but gold and silver were still underpriced in 1975, and were therefore poised for another rally as soon as the economy recovered. This argument doesn't affect diamonds, but they tend to follow gold and silver prices in any case.
3. Nelson Bunker Hunt tried to corner the silver market in 1980, which was one of the main reasons prices soared to $50 an ounce.

His fortune, which exceeded $4 billion at the peak of silver prices, quickly disappeared and he was later forced into bankruptcy. Not too many tears were shed, except by his creditors. It's unlikely, although not impossible, that another Nelson Bunker Hunt will come along.

4. The U.S. government was being run by a bunch of professional incompetents and malcontents who thought fighting inflation was none of their business. The Federal Reserve chairman, G. William Miller, actually eased monetary policy in the spring of 1979 even though inflation was in the double-digit range because he thought a recession was coming and he wanted to keep Jimmy Carter in the White House. Six months later, Miller was out of a job, and a year and a half later, so was his boss. In spite of an uneven and somewhat inept job by other Federal Reserve chairmen, notably Arthur Burns, I don't think the Fed will ever let double-digit inflation occur again without tightening policy.

If at some time in the future, another energy crisis—or a war, or a famine—sends inflation skyrocketing, and if at the same time someone tries to corner the gold or silver market, and at the same time the Fed abdicates its responsibility to curb inflation, then, yes, gold and silver could briefly become your best investment again. But the odds are against it. The proof of the pudding, I claim, followed the Iraqi invasion of Kuwait. Oil prices doubled within a matter of days, but gold and silver prices rose only a measly 10 percent and then hastily retreated.

Over the long run, the historical record clearly shows that gold, silver, diamonds, and other similar assets have failed to outperform the rate of inflation. This is true whether the rate of inflation is 0 or 20 percent. When inflation is *accelerating*, the price of these tangible assets will rise *faster* than inflation. For example, if inflation increases from 5 to 10 percent, tangible asset prices will rise substantially more than 10 percent. On the other hand, when the inflation rate levels off—even at 10 percent— so will the growth in tangible asset prices. And when inflation returns to 5 percent or less, as it always has in this country, tangible asset prices will decline sharply.

Bonds: Consistently Below Average

Besides foreign exchange, farmland, gold and silver, and gemstones, there is one other item that has a rate of return well below the average interest paid on a bank account: *bonds*.

If anyone can earn an average rate of 6.2 percent on money in the bank,

I don't know why they would bother with a 4.7 percent yield on bonds. However, bonds are apparently very popular. Whereas the total capitalized value of all listed equities in the United States is about $3.5 trillion, the total amount of bills, notes, and bonds outstanding is about $5 trillion. Somebody out there likes bonds. They are safe, and many institutional accounts are restricted to fixed-income securities. But you don't have to join that crowd.

In an era of stable inflation, the rate of return on bank deposits and bonds ought to be the same. You put $10,000 in the bank and earn whatever rate of interest the bank is offering. The amount of your principal does not fluctuate with economic conditions and is guaranteed by the U.S. government even if the bank goes belly-up. You always have $10,000 plus accrued interest.

Alternatively, you buy a $10,000 government bond of some stated maturity—15, 20, or even 30 years. Whenever the bond matures, you get your $10,000 back, plus all the interest you've earned in the interim. Just like the savings account. So if bonds always return 100 cents on the dollar, how could they yield a lower rate of interest than the bank account?

Simple—it happens whenever inflation rises.

Comparing Yields on Bonds and Bank Accounts

Suppose the current rate of inflation is 4 percent, and you are trying to decide between a 1-year CD that yields 6 percent and a 30-year government bond that yields 6 percent. So far, there is no difference.

Now assume that the rate of inflation jumps to 6 percent the next year. The CD rate follows inflation higher and increases from 6 to 8 percent. But you're locked into the 6 percent yield on the bond; if you sell it, that means a substantial capital loss. So over a 30-year period, you earn exactly 6 percent per year on the bond but almost 8 percent per year on the CD.

Since the rate of inflation has gradually been rising over the past 40 years, it logically follows that the rate of return on bank accounts has been greater than on liquid assets. This is precisely what's shown in Table 5. The rate of inflation now is just about what it was in 1970, so it should be no surprise that the rate of return on Treasury bonds and liquid assets over the past 20 years has been the same—8.4 percent.

If inflation were declining, the rate of return on bonds would be greater than it is on bank accounts. That is what happened from 1981 to 1986. But that era of disinflation has drawn to a close, and the long-term trend is toward higher inflation, so you should shun the bond market. Only if you honestly believe inflation is licked and will be declining in the years ahead would you conclude that bonds are a better investment than bank accounts.

Suppose inflation were expected to remain steady. Then a CD and a Treasury bond would yield the same rate of interest. Note that I said Treasury bond, because we're talking absolute safety of principal, guaranteed by the U.S. government. Of course, some corporate bonds allegedly pay a much higher rate of interest, and they are now well known as junk bonds. I'd rather spend my money at the track.

Of course, there is an intermediate class of bonds: corporate bonds from companies with very high ratings, such as IBM, AT&T, GE, Exxon, etc. These bonds generally pay slightly more than Treasury bonds, and the companies behind them are not about to default. However, most of these bonds are callable. If the price goes down because interest rates rise, you're stuck with the bond. However, if the price goes up because interest rates fall, the corporations have the right to "call" the bond, meaning they can buy it back from you at the price at which it was originally issued. It's tails you lose, heads they win. So when we're comparing government-insured CD rates and bond yields, let's compare apples and apples—which means Treasury bonds.

At midyear 1990, the average yield on both 1-year CDs and 30-year government bonds was approximately 8½ percent. Furthermore, the yield on CDs and Treasury bonds is always about the same during periods when investors expect the rate of inflation to remain unchanged.

Show this statement to a bond salesman, and he will undoubtedly regale you with stories of when the rate of return on a Treasury bond was substantially higher than on a CD. A prime example, favored by many bond salesmen, is May 1984, when the Treasury bond yield briefly soared to 14 percent at a time when short-term CD rates were only 12 percent. Most investors thought the rate of inflation was about to increase, because commodity prices had risen 25 percent the previous year. As it turned out, they were wrong. Tight monetary policy defused the inflationary threat, and bonds staged a tremendous rally.

However, every such story is balanced by an experience such as 1977, when Treasury bond yields were 7½ percent, compared with 5½ percent on CDs, because investors thought the inflation rate was rising. That time they were right: The inflation rate doubled, and the price of bonds declined by 50 percent from 1977 to 1982. Usually if the bond yield is substantially higher than the yield on CDs, it means inflation is likely to increase, not that bonds are a great buy.

Having said this, I will concede that bonds do play a significant role in cyclical investing. Since 1950, there have been six years when the rate of return on bonds was higher than either stocks or money market funds. Most of these were years of declining inflation, when most of the return stems from capital gains—an appreciation in the price of the bond.

Furthermore, it's extremely simple to buy and sell bonds; liquidity is excellent, and transaction costs are minimal. I haven't put them in the same class with foreign exchange, farmland, gold, silver, diamonds, and other precious metals and gemstones because approximately one year in seven, they're a good investment. But that's the only plug I'm going to give the bonds.

That takes care of the bottom half of the list. The top half includes domestic and foreign stocks, real estate, and collectibles.

ASSETS THAT PERFORM BETTER THAN BANK ACCOUNTS

Oil Prices: Rising Faster Than Inflation, But . . .

The rise in oil prices was one of the reasons that gold, silver, and diamond prices surged during the 1970s. Oil prices, of course, also tumbled during the 1980s, but still remained well above pre-1973 levels. Even before the spike in August 1990, crude oil prices were about $20 a barrel, compared with $3 a barrel during the early 1970s. That's an annual rate of return of 11 percent. This isn't spectacular, but it is double the overall rate of inflation, which averaged 5.5 percent over the same period. Does that mean oil is a good investment?

The problem is buying and storing it. Unless you just happen to have a large salt-dome cave in your backyard, physical storage of the oil represents a major problem. You can buy futures, which are very risky because of the extreme short-term volatility of oil prices, or you can buy oil wells either directly or through limited partnerships. Most of these deals are very complicated, have hidden tax ramifications that generally change every year, and are diluted by the syndicators by the time you get your part of the deal. Another possibility that works well—but only when oil prices are accelerating—is to buy stocks of oil-service companies.

Because of the additional costs and difficulties of buying the financial equivalents of "oil," plus its extreme cyclical volatility, I still don't recommend oil as a long-term investment. From the standpoint of cyclical investing, though, it is worth considering. Furthermore, if you think gold, silver, or diamond prices are about to rise again because oil prices are skyrocketing, buy oil instead.

Over the long run, oil prices will probably rise at about 10 percent per year, compared with the average inflation rate of about 5 percent. The demand for oil is rising faster than the current supply, and it would take substantially higher prices to curtail usage and attract enough investment to develop new sources of energy. In 1990, total world productive capacity was about 7 million barrels per day above demand, but that amount had been shrinking by about 1 million barrels per day since 1985. If these trends continue, that implies another energy crisis in the second half of the 1990s. These are average increases, and do not take into account such surprise shocks as the Iraqi invasion of Kuwait.

Collectibles: You Have to Know the Players

Most of the available evidence suggests that collectibles have done quite well over time, the major exception being stamps. For long-term investors who are knowledgeable about their particular field, collectibles are among the better investments. However, I have several pretty stiff caveats. Collectibles can't really be used for cyclical investments for two reasons: lack of liquidity, and much larger transaction costs. You really have to know the merchandise because fraud is rife; even the indexes that purport to show such magnificent gains are themselves highly suspect.

When you buy or sell a stock or bond, the transaction cost is usually less than 1 percent of the total value of the transaction. If it isn't, you should switch brokers unless you're specializing in low-price stocks or options. However, when you buy or sell collectibles, the minimum sales charge is a 10 percent commission when you buy and a 10 percent commission when you sell. These are the *lowest* rates offered by nationally recognized auction houses and high-quality merchandise. If you buy coins, stamps, or art from your neighborhood dealer, the markups will be in the 25 to 50 percent range—sometimes even more if they see you coming. In the standard Yeoman coin-book guides, retail prices are often double those at the wholesale level.

A 20 percent total commission can cut sharply into the rate of return unless you hold the item for generations. Suppose the value of your collectible has increased by 15 percent per year over the long run. Over a 40-year period, transactions costs reduce the rate of return only slightly— to 14.4 percent. Over 20 years the rate of return declines to 13.7 percent, and for ten years, it falls to 12.5 percent. Maybe even 12.5 percent sounds pretty good, but in essence the return has been whittled down to approximately the same range as stocks; the edge has disappeared. Collectibles therefore make good investments only if you plan to hold them for a long time.

Headlines were in order in May 1990, when Renoir's *Le Moulin de la Galette* sold for $71 million, plus the usual 10 percent buyer's commission. At the time, it was also revealed that the seller acquired this painting for $165,000 in 1929. A fantastic return, no?

Let's see. The net price to the seller, minus the 10 percent seller's commission, was $63.9 million, so the actual realized net gain was some 387.3 times over the past 61 years. That works out to a satisfactory but hardly overwhelming 10.3 percent per year.

This period did include the Depression years, when 0 percent was considered a good rate of return, so I'm not about to claim that Renoirs aren't a good investment. Nonetheless, this is one of the most famous pictures by one of the great masters, and it still returned only 10.3 percent per year.

Look at it another way. Suppose you had bought a market basket of the S&P 500 in 1929—yes, the year of the crash—and held stocks for the same 61 years. Your average annual rate of return, including the Depression years, would have been 9.8 percent, so the $165,000 would have been worth $50.7 million—not so shabby either.

Sometimes lightning does strike in the art world. The self-portrait *Yo, Picasso*, which was purchased in 1981 for $5.8 million, sold for $48 million in 1989, for a phenomenal 30 percent annual rate of return. But for every success story, there are thousands of failures that generally don't get much ink. In the same week that Renoir's masterpiece went for $71 million plus buyer's commission, and van Gogh's *Portrait of Dr. Gachet* went for $75 million plus commission, movie star Kirk Douglas offered 16 paintings by such masters as Picasso, Mondrian, Braque, Dubuffet, and Chagall. Only nine paintings sold, and the sale netted less than half of what had been expected.

Some global figures expose the rate of return on paintings in a harsher light. According to a study done at the University of Zurich, based on the prices of 1,200 masterpieces from 1635 to 1987, most paintings generated an annual rate of return of only 1 to 3 percent above inflation— or just about what you earn at the bank. And according to the Art Dealers Association of America, 99 percent of all works produced in a given year decline in value.

You should not be swayed by the truly remarkable record of Impressionist masters over the past five years. That's no more a trend than was the giant bubble in the Japanese stock market that burst in 1990; indeed, they are two sides of the same coin. A few Japanese, flush with cash from their stock market gains, decided to pay virtually any price for the "right" Impressionist painting. As the Japanese stock market settles back to normal, the demand for these paintings will diminish and prices will return to their long-run pattern.

Which brings up an important point. When you look at the various indexes of collectibles, including the ones listed here, be aware that they include only the successes, not the failures, and are therefore systematically biased upward. If a painting does not sell because the highest price received is unacceptably low, it isn't part of the index at all. And if a "masterpiece" later turns out to be a fake, no one goes back and revises the *Art Index* accordingly.

It's very simple to buy an index fund that will provide exactly the same rate of return as the overall stock market, but you can't buy an "index fund" of art. If you try buying art "by the yard," you're probably better off with wallpaper. Just because a few Japanese insurance executives decide to go on a wild spending spree doesn't mean the art market has suddenly become the world's best investment.

Over the long run, considering buying and selling commissions, paintings generally provide a better rate of return than stocks only to those with substantial expertise; it's worse for those without. Predicting which painting will set a world's record 20 years from now isn't appreciably easier than predicting which stock will rise the most in the future—and picking "average" art, unlike picking average stocks, probably means no gain at all in real terms.

Coins and Stamps: Beware of Fakes

Similar arguments can be made for coins and stamps. Coins had an exceptionally good performance record during the 1970s, when they rode the crest of higher gold and silver prices, but that was a onetime occurrence. Like paintings, coins and stamps have the disadvantage of high buyer's and seller's commissions. In addition, unless the coin or stamp in question has an unassailable provenance, you're likely to be hoodwinked into buying one that's listed in much better condition than is actually the fact—and you won't find out until it's time to sell again.

During the early 1980s, the situation in coins got so bad that a number of dealers formed an association that would clearly and unambiguously state the condition of the coin, guarantee it, and seal the coin in a special tamper-proof container. Except it wasn't. Crooks managed to break the locks, exchange the coins for others of poorer quality, and then seal them up again in such a way that it wasn't apparent the locks had been touched. In stamps, those uncirculated specimens where the gum backing was slightly worn (often from hinging) sold at a discount, so shady entrepreneurs quickly learned how to retouch the gum. As with objets d'art, you must have substantial expertise in coins and stamps in order to avoid being sold inferior merchandise.

Stocks and Real Estate: The Bulk of a Well-Managed Portfolio

That leaves domestic and foreign stocks and real estate, which are precisely the assets I suggest for the bulk of your investment dollars. Much of this book explains how and when you should buy and sell these assets. Only occasionally, when economic conditions dictate, is it worthwhile to switch into bonds or liquid assets.

I haven't made much distinction between domestic and foreign stocks here, because over the long run I don't think the value of the dollar will change very much. The same principles that apply for choosing a U.S. stock also apply to choosing a German, Japanese, or for that matter a Mexican or Thai stock. But since in many cases less information is available on foreign markets, most of my comments relate to the U.S. market. That doesn't mean some foreign stocks aren't excellent buys.

The Advantages of Leveraged Real Estate . . .

Over the long run, leveraged real estate—buying a home with a normal down payment—is your best investment. For purposes of calculating the rate of return, let's assume that closing costs on the house are 6 percent of the purchase price (mainly points, transfer tax, title insurance, and escrowed taxes), your down payment is 20 percent, and you sell it 10 years later and pay a 6 percent sales commission. Let's also assume that the cost of the mortgage payment is equal to what you would pay for rent, and that you have to live somewhere.

With housing prices down in New England, the New York City area, Los Angeles, San Francisco, and many of the country's tonier residential districts in between, it became fashionable in 1990 to denigrate the value of real estate as a good investment. Of course, it is possible to pay too much for real estate, and anyone who overpays at the peak of the cycle and then has to sell quickly probably will lose money on the deal. More common, however, is the case where someone bought a house for $50,000 many years ago, saw his neighbor's house sell for $500,000 last year, and now bitterly complains that he's "losing money" because his house can now be sold for only $400,000.

The underlying figures in Table 5 show that the rate of return on leveraged real estate is *not* based on some sky-high assumption about increases in housing prices. Instead, the average over the past 40 years is a surprisingly modest 6.6 percent—only 2.2 percent higher than the rate of inflation. So I'm not by any means assuming a 12 or 15 percent annual rate of increase. Blue smoke and mirrors aren't needed to tout the advantages of real estate. It's the combination of leverage and permanent inflation that boosts the long-run rate of return into first place.

To see how important the combination of leverage plus inflation is, first consider the case where you bought a house for $100,000 and paid $20,000 down—but the price of the house didn't change at all, so it was still worth $100,000 10 years later. If you sell it, you get your $20,000 back. Maybe the mortgage was paid down a little, but after selling costs, you didn't make a dime on your invested funds and probably would have been better off renting.

Of course, that's not how the real estate market works at all. Most of the time prices rise substantially over a 10-year period. On average, real estate prices rise almost 7 percent per year, which means they just about double in 10 years (the Rule of 72 again). Your $100,000 house is now worth $200,000, and your $20,000 down payment has grown to $120,000. Ignoring closing and selling costs, you've earned 20 percent per year on your investment—far better than the 12 percent average for the stock market—compared with a 5 percent rate of inflation. That's a 15 percent real rate of return.

Suppose you just happened to buy real estate during a decade when the average housing price rose 15 percent per year because the inflation rate had risen to 10 percent. This rarely happens; I'm just illustrating how higher inflation can help increase your *real* rate of return. The value of the house has gone from $100,000 to $400,000, and your original investment has risen from $20,000 to $320,000—a nifty 32 percent annual rate of return. The more inflation increases, the larger your *real* rate of return.

It is possible to calculate the rate of return for other assets on a leveraged basis. However, investors generally can't buy paintings or other collectibles on credit. When it became known that Alan Bond had purchased van

Gogh's *Irises* with only a 50 percent down payment, a major scandal erupted in the art world. More important, Bond couldn't make the remaining payments, so the painting had to be resold at a lower price, allegedly $35 million. Bond later resigned as chairman of his company in an abortive effort to save his remaining assets. So much for leveraging your art purchases.

If you put down 20 percent for your house and don't miss any payments, the bank won't come after you for more money even if the price of the house drops sharply. On the other hand, your creditors will definitely want more money for any other asset you buy with borrowed money if the price declines.

Federal Reserve regulations currently permit an investor to buy stock on a 50 percent margin. However, the broker will usually ask you to put up more money if the price drops 30 or 35 percent. As a result, marginable purchases carry a much greater degree of risk than all-cash sales. That's not true for real estate.

Perhaps calculating the leverage yield gives real estate an "unfair" advantage. However, that's how real estate is actually bought; other assets aren't leveraged.

. . . And One Disadvantage

The only drawback to the leveraged real estate approach is that, in most cases, your leverage is limited. Generally, you can't get a mortgage that's more than two—or at the most three—times your income, and your monthly payment shouldn't be more than 25 percent of your income.

Consider a simple example. Your income is $50,000 per year and you buy a $125,000 house with a 20 percent down payment. Your annual mortgage payments are $12,500 per year, including property taxes, or the maximum 25 percent. Let's say the value doubles in ten years, and to keep it simple, so does your income. You sell the house for $250,000, less $15,000 in commissions, pay off the $100,000 mortgage, and have $135,000 left. You use that as a 20 percent down payment to buy a $675,000 house, with a $540,000 mortgage and annual mortgage payments of $67,500.

Whoops. That's 67.5 percent of your income, and even if you could find a banker hungry enough to lend you that kind of money, you could hardly afford to eat, sleep, or drive to work—unless you pretend you are Donald Trump, who wangled an unlimited line of credit at the banks until they caught on to his little game. Thus your options are limited: You can either stay in the same house or purchase a more modest upgrade. Leverage can only carry you so far, at least in residential properties.

If you leverage a commercial property with steady cash flow, you may become a billionaire, but that's a much riskier proposition that requires an intimate understanding of the market. You almost have to be a full-time professional to earn that kind of return on commercial real estate, and I'm talking about investing your assets as distinct and separate from your regular job. Also, you become extremely vulnerable to any downturn in the economy, as many would-be billionaires found out in 1990. So leveraging up on real estate has its limits. If you want to join the multi-millionaire club, you'll need another vehicle to accomplish this goal.

Phony Reasons for Choosing Bonds Over Stocks

Apart from real estate—and unless you have a great deal of knowledge about collectibles—stocks are your best long-run investment.

Some people say they don't like to invest in the stock market. It makes them nervous to see their stocks go down, and besides—they claim—they always get into the market at the wrong time, buying at the peaks and selling at the troughs. When they listen to their brokers or invest in mutual funds, their rate of return always seems to be well below the average gain in the S&P 500.

Some or even all of these comments may apply to your stock market experience, too, but I claim they are all phony excuses. In this book I will show you how to pick stocks with above-average rates of return, and how to avoid the stock market during major downturns. But let's say that even after you finish this book, you remain skeptical, or confused about how to apply these principles. That's still no excuse. Buy a no-load, low-cost mutual fund that mimics the S&P 500. By doing so, you'll save on sales commissions. You'll ride the long-term wave of the stock market to prosperity and earn an average of 12 percent per year, just as you would have over the past 40 years. Naturally your portfolio won't increase in value every year, and there's no denying you would be better off avoiding the market during years of decline. But even a long-term buy-and-hold strategy in stocks will provide a much higher rate of return than would fixed-income assets. That's all I'm claiming.

Bonds, on the other hand, have turned in a putrid 4.7 percent annual average gain over the past 40 years, just barely managing to keep ahead of inflation. The difference between a 4.7 percent and an 11.9 percent annual rate of return over 40 years is enormous. If you saved $300 per month, the bonds would have produced a total of $423,000—but with your stocks, your market portfolio would be over $3 million.

Someone—probably a bond salesman—is likely to point out that over the past 20 years, bonds haven't done quite as badly relative to stocks. But they've still done 3.2 percent per year worse. Because the rate of inflation declined sharply during the early 1980s, bond prices rose quite rapidly. But unless inflation is really licked and will be declining over the long run, bond prices are going to fall again—and you'll be left holding the bag.

Big Stocks, Little Stocks . . .

In the long run, it doesn't matter whether you buy stocks of large companies or small companies. One myth holds that stocks of small companies outperform stocks of large companies. This claim is based on the hypotheses that (a) small companies are growing and dynamic, while large companies are lethargic and stodgy, (b) small companies entail greater risk, so the rewards are proportionately greater, and (c) small companies aren't covered as thoroughly by Wall Street analysts, so they contain more pleasant surprises.

Since the facts don't agree with these theories, there's no reason for you to believe any of them. As shown in Table 5, sometimes big-cap stocks run ahead of small-cap stocks, and sometimes it's the other way around. For example, big-cap stocks increased much faster than smaller stocks during the 1985–1990 period because of the proliferation of index funds; for the next several years, that pattern will probably be reversed. But don't buy small-cap stocks just because of a rumor that they outperform the giants. Sure, some of them do—but many others fall by the wayside completely. Inattention by Wall Street is no guarantee of success.

Analyzing Foreign Stock Markets

Over the past 40 years, the Tokyo stock market has substantially outperformed the U.S. market. That's not surprising; the Japanese economy has grown faster. In late 1989, Japanese stocks were clearly overpriced, and for once the vast majority of investment advisers said so—although many had been saying so ever since 1986. Even with the 39 percent drop in the Tokyo stock market during 1990, Japanese stocks remained overpriced. During the 1990s the Japanese and German economies will grow substantially faster than the U.S. economy, because these countries don't have the crushing burden of a huge government deficit—but their price/earnings

(P/E) ratios are well above the U.S. stock market, so they may not be much of a bargain. The best place to look for foreign stocks is in the emerging growth countries that have excellent future prospects but moderate P/E ratios.

To summarize, you should have most of your assets in stocks most of the time. But don't forget that no single type of asset is the best choice all the time. In the next chapter, I'll explain how to tell—in advance— when to switch in and out of the stock market.

Chapter 5

The R Factor: How to Predict Inflation and Recessions

It's no secret that your investment performance will improve if you stay out of the stock market, bond market, or real estate market when they're heading down. In theory, that's fine. In practice, it appears to be inordinately difficult. Only 20 percent of money managers are able to beat the market averages, and only 10 percent accomplish that goal when sales commissions are included.

Furthermore, it seems that economists aren't very good at forecasting. You've probably heard all the old jokes, although not as often as I have.

If all the economists in the world were laid end to end, they still wouldn't reach a conclusion.

If you must forecast, forecast often. Give them a date and a prediction, but never at the same time.

Two economists, three opinions.

Economists have predicted seven of the last three recessions.

And finally, What do you call an economist with an IQ of 60? Gifted. Very funny.

Yet in spite of these outrageous slings and arrows, I'm going to use the rest of the chapter to explain how to predict when stock, bond, and real estate prices are about to turn around. First, I'll outline some very simple rules of thumb that explain how economic factors affect various types of investments. Then I'll show you how to predict those factors.

PRINCIPAL ELEMENTS OF CYCLICAL INVESTING

1. Inflation is the enemy of both bonds and stocks. When inflation is about to accelerate, you want to get out of the stock market and into tangible assets.
2. In the United States, inflation has never been curbed without the economy plunging into recession, which is caused by tighter money. When the economy slows down but the recession hasn't yet started, you should be in liquid assets.
3. Recessions are the friend of bonds. When a recession is about to hit, you want to buy bonds.
4. The years immediately after recessions are the best times to buy stocks. Get into the market as the recession is about to end, and stay in until inflation starts to accelerate.

What Causes Inflationary Cycles

As noted in Chapter 3, there have been four principal bursts of inflation since the Korean War: 1956–57, 1966–69, 1973–74, and 1978–80. All of these started when the economy reached full employment and the Federal Reserve failed to tighten in a timely fashion—or initially tightened and then backed off too quickly. While the latter two dates may sound familiar because of the two energy crises, inflation had risen sharply even before energy prices started to skyrocket.

Similarly, there have been four periods when inflation declined markedly: 1959, 1971–72, 1975–76, and 1981–83. These are, of course, the mirror images of the four periods of higher inflation—and each one started about a year after a recession had begun. That's a pretty clear pattern.

Inflation doesn't necessarily have to accelerate when the economy reaches full employment. The government could show fiscal restraint, and the Fed could tighten before inflation worsens rather than afterward. But that has never happened in the past, so I'm assuming the leopard won't change its spots and it won't happen in the future either.

One pattern is very well established. Full employment plus easy money equals higher inflation. That eventually leads to a recession, which is followed by lower inflation. But that still leaves a gaping hole: How do you know when inflation is about to accelerate, and how do you know when a recession is about to begin? The consensus forecasts suggest that it can't be done.

Predicting Inflation and Recessions

I've been in the forecasting business since 1963, having issued forecasts every month since then, and am well aware that the reputation of economic forecasters is somewhere below weathermen and astrologers. Unfortunately, at least from my viewpoint, this isn't without some cause. Economists generally don't have a very good track record in predicting either recession or major changes in inflation.

Nonetheless, I've developed a very simple formula that, in the past, has been able to track all recessions and all major increases in inflation a year ahead of time.

I'm not claiming to have perfected the cure for cancer in my basement, or to have invented the Surefire Hot Fudge Sundae Diet. On the other hand, this formula has worked quite well in predicting inflation and recession over the past 15 years. If you're wondering why other economists don't use the same approach, I'll explain in just a minute.

The basic idea behind my formula is the concept of an *equilibrium interest rate*—what economists would call the natural rate—where demand equals supply, investment equals saving, and inflation and real growth are in balance.

When actual interest rates are above equilibrium, real growth declines and the economy usually heads into a recession. When interest rates are below equilibrium, one of two things happens. If the economy is in a recession, or the unemployment rate is still high, below-equilibrium interest rates can stimulate the economy with little or no inflation risk. However, if interest rates remain below equilibrium once the economy approaches full employment, inflation will always accelerate.

Since the Federal Reserve can influence short-term interest rates through monetary policy, it might seem like a marvelous idea for the Fed to set rates at this equilibrium level, thus avoiding both higher inflation and recession. Perhaps, but in the 77 years the Fed has been in existence, it has proved unable or unwilling to follow that discipline.

Some of the errors are unavoidable; real-world disturbances keep interfering. Sometimes inflation is affected by an outside shock, such as an energy crisis. Government spending or tax policies can throw the economy out of whack, particularly if there are rapid changes in defense spending. Occasionally the Fed is unable to determine how fast the economy is growing, or what the underlying rate of inflation is. And every once in a while, the Fed bows to the winds of political expediency. As a result, short-term interest rates are generally *not* at equilibrium—which is why the economy suffers recurring bouts of higher inflation and recession.

The Key to Successful Cyclical Investment Performance

Determine what the equilibrium interest rate is at any given time. Compare it with the actual rate, which generally is not at equilibrium because of the above factors.

If the actual rate is below its equilibrium value, expect inflation to increase. If it is above its equilibrium value, expect the economy to slow down. Of course there are many different interest rates, but I've chosen the commercial paper rate as representative of short-term interest rates. Using the federal funds rate, the Treasury bill rate, or the prime rate would give essentially the same results.

CALCULATING THE R FACTOR

Stephen Hawking, author of the best-seller *A Brief History of Time*, claimed his publisher told him that every formula he put into the book would cut the sales by 50 percent. Hawking said he demurred on most formulas, but one of them was so important that he included it even at the risk of losing half his sales. Since the book was on the *New York Times* best-seller list for 100 weeks, apparently he wasn't too heavily penalized. So I'll take a similar risk and include one formula here.

The equilibrium interest rate is equal to:

The current inflation rate +

½ times the change in real GNP over the past year +

the combined public sector deficit ratio.

The combined public sector deficit ratio is equal to the federal budget surplus or deficit plus the state and local budget surplus or deficit, all divided by GNP.

In 1989, for example, the inflation rate was 4.8 percent, the real growth rate was 1.8 percent, and the deficit ratio was 1.7 percent, which means the equilibrium interest rate was 7.4 percent. In fact, the commercial paper rate averaged 8.8 percent, which implied that the economy would head into a recession in 1990—as it did.

I have labeled the difference between the actual and equilibrium interest rate R (for residual, or remainder, or just rate of interest). The R factor is the key to cyclical investing. If R is near zero, real GNP will probably continue to change at its recent rate. If R rises well above 0, expect a recession the following year. And if R drops well below 0, expect more rapid growth—or, if the economy is near full employment, higher inflation.

Table 8
Annual Value of R, 1953–1990

1953	1.9
1954	−1.8
1955	−1.6
1956	1.9
1957	0.7
1958	−3.9
1959	−0.3
1960	2.6
1961	−1.7
1962	0.1
1963	−0.0
1964	0.2
1965	−0.5
1966	1.2
1967	−0.7
1968	−0.4
1969	3.6
1970	1.6
1971	−2.5
1972	−2.7
1973	1.3
1974	1.3
1975	−6.6
1976	−4.4
1977	−3.9
1978	−2.2
1979	2.3
1980	0.4
1981	4.4
1982	3.7
1983	−1.3
1984	0.5
1985	−0.7
1986	0.1
1987	−1.8
1988	−0.1
1989	1.4
1990	−0.2

Table 8 shows the values of the R factor for every year from 1953 through 1990. Before 1953, monetary policy wasn't independent, because the Treasury required the Fed to hold interest rates at artificially low levels; thus the methodology is irrelevant. As I'll show in the following pages, every time R exceeded 0.6, a recession or severe slowdown occurred the following year. No exceptions. And almost every time R fell below −0.6 and it wasn't a recession year, inflation accelerated the following year.

The R Factor and Inflation

Table 9 lists all the years in which R was less than −0.6 (values between −0.6 and 0 are insignificantly different from 0). Whenever R was negative, either the economy was in recession or inflation accelerated by more than 1 percent the following year—unless the government did something bizarre to interfere with the economy.

That happened in 1971. R was −2.5 in 1971, and inflation would certainly have risen in 1972 except that the Nixon administration froze prices for three months beginning on August 16, 1971, then kept price controls in effect through the end of 1972. However, that certainly doesn't invalidate the theory. When the controls were eased and later lifted completely, inflation soared into the double-digit range. Savvy investors at the time realized that inflation was being artificially depressed and would zoom as soon as controls were removed, which accounts in large part for the huge surge in gold and silver prices in 1973.

The other exception was in 1985, when R was −0.7. That's a borderline number, considering that the economy was still far away from full employment, with an unemployment rate of 7.1 percent. Nonetheless, inflation would have risen if crude oil prices hadn't fallen from $28 to $14 a barrel. Except for these two years, the R formula has a perfect track record. Furthermore, there are no years in which inflation rose more than 1 percent that were not preceded by a significantly negative R value.

The R Factor and Recession

The ability of R to forecast recessions is similarly impressive. Table 10 lists all the years in which R was greater than +0.6. In all cases but one, a recession started either late that year or the following year. Furthermore, when R was significantly positive for *two* consecutive years, the recessions were generally more serious: The years 1957–58, 1974–75, and 1981–82 saw the three most serious postwar recessions. By comparison, the

Table 9
Low R (< − 0.6) Indicates Higher Inflation Ahead
(Unless economy is currently in a recession)

Value of R		Changes in inflation the following year					
1955	− 1.6	1956	1.9%	1957	1.8%		
1965	− 0.6	1966	1.3%				
1967	− 0.7	1968	1.1%	1969	1.3%		
1971	− 2.6	1972	Price controls				
1972	− 2.8	1973	3.0%	1974	4.8%		
1976	− 4.4	1977	0.7%				
1977	− 4.0	1978	1.1%				
1978	− 2.2	1979	3.7%				
1983	− 1.4	1984	1.1%				
1985	− 0.7	1986	Oil prices fell				
1987	− 1.8	1988	0.5%	1989	0.7%	1990	0.6%

The years 1954, 1958, 1961, and 1975 were all recession years with R less than − 0.6.

recessions in 1954, 1960, 1970, and 1980 were briefer and less serious. And the formula predicted the 1990 recession on the nose.

The only time R was greater than 1 when a recession did not materialize occurred in 1966. However, real growth dropped from 6 to 2 percent and would have turned negative if it weren't for the Vietnam War buildup at the time. More important for our purposes, the stock market suffered a serious enough setback that it acted as if a recession had occurred.

The R values can also be used to predict general trends in tangible asset prices. The two times when R values were the most negative in nonrecession years were 1971–72 and 1975–78. Those were, of course, precisely the times when the prices of gold, silver, diamonds, real estate, and collectibles scored their biggest gains. Whenever the Fed pushes interest rates so low that they fall below the rate of inflation, it encourages excessive borrowing and speculation. That's precisely the story of the 1970s.

Why Can't Economists Forecast?

If this simple formula works so well, why can't economists seem to predict their way out of a paper bag?

Table 10
High R (>0.6) Causes Recessions

	Value of R	Recession started
1953	1.9	August 1953
1956	2.0	September 1957
1957	0.7	Recession continued into 1958, real GNP down −0.8%
1960	2.6	May 1960
1966	1.2	No recession but real growth dropped from 6% to 2%
1969	3.7	January 1970
1970	1.7	Economy grew only 1% excluding recovery from auto strike
1973	1.4	December 1973
1974	1.3	Real GNP down 1.3% in 1975
1979	2.3	February 1980
1981	4.5	August 1981
1982	3.7	Real GNP down 2.5%
1989	1.2	Recession started in 1990

I can't vouch for other economists, but a few anecdotes should shed some light on this perplexing issue—and suggest that most economists aren't as dumb as their forecasts would indicate.

In 1975, when I ran Chase Econometrics, I wrote a long-term forecast entitled "The World at the Brink," which predicted that inflation would reach a higher peak during the next business cycle than the 12 percent peak in 1974 (it rose to 13.5 percent in 1980), the prime rate would rise to 15 percent (it actually rose to 21½ percent), and the unemployment rate would soar to 12 percent (wrong there, it peaked out at 10.6 percent).

Many were not amused. David Rockefeller, who was then chairman of the Chase Manhattan Bank, our parent company, received several letters from heads of large multinational corporations questioning whether the bank ought to be associated with such drivel (these letters were of course routed to me). But it wasn't only the unfavorable comments that hurt. Even worse, a large number of clients canceled the forecasting service, costing me personally over $500,000—back in the days when that was enough to buy a mansion, not a 4-bedroom, 2½-bath tract house. One brokerage house canceled on the spot after I finished giving a speech predicting that the prime rate would rise to 15 percent. Another one who cancelled, Barton Biggs of Morgan Stanley, conceded that I was "creative as hell" but went on to point out that I must be dead wrong because if I was right, the Dow would drop to 400. Of course it didn't, but both Barton and Morgan Stanley have continued to do very well.

Did any of these companies resubscribe when these dire predictions came true? Of course not. Most economists had been fired by top management for not warning them of the recession. Not that it would have helped. I have known several forecasters who were fired for *correctly* predicting upcoming recessions. That's because there has been, and continues to be, a clear negative payoff for forecasts that diverge from the consensus, *whether right or wrong*. In spite of what they say, few business managers and corporate executives like to hear bad news. They think it weakens morale. In most cases, the ideal forecast is that while the economy may not be in such great shape, *their* sales will increase 15 percent next year.

The late Otto Eckstein, who headed a rival forecasting firm called Data Resources, Inc., once told me that as the largest forecasting firm, he had an obligation never to predict a recession because that might start a downturn that otherwise would not have occurred. Since Otto sold his share of his company for $20 million, compared with my relatively paltry $2.5 million, I guess he had a better handle on what the public wanted than I did.

Economists, like the rest of us, generally prefer to have a job, get a regular paycheck, pay the mortgage, and put food on the table. And like most people in staff positions, they take the path of least resistance.

The preceding paragraphs provide a possible rationale for explaining why, if such a simple and time-tested formula can accurately predict inflation and recession, the consensus forecast invariably misses the mark. As far as I'm concerned, the R factor works well, and I will continue to use it. I've already noted that R correctly predicted the 1990 recession; for 1991, according to this formula growth should be near zero.

Now that I have convinced you—maybe—that most economists could forecast more accurately if they weren't afraid of losing their jobs, let's look at the relationship between inflation, recession, and asset prices.

Table 11
Years During Which the Inflation Rate Changed More Than 1%

Years of rising inflation			Years of falling inflation		
	Return on			Return on	
	Stocks	Bonds		Stocks	Bonds
1956	6.6	−5.6	1954	52.6	7.2
1957	−10.8	7.5	1958	43.4	−6.1
1966	−10.1	3.7	1971	14.3	13.2
1968	11.1	−0.3	1972	19.0	5.7
1969	−8.5	−5.1	1975	37.2	9.2
1973	−14.7	−1.1	1976	23.8	16.8
1974	−26.5	4.4	1981	−4.9	1.9
1977	−7.2	−0.7	1982	21.4	40.4
1978	6.6	−1.2	1983	22.5	0.7
1979	18.4	−1.2	1986	18.5	24.4
1980	32.4	−4.0	Average	23.8	10.7
1987	5.2	−2.7			
Average	−1.0	−0.6			

CYCLICAL FACTORS INFLUENCING STOCK PRICES

Table 11 shows how bonds and stocks have fared during the years in which inflation rose more than 1 percent. In most cases, the answer is clear: very poorly.

There are a few exceptions, though. Bonds did well in 1957 because the recession started in September. By the end of the year, interest rates had already declined. But the R indicator gave a recession signal in 1956, so that wouldn't have been a surprise.

Bond prices have a very stable relationship with inflation and recession. When inflation rises, bond prices fall. Period. And when the economy goes into recession, bond prices rise, although usually with a slight lag.

This isn't true for the stock market, however. Stock prices are more prone to influence from other factors, which are discussed in the last section of the book. So I'm not offering a blanket statement that predicting inflation and recession correctly will always tell you what the stock market is going to do.

Sometimes stock prices are dominated by political events, particularly during election years. The main example of this occurred in 1980, when the market was so exhilarated by the election of Ronald Reagan that the total return on stocks that year was 32.4 percent even though there was a recession *and* rising interest rates that year.

Maybe that election was a surprise to the pollsters, but market analysts apparently knew about it well in advance. As one lifelong Democratic resident of New York City, who is now a top aide to Mario Cuomo, told me that August, "I don't know anyone who's voting for Jimmy Carter." In fact, from the recession-induced market trough in April of that year, stock prices rose over 35 percent by election time.

The market also rallied in 1968 because it preferred Nixon to Humphrey, although that rally was also due in part to an ease in monetary policy during the second half of the year as a quid pro quo for the 10 percent income tax surcharge passed by Congress.

Markets can't always predict elections, by the way. Stock prices generally rose in 1976, then abruptly reversed course and fell 25 percent in 1977 when Jimmy Carter turned out to be the victor. Presidential election results can disrupt that carefully planned economic analysis of the stock market.

As shown in Table 11, in years during which the inflation rate has risen 1 percent or more, the average rate of return for stocks has been -1.0 percent. In years when inflation has fallen, the average rate of return for stocks has been $+23.8$ percent. So before you get too fancy with election-year cycles or any other factors, look at the inflation numbers.

You should also check whether the economy is heading into a recession, and also consider changes in the capital-gains tax rate. A cut in the maximum capital gains tax rate from 49⅛ to 28 percent in November 1978 sent the market higher in 1979 in spite of higher inflation and slower growth. However, since that rate doesn't change very often, it's only an occasional tool for cyclical investing.

Stock Prices and Recessions

The total return on stocks was negative in 1949, 1953, 1957, 1962, 1966, 1969, 1973–74, 1977, and 1981, and was only 0.5 percent in 1960, which means prices fell that year. Recessions started in 1949, 1953, 1957, 1960, 1969, 1973, 1980, and 1981.

There's a good match between these two lists, but it's not perfect. Except for the 1980 exception noted above, the stock market has declined every time there was a recession (the mild 1960 recession reduced the total return to 0.5 percent, which means stock prices fell). So if a recession is imminent, the obvious strategy is to bail out of stocks for a while, as shown in Table 12.

Table 12
Return on Stocks, Bonds, and Liquid Assets (LA) in
Years Recessions Started and Following Years (Full Year Recessions Only)

	Starting Year				Next Year			
	Bonds	Bonds–LA	Bonds–Stocks	Stocks	Bonds	Bonds–LA	Bonds–Stocks	Stocks
1953	3.6	1.1	4.6	−1.0	7.2	5.6	−45.4	52.6
1957	7.5	3.7	18.3	−10.8	−6.1	−8.6	−49.5	43.4
1960	13.8	9.9	13.3	0.5	1.0	−2.0	−25.9	26.9
1970	12.1	4.4	8.1	4.0	13.2	8.1	−1.1	14.3
1974	4.4	−5.4	30.9	−26.5	9.2	2.9	−28.0	37.2
1981	1.9	−12.9	6.8	−4.9	40.4	28.5	19.0	21.4
Average	7.2	0.1	13.7	−6.5	10.8	5.8	−21.8	32.6

However, the market also declined in several years when recessions didn't materialize: 1962, 1966, and 1977. The 1966 episode is fairly easy to explain. The economy was overheating, and the Fed stepped on the brakes, causing a sudden lurch in interest rates and the first credit crunch.

The year 1977 marked a sharp acceleration in the inflation rate during the first year of the Carter presidency and higher interest rates. In addition, the capital gains tax had been boosted the previous year. So that decline can also be explained in terms of the overall economic environment as well as Carter's unpopularity with investors.

However, 1962 stands out as an unusual case of the market simply getting too far ahead of itself. Shortly after John F. Kennedy became president, the stock market rose to an unsustainable price/earnings ratio. This episode is discussed in some detail in the last section of this book, where I provide additional hints about how to exit the market ahead of the type of sharp decline that did occur in 1962. The reason I don't consider the failure of the R factor in 1962 to be serious is that during the 1960–65 period, the annual rate of return on S&P 500 stocks was 13.2 percent, bested only by the 20.3 percent rate of return on small stocks. Unless you got out at the bottom of the 1962 market slide, you still made good money in stocks until 1966. Just like the R factor would have predicted.

The 40-year average rate of return on the stock market has been 11.9 percent. Using the R factor permits you to identify years of recession and higher inflation in advance. If you had been out of the stock market during all the recessions that lasted a full year, as well as during nonrecession years when the rate of inflation rose more than 1 percent, and put your money in the bank during those years, your rate of return would have risen to 15.3 percent.

Maybe that doesn't sound like much of a difference. However, remember the miracle of compound interest. Starting in 1950, every $1 would have become $90 on a buy-and-hold strategy. By exiting the market during years of recession and higher inflation, every $1 would have become $297—more than three times as much.

All the years in which inflation fell more than 1 percent occurred either during or immediately following a recession; the lone exception is 1986, when oil prices plunged by more than 50 percent. However, inflation often continues to decline well into the recovery, particularly if it had been abnormally high during the previous business cycle.

Thus except for 1981, which was the beginning of a severe recession, years of declining inflation have been marvelous for stocks. Furthermore, even those investors who jumped into the market in 1981 would have been amply rewarded for the next five years. But in general, the rule is always to wait until the recession is coming to an end before reentering the stock market, as is also shown in Table 12.

The stock market generally does very poorly during years in which recessions start. That's to be expected, since profits crumble. However, note that the rate of return on bonds during recession years is mixed; the biggest gains often occur during the year *after* the recession. In spite of the daily fluctuations in bond markets caused by the latest economic indicators, bonds usually react to changes in inflation with a significant lag. Thus while recessions always reduce inflation and boost bond prices, the reaction is not always instantaneous.

Although the pattern of bond and stock prices shows a marked similarity during and shortly after a recession, it's also important to remember that they are not always correlated during all phases of the cycle. During a recession, stock prices are often declining when bonds are rising. More important, during a boom, bond prices generally start to turn down as inflation starts to accelerate, but stock prices will continue to climb as long as profits rise faster than bond yields. In the unusual circumstance when interest rates fall even as the economy is growing—such as in late 1985, when a coordinated worldwide attempt reduced interest rates and the value of the dollar—both bond and stock markets will surge at near-record rates.

Complete figures for annual rates of return from 1953 through 1989 for a variety of assets as well as stocks and bonds are given in Table 13. Those who are so inclined can see how other assets performed during years when the R factor was significantly positive or negative.

ASSET ALLOCATION THROUGH THE CYCLE

Now I'll trace the optimal portfolio allocation scheme through a typical business cycle. It doesn't matter where we start, but let's assume that a recession is under way, everyone knows it, and the Fed has already eased. Both short-term and long-term interest rates are declining, which means the recession will soon end. Here's what to expect.

Stage 1: Recession Ends

Stocks: Best buy. Will benefit from rapid growth, relatively low inflation, and stable interest rates.

Table 13
Annual Changes in Selected Assets

	Infl (CPI)	S&P w/DIV	Treas bonds	Liquid assets	S-F Home	Farm-land	Gold	Silver	Oil	DM	Frank-furt	Yen	Tokyo
1953	0.8	-1.0	3.6	2.5	5.0	1.5	0	-3.2	5.9		-10.5		46.0
1954	0.7	52.6	7.2	1.6	7.5	1.1	0	-4.3	3.4		-3.4		-15.3
1955	-0.4	31.6	-1.3	2.2	7.0	1.3	0	4.5	0.0		57.2		12.8
1956	1.5	6.6	-5.6	3.3	7.4	5.6	0	1.9	0.7		-2.9		35.8
1957	3.3	-10.8	7.5	3.8	3.8	8.0	0	0.0	10.8		-6.1		9.7
1958	2.8	43.4	-6.1	2.5	0.7	5.7	0	-2.0	-2.6		39.5		5.1
1959	0.7	12.0	-2.3	4.0	5.1	6.2	0	2.4	-3.7		83.5		45.7
1960	1.7	0.5	13.8	3.9	4.9	4.3	0	2.0	-0.7		72.8		15.4
1961	1.0	26.9	1.0	3.0	2.0	2.8	0	1.2	0.3		9.7		-3.6
1962	1.0	-8.7	6.9	3.3	2.6	5.0	0	17.2	0.3		-21.8		2.2
1963	1.3	22.8	1.2	3.6	3.2	4.5	0	18.0	-0.3		13.5		-2.7
1964	1.3	16.5	3.5	4.0	4.9	6.5	0	1.1	-0.3		-18.1		2.6
1965	1.6	12.5	0.7	4.4	5.8	6.1	0	0	-0.6		13.0		21.7
1966	2.9	-10.1	3.7	5.6	6.6	7.6	0	0	0.6		-14.1		9.4
1967	3.1	24.0	-9.2	5.1	6.2	6.2	0	59.8	1.4		45.5		-5.1
1968	4.2	11.1	-0.3	5.9	8.8	6.3	20.1	-5.2	0.7	-0.1	15.6	0.4	34.4
1969	5.5	-8.5	-5.1	7.8	6.3	5.6	-15.7	-7.8	5.1	1.7	15.4	0.6	39.9
1970	5.7	4.0	12.1	7.7	8.4	3.5	6.2	-9.5	2.9	7.6	-16.6	0.1	-13.9
1971	4.4	14.3	13.2	5.1	8.9	4.3	16.5	-14.7	7.6	4.7	12.3	3.0	37.8
1972	3.2	19.0	5.7	4.7	7.5	8.2	48.7	41.8	-0.6	9.2	24.8	14.8	103.6
1973	6.2	-14.7	-1.1	8.2	9.3	12.8	72.2	58.8	11.0	19.4	0.3	11.7	-21.8
1974	11.0	-26.5	4.4	9.8	8.8	24.5	66.3	40.0	187.0	3.3	5.3	-7.0	-6.8
1975	9.1	37.2	9.2	6.3	8.9	13.6	-24.9	-7.0	-3.5	5.1	42.8	-1.6	18.4

1976	5.8	23.8	16.8	5.3	8.2	14.7	-4.0	6.4	10.0	-2.3	-8.0	0.1	20.5
1977	6.5	-7.2	-0.7	5.6	13.5	16.3	22.4	8.3	9.8	8.4	18.8	10.4	-3.5
1978	7.6	6.6	-1.2	8.0	15.9	9.0	37.0	26.0	4.2	15.6	24.6	27.7	25.0
1979	11.3	18.4	-1.2	10.9	15.7	14.7	126.6	267.5	42.2	9.6	0.0	-3.9	3.7
1980	13.5	32.4	-4.0	12.3	13.4	16.0	14.5	-24.8	58.4	0.9	0.9	-3.4	8.4
1981	10.3	-4.9	1.9	14.8	7.6	9.0	-31.6	-49.2	25.5	-19.7	-18.4	2.7	16.9
1982	6.2	21.4	40.4	11.9	2.8	-0.6	13.9	25.6	-9.6	-6.8	9.9	-11.4	5.7
1983	3.2	22.5	0.7	8.9	3.2	-5.7	-16.5	-15.5	-9.0	-4.9	36.2	4.8	24.6
1984	4.3	6.3	15.4	10.2	3.5	-1.4	-19.2	-28.9	-1.2	-10.2	0.1	0.0	25.8
1985	3.6	32.2	31.0	8.6	5.6	-12.3	6.9	-8.9	-6.6	-3.3	70.3	-0.4	15.2
1986	1.9	18.5	24.4	6.4	8.5	-12.5	20.4	-8.0	-45.3	35.5	40.9	41.7	49.1
1987	3.6	5.2	-2.7	6.9	7.9	-8.0	21.9	24.8	22.1	20.7	-14.4	16.4	11.5
1988	4.1	16.8	9.8	7.7	6.1	3.1	-15.1	-10.1	-17.6	2.3	33.6	12.8	37.1
1989	4.8	31.5	18.1	8.8	4.3	5.9	-12.7	-15.9	22.1	-6.6	43.9	-7.2	27.5

Bonds: Most of the recession-induced gains have ended. Prices will improve for a little longer, but it's time to think about moving into stocks.

Liquid assets: Rates are generally declining toward their cyclical minimum.

Real estate: Won't be helped by inflation, but will benefit from relatively low interest rates. Buying now is a good idea; acceleration in prices probably won't start for another year or two.

Gold and silver: Prices are generally declining and will continue to fall for a while.

Stage 2: First Full Year of Recovery

The easing of monetary policy has accomplished its task and the economy, now back on track, is growing rapidly. Inflation is at its cyclical minimum. On an annual rates basis. This is the first year of the recovery. Short-term interest rates are probably near or slightly below their equilibrium value. If they are way below, be prepared for a big increase in inflation before the cycle ends.

Stocks: Still strong; generally the leader.

Bonds: Still rising if inflation has been high, but increasing far less than stocks. Since bond prices will probably drop soon, it's the wrong time to buy them.

Liquid assets: Rates are still near the cyclical minimum.

Real estate: Probably the best time to buy. Interest rates are still moderate, and prices are beginning to rise rapidly.

Gold and silver: Generally still flat; sometimes up a little, sometimes still declining if inflation in the previous cycle has been severe.

Stage 3: Economy Returns to Full Employment

The economy has moved back to full employment, bringing with it the likelihood of higher inflation. Now comes the critical question: Will the Fed raise interest rates enough to defuse the higher inflation? If it does, it runs the risk of recession.

Check the difference between the actual and the equilibrium interest rate. If it is significantly negative, inflation will intensify. If it is close to zero, the recovery will continue. If it is significantly positive, a recession is probably on the way. The Fed has several choices of monetary policy at this juncture. Depending on which choice it takes, your asset allocation will differ accordingly.

CASE A: INTEREST RATES SET TOO LOW

The Fed can try to prolong the recovery by keeping interest rates below their equilibrium level. This has often been tried—particularly during the 1970s—although ultimately it never works. If the Fed is currently pursuing this path, inflation will soon accelerate. Switch out of stocks and into tangibles. Real estate, gold and silver, and collectibles are all fine. This type of policy occurred primarily during the 1970s, although it also happened in 1987—note the big rise in gold and silver prices that year, as shown in Table 13.

CASE B: ECONOMY REMAINS IN EQUILIBRIUM

The Fed can raise interest rates proportionately with inflation, thus keeping the economy in equilibrium. Although this sounds like a good idea, it is seldom tried, partly because fine-tuning apparently is difficult. If the Fed is accomplishing this tight-wire act successfully, stick with stocks, it does occasionally happen—for a while.

CASE C: INFLATION-FIGHTING CAUSES RECESSION

The Fed can react vigorously to inflation by boosting interest rates well above equilibrium, thereby bringing on the next recession. Switch to liquid assets, but be prepared to buy bonds as soon as the downturn starts.

Note that in many cases the Fed goes from (A) to (C). If it does, first you want to be in tangibles, real estate, and collectibles; then in cash, and finally in bonds. That's quite a bit of switching to do in one cycle. But if interest rates are way below equilibrium, as they were in 1975–76, you can almost bet that inflation will skyrocket when the economy does reach full employment—in which case you can skip the stocks and go straight into the tangibles. The key remains the same: Watch the R factor.

Recessions usually begin approximately six months after short-term interest rates rise significantly above their equilibrium value. Admittedly, the R factor isn't published in the newspapers, but all the figures you need—inflation, real growth, and the deficit—are readily available in the financial pages of most newspapers. Besides, I'm talking about capturing major swings in the market, so you'll have some time to react.

Stage 4: Recession Starts

The recession is here. You're in liquid assets, or perhaps you've already shifted to bonds. This is the one time the bonds pay off. Avoid stocks until the economy shows signs of stabilizing—or until the market gives an undeniable buy signal, as discussed in the last section of the book.

The size of the payoff in bonds will depend primarily on how much the inflation rate rose during the preceding boom. If inflation hasn't gone up very much, the gains in bond prices will be unexciting. On the other hand, a recession doesn't usually develop unless inflation has risen substantially. During years of severe recession and the year immediately after, the average annual rate of return on Treasury bonds has been 16.1 percent. During all other years, it has been 1.4 percent.

Table 14 provides a summary of what to buy and what to avoid in each phase of the business cycle. When the recession starts, you should clearly be out of stocks. When it ends, you should move back into the stock market and stay there until inflation starts to accelerate. When it does, then—and only then—switch into gold, silver, or other tangible assets. As soon as the recession starts, move into liquid assets or bonds. Note that inflation generally remains high through the recession and starts to decline only with a lag of a year.

MONETARY POLICY: HAS THE FED
LEARNED ITS LESSON?

One of the most explosive periods of monetary expansion occurred in 1976 and 1977. Real growth averaged 4 percent, inflation was 6 percent, and the deficit ratio was 2 percent, which implied the equilibrium short-term interest rate should have been about 10 percent. However, short-term interest rates averaged only 5½ percent in those two years. That led to an unprecedented binge in the price of tangible assets and unprecedented inflation—and eventually to the most severe downturn in 50 years.

In the recovery that started during late 1982, the Fed did a credible job of keeping the short-term interest rate close to its equilibrium value through 1986. However, after the switch from Paul Volcker to Alan Greenspan, the economy boomed and inflation rose, but short-term interest rates didn't rise.

Thus the R value turned significantly negative in 1987. The result was a boom in the stock market beyond sustainable levels, followed by the dramatic crash. Because the R factor was negative, real estate and collectibles also did well, although the surge in paintings was due more to runaway gains in the Japanese stock market, which came to a sudden end in 1990.

Table 14
Rates of Return During Various Phases of the Business Cycle

	Stocks	Bonds	Liquid assets	Single-family home	Silver	Inflation
Phase 1: Recession ends	28.2	6.2	6.4	6.2	−2.8	5.6
Phase 2: Recovery with stable inflation	19.6	8.9	5.8	5.6	−2.0	2.7
Phase 3: Recovery with higher inflation	3.7	−2.1	6.6	10.1	35.4	5.2
Phase 4: Recession starts	−6.3	5.1	7.6	7.4	−5.9	6.6

All figures are average annual percentage change (geometric averages) as calculated from Table 13. Silver is generally used for tangible assets because annual figures for most other types of tangible assets are not available before 1970.

During the first half of 1989, short-term interest rates rose more than 2 percent above their equilibrium level. As a result, the economy slowed down, then dipped into a recession. Real estate prices leveled off and gold and silver, after a brief uptick following the oil shock in August 1990, also retreated. Stock prices didn't fold immediately, but during 1990 the market did indeed decline. In 1990, liquid assets and bonds were the best performers—just what you would expect in a recession year. Some things never change.

SUMMARY: THE INFLATION CYCLE

Inflation never rises at the beginning of the recovery. Wait until the economy begins to approach full employment. If the R factor has been negative during the previous year, inflation will start to accelerate and will continue rising until the Fed steps on the brakes.

The four years in which inflation significantly declined correspond precisely to the years after a recession occurred. That one's easy.

Someday we may go through a period where inflation declines without a recession—but don't hold your breath. It has never happened in this country. If the Fed doesn't tighten enough to bring about a recession, inflation won't decline. On the other hand, whenever a recession does occur, inflation usually drops sharply the next year.

Inflation rises when the economy is near full employment and interest rates are below their equilibrium value, and it falls after the economy heads into a recession. In 1986, inflation declined all the way to 2 percent. At this point the Fed figured inflation was licked. It eased, and by 1990 inflation had returned to 6 percent. Some lessons are never learned.

Chapter 6

Pitfalls Every Investor Faces— and How to Avoid Them

IF YOU WANT A FRIEND, GET A DOG

When you buy a new car, TV set, or pair of shoes, eat out at a restaurant, purchase an airline ticket, visit the dentist, buy the daily newspaper, or call the plumber, you have a fairly good idea of the details of the transaction that is taking place. You're buying a specific product or service and you're being charged a specific price that's generally known in advance of the actual transaction. If the item you buy is defective, you'll probably get a replacement or your money back. And if the item isn't what's advertised and the seller remains recalcitrant, you can usually obtain relief through legal action.

Furthermore, you've probably done some shopping around to compare prices. It doesn't matter whether the cost is large or small; most people aren't willing to pay 50 cents for the daily newspaper if they can get it for 35 cents. And on big-ticket items, shopping for the best price—and haggling for the last dollar—is part of the ritual.

One other important thing. While the person selling you this product or service will be friendly, since that increases the chances of a sale, there is no illusion that he or she is your personal friend. It's a straight business transaction: You would like to buy something, and the merchant would like to have your money.

For some reason, though, most people don't shop around when they invest their money. They don't research their acquisitions, and they don't apply the same rules and tests to choosing an investment adviser that they would apply to an electrician or painter. Finally, they often make the serious error of pretending that the person to whom they have entrusted their life savings is a friend.

Perhaps there's some deep psychological reason for this. Discussing the amount of your income and assets with someone is apparently a very intimate step. Apropos of this, I sometimes use the old line that "everyone has more sex and less money than you think." And sure enough, people who hear that invariably end up discussing their sex lives, with nary a word about their financial position. In any event, telling someone what you are worth apparently carries with it some subliminal message that such a person must be your friend, because you wouldn't discuss such matters with just anyone.

If you're going to become wealthy, you'll have to wean yourself away from any psychological dependence on an investment adviser or any other financial professional you deal with and learn to treat the relationship as strictly business. If you hired someone to remodel your bathroom and he asked for more money when he said the job was half finished—but had actually done nothing—you would certainly demand proof of progress before advancing another dime. Yet otherwise astute people are apparently willing to accept sweet talk in lieu of certified financial statements explaining precisely how much money they have in their investment account. By the time they find out that the figure is zero, of course it's far too late.

I'm not saying you should choose as your investment adviser some poor slob who's down at the mouth and just had his car repossessed. If he couldn't make money for himself, he won't be able to make it for you. On the other hand, a smooth talker and a sharp dresser in this business means absolutely nothing. Maybe the money for those expensive accessories was swindled from his previous clients.

Choosing the Right Investment Adviser

As an article in *Forbes* magazine admonished, "Pick, if you want, a financial planner who is successful and famous—but not one like Houston's Venita VanCaspel, who is successful at the expense of clients." The article went on to state:

> Venita VanCaspel is about as famous as a financial planner can be, and she has an almost saintly reputation to go with the fame. But she

has had so many lawsuits and complaints brought against her and her firm that regulators say she is almost in a class by herself. Since 1984 investors suing VanCaspel allege that following the advice of the 'First Lady' cost them more than $4.5 million.

Most of the allegations centered around selling tax shelters that are now practically worthless.

VanCaspel's clients apparently confused an investment adviser with a salesperson. When you go shopping around for a Cadillac, it's the rare Cadillac salesman who will tell you that the Mercedes, BMW, Acura, and Lexus are actually all much better cars.

Securities salespeople, like other sales personnel, rarely tell you about the risks involved. If you ask—and sometimes even if you don't—they will hand over the prospectus, which does indeed list all the risks. The first time I read one of these, I was quite surprised, and started asking the broker about all the caveats contained therein. "Oh, never mind that stuff," he told me, "the SEC requires a lot of silly legal language." I thanked him and headed for the door as quickly as possible. Now I always read the prospectuses.

But many don't, and never will. So I'll get back to my main point: Salespeople don't tell you what's wrong with the product unless they're forced to. And when an investment adviser is also a salesperson, that means, very simply, he isn't an adviser at all: He's *only* a salesperson.

To avoid choosing a salesman, pick an investment adviser who gets paid by the hour, not by what he sells you. After all, you wouldn't want a surgeon who got a commission for each limb he sawed off. Of course, that leaves you open to the risk that the adviser you pick just sits there and drones on endlessly for hours, running up your bill, while his recommendations turn out to be worse than useless.

I do have a better idea, which is that you become your *own* investment adviser. I'll go into that further at the end of this chapter. But for the time being, it's important to acknowledge that if you're going to get rich, you will have to deal with financial professionals. So choose your investment adviser, banker, or broker with the same care you use in choosing your dentist, plumber, or butcher. And please don't make the mistake of thinking that these people are your friends. They are in business to make money. Period. As Harry Truman once said in a different context, if you want a friend, get a dog.

THIS ONE'S GUARANTEED

If someone sidled up to you on the street corner and said if you paid him $100 he would guarantee that it wouldn't rain tomorrow, you'd probably move on in a hurry—if you didn't call the cops first. The same reaction would be appropriate if he guaranteed that you would meet a wealthy stranger tomorrow, or that the Cubs would win the pennant. Most people above the age of three know better than to believe stories like these. Nonetheless, when this someone flashes a business card with a well-respected name—such as Merrill Lynch, or Citicorp, or Morgan Stanley, or Salomon Brothers, or American Express, or Dean Witter—many people put on the blinders.

Every so often, when I'm in the mood—which means only a small fraction of the time—I clip an article from the *Wall Street Journal, Forbes, Business Week,* or some other major business publication that relates yet another story of how some guarantee didn't quite mean what it said. The last time I looked, there were over 100 clippings in that particular file. There could just as easily have been 1,000. Here are a few examples:

From the *Wall Street Journal*: In May 1986, Dr. Richard Blumenfeld, a New Jersey dentist, gave Merrill Lynch about $40,000 for a *federally insured* CD with an effective yield of more than 9 percent. But nearly 3½ years later, the annual return was just over 2 percent. It turned out that while the principal was insured, the interest wasn't.

From *Forbes*: In 1985, Frank Gallo's broker recommended that he buy four $1,000 units of Dean Witter Realty 2. Part of the broker's pitch was the assurance that if Gallo ever wanted out, Dean Witter's secondary market would deliver. Yet although Gallo's Dean Witter statement had appraised these units at $950 each, the market price was a shocker; he was offered around $450 each. In that case, liquidity meant a 50 percent discount.

From the *Wall Street Journal*: In the wonderland of Wall Street, "highly confident" isn't always what it seems in the battle between Morgan Stanley and a onetime client, John B. Coleman & Co. A judge says Morgan seems to have taken actions that appear to be "without precedent" on Wall Street. Morgan Stanley used language that in the arcane world of finance means they promised him the money and then said "just kidding."

From *Business Week*: "How Pushing Real Estate Backfired on Pru-Bache" (headline). Stunning losses have many investors up in arms. In spite of specifically requesting "no-risk" investments, which usually means

Treasury securities or insured bank accounts, many clients lost almost 80 percent of their invested capital.

From the *Wall Street Journal*: "Troubles Mount for $5 Billion of Public Partnerships" (headline). "This is a nationwide problem," says Atlanta lawyer Marion Smith II, who recently won a $3.1 million arbitration award from the Shearson Lehman Hutton Inc. unit of American Express. The limited partnerships, which were touted as highly profitable, in fact turned out to be virtually worthless.

From *The Economist*: "Trust Nobody, Especially Your Advisor" (headline). The SEC estimates that Americans are being defrauded of at least $200 million a year by their investment advisers. The commission found fault with six out of every seven investment advisers who were examined in 1989.

From the *Wall Street Journal*: "Salomon Is Censured for '87 Crash Trading" (headline). According to the SEC, Salomon sold stocks short during the big crash in a way that clearly violated the rules. Salomon claimed that their mistakes were only "technical violations."

From the *Wall Street Journal*: " 'Money-Back' Guarantees on Commodity Funds May Not Be Worthwhile; Still No Guarantee in Commodity Funds" (headlines of a two-part series). This brouhaha was stirred up by claims from Dean Witter and others that commodity funds were "guaranteed," which means you would get your principal back no matter what happened to the fund. And who provided the guarantee? Dean Witter said it was an irrevocable letter of credit from Citibank, but in the fine print it turned out to be only a subsidiary of Citibank that had no assets and would presumably fold if it actually had to pay out any money.

The list goes on . . . and on . . . and on. I'm not trying to pick on the big names. It's just that a well-known reputation and a slick Madison Avenue campaign don't make your money any safer. Of course, many smaller financial institutions are even more disreputable, and everyone presumably knows enough to stay away from boiler-room operations that try to solicit your business on the phone. If you're not quite sure who is on the line, just ask them to leave their number and say you'll call back later.

If all these big-name firms I've just mentioned aren't to be trusted, where are small investors to put their money?

Read the fine print. Don't be fooled by a pleasant smile. And when in doubt, always take 24 hours to think it over. A broker who wants your signature on the line today—unless you owe money for assets you already purchased—is up to no good.

Here are a few other common pitfalls to avoid.

Don't Get Yield Myopia

The maximum rates paid by banks on federally insured deposits on any given day can easily be determined; they appear in every issue of *Barron's* and other sources. Thus it logically follows that if someone purports to offer you a higher rate on federally insured deposits, it can't be done. Several possibilities might explain why the rate seems to be higher.

1. These aren't bank deposits at all, but unsecured commercial paper.
2. Some of the deposits are in foreign currencies, in which case you run the risk of the dollar appreciating and your principal depreciating. Sure, it could go the other way. You want to play in the foreign exchange market, go ahead. But don't call it a riskless investment.
3. The principal is insured, but the interest isn't.
4. The "return" you are promised is actually eating into your principal. In other words, if the maximum CD rate is 9 percent and you are promised 11 percent, that's because your $1,000 at the end of the year is worth only $980.
5. You are a victim of a classic Ponzi scheme.

Steering Clear of Ponzi Schemes

The original idea has probably been around since the first prehistoric "crop doctor" guaranteed to increase the yields in the field upon payment of a suitable retainer up front, but this genre of scam is named after one Charles Ponzi, a financier of sorts in the 1920s. The idea is very simple. You promise some unwitting sucker a fantastically high rate of return, usually 40 to 50 percent or more per year. Of course, you have no intention of earning any such lofty rate of return. Instead, you pay the money from the principal "invested" by the next unwitting sucker. Anyone who invests $10,000 of his hard-earned money and gets $5,000 back at the end of the year is really getting half of the $10,000 that someone else just invested.

Naturally you're delighted with a 50 percent annual return on your money, and tell all your friends about it. They invest, too. The promoter waxes fat and amasses the suitable number of mansions, Lamborghinis, yachts, other accoutrements, and—although he doesn't tell you about it—foreign bank accounts.

Soon enough, of course, there's nothing left to pay anyone, and the whole scheme unravels completely. By then it's perfectly obvious what happened, but you're left with no defense because the scam artist himself is either bankrupt or has transferred all his assets, along with his corpus, to Liechtenstein.

It's so obvious in retrospect. But year after year, otherwise sophisticated investors fall for the same scheme over and over again. Even the mythical little old lady in tennis shoes knows that you can't earn 40 percent or more per year in bank accounts, bonds, or stocks. So there must be some additional risk involved. In fact, most of the hucksters who promise these rarefied rates of returns claim they are operating in the options and futures markets.

In spite of the near impossibility of anyone except a few financial geniuses generating these kinds of returns, I will concede that the lure is impressive. I've sat at the screen many times and watched how some options, soon to expire, increased 10 or even 100 times their value within a few days—sometimes even within a few hours. If you had bought put options just before the October 1987 crash, you could have made 1,000 times your money within two days.

No, I've never had that kind of day at the options track. My all-time record is making 10 times my money in the days before the minicrash in October 1989, and I didn't have very much at stake because it was obviously gambling. These long shots pay off about as often as the 200–1 shot at the other kind of track. But such events do occur from time to time, and an unscrupulous entrepreneur can carefully gather the records and pretend he participated in those big moves. In fact, it's not unlikely that someone could place a small bet on many such events, trash all the brokerage house slips for the losers, and just show you the few big winners he had, pretending all the time those were his only trades.

So the fact that someone shows you a "documented" track record of 50 percent gains per year means nothing—unless he can also show you at the same time that the total amount of money under his management has increased by the same rates, and the amounts are substantial—$100 million instead of $100,000. After all, almost anyone can get lucky once.

So how do you avoid these Ponzi schemes?

1. Don't bite in the first place. As I said before, save early and often and you'll have plenty of money in the long run.
2. If you must bite, try to get an individually managed account. That way you'll actually have a record of all the buy-and-sell transactions so you can verify that your money is actually being traded rather than just siphoned off to the next sucker in line.
3. However, the trouble with this idea is that if you have only a small amount of money, like under $100,000, few if any star traders

want to be bothered with your piddling account on an individual basis. In that case, go with the track record. The Barclay Trading Group of Fairfield, Iowa, publishes the track record of top commodity traders over the past five years. This list shows that several traders have been able to compile average annual gains of over 50 percent per year for the past five years. I have no idea whether they'll be successful in the future. But it's a sure thing that those with poor track records aren't about to become financial geniuses "next" year.

If you decide to hitch your wagon to the 40 percent per year or better yield, at least invest your hard-earned funds with someone who has a documented track record, is already well known in the particular field of endeavor, and not only has at least $25 million of assets under management but has had that amount for several years. At least that reduces the chances of becoming part of another Ponzi scheme.

Fear, Greed, and Tulip Bulbs

In 1636, at the height of the Tulip Bulb Mania, a house could be purchased for the price of three tulip bulbs.

All right, land values weren't what they are in Beverly Hills today, and the houses in question were little more than shacks. But the syndrome is still the same. Greed and fear are what run Wall Street. Anyone who thinks differently has lost his way, if he hasn't already lost his mind.

People will invest in stocks at the most unreasonable prices because they think they will go still higher. The Greater Fool Syndrome. There's always someone stupider than you who will buy the stocks, or the tulips, at a higher price.

Maybe this doesn't apply to you, but it apparently applies to lots of other people. Every year the *Wall Street Journal* and others publish the 10 best and 10 worst performers of the previous year. Of course the names and faces change, but there are always companies whose stock has declined 90, 95, or even 99 percent over the previous year; the results never change. Apparently some folks just couldn't manage to get out at the top. In 1989, it was Integrated Resources that headed the list, tumbling from 13⅞ to ³/₁₆. That's zero and ³/₁₆. Yes, they had their day in the sun: The stock rose from a low of ⅜ to a peak of 46. But in the end, their junk bond portfolio turned out to be just another collection of tulip bulbs.

Another story of greed, fear, and tulip bulbs. Last year my bank went bankrupt. Actually, it was my former bank, because for once I had the good sense to yank all of our personal and corporate deposits out before they closed their doors. In this day and age of S&L scandals, a bankrupt financial institution may seem as commonplace as a subway murder in New York City. But there is a little more to this story.

The name of the bank was the National Bank of Washington, and six months earlier, the stock had been at about 15. It wasn't making any money, but an LBO (leveraged buyout) at 19 was a "done deal." Thus encouraged, some of the insiders at the bank—big names in the Washington financial community, with individual net worth in excess of $10 million—bought heavily in order to take advantage of a sure thing.

Except it wasn't. The deal was never consummated, and by July 1990, the stock was worth zero. And the local press published the names of all these former hotshots who had lost millions of dollars.

NBW, unlike most companies listed on the stock exchange, was one I actually knew something about, having served on its board of advisers in its palmier days. I was tempted to take a flyer myself. But something didn't quite fit. If the price of 19 was a sure thing, today's price would be 19. The spectacle of instant wealth—and most of these wheeler-dealers were heavily leveraged, so they stood to make a whole lot more than 30 percent on their money—clouded their vision.

A few people made lots of money on tulip bulbs back in the 17th century; they got out before the top. Some people in the 20th century think they're just as smart. Lots of luck.

DON'T BE HORNSWOGGLED BY THE TAX CODE

This isn't as much of a problem as it was before 1986, when top marginal rates were 50 percent but the tax code was riddled with loopholes. But I still frequently see ads in the financial press asking the same dumb question: Why should you pay taxes?

Because, as the philosopher said about getting old, it beats all the alternatives.

My view of taxes is very simple. I don't like paying them. On the other hand, I like wasting money even less. If someone can show me how to save $1,000 in taxes by paying them $500, they have a deal. Even maybe at $900 they have a deal, although as the amount approaches the $1,000 mark, you have to weigh the probability that the IRS will audit your scheme, and you'll not only have paid someone else $900 but will end up paying the IRS $1,000 plus penalties plus interest, plus they will be on your case until the 21st century. But if someone wants to charge me $1,200 to save $1,000 on taxes, it's strictly no deal.

That may sound so obvious that it's hardly worth mentioning. But I have several rich, sophisticated acquaintances who fell for precisely that scam. Of course, it's not couched in quite that way. You get the $1,000 saving immediately. Somewhere down the road, mind you, some taxes may be due, but time is money and all that blarney. Count your fingers after you shake hands with those types.

I invested in several garden-variety tax shelters back in the early 1980s. They weren't very exciting, although they also weren't very risky. I paid the tax-shelter syndicate $40,000 per year and in return for that saved about $60,000 per year in taxes, including state and local taxes. It sounded like a reasonable trade-off.

Yet in mid-1986, Congress changed the rules retroactively, saying you couldn't deduct those payments even though you had to keep making them. Luckily, my payments were completed in 1987, so the penalty I faced wasn't very severe. But there's an important lesson here. No matter what the salesman tells you, Congress can change the laws on you in midstream anytime it wants. If Congress feels like it, it can take away your tax exemption for municipal bonds, your mortgage deduction, your charitable contribution deduction, and anything else it wants. I'm not saying all these terrible things will happen this year, or next, or even in the long run. What I am saying is that they are possible and, after the experience of 1986, plausible.

The Investment Must Be Viable Without Tax Advantages

None of this should be taken as an excuse to ignore the tax code. It is as vitally important as ever. In fact, much of the strategy described in the rest of this book is built on accumulating wealth in tax-deferred form, whether it be IRAs, pension plans, or life insurance. But there is one inviolate rule of thumb. Ask yourself: If the tax deduction were eliminated, would this still be a sound investment? If the answer is no, you know what to do.

Buying a home is a sound investment whether you get any tax advantage or not, although it's even better if you can deduct the mortgage interest. Putting aside money for retirement is a sound idea whether the funds can build up on a tax-deferred basis or not, although it's even better if you don't have to pay tax on the earnings as they accumulate. But "investing" in an oil well, or a cattle ranch, or a new franchise operation that will never make a dime on its own just because someone told you there would be some lucrative tax benefits—well, you know better than that. Even though, apparently, millions of others don't.

Since 1986, the IRS has almost completely stamped out tax shelters per se. If someone tries to interest you in making an investment on that basis, suddenly recall that you have an important appointment a half hour ago.

HOW TO BE YOUR OWN INVESTMENT ADVISER

As you've probably gathered, I'm pretty negative on most brokers, investment advisers, and financial planners. This notion discourages some folks. They figure if these professionals—who spend most of their working lives trying to uncover investment opportunities with above-average rates of return—can't pull it off, what's the chance for us mere mortals who have to work for a living?

It's true that most people don't beat the market. On the other hand, most people who get bamboozled by brokers, investment advisers, and financial planners do far worse than the market, often losing their principle as well as receiving a sub par rate of return. You must learn to avoid these traps before you can engage in intelligent financial planning that will provide above-average returns over the long run.

But what if you manage to sidestep such pitfalls? Can you beat the market?

When economists and financial analysts get together, being of similar curmudgeonly bent, they like to argue about whether the stock market is "efficient"—whether any single individual, over the long run, can beat the market averages. The theory behind the *efficient market hypothesis*, as it is called, is that a great many people are trying to make money in the market, and once a useful piece of information has been divulged, prices react almost instantaneously. So by the time *you* find out about it, the profits have long since been made. Even worse, someone may be trying to unload his stock, telling you how marvelously the stock is going to perform at precisely the moment it starts to head downhill.

There is a lot of wisdom in the efficient market hypothesis. It doesn't hold for everyone, however.

Warren Buffett beat the market. He started with $100,000 in 1956. Thirteen years later, the per-share value of his investment holdings had increased 30-fold. But Buffett said he couldn't find any stocks worth buying in 1969, so he disbanded his fund and sent the money back to the shareholders. Five years later, after the market had dropped 50 percent, Buffett was back in. According to *Forbes* magazine, he's now worth more than $4 billion.

John Templeton beat the market. He started a little earlier, in 1939, when he was convinced that stocks were undervalued because of wartime fears. He built up his fund to $300 million, sold out, and started all over again, specializing in international funds—where he has also done exceptionally well.

George Soros beat the market—and he did it with market timing, which many of the "experts" say can't be done. His Quantum Fund took big positions in fixed-income assets and rode them to glory when interest rates came down.

Paul Tudor Jones beat the market—in commodities, futures, and options. His documented track record shows an average gain of over 100 percent for the past five years. Jones is still young, so he was worth "only" about $300 million when this book went to press. But at 100 percent per year, he'll be a billionaire soon enough.

Peter Lynch beat the market. The Magellan Fund, which he directed from a $100 million fund in 1977 to a $14 billion fund in 1990, beat the S&P average by better than 5 percent per year over this period. No other public fund of that size has ever approached this record. Then, suddenly, in April 1990, Lynch announced that he was quitting—burned out at age 46, he said. Maybe that's true. But it's an interesting coincidence that Lynch rode the biggest bull market in history to its peak, then decided to quit just as the market was peaking.

There are lots of others who beat the market, but these are the most famous. Based on mutual-fund track records over the years, it would appear that between 10 and 20 percent of the fund managers can beat the market on a consistent basis. So it can be done, although obviously it's not easy.

Each of these men—no woman has yet emerged with this kind of track record—follows a different investment strategy. Warren Buffett generally likes to hold on to a few stocks forever, or at least for 20 to 30 years. Paul Tudor Jones, on the other hand, changes his mind every three weeks. Peter Lynch, as the saying goes, never met a stock he didn't like. George Soros took huge risks in forecasting the economy correctly. And John Templeton decided to eschew domestic stocks and move into foreign stocks at a time when virtually no one else was following that area. So obviously there is no single optimal investment strategy for everyone; different financial geniuses have different strategies that work best for them.

Nonetheless, I will tell you in this book how to generate an above-average rate of return—*on your own*. This doesn't require that you become a Certified Financial Genius, or that you devote most of your waking hours to managing your assets. It can be done by observing a few simple rules—which I'll summarize in the next few pages—and investing the bulk of your assets in real estate and stocks, which are covered in the remainder of this book. The most important aspect of successful investing is not making all the right moves all the time—no one can do that—but avoiding the traps and pitfalls that always await the unwary.

1. **Discipline, discipline, and discipline.** Pick your own investment strategy—and stick to it. You may be the type who uses a buy-and-hold strategy, you may follow the precepts of cyclical investing, or you may simply like to trade in and out on a frequent basis. As the track records of the above five financial geniuses attest, no single style is necessarily the best. But *don't* change styles in the middle of the stream. Don't decide that you're a buy-and-hold investor and then, just when it's darkest before the dawn, sell out your portfolio just as the next market rally is starting.
2. **Check it out.** Don't buy a stock—or a bond, or a future, or any asset—without checking it out first. Is the stock overvalued? Has it just had a big run-up in price and is it about to decline—even though the company and its earnings may be sound? Have the insiders been deserting it like a sinking ship? At a minimum, check the basics. They are in the *Wall Street Journal, Investor's Daily, Barron's*, the *Standard and Poor's Corporation Stock Guide*, or—if you want to spend a little more money—the *Daily Graphs* from William O'Neil and Company. I would avoid any publications from *Value Line*, though; I think their work has gone downhill recently.
3. **Look for conflicts of interest.** Of course, the broker wants to sell you something because he's making a commission. That's human nature, and it's true of the used-car or TV salesman, too. But is he trying to unload the "stock of the day" on your backside? Is his firm desperately trying to get out of a big position? Does the product being pushed carry an unusually large commission? The high-pitched request to buy a bargain "right now" should raise all sorts of warning flags. Wait a few days. The only time you'll miss out is if your broker had inside information on a pending takeover, in which case his next call may be from Lompoc. Be particularly suspicious of financial advisers who try to put you in exotic types of investments with large commissions.
4. **The hairdresser syndrome.** Don't buy stocks just before the economy heads into a recession, and don't buy bonds just before the inflation rate starts to heat up. No one gets these right every

time, but right after the market has just had a major bull rally, profits start to slide, and interest rates start to rise seems a mighty poor time to get into the market.

I call this the hairdresser syndrome because an old Wall Street tale holds that when your hairdresser starts asking you for stock market tips—or even worse, tells you what he or she is buying— the market is just about to peak. It's not an infallible indicator, but when the average Joe or Josephine in the street gets caught up in market euphoria, I'd say it's time to bail out.

5. **Go with the track record.** Don't invest your money with anyone who doesn't have a proven track record. Sometimes you'll miss out on some spectacular successes. John Train, in his book *The Money Masters*, reveals how he failed to invest his funds with Warren Buffett at the beginning because Buffett didn't have a track record, and his crummy offices and lack of a secretary didn't help the impression. Nonetheless, with the increasing number of charlatans in this world, I'll stick with this rule.

All brochures and prospectuses are required to say, "Past performance is no guarantee of future results," or something very similar. Of course it isn't. However, lousy past performance is certainly no harbinger of great results either. If someone has performed well above average in both up and down cycles—and is still heading the fund where he accomplished that record—I'd say that's a fairly powerful recommendation.

6. **Free recommendations are worth what you pay for them.** Recommended lists of stocks from large brokerage houses aren't worth the paper they're printed on. It's not that all the stocks are wrong; many of them are good picks. But they don't tell you in advance which ones will outperform the market. I've studied these lists from the major brokerage houses, and all they ever do is mirror the market averages. The efficient market hypothesis is alive and well at big brokerage houses. If a broker tells you about a "hot" stock, he didn't discover it himself. It came from the "research" department, where at least 20 other firms have pawed over the same information. Some of the picks will turn out to be good; those are the ones you'll hear about next year. But just as many will be bad.

7. **You can make your own stock selections. . . .** Don't be afraid to buy a stock if you've done your research and found one that's selling at a moderate price/earnings ratio and has the potential for stupendous growth. If your broker never heard of it, so much the better.

8. **. . . . So long as you don't think you're a genius.** On the other hand, don't make the mistake of thinking you're smarter than everyone else. That happened to a chap named George G.W. (Gerry) Goodman, who published a famous book called *The Money Game* under the pseudonym of Adam Smith. For pure

enjoyment, it's the best book about Wall Street I've ever read. But evidently all the fame and publicity went to Goodman's head, because he invested almost all of his rather substantial royalties in a little-known and poorly managed Swiss bank that eventually went bankrupt, wiping out his entire stake. Goodman confused wit and erudition with financial savvy. He wrote another book about it, but that one wasn't as sparkling, and since then he's been reduced to uttering occasionally humorous comments on public TV.

9. **Moderate diversification works best.** This is a corollary to Goodman's Disgrace, most commonly known as Don't Put All Your Eggs in One Basket. Mindless diversification doesn't make any sense either, but I would suggest never putting more than 20 percent of your assets in any one particular stock. And if it's a little-known stock of a privately traded company where the books aren't available to you—say a small Swiss bank, just to pick an example—I'd knock that 20 percent figure down to 10 percent.

10. **Admit your mistakes.** The best investors in the world make mistakes—and will tell you about them. Peter Lynch is a good example. To read his book, *One Up on Wall Street*, you might be pardoned for thinking he picked more clunkers than winners. And this is the man whom *Barron's* called "the Babe Ruth of investing." One of the hardest things to do is sell your onetime "favorite" stock at a loss. It forces you to say to yourself, "I made a mistake." But if that's difficult, just remember another old favorite of mine: The biggest business errors are made trying to redeem past mistakes. Take your loss, and redeploy your assets where they will make some money. Sure, sometimes the stock you just sold will come back. Much more often, it won't.

11. **The stock doesn't know you own it.** As a corollary to admitting your mistakes, shed yourself of any emotional illusions that the stock will do what you want it to do. How many times has the broker said to you—or you've whispered to yourself—"It's bound to double"? It's "bound" to do nothing of the sort. Maybe earnings will rise so much that it will double, or maybe the company will be bought out. But just because you've purchased the stock doesn't mean it will act one iota differently than if you hadn't purchased it. If the stock doesn't behave the way you expected, sell it and move on to the next issue. The stock won't care.

12. **Never add to a losing position.** This one should be the easiest to remember and observe, but in fact it's the one that is most often violated. You bought a stock at $30 and its price has fallen by half. The theory is apparently that if you liked it at $30, you'll love it at $15.

In the first place, you shouldn't hold any stock that declines

50 percent. But your failure to sell it soon enough is hardly a guarantee that it will come back. It might be that the company has turned around, or the industry has turned around, or the market has turned around so much that it will eventually go back to $30. But the *last* thing you should consider doing is throwing good money after bad.

13. **"This time it's different."** John Templeton has dubbed these the four most dangerous words in investing. Never buy an asset—or invest in any market near its peak—just because someone tells you this. They said it about gold in 1980, about domestic stocks in the summer of 1987, and about Japanese stocks at the end of 1989. That phrase is the last refuge of either a scoundrel or a moron.

That's enough from the homily department. Let's move ahead to the next two sections of the book, where I'll explain how to build those modest assets you now have into many millions by the time you retire.

FUNDAMENTALS OF

MONEY MANAGEMENT

Chapter 7

A Time to Save
and a Time to Borrow

It's money in the bank!

That phrase, which used to denote so many of the good things in life, now has a hollow ring to it. Leave your money in the bank, and you'll never be rich.

Nonetheless, no matter how astute a money manager you are—and how much this book can help—you've got to set aside some of your hard-earned income for savings and investment. To become very wealthy, you must accomplish something highly creative, imaginative, and lucrative in either the stock market, real estate, or your own business. But most people can't act rationally if they are always squeezed down to their last dollar, worrying about how to pay for those inevitable contingencies that always crop up when they can least afford them.

So one of the keys to creation and preservation of wealth is peace of mind. That means putting aside enough money in the bank to cover contingencies, buy your own home, and purchase adequate life insurance. Once that's done, we can begin to talk about how the rich got that way. But first things first.

REASONS FOR SAVING

1. **Emergencies and contingencies.** You or your spouse might be laid off, or your bonus or overtime could be cut back. Or the roof

collapses or the furnace blows up. Or the car suddenly lurches to a halt before you've finished the payments. Such disasters do occur. I assume you and your family are adequately covered for medical care, so those astronomical hospital bills don't fall into this category.

2. **Buying a home.** After contingencies are taken care of, this is the key investment everyone should make. Considering you have to live somewhere, buying a home is better than renting unless you plan to move within three years. Even if you just have average luck, with the normal 20 percent down payment, buying a house will earn you an average of 20 percent on your investment. No other class of investment can make that claim.

3. **Purchasing adequate life insurance.** It's true that many life-insurance salesmen make used-car salesmen look like saints, but that doesn't mean you should ignore them. Just don't get taken in by their blather.

4. **Buying cars for cash.** Yes, I know it's easy to get carried away with the flashy new wheels that you can drive off the lot for next to nothing down. Yet under the more or less standard four-year loan at 12 percent interest, you end up paying 50 percent more for the car. That $16,000 car really costs $24,000. It always amazes me how some people will argue for hours over that last $100 and then spend an extra $8,000 on the financing charges. If you do need a car and don't have much money, buy an inexpensive one, put down as much as you can, and pay off the balance within two years. For the *next* two years, put what would have been the monthly payments into a savings account, so the next time around you won't have to borrow as much.

5. **Planning for your children's college education.** Next to your house, that's probably the largest amount you'll spend on any single item. Start now or pay the piper later.

6. **Setting aside money for retirement.** Here again, the law of compound interest is so heavily weighted that it is essential to start early. Assuming you retire at 65, every $1 set aside at age 25 will compound to the same amount as $10 set aside at age 45. Most people don't realize this; they will get around to saving "later," when they have some extra cash. Most of the time, later is never.

Once you're 65, your earning power, and your desirability to employers, declines dramatically. Besides, you should be able to enjoy your leisure time in a manner befitting your previous lifestyle. I'll admit that having to scrimp for 40 years just to have a more than adequate retirement income has the priorities all backwards. But not having to scrimp in your golden years is one of the goals this book is all about.

How Much of Your Income Should You Save?

I know lots of people who say they can't save anything at all, and so do you. They live from paycheck to paycheck—and balloon the balances on the credit card in the meantime. It's easy to sympathize with those who have suffered unexpected expenses or a severe drop in income, or even those who have plowed their savings into starting their own business and are temporarily having trouble making ends meet. But being unable to save anything year after year is just a bad habit; if that's your problem, I'm not going to be able to help you very much—unless, of course, I get you to change your mind.

So here's my rule: Save 10 percent of your after-tax income.

Yes, I know. Not many people save that much. Also, not very many people are rich.

To see how this works, let's start at age 25, with a salary of $50,000; after taxes, that's about $36,000. That means saving $300 a month. Over the long run, inflation has averaged 5 percent per year; an average salary rises 2 percent per year in real terms, due to promotions and increases in productivity, or 7 percent in nominal terms. I'll also assume you earn the average rate of return of 12 percent per year in the stock market, and all your savings are done in tax-deferred form. Under these assumptions, how much money will you accumulate by the time you're 65?

(A) $335,000
(B) $900,000
(C) $2.44 million
(D) $6.3 million

Actually, there are two right answers. The actual amount of your cash on hand will be $6.3 million. However, because of inflation, this will be equivalent to "only" $900,000 in today's dollars. Nonetheless, putting aside 10 percent of your income starting at $300 a month doesn't seem like an undue burden if you'll end up with $900,000 in inflation-adjusted dollars at retirement time. Furthermore, that's just for openers. In the rest of this book, I'll show you how to increase your rate of return far beyond 12 percent. But if you don't start saving early, you will never end up on Millionaire's Row.

I realize not everyone makes $50,000 at age 25. However, you can also think of it as representing the combined income of two people living together. Even if you haven't found anyone you want to spend the rest of your life with, that person—whom you haven't met yet—is also earning, and presumably saving, part of his or her income. In any case, all the results are proportional: If your income is $25,000, divide by 2; if it's $75,000, multiply by 1½, and so on.

I chose $50,000 for two reasons. First, if you're earning less than that, I will concede that saving is probably difficult. Second, I want to show that given even this relatively modest income, you can eventually become rich if you are willing to discipline yourself to follow a few simple rules. The first one is seeing your way clear to saving 10 percent of your after-tax income.

Keeping Your Contingency Fund in the Bank

If you're young, single, and are renting your accommodations, a contingency account probably isn't very important. Relatively few emergencies will arise, and if you are fired, your expenditure level can easily be reduced until you find a new job. In extremis, you can always shower with a friend. But once you've got a spouse, children, and house payments, it's time to take those financial obligations more seriously. But in what form should you hold these contingency funds?

Back in the 1930s, as the banking industry was being reformulated in the wake of the massive bank failures of the Great Depression, it lobbied aggressively for ceilings on deposit rates and a ban on interest payment for checking accounts. This legislation would have been called price-fixing if anyone else had tried it. As it turned out, the bankers outsmarted themselves, which admittedly wasn't very difficult. During the 1960s and 1970s, interest rates rose so far above those self-imposed bank-deposit ceilings that many investors withdrew their money from the banks. Eventually the banking fraternity realized it had been hoist with its own petard. The ceiling rates, which they had thought were for their own protection, were denuding them of their deposit base. So they started lobbying for an end to interest-rate ceilings, which they received—but had to give up the prohibition on paying interest on checking accounts.

With the deregulation of the banking industry in 1980, these restrictions were indeed lifted, and banks can now offer any interest rate they choose to pay. Of course, if that rate is higher than the amount earned on their money, they will eventually go bankrupt, as thousands of banks and S&Ls discovered during the 1980s. But then again, no one ever said bankers were intelligent, although until the recent scandals some of us were under the misapprehension they were honest.

Nowadays, most banks pay interest on checking accounts. If you really shop around, you can find a bank that won't pay you interest, but that's very unusual unless you plan to keep a fairly small balance. Most personal checking accounts are actually NOW accounts (which stands for *negotiable orders for withdrawal*, a negotiable order in this case being more commonly known as a check). Most NOW accounts currently pay about 5 percent interest.

In any case, we're talking small potatoes here. Most people who have a reasonably smooth monthly flow of income and expenses keep a maximum of one to two months' worth of after-tax income in their checking account; usually it's closer to one month. That doesn't mean your liquid assets are that meager; it's just that your other savings are invested in some other type of instrument that yields a higher rate of return.

For an average balance of, say, $3,000, the difference between a 5 and 6 percent rate of interest is $30 a year. Unless you value your time at a very low hourly rate, it isn't worth shopping around for a NOW account that pays a slightly higher rate of interest. Choose a bank that's convenient, one where the bank officers are competent and friendly, where they will be accommodating if somehow a check bounces that wasn't your fault, and where they won't put a hold on your deposits. That's all I'm going to say about checking accounts because, frankly, that's all the space they deserve. I don't waste my time worrying about saving $2.50 a month by getting a better rate on my NOW account, and you shouldn't either.

When it comes to the bulk of your savings, however, choosing a financial institution is a different story. If we're talking a $25,000 account, and rates vary by as much as 2 percent a year—as they often do—that's $500 a year. Not the difference between being rich and poor, but it is worth a little bit more of your time.

First, I assume you know as well as I do, after all the well-publicized scandals and failures, that you should put your money only in a bank whose deposits are federally insured. A savings account is not supposed to be a risky investment; the principal should be totally safe. Also, since this is the contingency fund, you want total liquidity. That means not tying up your money for a certain amount of time, such as three to five years, where, as they say, "premature withdrawal" carries with it a "substantial penalty."

In other words, you should be willing to earn a slightly lower rate of interest on your contingency-fund balances so you can get them out anytime you want. Money you won't need for a while generally belongs in the stock market. If prices are going down and your cash is on the sidelines, you still want the flexibility to get back into the market when it turns up again.

CDs or Money Market Funds: Which Is Better?

The two principal types of bank deposits designed primarily for savings—as opposed to checking accounts—are *certificates of deposit* (CDs) and *money market accounts*. CDs are deposits for a fixed term, usually from three months to five years, and carry those penalties for early withdrawal. Technically, a CD could be for any fixed length of time. If you knew, for example, that you would need the money precisely two years and 337 days from now, you could arrange a customized CD with your banker. But few people can plan their lives quite that well, so instead they opt for the standard maturities offered by the banks. Generally I don't recommend these, because you are giving up flexibility for a very small additional return.

Money market accounts have no fixed time period for deposits, and most of them carry checking-account privileges, but only for checks above a certain limit, usually $250 or $500. Banks do provide these types of accounts, but most money market accounts are offered by brokerage firms and similar institutions, so those deposits generally aren't insured by the federal government. If this bothers you, put your money into a money market fund that invests only in government securities; the rate will be about ½ percent less.

These rates fluctuate daily with the market, so there's no point in quoting specific rates. However, I can give you the general ranges. The key short-term rate is the federal funds rate, the rate banks charge each other for lending funds overnight. It is very closely controlled, as the name might suggest, by the Federal Reserve Board. Most of the time, the average rate paid on money market funds is the same as the Fed funds rate, and the rate on CDs is ¼ to ½ percent higher. For 1988 and 1989, the Fed funds rate fluctuated between 8 and 10 percent. Over the longer run, it tends to run 3 to 4 percent above the rate of inflation, but is higher during booms and lower during recessions; for example, it fell to 6 percent in early 1991. The rate is also higher when inflation is accelerating and lower when it is receding. So these are only general guidelines.

Rates on CDs and money market funds are very similar, so if you think there is any reasonable chance you might need the funds before the maturity date, choose the money market fund.

If you want to shop rates, every week *Barron's* has a list of the banks that pay the highest rates on 90-day, 6-month, 1-year, 2½-year and

5-year CDs, and on money market accounts. It also lists the various money market rates offered by over 400 money market mutual funds: such big names as Fidelity, Vanguard, Dreyfus, and Dean Witter, plus many smaller funds.

On a fairly typical day in 1990, when the federal funds rate was at 8¼ percent, *Barron's* gave the following quotes. The top rate on a money market account at a federally insured bank was 8.85 percent. The top rate for a 90-day CD was 8.83 percent; for a 6-month CD, 8.89 percent; for a 1-year CD, 8.77 percent; for a 2½-year CD, 8.89 percent; and for a 5-year CD, 8.90 percent. The highest money market rates outside the banking system were 8.8 percent, offered by the Dreyfus Worldwide Dollar money market fund and the Fidelity Spartan money market fund. In other words, for practical purposes, your highest rate was around 8.8 percent whether you chose a money market fund or a CD of any maturity. In that case the choice is easy; go with the money market fund because it gives more flexibility.

If you're purchasing a CD of a fixed length, and the bank is federally insured (all of those in the *Barron's* listing must satisfy that criterion), there's nothing wrong with picking the highest rate. Be aware that banks with the highest rates are probably in trouble and desperately need deposits to stay afloat; but if the bank is insured, you will get all your principal and interest back even if they do belly-flop.

Money market funds differ from CDs in two principal aspects, besides the flexibility of immediate withdrawal. First, not all of the investments are federally insured; certainly the ones with the highest rates aren't. Second, since these rates vary all the time, what appears to be a pleasingly high rate now could very well become a mediocre one next month. Of course in that case, there's nothing to prohibit you from switching funds, but there are costs attached to wiring the money and keeping up with the quotes, so in general it doesn't pay to switch to a fund with a peak rate just when market rates are starting to turn down.

The yield you receive also depends on the expense ratios various firms charge. All funds have some expenses; that's how they make their money, and that's also what pays for the advertisements. Most firms hold the expense ratio constant over time, but some funds could defer expenses for a while to build up business with a high yield, and then lower the boom.

This isn't illegal; quite the contrary. In fact, some big firms will advertise that, for a limited time only, they are reducing or entirely waiving the expenses in order to increase the yield and attract new business. You just have to read the fine print.

The yields on the 400 funds listed in *Barron's* and other sources generally fall into three groups. The highest are a few funds that invest part of the money in foreign securities, where short-term rates are higher. The vast majority in the middle invest in CDs, commercial paper, and bankers acceptances. Those with the lowest yields generally invest only in Treasury securities.

Do Tax-free Money Market Funds Save You Money?

One alternative that remains popular is the tax-free money market fund. The rates vary by state, depending on variations in the income tax rates. Before the 1991 tax hike, funds for investors who live in states that have no income taxes were yielding about 71 percent of the average taxable money market fund. Since the top marginal tax rate was 28 percent, you're a little bit worse off with the tax-free fund—so why bother. In states with large income-tax bites, such as New York and California, the tax-free yield manages to drop just enough that it too is just below the equivalent taxable money market fund adjusted for the combined marginal tax rates. That's why I don't think the tax-free funds are worth it.

At this point you may be more than ready to point out that Congress raised the top marginal tax rate to 31 percent in 1991. But guess what. As soon as the particulars of the new tax bill were known, the ratio of the yield on municipal to comparable corporate bonds fell from 71 to 68 percent.

Until the recent S&L scandals, many banks would advertise rates for so-called Jumbo CDs, which are $100,000 or more. Since the federal guarantee applies up to $100,000, there really wasn't any risk even if the S&L did happen to fold. My beef with this type of investment is that if you have $100,000, it should be in some other form of investment, such as stocks or real estate—not in the bank. So I'm not recommending Jumbo CDs either.

Bank Guarantees: Another Oxymoron

Furthermore, just because the bank "guarantees" you a high rate for the life of the deposit doesn't mean it will honor that guarantee. In case you think I'm being too cynical here, and are sure that large New York money-center banks would certainly honor their commitments, I refer you to the case of Irving Trust, as reported in the *Wall Street Journal*. Since the article needs no embellishment, it is reprinted here verbatim.

Here's a Guarantee You Can't 'Always' Take to the Bank

BY RANDALL SMITH
Staff Reporter of THE WALL STREET JOURNAL

NEW YORK—How long is "always" on Wall Street?

At Irving Trust Co., it seems, always is about seven months. That's how long ago the bank promised to "always" pay a special high interest rate on its biggest deposits. Now, however, Irving has decided to renege.

In a brochure last September promoting its special "One Wall Street" account—named after the bank's address—Irving said balances of $15,000 and up were "guaranteed always to pay you" at least one half of a percentage point over the Donoghue Money Fund average, a standard benchmark for short-term interest rates.

This month, however, Irving Vice President Cynthia Cole sent out a letter saying, "Dear Customer: I am writing to inform you of some changes in the way in which interest will be calculated on your One Wall Street Account."

Effective April 14, Ms. Cole said, balances under $50,000 will receive interest equal to the Donoghue average. Balances between $50,000 and $100,000 are entitled to the same average plus one tenth of a percentage point. Beyond that, balances earn a maximum of one quarter of a percentage point over the average.

So what happened to that half of a percentage point premium "guaranteed always?"

A spokesman for Bank of New York Co., which acquired Irving and its parent Irving Bank Corp. last December following a bitter year-long takeover battle, noted that Irving had always "reserved the right to change the spread and the way the spread was calculated."

The spokesman said that the new management at Bank of New York "probably felt there was too great a disparity between this yield and what is available in the markets."

The spokesman added: "I think it was a little enthusiastic language. I think it's understood that it's 'guaranteed always' until the terms and conditions are changed, which in fact they were. In business, nothing is forever."

Remember what is written on square one: Higher yield means higher risk. If you do stumble across a money market instrument that pays 2 percent more than the going rate, refer back to page 68 to find out why.

There's a time to speculate and a time to play it safe. I'm not averse to speculating if the odds are right. I've made ten times my investment—or lost it all—in overnight trading in options. But when it comes to bank accounts, I'm old-fashioned. That's money for paying the household bills, not for risk-taking. I take it to the bank around the corner where I can keep my eye on it, so to speak, and earn only the average rate of return. My wealth comes from real estate, the stock market, and building my own companies—not from an extra 1 percent yield on bank accounts. I know from personal experience, some of it bitter, that banks seldom feel any obligation to honor their written commitments.

BORROWING FROM THE BANKS: DOING BUSINESS WITH YOUR ADVERSARY

What differentiates a banker from a used-car salesman?

The used-car salesman knows when he's lying.

At least once, and probably several times in your life, you will have to borrow money from a bank or some other financial institution. Except for truly unusual circumstances, you are foolish not to borrow to buy your home, because over the long run it is an appreciating asset. The interest on home mortgages is still deductible, while most other interest isn't. Borrowing for your children's education is also a worthwhile investment. Many people borrow on a regular basis to buy cars, although, as I've indicated, that practice is more questionable. Other borrowing, especially for nonessentials at usurious interest rates, is just plain foolish. But almost all of us borrow at one time or another.

Let's get one thing straight. Bankers and other money lenders are in business to make a profit, and they don't give a damn about you personally. This shouldn't come as a total shock. When you go to buy the weekly roast at the supermarket, the butcher doesn't care about your personal life. Neither does the plumber when he fixes your toilet, nor the salesperson at the shoe store.

For some reason, though, the banks have chosen as their advertising message the idea of "relationship" banking, which seems to suggest that if you do all your banking at one institution, the bank will look upon you more fondly when it comes time to borrow money. That's a total crock. Banks want your business for one reason only: They plan to make money on the deal. They have no greater interest in your personal happiness than does the butcher, plumber, or shoe salesman.

I'm not knocking bankers particularly. As a class, they are no worse than, say, insurance salesmen. But most of the ones that you deal with— as opposed to the ones who lend Amalgamated Xygots $100 billion for an LBO—are poorly paid, unmotivated, and not particularly intelligent. Someone sitting behind a big desk with a dark blue suit, a white shirt or blouse, and an impressive title is not necessarily your friend. You are in there for a business deal. If the person on the other side of the desk thinks the bank can make money off it, you will probably get the loan; if he doesn't, you won't. Just don't confuse the face behind the desk with all those Madison Avenue commercials that suggest this empty suit actually wants to help you. The people who write the ads don't make the loans.

I have done business with many banks—and borrowed millions of dollars—and while a few banks were a pleasure to work with, most were despicable. In almost every case, the loan that I finally did get was rejected by some other bank, so don't take it personally when Mr. or Ms. Subnormal Loan Officer says you aren't a good enough credit risk for the likes of their bank. I once got turned down for a $250,000 loan at a bank where the company I owned had a $250,000 deposit; naturally I pulled the deposit. And the next week the banker actually phoned to ask if there was a problem.

Admittedly, if you get turned down by five banks in a row, there may be something questionable about your financial situation. In general, though, I would strongly suggest that you contact at least three banks when borrowing money. I presume you wouldn't buy a new car from the first dealer without checking out the prices others are offering. Believe me, all loan rates are not created equal.

In fact, about the only rule of thumb I learned from working with the banks was reinforcement of the old saying "familiarity breeds contempt." When I went to bankers whom I knew well and who had had my accounts for many years, I usually got turned down for further loans. On the other hand, when I went to a fresh bank—and offered vague hints that they might get all of my business if their terms were favorable—I initially got the royal reception.

You might think this is backward. Wouldn't a bank be more likely to give favorable treatment to someone who has had an account with it for many years, whose income has grown steadily, who has steadily increased the size of the balance, and who has never missed a payment?

You might answer yes, but then you aren't in the banking business. In over 30 years of dealing with banks, my experience has been that banks *will* work hard to bring in the new account; but once they've done that, they generally lose interest in staying on good terms. I once asked a banker who was a close personal acquaintance why, and he mumbled something about the bank not wanting to loan me and my various companies too much money, and would prefer that I spread the risk around to others. That's why I say that relationship banking is a joke.

It's fairly important to recognize this fundamental failure of bankers, because most people, being creatures of habit, tend to go to the bank where they already do business to ask for another loan. There's certainly nothing wrong with including your current bank on the list of possible sources of funds. But you will almost always do better if you also try to obtain credit from three other banks or similar institutions. At least in my experience, one of them will give you a better rate every single time.

Since buying a house is probably the single most important investment decision you will make, I'll discuss the various types of mortgages you should consider in the next chapter. But what about other borrowing?

No short list of comments can cover all the chicanery of bankers, but there are a few hints that should make life a little easier for you—besides the obvious one of looking for the lowest rate.

1. If the bank says you can borrow money at a certain rate, such as for a mortgage, often that rate is not fixed until the money has actually been transferred, regardless of what your written document says. The only time some bankers believe written documents is when these documents are in their favor. If market rates rise between the time the bank signs and the time you borrow, your rate goes up. Your only recourse is to refuse the loan and start all over again. Naturally, there is no similar flexibility in the downward direction.

2. If you borrow money from the bank for your business and the bank later decides it does not like you, it can demand its money back. Immediately. This can happen even if you have a perfect credit record and have never missed or been late with a payment. If that leaves you in a hole, too bad. It happens all the time, it has happened to me, and it has happened to many other people I know. The practice is known as calling your loan, and if you have signed a document permitting the bank to do this, you have no legal recourse. If you don't agree to that clause, and the loan is not secured by your home or other valuable assets, you probably won't get the money at all.

3. If the bank guarantees to pay you a certain rate of interest, the guarantee means nothing, as I've already shown. They may decide to change their minds later. Similarly, if you sign up for a credit card at what appears to be an unusually low rate, the bank will probably raise the rate fairly soon.

Why are banks so unscrupulous?

It's all a matter of simple economics. When you buy a car, a VCR, or a new coat, the seller doesn't want the merchandise back. He would have to sell it on the secondhand market at a small fraction of the price you paid for it. However, if the bank gets its money back, it can turn right around and lend it to someone else at the same rate—there is no discount on returned funds. Furthermore, these days banks make most of their money by charging you fees up front for setting up the loan. In plain and simple English, that means that the more often they can turn over the money, the higher the rate of return they can earn. Remember, I told you banks are in business to make a profit, although admittedly some of them aren't very good at it.

Banks are still a useful place to borrow money, however, because they have the most to lend. And their terms are, by and large, usually better than those of other lenders. But please don't make the mistake of thinking that you have a friend at the bank.

CREDIT CARDS: BORROWER BEWARE

I probably use a credit card virtually every day of my life, and for a very simple reason: I don't like to carry lots of cash in the big city. This way, if I'm mugged I'm only out $40 or so. The credit card comes in very handy as a substitute for cash. But that's all it is. It is not—or at least should not be—considered a way to borrow money.

Look at it this way. Suppose you were to receive in the mail a beautifully embossed envelope that turned out to contain a perfect replica of a $10 bill. The smoothly written prose in the accompanying letter explains that if you'll just send in $20, you'll receive an actual $10 bill by return mail. That probably wouldn't get too many takers—but that's precisely the kind of deal banks are proposing on the credit cards they offer these days.

Don't get me wrong. It's virtually impossible to operate in the business world without a suitable choice of plastic. Try buying an airline ticket, checking into a hotel, or renting a car without a credit card; you're lucky if they don't summon an officer of the law. Or try to explain to the corporate accounting department—or, if you're self-employed, the IRS—that the light business lunch of $174.32 was strictly business, but no, you don't have a credit card receipt. Somehow the restaurant receipt, on which you wrote in the amount yourself, doesn't have the same ring of credibility.

Because computers are less than human, I always carry a minimum of three working credit cards, since every so often some dumb machine screws up my account. It happens with the biggies, too—in the past, American Express, Chase Manhattan, and Citicorp have all refused to honor my card at one time or another because of some back-office goof-up. You can either have a temper tantrum on the spot and demand to speak to a supervisor, which is often difficult at 10:30 P.M. after a leisurely dinner, or you can pull out another card that still works and straighten the mess out later. In my case, American Express actually straightened out the problem, so I still have their card, but Chase and Citicorp couldn't have cared less, so I just moved on to the next bank on the list. My new cards came by return mail.*

Borrowing at 18 to 20 percent, when other sources of borrowing are available at 10 to 12 percent, just doesn't make any sense to me, unless the amount you're borrowing is so small that the transaction costs wipe out the difference or no one else will lend you money.

I'll concede that can happen when you're just starting out on your own. Many recent college graduates, who have not previously held full-time jobs or established credit ratings, are not considered suitable risks by banks. On the other hand, most of them are deluged by credit card applications. For those who are setting up their own households but don't yet have much income from their new job, borrowing on a credit card sometimes makes sense. What should obviously be avoided is keeping up that bad habit long after your income and credit rating have been established—or even worse, becoming a credit-card junkie, increasing your revolving debt to the limit, getting a second card and doing the same, ad nauseum.

Getting the Lowest Rate—Watch Your Step

While the average rate on credit card debt has been about 20 percent for several years, some banks appear to offer much lower rates. Once again, you have to be very careful here. Many financial advisers will steer you to an organization called the Arkansas Federal Savings Bank in Little Rock. It so happens that Arkansas still has a state usury law that says banks can't charge an interest rate more than 5 percent above the Federal Reserve discount rate. Most credit cards carry an interest rate that is 10 to 12 percent above the discount rate, and in fact, it's difficult to make any money on a 5 percent spread, considering processing costs and allowances for bad debts. As a result, most Arkansas banks restrict the issuance of credit cards to their best customers. However, Arkansas Federal is differ-

---

* Just as this book was going to press, I received notification from Citicorp that they had straightened out my account. It only took them 17 months. But Citicorp had the last laugh. Just to make sure I still couldn't use the card—in the unlikely chance I wanted to—the statement showed a net balance of 50 cents overdue, and hence an available credit line of zero.

ent; it welcomes out-of-state business, and just to show its goodwill, actually charges ⅛ percent less than the maximum permitted rate. So what's the catch?

It's very simple. Almost all banks give you a grace period of 25 to 30 days between the time you're billed and the time you must pay before interest charges start to accumulate. But Arkansas Federal's grace period, except for their special in-state customers, is a big flat *zero*. So let's say you charged $500 a month on your card and paid each monthly bill within the usual grace period. You would end up paying $60 per year in interest to Arkansas Federal, compared with zero at most other banks. Far from being the best deal in town, it's actually close to the worst.

The lowest credit-card rates with the normal 25- to 30-day grace period are usually about 7 percent above the discount rate, which means they are about 5 percent below the average rates. There are a few catches here, but they aren't nearly as serious as the Arkansas trap. Here's what to watch for:

1. Bait and switch. The bank will offer a very low interest rate for a year or so, then suddenly move it up to the average 19.8 percent rate. Chevy Chase Savings and Loan in Maryland did exactly that; they successfully bought market share and then hiked their rates.
2. Rates on cash advances may be quite a bit higher than on credit card purchases, and the interest on advances almost always starts from day one. So if that's why you signed up for a particular card, check the fine print.
3. The rates are variable, tied either to the discount, federal funds, or prime rate. Thus if interest rates rise, you could find your carrying charges mounting in a big hurry. Of course, the 19.8 percent rate could also increase, but in practice it is seldom changed. Even with an increase in the variable rate, you will still be below the average; it's just something to check carefully.

The list of banks that offer the best rates changes from time to time, of course, but you can find a list of bank credit cards with the lowest rates, annual fees, and grace periods in *Barron's* every week. If you're shopping price, that's where to start. Just remember, the rates aren't guaranteed for any specific length of time.

Credit-Card Premiums: Not Worth a Detour

Most banks, however, don't bother to compete on price; instead, they try to dazzle you with all sorts of extras. Many banks will waive the annual fee for the first 6 or 12 months in order to get your business; others charge an unusually low rate of interest for the first few months. If you don't mind opening new accounts quite often, you could save enough—to order a better bottle of wine at your next dinner.

Others offer free travel and auto insurance, lost-luggage insurance, or sweepstakes offering exotic first-class vacations for two to your choice of paradise. On balance, these gimmicks are not worth more than $10 to you. Not worth a detour, as the Michelin folks might say.

Most of the time, then, you should use your credit card for convenience only, taking care to pay all of your outstanding balance before the grace period has expired. Once in a while, though, you might use your credit card as a source of money for personal loans, providing you have one of those credit cards where the interest rate on cash advances is 7 percent above the discount rate, compared with the 10 to 12 percent average.

Ordinarily, any given bank will charge you a higher rate of interest on a credit card loan than on a personal loan that you have signed for—even, one that's not backed by specific collateral. A bank in Connecticut or Texas probably isn't about to make an unsecured personal loan to someone in Los Angeles or Omaha whom they have never even met. And you are not likely to travel hundreds or even thousands of miles just to save a few percent on interest charges.

Yet since many out-of-state banks are soliciting your credit card account, it's quite possible that you can borrow on that card at, say, 14 percent, whereas your neighborhood bank will charge you 17 to 18 percent on a personal loan. In that case, providing you are just borrowing the money for only a few months, the credit card is the better deal.

Most of the time, though, except for borrowing for a mortgage, the rates are so high that they will cut into your ability to accumulate wealth. So my rule is: Borrow only for your house. In that case, because it's an appreciating asset, the sooner the better. I'll explain why in the next chapter.

Chapter 8

Buying a Home—
Your Most Important Investment

Over the long run, buying a home will probably be your best investment for two reasons: leverage and the tax laws.

Leverage allows you to buy an asset with only 10 to 20 percent down—without having to worry about margin calls.

The tax laws allow you to build up the value of the asset without paying taxes as the value increases, and in many cases even without paying taxes on the accumulated gain when you decide to sell.

No other asset provides you with both these benefits.

The benefits of owning real estate do *not* depend on some superheated real estate boom. Tax laws and leverage will turn your real estate into a superior investment even if it only keeps up with the rate of inflation—and historically it has done much better than that.

You have to live somewhere. Rent and the monthly mortgage payment for any particular house or condominium are usually about the same amount after taking into account the tax deductions for mortgage interest and real estate taxes. But owning the house gives you an equity buildup. So the choice should be an easy one.

Unless you can't afford any mortgage at all. But it's well worth scrimping and saving for a few years so you can at least get a seat on the Real Estate Express, even if it's in the boiler room. And if you can't save, find an investor who will put up the down payment. For even with an ordinary investment—a house whose price rises no faster than the national average—a 10 percent down payment means your equity will still earn about 20 percent per year. Even if you have to borrow the down payment or share the equity with a stranger, it's still your best long-term investment.

I will concede that if you try, it is possible to buy a house that will not appreciate in value. In the short run, in fact, this happens on a fairly regular basis. Real estate prices go through cycles just like the prices of all other types of financial assets. But in the long run, it's a rare occurrence indeed.

From 1946 to 1990, the overall rate of inflation averaged 4½ percent per year, while real estate prices have increased an average of 7 percent per year. Using the Rule of 72, that means housing prices doubled every 10 years. Seven percent is no better, and probably somewhat worse, than you can get from an insured money market account. But in that case, you don't have leverage working for you. It makes all the difference.

LEVERAGE MAKES ALL THE DIFFERENCE

Time for some simple arithmetic. Suppose you buy a house for $100,000 with $10,000 down, plus another $6,000 for closing costs. Ten years later, it's worth $200,000, and the equity in the house—even if you haven't paid off any of the mortgage—is $110,000. Your initial $16,000 investment has risen more than 6-fold over the 10-year period, which works out to an average annual rate of increase of 20 percent per year. At 7 percent, $16,000 in the bank grows to $32,000 in 10 years—in a house, it grows to $110,000. That's really all you need to know in order to get started in real estate.

Not everyone has $16,000 free and clear to invest. And not everyone can afford the monthly payments of approximately $750 a month—closer to $900 a month including insurance, real estate taxes, and repairs. Furthermore, decent $100,000 houses aren't available in all parts of the country. Of course, the same arithmetic applies for a $200,000 house, except that you need a $32,000 nest egg.

Some people always have excuses for not buying. If you want to stay poor, make excuses. But if you want to start building your assets to the point where one day you'll be rich, start by investing in your own home.

DO REAL ESTATE PRICES ALWAYS RISE?

I've made it clear enough that there are no ironclad guarantees in this book. But if you hold on to a house for eight years or more—the length of the average mortgage—the historical record shows that, 99 percent of the time, you will make money.

Table 15 illustrates three key facts about real estate prices. First, in every year since World War II—except for 1949, when the CPI declined—the average housing price has risen. And that includes the real estate "depression" year of 1990. Second, on balance, housing prices have risen 2½ percent per year faster than the overall rate of inflation. Inflation is the driving force behind housing prices; a 1 percent increase in inflation will also boost housing prices by 1 percent.

Third, if you look closely at the numbers in this table, a more subtle pattern emerges. When housing prices rise much faster than inflation in any given year, the rate of inflation and interest rates usually rise during the next year or two. (See 1954–55, 1971–72, and 1986.) Conversely, when housing prices rise about the same or less than inflation, inflation and interest rates usually drop during the next year or two. (See 1972–75, 1980–82, and 1989.)

Thus the gap between the gain in housing prices and the overall rate of inflation is a fairly reliable, although by no means infallible, guide to how inflation and interest rates will change over the next two years. Few forecasters know this, but it will help you to determine whether "now" is a good time to buy a house. If the gap between the change in housing prices and inflation has been well above average for the past three years, be cautious about buying, and if that trend has continued for five years, *watch out!* If, on the other hand, housing prices have risen about the same or less than inflation for the past three years, you're probably looking at the beginning of another cyclical boom in prices.

These figures, and some others that aren't shown here, can be summarized in five very simple rules.

1. Over the long run, the average price of a house rises at the same rate as the average family income.
2. Because of long-term increases in productivity and the number of people working per family, income rises about 2½ percent per year faster than inflation. That means housing prices rise about 2½ percent per year faster than inflation.
3. Sometimes income grows faster than usual, or interest rates don't keep up with inflation. During those times, housing prices rise

Table 15
Change in Housing Prices and Inflation, 1946–90

	Federal Housing Administration Data				National Association of Realtors Data		
	Average Price	% Gain	CPI Inflation		Average Price	% Gain	CPI Inflation
1946	6,300	..	..	1968	22,300	8.8	4.2
1947	7,400	17.5	14.4	1969	23,700	6.3	5.5
1948	8,600	16.2	8.1	1970	25,700	8.4	5.7
1949	8,300	-3.5	-1.2	1971	28,000	8.9	4.4
1950	9,400	13.3	1.3	1972	30,100	7.5	3.2
1951	10,000	6.4	7.9	1973	32,900	9.3	6.2
1952	10,100	1.0	1.9	1974	35,800	8.8	11.0
1953	10,600	5.0	0.8	1975	39,000	8.9	9.1
1954	11,400	7.5	0.7	1976	42,200	8.2	5.8
1955	12,200	7.0	-0.4	1977	47,900	13.5	6.5
1956	13,100	7.4	1.5	1978	55,500	15.9	7.6
1957	13,600	3.8	3.3	1979	64,200	15.7	11.3
1958	13,700	0.7	2.8	1980	72,800	13.4	13.5
1959	14,400	5.1	0.7	1981	78,300	7.6	10.3
1960	15,100	4.9	1.7	1982	80,500	2.8	6.2
1961	15,400	2.0	1.0	1983	83,100	3.2	3.2
1962	15,800	2.6	1.0	1984	86,000	3.5	4.3
1963	16,300	3.2	1.3	1985	90,800	5.6	3.6
1964	17,100	4.9	1.3	1986	98,500	8.5	1.9
1965	18,100	5.8	1.6	1987	106,300	7.9	3.6
1966	19,300	6.6	2.9	1988	112,800	6.1	4.1
1967	20,500	6.2	3.1	1989	118,100	4.7	4.8
				1990	118,600	0.4	5.4
22-year average		5.9	2.6	23-year average		8.0	6.1

more than usual. If that happens five years in a row, it's a bad time to buy.

4. Sometimes income grows slower than usual, or interest rates rise faster than inflation. During those times, housing prices rise less than usual. If that happens three years in a row, it's a good time to buy.

5. These national trends are often exaggerated in certain regions where growth in income has been much higher, or much lower, than the national average. Housing prices follow accordingly.

The results in Table 15 don't necessarily mean your house will always appreciate in value every year. You could buy in the wrong year. For that matter, it is possible to buy a house in what will soon become a ghost town, or in a section of town that is just about to be turned into a slum, or one that is about to be hit with a depression. Some people manage to overpay for real estate even in the best areas. Obviously you can't buy real estate with your eyes closed. If half the storefronts in town are boarded up, it's not a growth area. And if you have to step over drug addicts to get to the front door, the neighborhood is probably not improving. But you already know that.

Occasionally prices in entire regions decline. Some people who bought houses in Houston in 1981 couldn't get their money out even 10 years later. Many other cities in the Energy Patch carry the same tale of woe. Average prices in Houston and Oklahoma City were indeed lower in 1990 than in 1982, as is shown in Table 16. During the late 1980s, prices in the Northeast also started to soften, although most 1990 prices were still above 1987 levels. However, while these episodes do point out that in the short run real estate is not always a one-way street, they don't change my opinion about the long-term desirability of investing in real estate.

Furthermore, the spectacular rise and fall in oil prices from 1973 to 1986 was a once-in-a-lifetime event that will not be repeated. The optimism in the Energy Patch after the second energy crisis boosted oil prices to $34 a barrel became irrational, and the amount of overbuilding that took place was so severe that a real estate glut would have developed even if oil prices had kept rising. But that was almost impossible, given that higher oil prices were already raising domestic production, reducing imports, and putting downward pressure on OPEC prices. Five years later, the whole house of cards collapsed.

In retrospect it seems so simple, yet many of the best economic and business minds were fooled at the time. And if they didn't know, how can the average home buyer foresee the dramatic reversal in trends?

I'm not asking you to be a forecaster, but I will give you the Evans Rule of Real Estate Markets: If home prices in a given area have tripled during the past five years, don't buy. Wait until prices decline. If prices have risen less than inflation in the past three years, it is definitely time to buy.

Over the past 40 years, there have been no exceptions to that rule.

Thus unless you buy at the top, over the long run real estate will always be a good investment. While the price of every single house in the United States won't rise steadily forever, the average price will continue to outpace inflation. Unless you buy dumb, you will benefit by that trend.

Table 16
Housing Prices by Metropolitan Area

	1982	Third Quarter 1987	Third Quarter 1989	Third Quarter 1990	Average Change(%) 1982–1990
Northeast					
New York	70.5	183.0	183.8	176.7	12.2
Boston	80.2	181.6	183.3	175.9	10.3
Hartford	71.1	165.4	168.5	159.4	10.6
Washington	87.2	108.4	145.3	153.4	7.3
Providence	49.7	126.6	132.0	129.8	12.7
Philadelphia	58.1	84.4	108.4	120.0	9.5
Albany	47.1	88.6	92.2	109.4	11.1
Baltimore	62.0	87.9	98.9	108.4	7.2
Rochester	49.5	74.1	80.8	81.2	6.4
South					
Dallas/Ft. Worth	74.0	89.3	94.7	90.7	2.6
Miami	74.9	83.5	86.6	92.3	2.6
Ft. Lauderdale	74.2	80.8	83.9	93.6	2.9
Birmingham	60.6	71.6	80.3	83.3	4.1
Memphis	59.3	75.2	78.3	78.9	3.6
San Antonio	58.3	72.1	68.2	65.5	1.5
Houston	77.2	67.3	70.9	72.2	−0.8
Tampa	53.9	65.0	73.8	72.4	3.8
Oklahoma City	58.4	61.4	56.2	55.0	−0.7
Midwest					
Chicago	73.0	91.2	111.4	122.0	6.6
Minneapolis/St. Paul	72.4	80.9	87.8	88.2	2.5
St. Louis	57.0	75.7	78.3	82.7	4.8
Columbus	57.8	72.7	81.3	83.1	4.6
Milwaukee	65.8	70.9	80.0	85.2	3.3
Kansas City	58.1	69.2	69.1	75.6	3.3
Cincinnati	56.5	68.8	77.9	81.9	4.8
Cleveland	63.0	68.5	77.8	83.9	3.6
Detroit	47.5	65.9	76.2	78.6	6.5

Table 16
Housing Prices by Metropolitan Area (cont.)

	1982	Third Quarter 1987	Third Quarter 1989	Third Quarter 1990	Average Change(%) 1982– 1990
Indianapolis	50.6	62.8	72.8	75.8	5.2
Louisville	46.0	53.3	59.3	62.0	3.8
West					
San Francisco	124.9	175.9	269.4	261.6	9.7
Orange County	133.3	167.7	249.1	241.7	7.7
Los Angeles	113.4	145.4	224.6	211.4	8.1
San Diego	98.6	131.7	178.4	186.6	8.3
Denver	76.2	91.0	88.5	87.8	1.8
Salt Lake City	64.6	71.1	70.3	71.0	1.2
Phoenix	66.7	82.7	76.8	85.8	3.2

Prices in thousands of dollars.

GOOD REAL ESTATE IS ALWAYS "TOO EXPENSIVE"

Approximately 40 percent of the total population, or over 100 million people, live in the 20 largest metropolitan areas of the United States. Naturally, housing is more expensive in these areas than in the less densely populated parts of the country. In each of these areas, there are a few sections that are most desirable, because of their central location, cultural amenities, or low-crime environment. "Everyone" would like to live in these areas, but obviously there isn't room. As a result, the price of land in these areas is bid up to the point where most people cannot afford housing there. The pricing system serves its proper function of rationing scarce resources. If real incomes in the area suddenly rise rapidly, housing prices will increase proportionately. While you can buy more cars, vacations, and fine clothing if your income increases, your housing dollar in the most desirable neighborhoods hardly stretches at all, because the amount of land is fixed.

At the beginning of 1990, an unprepossessing town house in the Georgetown section of Washington, D.C., cost $500,000 to $600,000.

A house of the same size way out in the suburbs costs about a quarter of that price—and probably needs fewer repairs. Is it worth scraping to aspire to the more expensive house, bearing in mind that the actual living quarters will be no larger?

You have to make that decision yourself; it depends on the trade-off between current and future consumption. But I will offer the following guideline. Whereas real estate prices have increased about 7 percent per year over the long run, prices in the best sections of town have increased about 12 percent per year over the past 40 years. Over a lifetime, this makes a fantastic amount of difference. For purposes of comparison, consider two homes, each selling for $100,000, one of which appreciates at 7 percent and the other at 12 percent per year. In fact, the home in the better neighborhood wouldn't be selling at $100,000, but this comparison keeps the arithmetic simple.

	Value of $100,000 home after			
	10 yrs.	**20 yrs.**	**30 yrs.**	**40 yrs.**
7% annual appreciation	$196.7	387.0	726.2	1,400.7
12% annual appreciation	310.6	964.6	2,996.0	9,305.1
7% adjusted for inflation	128.0	163.9	209.8	268.5
12% adjusted for inflation	206.1	424.8	875.5	1,804.4

All figures in thousands of dollars.

At first glance, you may think the compound-interest button on my calculator went berserk. How could a $100,000 house ever be worth almost $10 million, even 40 years later?

I'll give you a few examples. A stand-alone house in Georgetown that sold for $10,000 right after World War II recently changed hands at $1.5 million. Town houses in midtown Manhattan that sold in the $50,000–$100,000 range right after the war are now bought and sold at $5 million, even with the real estate slump. Beverly Hills is even pricier; those $3 to $4 million homes sold for under $100,000 just 30 years ago.

Since these gigantic figures often seem a bit difficult to comprehend, I have also calculated them by deflating for the rise in inflation—the deterioration in the purchasing power of the dollar. Even so, the investment performance is still magnificent on a house that appreciates 12 percent per year. The $100,000 house would still be worth $1.8 million in inflation-adjusted dollars 40 years later. When you're ready to retire, buy a similar house in a less classy neighborhood for about $270,000, invest the remaining $1.5 million in blue chip stocks, and enjoy the rest of your life.

The problem, of course, is that houses in the most desirable parts of town are already too expensive or, if they are reasonably priced, far too cramped. So some sort of compromise is necessary until you can build up your wealth from other sources. But my general advice, in contrast to what many other financial planners will tell you, is to buy at least as much house as you can afford. If you find you need money later on, you can borrow on the built-up equity in the house at a much lower rate than that equity is appreciating.

HOW FAST DOES YOUR EQUITY BUILD UP?

Few of us live in the same house for 40 years. In fact, the average length of a mortgage is about eight years. The stated term of the mortgage is usually 30 years, but in practice it is an average of eight years until the house is refinanced or sold to someone else. For that reason, Table 17 shows the rate of return earned on equity, year by year, for the first 10 years.

All figures are for a $100,000 house; the results are proportional for more expensive homes. The assumptions assume 6 percent closing costs on buying and 8 percent settlement costs on selling, including the broker's commission. Figures are provided for 7 and 12 percent annual appreciation, and for 20 and 10 percent down payments. I've also included a line for a shared equity mortgage, where you pay only the closing costs and some other investor puts up the money for a mortgage; that concept is discussed below. These results show that:

1. Even with the most conservative assumptions—20 percent down and 7 percent annual appreciation—your equity earns almost 15 percent per year. However, note that this doesn't apply until after the third year. So if for some reason you are planning to live in the house for less than three years, that is one of the few times it's actually better to rent than to buy.
2. The maximum rate of return generally occurs during the seventh or eighth year, which is hardly startling news given that this is the life of the average mortgage. Beyond that, if you stay in the same house, it pays to refinance and put your equity to work elsewhere— or buy a more expensive house.
3. Of course the rate of return on equity is larger with a smaller down payment, but this has to be balanced against a larger monthly payment. With a 10 percent mortgage rate, you would pay $1,000

Table 17
Rate of Return on Equity Invested in a House

7% Annual Appreciation

Year Number	1	2	3	4	5	6	7	8	9	10
Value of home	107.0	114.5	122.5	131.1	140.3	150.1	160.6	171.8	183.8	196.7
less: selling costs	−8.6	−9.2	−9.8	−10.5	−11.2	−12.0	−12.8	−13.7	−14.7	−15.7
equals: net value	98.4	105.3	112.7	120.6	129.1	138.1	147.8	158.1	169.1	181.0
Return on $26,000 investment (20% down)	neg	neg	7.9	11.8	13.6	14.3	14.7	14.7	14.7	14.5
Return on 10% down	neg	neg	12.4	17.6	19.6	20.1	20.1	19.8	19.4	19.0
Return on no down payment (only closing costs; equity split)	neg	neg	1.9	14.5	19.4	21.3	21.8	21.8	21.5	21.0

12% Annual Appreciation

Year Number	1	2	3	4	5	6	7	8	9	10
Value of home	112.0	125.4	140.5	157.4	176.2	197.4	221.1	247.6	277.3	310.6
less: selling costs	−9.0	−10.0	−11.2	−12.6	−14.1	−15.8	−17.7	−19.8	−22.2	−24.8
equals: net value	103.0	115.4	129.3	144.8	162.1	181.6	203.4	227.8	255.1	285.8
Return on $26,000 investment (20% down)	neg	16.7	23.7	25.6	25.9	25.2	24.9	24.3	23.6	23.0
Return on 10% down	neg	26.0	34.9	36.0	35.1	33.8	32.3	30.9	29.6	28.5
Return on no down payment (only closing costs; equity split)	neg	13.3	34.7	39.0	38.9	37.6	36.0	34.4	32.9	31.5

* Based on $100,000 house. "Return" is average annual rate of return on investment.
Prices in thousands of dollars.

more per year for a $100,000 home with a 90 percent than an 80 percent mortgage, even if the rates were the same. In many cases, the mortgage rate is ½ percent higher if you select the smaller down payment, which would mean another $450 per year.

Nonetheless, the rate of return is better—10 percent is a lot easier for most people to scrape together.

4. It may look as if the no-down-payment option is the best of all. However, if you could somehow borrow the 10 percent down payment at less than a 20 percent interest rate, you would still be better off making the down payment yourself instead of having someone else share the gains; I'll explain this later. But if you can't, a shared-equity mortgage is still well worth it, since you only have to put down the closing costs.

Now have I convinced you to buy a house? Good. Let's get started.

FINDING THE DOWN PAYMENT

Lenders prefer that you have a 20 percent down payment in hand and a high enough income so that the monthly payment isn't more than 25 percent of your pretax income. If you meet these criteria—and if you have had a steady job for several years—there are plenty of financial institutions that would love to have your business, even in these days of stricter lending standards. Just shop around for the best deal.

However, I realize that most young couples, unless they have rich and generous relatives, don't have that kind of cash when they first start out. We certainly didn't. We bought our first house with 5 percent down and our second house with 10 percent down. They were modest houses in average neighborhoods, and in fact their prices only appreciated at the usual 7 percent per year. But the buildup in equity allowed us to leverage into much more spacious and expensive homes later on. So initial lack of capital is no excuse for not buying a home.

With skyrocketing housing prices in many areas and mortgage rates in the 10–12 percent range instead of 6 percent, many first-time would-be home buyers cannot qualify under these standard terms. For a $200,000 house, a 10 percent down payment, and a 10 percent interest rate, the mortgage payment including taxes and insurance would be about $1,700 per month—which implies a monthly income of $6,800 per month to qualify. Many young families don't meet that requirement.

In that case, you can utilize one of a number of options to buy a house with a smaller down payment or—at least for a while—a reduced mortgage rate. Of course, there's no free lunch in mortgages any more than in any other financial market. Eventually you will have to make up the interest that wasn't paid earlier. But it's reasonable to assume that your income will continue to grow, so you'll be able to afford those higher monthly payments later on. At the same time, your equity is busy growing at 20 percent per year.

Since it's important to start investing in real estate as soon as possible, the rest of this chapter discusses in some detail how you can reduce your down payment and select the right mortgage.

HOW TO REDUCE YOUR DOWN PAYMENT

1. Get an FHA loan.
2. Convince some lender you should qualify for a lower down payment.
3. Persuade the seller to take back a second mortgage, or in a few cases, assume his mortgage.
4. Rent with an option to buy.
5. Buy run-down, foreclosed, or distressed property.
6. Use a shared-equity mortgage.

FHA Loans: The Best Deal for Low-Cost Houses

The FHA loan program is alive and well and helping many first-time home buyers to get started. It won't help those who live in high-rent districts, because the maximum amount you can borrow is $124,875. (This figure is indexed annually for inflation.) But below that limit, it's only 3 percent down; although most lenders require 10 percent down, so I've used the latter figure in my calculations. In most regions of the country that's enough for a starter house. The major area of the country where this amount is inadequate is California. The state has on occasion offered some state-subsidized low down-payment loans, but is generally so swamped with applicants that only a small percentage who sign up ever get these preferred mortgages. It's like winning the lottery—not something you can bank on.

It's also rumored that Congress might raise the limits so that FHA mortgages would be available for starter homes in almost all areas of the country. Stay tuned, because if that happens, the FHA program will be an even better source of a low down-payment mortgage.

Talking Bankers into a Low Down Payment

During the 1980s, as we now know all too well, many bankers made loans that, to put it politely, couldn't stand the scrutiny of daylight. Not only were many loans made for much more than the reasonable value of the property, but money was sometimes loaned on real estate that never even existed. However, with the recent rash of bankruptcies in the S&L industry, mortgages are now being scrutinized with a more jaundiced eye, and lenders may be quite uninterested in hearing about how, although you don't have any money now and have gone bankrupt in the past, you still qualify as an excellent credit risk in the future.

Nonetheless, banks still have the discretion to grant you a mortgage with a 10 percent down payment even if you're outside FHA limits. The odds of obtaining a mortgage with less than 20 percent down are improved if:

1. You are young and have recently obtained a high-paying job with rapid potential for advancement, so that your monthly income will soon be far more than four times your monthly payment. If there are two wage earners in the family, so much the better.
2. The house is a standard, fairly modern one in what has been a rapidly appreciating neighborhood, and is reasonably priced.
3. Often a builder, in order to move his excess inventory, will offer you a 10 percent down payment on a new home.
4. You are willing to pay a few extra points, a higher-than-market mortgage rate, and the bank is hungry for business.

Getting information on this last item used to be an annoying, time-consuming matter, since it meant calling dozens of financial institutions and pleading with each of them to give you a 10 percent down-payment mortgage. But in this day and age of electronic information, that isn't necessary anymore. Virtually every large city has a touch-tone activated computerized data base, telling you which lenders are willing to offer the best terms. Furthermore, they no longer need to be in your particular area. If you live in New York, the best deal might be from a Florida or Texas bank or S&L, providing of course they are still in business.

This out-of-town information can be accessed in two ways. First, you can go to a real estate broker who participates in one of these nationwide data bases; it's much easier to call the brokers than to call the banks directly. Second, a company known as HSH Associates, with the usual acronym-type 800 number (call 800-information for details) will send you a list of the terms of loans from dozens of financial institutions in the state or major metropolitan area of your choice. The cost of the list as this book went to press was $18, although this figure has probably risen in the meantime. If you're serious about getting the best mortgage, $18 is a fairly modest price to pay for that information.

Seller Financing

We now turn to the art of personal negotiation, where you convince the seller to take back part of the mortgage. In many cases, the bank or other primary lending institution will provide an 80 percent mortgage, while the seller will offer a second mortgage for an additional 10 percent—leaving you with only a 10 percent down payment plus closing costs.

The seller, by the way, can be either the previous owner in person or a financial institution that has repossessed the property. Sometimes these institutions are so anxious to get the house off their list of nonperforming loans that they allow you to buy it with next to nothing down. Not always, of course—although you'll never know if you don't ask. Most of the time, however, this method works best if you deal directly with the individual family selling the house.

You might reasonably expect that the only properties where the seller would take back the mortgage would be undesirable or subpar investments. But this isn't necessarily the case. Luxury properties can often be purchased with a small down payment because the market is thin for those types of properties and the seller wants to move elsewhere. It happened to me.

We once owned a house out in what some people considered to be the ritzy part of the Washington suburbs. After a few years, the entire family got tired of commuting, so we sold the house and moved into Georgetown. When we put the old house on the market in 1983, the only offer we got at what I considered to be a fair price was one where we would take back a 10 percent mortgage. The buyer got an 80 percent mortgage from the bank and another 10 percent mortgage from us, so he only had to put 10 percent down on a $640,000 house.

We took his note for $64,000 at a 12 percent interest and received a check every month for $640 until he refinanced at a lower rate of interest. In 1989, the buyer sold the house for $1.4 million, which means he walked away with $824,000 in equity after six years with an initial investment of $64,000—or a phenomenal 53 percent per year.

Was that rate of appreciation in the price of the house unusual? Only slightly. It works out to 14 percent per year, whereas the average appreciation of housing prices in that area of suburban Washington for the same period was 12 percent per year. So our old property did a little better than average, but not much.

Am I sorry we sold in 1983? Not really. We liked it better in Georgetown before moving to Florida, and besides, the value of our next house went up almost 18 percent per year, so we came out ahead anyhow.

Perhaps not too many of you will be buying houses for $1.4 million in the near future, even at 10 percent down. The monthly carrying costs for interest alone, at a 10 percent rate of interest, would be $10,500 per month. But I brought up this little story because (a) at least in Washington, how much you bought and sold your house for is even more interesting to most people than the details of your sex life, and (b) it does illustrate that even in high-priced deals, the seller will often take back part of the mortgage, providing you will pay an above-market interest rate on the note and also can convince him that you are a viable risk.

How do you know whether a seller is willing to take back part of the down payment? The easiest method is simply to inform any competent real estate agent (assuming that's not an oxymoron) that you are interested in listings that have some flexibility in seller financing. That should give them a pretty good idea which properties to show you. Sometimes the classified ads will state explicitly that seller financing is available; other times will merely mention "motivated seller" or some other oblique phrase.

In some areas of the country, builders who are having trouble unloading new homes may also carry part of the down payment for you for a while. Those areas change over time, of course; in 1990, the area where you were most likely to get help from the builder was New England. Again, you simply have to ask. If you are trying to obtain an unusually small down payment and the sales representative for the builder suggests you talk to a bank about financing, simply move on to the next builder. These days there's no shortage of builders with unsold homes.

Finally, the best bet for take-back financing is often from those who are selling a larger house and are about to retire to a smaller one. Often, these sellers are planning to live off their investment income in the future, and have no need for the capital since they are downgrading the size of their home. The best they think they can earn on their capital is the money market rate of 7 or 8 percent. In that case, they might be delighted to earn 12 percent on a second mortgage.

Renting with an Option to Buy

Occasionally you can find an even better deal, which is to rent with an option to buy. Consider an example of a $200,000 house with a rental payment of $1,500 per month, which would be about the same as the mortgage payment with 10 percent down and a 10 percent interest rate. However, because you are renting, there is no down payment except for a one- or two-month security deposit. The $1,500 rental payment is then applied to your down payment, so by the end of the first year, you will have built up $18,000 in equity, plus the $3,000 initial deposit, which gives you almost enough money to go to the bank and get a regular mortgage.

In this case, the seller would be carrying the house for an entire year without earning a nickel. That's extreme; a more likely arrangement is that half of the rent would be applied to a purchase option. That way, it would take you two years to build up the required 10 percent deposit. In many cases, the seller bought the house at a much lower price, so $750 a month will actually cover his mortgage. But either way the idea is the same—you get to buy a house with no money down, although it means renting for an extra year or two.

Admittedly, deals like this don't come along every day. You have to search carefully for them. But if you don't have the cash, this approach provides an excellent opportunity to start investing in real estate.

Buying a "Bargain" House

Three separate types of below-market transactions can be considered: run-down homes, distress sales, and actual foreclosures.

Fixing up run-down homes is a great idea if you are handy and willing to invest sweat equity. Not everyone is, of course. But if you know something about the construction business and are willing to endure hassling with sloppy, tardy, and dishonest tradesmen, the return can be very rewarding. You benefit in four ways.

1. On most contracting jobs, the general contractor takes 15 percent, which is built into the price of the house. Those who are willing and able to serve as their own general contractor save that amount—as long as they know what they are doing.
2. Most larger builders must pay "scale," whether that means union rates or the going rate to craftsmen. If you are careful and shop around, and are willing to wait awhile, you may be able to hire workers for less. In many cases you can hire competent professionals who are working on their own time; just don't expect to get the job done in a hurry.
3. You save the interest on the money you would otherwise borrow to pay for the improvements that someone else has already done.
4. Most people don't like to buy a dump. As a result, the price of a house that's in need of repairs is often less than comparably situated homes minus the cost of these repairs. You are buying the house at a discount.

Of course, you have to know whether the workers you have hired are doing an inferior job. Also, this generally works better if the house is run-down but is otherwise in a good neighborhood; it's the same idea as "buying the worst house on the block." Renovating a house in a slum—thereby creating the best house on the block—is a much riskier idea. Some real estate operators have become rich by renovating just ahead of regentrification, but that involves a sixth sense about which sections of town are coming back. This is a much more speculative gamble, and although it has worked for some people, I don't recommend it.

You might wonder why someone would let a valuable property, such as a house in a good neighborhood, deteriorate. Often the owner is someone who needed the income and rented the house out for years, failing to perform the necessary maintenance. By the time he or she finally sells it, the house is a mess, although still structurally sound.

You can either live in such a house or turn it for a quick profit. It is not uncommon for a $100,000 house, plus your cost of $50,000 in improvements, to sell for $200,000 after renovation. The $50,000 profit can then be used for a down payment on a more expensive house.

In fact, that's the rule of thumb I follow. Find out what comparable houses in the neighborhood recently sold for ($200,000); make sure that is the selling price, *not* the asking price. Find out how much it would cost to repair the place ($50,000). The discount on the house should be at least twice the cost of repair, so in this example you shouldn't pay more than $100,000. If you're handy, good luck.

If you're not, but still would like to buy a house at a discount, consider distress sales. You have to keep a sharp eye peeled for these, since most sellers can sell their homes in short order if they are willing to take less than the market price. However, the market isn't perfect, and every once in a while the owner will need to sell in a hurry but will not receive any acceptable offers because of some combination of economic conditions and location. One usual case when the family income has declined precipitously and the mortgage payments can no longer be met; another is the need for quick cash to pay estate taxes. It stands to reason this sort of circumstance occurs only in an area where housing prices are stagnant or falling. If the price has risen, the owner can sell at a profit no matter how much his personal financial situation has deteriorated. Thus you would be buying a house whose value has recently declined. While that could be due to a general slump of housing prices in the region, the house might be a dud, so there is an additional element of risk in buying a house no one else wants.

There are two ways to play this game. One is to approach the owner before the lending institution forecloses, and the other is to wait until afterward. No hard-and-fast rules apply, but in general if you buy from the owner before foreclosure, you will pay a slightly higher price but can probably negotiate a small down payment; in some cases, you can simply assume the mortgage with no down payment at all. If you wait until foreclosure proceedings have started, the price will probably be lower, but you will often be required to put up a fairly substantial down payment because the lender doesn't want to get stiffed twice in a row.

Distress sales, of course, are not advertised as such. However, most real estate brokers will know who is desperate to sell and what sort of offer might be acceptable. Sometimes ads that claim "must sell today," "make offer," or "motivated seller" are just come-ons, but it is in this group of houses that you will in fact find the distress sales. Since brokers also know this, they may write the ad this way when they are about to lose their listing. But what's a little exaggeration among friends?

If you decide to wait for actual foreclosures, some brokers may also be able to direct you to those listings. Often, though, it's not in their best interest, so they feign ignorance. Don't let that bother you. Head for the county recorder's office and ask for the current listings of foreclosures and auction dates. Sometimes these are published in the regular newspaper, but more often they appear in a small-circulation legal newspaper that is not otherwise worth reading unless you happen to be a lawyer.

Once you have obtained this list, you still have a choice of tactics. You can approach the owner before the sale, attend the auction, or if there are no bidders at the auction, negotiate with the lender/seller afterward.

There are no hard-and-fast rules here; everything depends on how previous foreclosure sales in the area have been going. If there has been spirited bidding at previous auctions of similar property, you'll probably want to strike a deal with the owner ahead of time. On the other hand, if most of the auctions are attended by no-shows, it pays to wait until afterward. Your own personal preferences might also enter into the decision: If you see "just the house" for you and your family, it might pay to purchase it before the auction. Usually, however, these aren't choice houses or locations but starter homes for those with limited capital resources who want to accumulate equity on a modest base.

HOW TO AVOID BUYING A TURKEY

This section applies to any house you purchase. I've put it here, however, on the grounds that if a house is selling at distress prices without any visible buyers, it may have some grave defects that are not immediately apparent.

Certain sections of the country have recently been inundated by foreclosures where the previous owners simply mailed in the key and disappeared. It may be that the family fell on economic misfortune or had unusually high medical bills, or the wage earner had to obtain employment in another area. However, the odds are considerably higher than usual that these properties are substantially less than choice. The house may have been constructed by a builder who was notorious for cutting corners; or it may have been built over a sinkhole, an earthquake fault, or even a toxic-waste dump. Theoretically you could make a case that the seller or their agent is supposed to tell you all these things, but don't bet on it.

Historically, the law of buying real estate has been the law of the jungle. If you don't notice the defect beforehand—and the seller has made no obvious effort to cover it up—you're probably out of luck. In some states the laws are changing in this regard, but not very fast. California now requires the seller to list all known defects in writing—a law that could only make a lawyer happy. What is a "known" defect, and when did the seller knows it? Furthermore, litigation against someone who has moved out of state, and who in any case can claim the house was in perfect condition when he left, is not a profitable way to spend either your spare time or your hard-earned dollars. It's obviously much better to find out ahead of time.

Most financial advisers will tell you to hire an inspection service and have them go through the house with what is purported to be a fairly fine-tooth comb. They will spend several hours, issue you a written report, and charge you some fee that usually ranges from $250 to $500.

It can't hurt. They might discover some major structural defect, and it doesn't cost that much more than a good dinner for two these days. But most of the time, it won't help either. The problem is that most of these inspection services are in the pockets of the real estate people who recommend them. If the wall is falling down, which you can see yourself if your vision is better than 20/200, they will probably mention that fact. If there are puddles on the floor where the roof leaks, presumably they will also note that, too. But the hidden traps are generally overlooked by these services. Yes, I am also writing about this from personal experience.

So after getting ripped off by one of these services—and finding that the house needed $5,000 of repairs after obtaining a "clean bill of health"— we decided on an alternative plan, which admittedly is somewhat more expensive and cumbersome. We now have an independent electrician, plumber, roofer, and general contractor look at the house and prepare separate reports. In one case, as it turned out, they found several minor problems, which we were then able to convince the seller to fix, so we actually came out slightly ahead on the deal. Of course, this won't always happen. More important, though, we avoided the risk of there being any major structural damage.

The amount of precaution you decide to take before buying a house is a function of your own personal risk/reward ratio. The more expensive the house, the more thorough an inspection you should be willing to finance. If you have lived in a neighborhood for some time, are staying in the same general area, and know the location to which you will be moving, you may have a good enough feel for the property to require only a cursory inspection. But my advice is that if you are a first-time buyer of a property in a region that is not well known to you, and in addition you are buying foreclosed property, you're taking much too big a risk not to have it thoroughly inspected by independent tradespeople rather than a so-called inspection service.

One final note of caution. Whenever you are buying a house, whether it is at full price or one of these distress specials, just remember the obvious: The broker works for the seller, not the buyer.

Many people strike up what they think is a friendship with the broker during the months of travail looking for just the right house, and they sometimes forget that brokers are just salespeople and not real estate or investment counselors. Their job is to move merchandise and collect commissions, and they are paid by the seller. When in doubt, use the used-car salesperson test: If the information I have just heard was given to me by a used-car salesperson, would I believe it? If the answer is yes, you may proceed. But remember that all salespeople engage in a certain amount of puffery, and that doesn't change just because the product is real estate.

A SHARED-EQUITY MORTGAGE

As I've noted above, you will find below-market prices primarily in those areas where real estate prices generally have been stagnant or declining. If prices have been rising rapidly, then by definition it won't be a distress sale. Furthermore, it is in those booming areas that scraping together an adequate down payment becomes most difficult. Almost anyone who has a steady job can manage $5,000 for a down payment on an average-priced home in a small town in the Midwest. But coming up with $50,000 for the average starter home in Orange County, California, is a completely different matter. For this reason, there has recently been a proliferation of investors offering shared-equity mortgages in the rapidly appreciating areas of the East and West coasts.

The concept is fairly simple, although in practice there are hundreds of different options. You put no money down at all when purchasing a house, except for paying the closing costs; someone else furnishes the down payment. In return for that, this other party owns part (usually half) of the house, and you share the appreciation in the equity that occurs over time. When you sell the house, you get half the appreciated equity, and the investor gets the other half. You end up with half instead of all of the gain—but on the other hand, the only investment you have to make is the closing costs. If you are cash-poor, it's one of the better deals around. Because the maximum rate of return stalls out after seven or eight years, these are not long-term deals. Indeed, because the investor isn't putting up the closing costs, his maximum rate of return peaks at five years, so many contracts are structured for that amount of time.

One of the major risks of owning any home is that its value could decline soon after it is purchased. A sudden change in your personal or family situation that requires a transfer to another location might mean selling at a loss. In that case, you lose some or all of the down payment. Some people simply mail the key back to the bank and walk out with no equity— which does not do much for their credit rating the next time they try to buy a house.

Under a shared-equity arrangement, the financial risk is shifted to the investor. Naturally you won't be overjoyed if the house declines in value, because that wipes out the chance to share in the gains. On the other hand, it's not your down payment on the line. As a trade-off for a smaller return, the home buyer passes off the risk to the investor.

Before signing up for such a deal, be sure to check the fine print in any agreement. Would-be buyers could run an advertisement to find an individual investor, but that's not what usually happens. Instead of dealing with an individual, you probably will work with a company or partnership that does hundreds of these deals, and whose lawyers have already honed the agreements to a fine edge. The specific terms in the fine print can make a substantial difference over the period of your agreement. Here are some major areas to check.

First, find out who pays the closing costs. You will always pay the normal closing costs—title insurance, homeowner's insurance, real estate escrow, transfer tax, and points for the mortgage. However, some of these partnerships also charge a fee for bringing the buyer and the investor together. You shouldn't have to pay that fee in addition unless you get some other concessions in the arrangement.

Second, even if the monthly amount is the same, it makes a great deal of difference whether your payments are called "mortgage payments" or "rent." Whoever makes the mortgage payment is able to claim that important mortgage-interest deduction; if you are paying rent, the tax advantages go to the investor. Obviously the after-tax costs will be much lower if you can claim the interest and real-estate tax deductions.

Third, determine who pays for repairs. Most of the time, it's you. However, if you are paying rent and not getting the tax deductions, you certainly shouldn't be liable for the repair bills, too.

Fourth, check to see what happens when your agreement expires. You may have grown accustomed to the house and want to stay there. In that case, you will probably have to obtain another mortgage; the old one might have been for a slightly lower interest rate but with a balloon payment at the end of five years. If the house has appreciated enough, your accumulated equity will be sufficient for the requisite down payment, and all ends well. On the other hand, if it isn't, you may find yourself being evicted if your rights to remain in the house aren't clearly spelled out.

Fifth, what happens if you walk—maybe you and your spouse split. Are you obligated to continue meeting the monthly payments, or does the title revert to the investor? Presumably you want to keep your credit rating clean. If not, you can just disappear. But that's no way to accumulate wealth.

You probably won't get your way on all of these points, but as with mortgages, don't be afraid to shop around. Ask your real estate agent for names of investment partners, or simply check the real estate section of the newspaper on weekends. Not surprisingly, most of these firms have sprung up where home-price appreciation has been the greatest, which is to say California and the Northeast corridor. Don't waste your time looking for any such investors in Houston or Oklahoma City, or for that matter in Louisville or Youngstown.

CREATIVE FINANCING OF YOUR DOWN PAYMENT

Assuming that you are able to find one of these investors and can agree on terms, you will boost your return on equity substantially. Even so, it's still better to scrape together the 10 percent down payment without having to give up half of your equity—even if that is a riskier deal than is usually the case for real estate.

Let's go back to the example of the $100,000 house that appreciates in value to $140,000 over the next five years, but this time an outside investor puts down the 10 percent, or $10,000, and takes a mortgage for $90,000. All you do is put up the $6,000 in closing costs. After five years, the house will be worth $140,000 and the equity will be $50,000. The investor takes back his original $10,000, and you split the difference. He gets back $30,000 on a $10,000 investment, which is terrific, and you get $20,000 on a $6,000 investment—which is also a terrific deal that works out to 27 percent per year. And that's if the house only appreciates by the national average rate of 7 percent. Most of these deals take place in such high-priced areas as California, where the appreciation is closer to 12 percent per year, so the payoff is correspondingly greater, almost 40 percent per year.

Earning $20,000 on a $6,000 investment in five years may seem like a nifty trick, and it is. But just suppose you could borrow the $10,000. At what rate of interest would it be worthwhile to borrow that money instead of splitting the equity gain with some investor?

If you could borrow the money somewhere else, you would earn $30,000 on a $10,000 investment in five years—just like the investor—which is a 25 percent annual rate of return. So if you could borrow money at less than 25 percent per year, you would be better off doing so.

The trouble is, you're not supposed to borrow the down payment. The bank providing the mortgage would presumably be very unhappy if they found out, and the bank that loaned you the original $10,000 might just ask for its money back ex post haste pronto. Remember, it has the legal right to do so. Now I'm not telling you to lie or cheat or anything like that. Just observe the same code of ethics that is observed by the banking fraternity, and you shouldn't get into any trouble. It goes something like this.

First, borrow the money from Bank A for some "other" purpose. Don't try anything that's too farfetched; college education for your children when you've only been married for four months probably won't cut the mustard. And obviously if you say it's for the car, the bank will want to hold the title. However, there is a category called "unsecured personal loans," where you must sign personally but don't have to offer any collateral. It could be for continuing education, or furnishing your apartment; maybe even buying a computer for your own business. Different bankers have different hot buttons; the same story doesn't work everywhere. But if they want to lend you money, they will accept any reasonable story that doesn't make them look like idiots.

Put the money in your bank account. Now go to Bank B, preferably across town—or, for that matter, across the country—and tell them you want to buy this house with 10 percent down. Oh yes, we have saved up that amount because we are hardworking, thrifty citizens.

But won't the credit police zap you?

In one of my mortgage applications, right there on the form it said "average monthly amount outstanding on your credit card." It so happens that I do a fair amount of speech-making and traveling in my business and charge all the expenses to my credit card. All of these are later reimbursed; I never pay for the trips myself. But buying the tickets pushes the average monthly tab up to about $5,000.

Considering that I offer financial advice for a living, I presumably should have known better, but maybe I was under the influence of some truth-inducing hallucinogens that day, so in the appropriate column for "average monthly credit balance," I wrote $5,000. The loan officer handling the application, who in this particular case was an old acquaintance of mine instead of your usual mindless blow-dry type, was appalled. "You'll blow the whole application," he said, quickly crossing it out and writing in $250, which was evidently the amount the computer expected to see.

So do they check your outstanding monthly credit balances? You be the judge.*

Having said all this, it is in fact extremely important to have some sort of credit record so the lender can check to see whether you pay your bills on time. It could be Visa or MasterCard, American Express, the local department store, car payments, even the gasoline credit card. Be sure to give them *something* to check. But that doesn't mean you have to give them *everything* to check.

If you are the nervous type who, whenever you see a policeman on the block, is sure he has come to arrest you, if not for murder, at least for indecent exposure, then just skip this advice and let someone else walk off with half the equity buildup. In most cases, however, I think you will be better off borrowing the down payment first, with one important caveat: Be *sure* you will be able to pay back your debts. If you obtain funds under questionable circumstances and then can't pay them back, the lender could turn from Dr. Jekyll to Mr. Hyde overnight. But of course you do plan to pay all your debts; you're just trying to accumulate wealth faster.

One other point on the down payment, no matter what other financial

---

* I should piont out this won't work all the time, because many mortgage bureaus will run a credit check on you and find those $5,000 monthly balances on your cards. In that case, you demurely explain that of course these are "business and travel" expenses that are indeed repaid monthly.

arrangements you make. Make sure the money is in the bank *before* you start to apply for the loan. Once when I applied for a mortgage, my bank account increased by an unusually large amount between the time of the original application and closing time because I had given several speeches and was paid for all of them in the same month. The bank was sure I had borrowed the down payment and deposited it into my account, and I had to show them the contracts to get them off my back.

Throughout this chapter, I've suggested various ways to cobble together the minimum down payment so you can start sharing in that 20 percent annual return on equity that real estate provides over the long run. However, you also have to meet the mortgage payments without starving. There aren't as many ways to skin that cat—after all, you did borrow the money—but there are ways to pay less interest now and more later. Some people will advise against that strategy on the grounds that your total interest payments will be more. That's true, but irrelevant. If you want to create wealth, the key is not to borrow less, but to make sure the rate of return you are earning on your investment is greater than the rate you are paying for borrowed funds. If that key test is passed, it's beneficial to borrow more now and pay it back later.

So let's assume that one way or the other, you have managed to accumulate a down payment. Now let's talk about what kind of mortgage you should get—fixed or variable rate? If it's the latter, which one of hundreds of options is the best? And after you have had the house for a while, how do you leverage your equity into real wealth?

Chapter 9

Leveraging Your Way
to Wealth Through Real Estate

THE THREE BASIC TYPES OF MORTGAGES

Now that you've selected the appropriate down payment, here comes the difficult part of the process—selecting the right mortgage. I get more questions on this than on any other facet of money management or investment strategy.

The Federal Trade Commission has prepared something called "A Concise Guide to Mortgages," printed at your expense, which lists the 15 major types of mortgages. Naturally there are variants on almost all of these types. Since this book is something more than a handbook on mortgages, I won't discuss all 15 in detail. In fact, I won't even discuss most of them at all. But these mortgages, and their first cousins, can essentially be broken down into three major categories.

1. **Fixed-rate mortgage.** You pay the same amount every month until the mortgage is completely paid off or you move.
2. **Adjustable-rate mortgage.** Usually, the first year's rate is very low, then it increases and moves in step with some market rate, such as the one-year treasury bill rate. After the first year, if interest rates were to remain fixed, so would the monthly payments.
3. **Graduated-payment mortgage.** The monthly payment increases over time even if rates stay the same. This may be either a fixed- or variable-rate mortgage. It is designed for those who are

financially strapped now but have good reason to expect their income to grow rapidly in the near future. It is particularly appropriate for young couples with first-time mortgages.

Fixed or Variable Rate: How to Choose

In terms of choosing between a fixed- and a variable-rate mortgage, the single most important factor to remember is that a variable-rate mortgage is only a good idea on a temporary basis. Since interest rates do fluctuate, the idea is to lock in a fixed-rate mortgage when rates are relatively low so you won't be penalized when they go back up again.

Now this particular piece of advice might appear empty, similar to the fatuous suggestion to "buy low and sell high." Not so. This does not mean I have discovered the secret, previously unknown to anyone, of how to predict interest rates. It does mean that at any given time, it is possible to make an informed guess about whether interest rates are above or below their average values. Furthermore, it's not that difficult—as judged by the fact that consumers, as opposed to economists or journalists, had a pretty batting average during the 1980s.

The equilibrium value of the mortgage rate—where the rate would be if Fed policy were neutral—is based on a fairly simple formula, similar to the formula given on page 53. It is equal to the average rate of inflation, plus half the average rate of growth in real GNP, plus the ratio of the public sector budget deficit to GNP in percentage terms (e.g., 3 percent), plus 2 percent. In other words, the equilibrium short-term rate plus 2 percent.

To take an example, suppose the average inflation rate were 5 percent, the growth rate 3 percent, and the budget deficit ratio 2 percent. Then the equilibrium value of the mortgage rate would be 10½ percent. That certainly does not mean the mortgage rate would always be 10½ percent at the time when those economic conditions existed. It does mean that if the mortgage rate were well below 10½ percent, you should hustle and line up a fixed-rate mortgage, while if it were well above 10½ percent, stick with the variable-rate mortgage for a while.

In fact, this relatively simple rule would have been quite valuable several times during the past decade. During the latter half of 1984, the mortgage rate exceeded 12½ percent even though inflation was around 4 percent. During that time, fixed-rate mortgages should have been avoided like the plague—and they were; almost all mortgages written that year were variable-rate. In 1987 and early 1988, by comparison, the mortgage rate declined to 9¼ percent. That was the optimal time to lock in that fixed-rate mortgage, and many people did precisely that. Ordinarily, the FHA processes about 600,000 mortgages a year. In 1987, when rates were well below their equilibrium level, the FHA processed 1.2 million. And when rates declined to 9¼ percent again in 1991, mortgage applications surged again. Consumers apparently knew when rates had troughed, and using this simple formula you can, too.

Does this mean the average consumer is brighter than those geniuses on Wall Street who are paid hundreds of thousands of dollars a year to predict interest rates? Evidently so, because when interest rates started rising rapidly in 1988, most economists and bond traders were surprised—but homeowners weren't. But in this case, there is some justice. You still have your job—and they don't.

You may wonder why the mortgage rate dropped from 13 percent in mid-1984, when inflation was 4½ percent, to 9 percent in 1987 and early 1988, when inflation was also 4½ percent, then rose back to 10½ percent in mid-1989, when inflation was still 4½ percent. The short answer is because the Fed first eased, then tightened. But when did it do that if the inflation rate stayed the same?

That's a much more difficult question, and one analysts are paid a lot to solve. Not that they get it right, you understand. Again the short answer is the Fed thought inflation was declining the first time, and thought it was rising the second time. But my point is that the precise reasons don't matter. In both cases cited above, mortgage rates did move back toward their equilibrium levels after consumers had made their move. Using this one simple rule collectively saved homeowners billions of dollars.

Just in case the decision isn't so clear-cut in the future, here are a few more hints to help you tell when mortgage rates are likely to rise or fall.

1. Ordinarily, the mortgage rate is about 1 percent above the prime rate. Sometimes, though, it's below the prime rate. When that happens, the mortgage rate is out of line and will soon rise. Run, don't walk, to your lending institution and lock in a fixed-rate mortgage if you haven't already done so. Conversely, when the mortgage rate is more than 2 percent above the prime rate, choose the variable-rate mortgage, because rates will soon come down.

   As a corollary to this rule, when the spread between a fixed- and a variable-rate mortgage is more than 3 percent, take the variable rate. When the spread declines below 2 percent, take the fixed rate.

2. The inflation rate will probably average about 5 percent during the 1990s. Thus if inflation temporarily declines below 4 percent

and interest rates follow, they will not remain there very long but will soon increase again, which means it is time to lock in those low fixed rates. Similarly, if inflation exceeds 6 percent, rates will rise well above their average levels; that's when it pays to take the variable-rate option.

During the 1980s, you would have done quite well by using this rule and taking 10½ percent to be the equilibrium mortgage rate. Of course, that level may change; before 1966, the average mortgage rate was 6 percent, because the average inflation rate was 2 percent, the growth rate 4 percent, and the budget deficit ratio was close to zero. In the future, the average rate of inflation could rise or fall, the economy could grow at a faster or slower rate, or (don't bet on it) the government could even reduce the deficit. But if these events do occur, you will be able to plug the new values into this simple formula to determine whether mortgage rates are currently above or below their equilibrium value.

Let's say that you have now made the proper choice of mortgage: variable rate if mortgage rates are above their equilibrium value and fixed rate otherwise. You're well on your way, but that's just the beginning of your odyssey through the various types of mortgage rates.

Graduated Payment Mortgages: Procrastination or Wise Investment?

In the olden days, dime-store novels often contained one of those "heart-warming" scenes where the family, having scrimped and saved to make those mortgage payments for the past 25 years, was finally able to have a mortgage-burning party. Maybe that made sense in the days of zero inflation when "a penny saved is a penny earned" did not mean "21,000 pennies saved are cluttering up my dresser." Nowadays, though, having no mortgage means you are penalizing your investment performance and your ability to create wealth. Unless you are already retired and living off your income, you are better off with a mortgage—regardless of how wealthy you are.

Furthermore, putting down less money now and carrying a larger mortgage permits you to buy a more expensive house and have more equity working to increase your net assets. If you can't handle a big monthly payment right now, consider the option of a graduated-payment mortgage. The obvious advantage is that the mortgage payment expands in line with your income, thereby lessening the financial burden when you first buy the house.

Of course, you know that in spite of all those beguiling ads, bankers are in the business of making money, not making friends. It naturally stands to reason that if you pay less interest now, you will eventually pay more interest later. And since the bank will charge you interest on the deferred amounts, the total amount paid is considerably larger. But then again, so is your total equity. A graduated payment schedule works especially well for first-time home buyers.

There are almost as many different kinds of options on variable-rate mortgages as there are lending institutions. Furthermore, they are all subject to change, often without notice, so by the time you read this, any such list I could give would be roughly as useful as last year's classified ads. Then too, figuring out which rate is the best would require not only accurate predictions of interest-rate trends several years into the future, but forecasting changes in the spreads between various maturities of interest rates—which is even more difficult than predicting the direction rates will move.

If you want low payments now but figure you can live with higher payments later on, get a mortgage that keeps the interest rate low for the longest possible time, which is usually five years, and then caps the maximum jump at 2 percent or less per year. Remember, you're not really paying less, because it all catches up with you at the end. However, if the value of the house is appreciating rapidly, you will have a healthy equity buildup to apply to your next house, a worthwhile goal. Just don't be dazzled by some banker who tells you his mortgage is "better" than someone else's because the monthly payments are lower. It just means you pay more later.

Fighting the Point Spread

One important factor to consider when determining which mortgage to take is the number of "points" you have to pay. Virtually all mortgages now carry some points; that's how lenders make most of their money. This is strictly a fee, so unlike the lower mortgage payments, there's no trade-off with higher equity later.

Points are the fee you pay up front to obtain the mortgage. Sometimes they too can be wrapped into the financing, although lenders will take their fees up front either way. One point equals 1 percent of the mortgage, i.e., on a $100,000 mortgage, 1 point would mean a payment of $1,000 up front. The most common rate is 3 points, with the usual range from 2 to 4 points. Usually the buyer pays for the points, but if the seller is anxious to unload the property, he may pick up some of the points as well. The higher number of points is usually associated with mortgages that have a lower down payment—the presumption is greater risk—or a lower interest rate.

One point is equivalent to about ⅛ percent on the mortgage rate for a 30-year mortgage. In other words, a mortgage with 2 points and a 9¾ percent rate would be roughly equivalent to a mortgage with 4 points and a 9½ percent rate. These figures apply only to those who hold the mortgage for its full term, so if you don't plan to keep the house or the mortgage very long, the points boost the effective rate much more. Don't waste all your energy bargaining for a lower rate and then neglect the points.

Refinancing the Mortgage

People often ask me when they should refinance. Let's say they got a fixed-rate mortgage at 12 percent and now the rates are 10 percent. Or maybe they got a variable-rate mortgage and want to lock in the 10 percent fixed rate. When is it advantageous to switch?

The key here is that it's not costless; you almost always have to pay points to switch. While each point paid is equivalent to only about ⅛ percent on a 30-year mortgage, that figure rises to ¼ percent if you keep the house for only five years. If you pay 3 points, which is fairly normal these days, that adds slightly more than ¾ percent to the true interest cost. If you are shedding more than 1 percent on the fixed-rate mortgage, then it's worth the move. But if you are paying 10 percent on a variable rate and are considering a crossover to a fixed rate at the same level, the move will probably cost you money unless you plan to keep the house for a long time. In that case, wait until the fixed rate drops to 9½ percent; then switch.

PAYING DOWN THE MORTGAGE: THRIFTY OR FOOLISH

Another popular question: If I do have extra money, is it a good idea to pay down some of the mortgage and reduce the total amount of interest I have to pay?

This is an important question, because the great bulk of your total mortgage payments is interest, not principal. For a 30-year $100,000 mortgage at an interest rate of 10 percent, your total payments would be

$315,925.20 over the life of that mortgage. In other words, you would have paid almost $216,000 in interest compared with the $100,000 in principal. Finding some way to reduce those interest payments could save you hundreds of thousands of dollars over the long run. But is it really saving?

Suppose that soon after starting your mortgage payments, you happen to come up with an extra $10,000, and apply that to the loan. If the mortgage payments stayed at the same level, that one $10,000 payment would reduce the term of the mortgage to 19 years, slicing the total amount of interest paid by $116,000. Then for years 19 through 30, you could bank the money you would have used for mortgage payments, and 30 years from now end up with not only the extra $116,000 but the interest on that money; let's assume an extra-generous 10 percent money market rate, putting the best face on this situation. The total would amount to $175,000.

Sounds great, right? You plunk down $10,000 now and end up with a $175,000 payoff 30 years later. You earn interest instead of paying it to the bank.

Guess what? It's just our old friend the Rule of Compound Interest in disguise. Suppose you had taken the $10,000 and invested it at 10 percent for 30 years instead of paying off the mortgage; you would have had precisely the same $175,000. It's two sides of the same coin. That shouldn't come as a surprise, though. A 10 percent rate of return is a 10 percent rate of return whether it is in a mortgage payment, a money market fund, or any other investment.

Suppose you had invested the $10,000 in the stock market and earned the average 12 percent rate of return in a tax-deferred account instead of paying down the mortgage. At the end of 30 years, you would have had $300,000. So why bother to pay down the mortgage early?

Here's the lesson to be learned. It pays to reduce your mortgage if and only if the rate of interest you are paying for your mortgage is higher than the rate of return you could earn by investing your funds elsewhere—taking into account the tax angles, including the fact that your interest is deductible. If not, keep the mortgage and invest the money somewhere else. For example, if you were fortunate enough to earn 20 or 25 percent per year, you would have had $2.37 million or $8.08 million by the end of 30 years, rather than $175,000.

No matter how you structure the extra payments—a lump sum, a little bit more every month, or accelerating your payments—the arithmetic is always the same. Some of the better-known money market guides will tell you that if you take the monthly payment, divide it in half, and pay half every 14 days, instead of twice each month, you will also reduce the length of the mortgage from 30 to 19 years. It sounds great, almost like getting something for nothing. However, it's the same old arithmetic in disguise. Don't be fooled.

Admittedly, if you are the type who spends any extra money left in the bank account at the end of the month—or for that matter, spends it before it even makes its way into the account—prepaying the mortgage interest may be a clever way of forcing yourself to save more. But there are lots of investments that pay a higher rate of return than your current mortgage, including buying a bigger and better house, a second house, other real estate, or the stock market.

So here's the Evans rule on this subject: No one gets rich paying back their mortgage early. In fact, I recommend just the opposite: *Increase* your mortgage and invest the money elsewhere. That works every time, *providing* that you invest the money in some other asset with a higher rate than your mortgage rate. As it turns out, that's quite easy for several reasons. First, your mortgage interest is deductible, while most of the time the funds can be invested in tax-deferred savings plans. Second, over the long run, the rate of return on stocks has always been higher than on bonds, even disregarding tax advantages. Third, having additional liquidity provides you with a cushion in case of unexpected emergencies so you don't have to borrow at 18 percent personal-loan rates.

For most people, a mortgage is the least expensive way to borrow money. Maybe Polonius or Ben Franklin wouldn't have approved, but they didn't live in inflationary times.

HOME-EQUITY MORTGAGES

There are two major ways to use the equity buildup in your house for additional investment opportunities. One is to sell and move. However, many people are relatively happy where they are, or don't like the hassle of moving, and don't want to exercise that option. That's quite all right, because another viable option exists today. Indeed, you can hardly read the newspaper, open your mail, listen to the radio, or watch TV without being bombarded by offers to refinance your home. It isn't only the banks that are doing the advertising either, because the larger brokerage houses have moved into this field in a big way.

According to The Evans Rule of Commerce, the amount of advertising is directly proportional to the expected profits, so these loans are obviously a good deal for the banks and brokerage houses. But are they a good deal for you?

The answer is yes, no, or maybe, depending on your tax situation. Most of the time, however, it's yes.

The basic idea behind the home-equity mortgage is as follows. Suppose someone came to you with a proposition: You can borrow money from me at 5 percent and reinvest it at 10 percent. How much would you like to borrow? I assume that most people would go for a zillion dollars. It's a no-lose situation.

Of course, the catch is that no one in their right mind would offer you a proposition like that. But once again, here's where the distorting effects of the tax laws come in. Suppose you can borrow at 10 percent, and the interest is deductible, so that your net borrowing cost is 6 to 7 percent, depending on your precise tax situation. Also, suppose you can invest this money in the stock market through a tax-deferred scheme so that your money earns 12 percent and isn't taxed until retirement. Now all of a sudden the proposition makes sense to everyone—the lender and the borrower. So go for it!

Naturally there are a few restrictions. Usually you can't borrow more than 80 percent of the value of the house, although I've recently seen some ads for 100 percent financing. Since that leaves you no cushion, I wouldn't go above 80 percent. Second, the tax benefits don't extend out to infinity; the largest home-equity mortgage for which the interest is still fully tax-deductible is $100,000. At least to date, that ceiling doesn't apply to your original mortgage. Third, the usual costs of obtaining a mortgage apply— usually about 3 percent of the face amount. This won't be much of a burden, providing you refinance only once every 8 to 10 years. Fourth, I want to make it crystal clear that the money you draw out is strictly for saving, not spending. By increasing your debt burden, you run the additional risk of facing a financial squeeze if your income dips temporarily. If you invest all of the money, your financial risk hasn't increased at all; you've merely transferred it to a form that earns a higher rate of interest.

Most home-equity mortgages are variable-rate loans; they are tied to the Treasury bill rate or the prime rate. So you could conceivably be behind the eight ball if short-term interest rates soared to 20 percent again someday; your stock market portfolio would probably look pretty sick, too, unless you went short. So there is some financial risk involved in this strategy, which is why it's important to understand the principles of cyclical investing. Nonetheless, over the long run, borrowing on the equity buildup in your home is one of the best ways to accumulate wealth.

When John D. Rockefeller IV, known as Jay to his friends and constituents, moved to Washington, D.C., he bought himself a tidy villa in what real estate brokers in this town quaintly call the "upper brackets." The Rockefeller wealth has been split a few ways since Old John D. the First made his billion, but without question, John D. IV could have paid cash. In fact, he did nothing of the sort. He got a mortgage of over $10 million, which costs him some $111,000 every month. Why would he do that? Simple. After tax, he earns a much better rate of return with his funds than he would if the house weren't leveraged. Whether or not you subscribe to Jay's brand of politics—or his late uncle's, for that matter—we could all do a lot worse than emulate the Rockefeller family in their creation and preservation of wealth. The way you get rich is by putting your money to work at the highest rate of return.

So there's nothing shameful about taking out a second mortgage if the funds are being invested at a higher rate of return elsewhere. Of course, that means you aren't spending those funds—unless it's for your children's college education, which I consider a worthwhile investment both in dollars and cents as well as for the intellectual and social benefits.

In selecting a home-equity loan, you also have to check the trade-off between a lower rate and higher points. Most of these loans will have some up-front origination fees, so the true cost of borrowing will be substantially higher if you plan to repay the money in a hurry. Home-equity loans are for long-term investing, not short-term cash flow.

Here's what you can do with the money from your home-equity mortgage.

1. If you have borrowed money at a higher rate of interest, the obvious first step is to pay off those loans. This includes loans for a college education.
2. Use the money as a down payment on other types of real estate, such as residential real estate that you can then rent.
3. Use the money to set up some sort of retirement plan and invest the money in the stock market. You can't profitably invest it in the bond market because the rate of interest on the mortgage is higher than on the bonds—unless you can deduct all of the home-equity mortgage and invest the bonds in a tax-deferred scheme. But since over the long run the rate of return on bonds is always lower than on stocks, I'm not recommending this option.
4. Start your own business. Of course, this is risky—but it's not quite as bad as it sounds. After all, unless the value of your house

plummets, the loan is collateralized by the value of the house. Under the worst circumstances, you have forfeited the gain in equity and are left with monthly payments. However, they are still at the best rate in town.

None of this is free. If you originally had a mortgage payment of $1,000 per month, combining it with the home-equity loan might boost it to $2,000 per month. In many cases, though, your income has also doubled since the time you obtained the original mortgage. The relative burden won't be any higher, since over the long run home prices and average income rise at the same rate.

You may argue that in the meantime the children have come along and made a travesty of your budget, so you can't afford to set aside any more for saving. Here as elsewhere, you will always have to make the decision between current consumption and wealth creation. I promised no guarantees in this book, but I will guarantee that you will never get rich if you don't save. If you are willing to save 10 percent of your after-tax income, though, taking advantage of the tax breaks on a home-equity loan and reinvesting the money is one of the best ways to enhance your rate of return.

WHAT SIZE MORTGAGE SHOULD I CARRY?

As much as you can afford—and as much as lenders will allow.

There are two separate issues here. First, how do you want to divide your income between spending and saving? Second, given that decision, how much of your savings should be in your own home, and how much should be in other types of assets, such as the stock market?

Earlier in the book I suggested the fairly standard proportions of 25 percent of your pre-tax income for total housing costs—mortgage payments, real estate taxes, home insurance, and utilities—and 10 percent of your after-tax income for savings. However, once you have built up a reasonable contingency fund there is no good reason part of that 10 percent can't be an investment in your home, or for that matter in other real estate. Since interest payments on the primary mortgage are tax-deductible, you could spend as much as 35 percent of your income on housing costs. If the value of your home is two to three times your income, the cost of real estate taxes, home insurance, and utilities will be anywhere from 6 to 10 percent of your income; these must be considered consumption rather than saving. Using the upper figure, that would leave 25 percent of your income for the mortgage payment.

As it turns out, 25 percent of your income is the maximum that most lending institutions will permit for the monthly mortgage payment, so the two answers really coalesce into a single number.

Admittedly, this answer makes sense only if real estate values continue to appreciate and if, when you take out a second mortgage, you invest rather than spend the proceeds. But over the years I have found that for most people, regular mortgage payments are one of the better ways to save. You have to meet those payments, so the money isn't spent on other things.

The downside risk could occur if you or your spouse were laid off. You'd be faced with an outsize monthly payment and sharply reduced income. Most of the time, you can dip into the extra money you invested from the second mortgage. In the worst scenario, though, you might have to sell your house and downgrade, which does nothing for your wealth, your ego, or your family standing.

If you have just bought a house with the maximum affordable mortgage payment and you suddenly lose your job, there's no cushion to fall back on. Life has dealt you a low blow. If in fact you are in a profession or industry that does suffer frequent layoffs—such as a Wall Street broker—it would be prudent to be a little less aggressive initially on the mortgage payments.

However, most people who are just starting their career can find another job at comparable pay fairly quickly. The serious problems generally occur for those who have moved up the job curve, are highly paid for performing a very specialized skill, and are at an age where, in spite of anti–age-discrimination laws, no one is very anxious to hire them.

However, it is precisely at that point you can draw on the money that has been invested from the home-equity mortgage. Let's say you bought a house at $50,000 many years ago when you were 25, and it is now worth $400,000. Your total mortgage is $250,000, and you're not even close to being able to afford the $2,500 monthly mortgage payment when your income *suddenly drops*. Your original mortgage is now well below $50,000; it's the payments on the additional $200,000 home-equity mortgage that are the backbreaker. However, if you have invested that money prudently, the $200,000 should be in the $500,000 to $600,000 range, giving you adequate capital reserves until you can find another job. You aren't really "spending" more on your mortgage at all. You have simply used the benefits of leverage and the tax laws to reinvest the money elsewhere more profitably, then drawn it down when it was needed.

I will concede that using a full 25 percent of your income for the mortgage payment is borrowing right up to the limit and doesn't leave much room for flexibility in case your income is temporarily impaired—or, in the case of a variable-rate mortgage, interest rates rise. Thus for the purposes of the next section of this chapter, I will take a slightly more conservative stance and assume that your mortgage payment is 20 percent of your income. With a mortgage rate of 10 percent and the standard 20 percent down payment, that means you can afford to buy a home worth 2½ times your income at the time of the original mortgage. Even with a slightly more conservative approach, the figures are eye-popping—providing you start early and stick with your plan until retirement.

HOW LEVERAGE BENEFITS YOU

Step 1 to accumulating wealth, as I've pointed out before, is to buy your own home. Step 2, which we'll consider now, is to use leverage to increase your wealth faster.

To keep the arithmetic simple, I've used the standard assumptions here. The value of your house and your income both grow at about 7 percent per year, which is the long-term historical average, so they double every 10 years. Inflation is assumed to be 5 percent per year, and the mortgage rate is 10 percent per year. Current tax rates are also assumed, which means a top federal marginal tax rate of 33 percent, and an average state and local income tax rate of 4½ percent. If you live in an area that has higher or lower tax rates, the figures can be adjusted slightly, but the overall results are just about the same. I've also assumed that at age 25 you bought a $125,000 house with $25,000 down and had a $50,000 income. However, Table 18 shows the intermediate results every 10 years, so if you are just reaching these financial milestones at age 35 instead of 25, the arithmetic will still be the same—except that you'll only have 30 years to accumulate wealth instead of 40.

According to these assumptions, when your income is $50,000, your annual mortgage payment will be $10,000. When your income rises to $100,000 10 years later—remember that most of that increase is due to inflation—your total saving will rise proportionately to $20,000. That could consist of the original $10,000 mortgage plus another $10,000 in stocks; or it could represent an increase in the mortgage payment to $20,000. Either way, one of the key assumptions is that your saving keeps pace with the growth in your income.

To simplify matters a little, I've assumed that increases in saving occur only once every 10 years, not instantaneously. After all, you can't take on a new second mortgage or buy a new home every year. This also provides some additional leeway for temporary dips in income or increases in interest rates. I've also assumed all of the mortgage payment goes for interest and none for principal, which is a very close approximation for the first few years of the standard 30-year mortgage.

Back to the basic premise. You buy the house for $125,000, and 10 years later it's worth $250,000. At that point, you face the following options.

1. Do nothing. In essence, save a smaller proportion of your income. Of course, you will never get rich that way.
2. Leave the mortgage alone, but set aside an extra $10,000 a year and invest it in the stock market, where it will earn an average of 12 percent per year. If you are able to develop the right kind of retirement plan (discussed later in this section), the funds will accrue on a tax-deferred basis.
3. Same as 2, except that you invest after-tax dollars in the market and pay taxes on the dividends and capital gains as they are earned.
4. Use the accumulated equity in the home to get another $100,000 home-equity mortgage, then invest the proceeds in the stock market. In most cases, the interest on this mortgage is entirely deductible. If you can then invest the stock in a tax-deferred plan, you will have the best of all possible worlds.
5. Same as 4, except that the funds are not invested in a tax-deferred plan.
6. You just don't trust the stock market, or you would like a better house—and don't mind moving. Take the accumulated equity as a base for the down payment on a more expensive residence. My only restriction here is that the mortgage payment can't exceed 20 percent of your income.

Table 18 shows how much wealth you would accumulate for each of these six options over a 40-year period. Even in the do-nothing case, the value of your home appreciates from $125,000 to $2 million. This may sound highly unlikely, but just remember that 40 years ago the average new home sold for just over $10,000, and now the figure is almost $150,000. So we're talking the same 15-fold increase over the next 40 years. Since much of this is due to inflation, I've also deflated the figures, assuming a 5 percent annual rate of inflation, to show how much your wealth would be worth in today's dollars.

There are some important tax consequences when you're 65, which are

Table 18
Investment Strategies—I

	Plan 1: Do Nothing	Plan 2: Invest in Stock Market, Tax-Deferred	Plan 3: Invest in Stock Market, No Tax Deferral
Age 25 $50,000 income	$125,000 value of home 100,000 mortgage 25,000 equity	$125,000 value 100,000 mortgage 25,000 equity	$125,000 value 100,000 mortgage 25,000 equity
Age 35 100,000 income	250,000 value of home 100,000 mortgage 150,000 equity	250,000 value 100,000 mortgage 150,000 equity Take extra 10,000/yr. Invest in stock mkt. at 12% Total after 10 yrs.: 196,500	250,000 value 100,000 mortgage 150,000 equity Take extra 6,250/yr. after taxes (same as 10,000, pretax) in stock mkt. at 7.5% Total: 95,000
Age 45 200,000 income	500,000 value of home 75,000 mortgage 425,000 equity	500,000 value 75,000 mortgage 425,000 equity Boost investment in stock mkt. to 20,000/ yr. at 12%. Total after 10 yrs.: 393,000 *plus* 196,500 now worth 610,300. Total stock mkt. value: 1,003,300	500,000 value 75,000 mortgage 425,000 equity Boost investment in stock mkt. to 12,000/ yr. at 7.5%. Total after 10 yrs.: 190,000 *plus* 95,000 now worth 195,800. Total: 385,800
Age 55 400,000 income	1,000,000 value No mortgage	1,000,000 value No mortgage 1,000,000 equity Boost investment in stock mkt. to 40,000/ yr. at 12%. Total after 10 yrs.: 786,000 *plus* 1,003,000 now worth 3,116,100 Total: 3,902,100	1,000,000 value No mortgage 1,000,000 equity Boost investment in stock mkt. to 25,000/ yr. at 7.5%. Total after 10 yrs.: 380,000 *plus* 385,800 now worth 795,200 Total: 1,181,000
Age 65 Retired	2,000,000 house value 284,000 deflated	2,000,000 house 3,614,400 stocks after tax 5,614,400 total wealth 655,000 in today's dollars	2,000,000 house 1,181,000 stocks after tax 3,181,000 total wealth 452,000 deflated

Table 18 (cont.)
Investment Strategies—II

	Plan 4: Home-Equity Loan, Tax-Deferred Stock Market Investment	Plan 5: Home-Equity Loan, No Tax-Deferred Investment	Plan 6: Move to More Expensive House
Age 25 $50,000 income	$125,000 value of home 100,000 mortgage 25,000 equity	$125,000 value 100,000 mortgage 25,000 equity	$125,000 value 100,000 mortgage 25,000 equity
Age 35 100,000 income	250,000 value of home 200,000 mortgage 50,000 equity Take 100,000 home-equity mortgage, invest in stock mkt. at 12%. Total after 10 yrs.: 310,600	250,000 value 200,000 mortgage 50,000 equity Take 100,000 home-equity mortgage, invest in stock mkt. at 7.5%. Total after 10 yrs.: 206,100	250,000 value of existing home 100,000 mortgage 150,000 equity 200,000 new mortgage 350,000 value of new home
Age 45 200,000 income	500,000 value of home 400,000 mortgage 100,000 equity Take 200,000 home-equity mortgage, *interest no longer tax-deductible* so equivalent is 150,000. Invest in stock mkt. at 12%. Total after 10 yrs.: 465,900 *plus* 310,000 worth 964,700 Total stock mkt.: 1,430,600	500,000 value 400,000 mortgage 100,000 equity Take 200,000 home-equity mortgage, *interest no longer tax-deductible* so equivalent is 150,000. Invest in stock mkt. at 7.5%. Total after 10 yrs. 309,200 *plus* 310,000 worth 424,800 Total stock mkt.: 734,600	700,000 value of existing home 200,000 mortgage 500,000 equity 400,000 mortgage 900,000 value of new home
Age 55 400,000 income	1,000,000 value 800,000 mortgage Extra 200,000 equity Take 400,000 home-equity loan. 300,000 invested in stock mkt. at 12%. Total after 10 yrs.: 931,800 *plus* 1,430,000 worth 4,443,200 Total stock mkt.: 5,375,600	1,000,000 value 800,000 mortgage Extra 200,000 equity Take 400,000 home-equity loan 300,000 invested in stock mkt. at 7.5% Total after 10 yrs.: 618,400 *plus* 734,000 worth 1,512,800 Total stock mkt.: 2,131,000	1,800,000 value of existing home 400,000 old mortgage 1,400,000 equity 800,000 mortgage 2,200,000 value of new home
Age 65 Retired	1,200,000 equity in home 3,601,700 stock mkt. after tax 4,801,700 total wealth 682,000 deflated	1,200,000 equity 2,131,200 stocks 3,331,200 total wealth 473,200 deflated	4,400,000 value of home *less*: 800,000 mortgage 3,600,000 equity 511,200 deflated

covered in more detail in the following chapters. First, if the funds have been accumulated in a tax-deferred account, of course you will have to pay taxes when you withdraw them; I've assumed that would be at a 33 percent marginal rate, since your income that year would be well into the upper brackets. Also, I've assumed that by retirement time you've moved to a state that has no income taxes. Second, you may want to get your money out of the house but don't want to pay the capital-gains taxes. That's simple. Suppose your house has appreciated to $2 million; sell it and buy another house that is also worth $2 million. Sell it a minimum of two years later, perhaps even at no profit after sales commissions, and move to a smaller house. That way, you won't have any profit to show on your last sale and you will avoid all capital-gains taxes. That's one of the major benefits of the rollover rule for real estate.

The results of Table 18 are summarized below for those who don't particularly enjoy reading long columns of numbers. I've used the constant-dollar figures here to provide a more realistic estimate of how fast your wealth has really grown, although the current-dollar figures are more mind-boggling.

Even if you're a do-nothing spendthrift who uses no leverage and consistently decreases your saving rate over a lifetime, you still come out reasonably well, with a $284,000 nest egg in constant prices compared with an original $25,000 investment for the down payment. You can then live in the old house mortgage-free, or trade down to a more modest residence or apartment and invest the rest.

Plans 2 through 5 illustrate the benefits of being able to accumulate wealth on a tax-deferred basis and pay taxes only near retirement age. For those who invest directly in the stock market, the constant-dollar payoff is $655,000, compared with $452,000 if you have to pay taxes on the money up front. Of course, in current dollars the figures are much more exotic: $4.6 million compared with $3.2 million. But don't forget that over a 40-year period, prices will rise 7-fold.

As it turns out, it doesn't make much difference whether you get a home-equity mortgage or not, providing you have the discipline to put aside the savings every year. Since only the interest on the first $100,000 of the home-equity mortgage is deductible, your tax deduction drops sharply after that level; I've taken that into account in the calculations. However, I still recommend the home-equity mortgage because it more or less forces you to make those payments—particularly if the funds are tied up in a tax-deferred account where you can't get at them easily before retirement. Otherwise, it's far too easy to postpone investing during a year when expenses are high; pretty soon it gets to be a bad habit, and wealth accumulation is out the window.

Plan 6 isn't precisely comparable because every 10 years you move to a more expensive house. Presumably the value of living in a bigger house, or one in a better neighborhood, is greater than zero. Furthermore, unless you can put those investment funds away in tax-deferred status, the equity buildup in the house—always keeping the mortgage payment at 20 percent of your initial income for the decade—is greater than the stock market because of the increased leverage. Besides, even if you end up with slightly less money, the accommodations have been plusher along the way.

Whether you leverage real estate by buying a more expensive house or by taking the money out and reinvesting it in the stock market or other real estate, the returns will be quite handsome. Unless you really need to spend each available dollar as it comes along, this represents one of the most important ways to accumulate wealth over your lifetime.

SELLING YOUR HOUSE(S) AT THE END OF THE LEVERAGED STAIRCASE

So far we've generally ignored the favored tax treatment of real estate, other than to note that interest payments are tax-deductible; so are property taxes. However, tax treatment when you sell can be of great importance. No use paying the government 33 percent of your gain if there's a palatable alternative.

The standard rule, which virtually all homeowners know, is that the capital gain on your principal residence isn't taxed if you purchase a home of equal or greater value sometime within the next two years. That assumption has supported our way up the stairway to wealth through leveraged real estate. However, it doesn't hold when you cash out that last house and downgrade for your retirement—unless you use a little foresight.

If you are over 55, the current tax laws state that $125,000 of the gain won't be taxed. Maybe a long time ago that was a lot of money, but in most cases it will apply to only a small fraction of the bill in future years. Also, this applies only to your principal residence, and you can only use it once. If you're using real estate for wealth accumulation, that tax break will make very little difference. You need more help from the tax code—if it exists.

In the case of the principal residence, it's easy to sidestep the tax code.

As I've already mentioned, take the $2 million house you have at retirement, sell it, and move into another $2 million house, which you can then sell after two years—with no profit and no taxes.

However, that doesn't apply to any other houses you might own; the tax-free rollover applies only to the principal residence. Don't despair—the tax code is still reasonably friendly to real estate, although that, too, could be changed someday, so check before you go ahead. The way it works now involves transferring your home from residential to business property. This is accomplished by renting out the property. All of this is explained in Section 1034 of the IRS Code, which also contains the more popular "rollover residence replacement rule." I'm citing the specific section so that when you are ready to try it you can check with your tax adviser to make sure it's still there.

Here's how it works. Suppose you have a house worth $500,000, which you purchased many years ago for $200,000. You rent it out for a year or more; the rate you get really isn't of great importance because this is mainly for tax purposes. The market value of a $500,000 house would be about $4,000 a month rent, but that's a little steep for most people. At $2,500 a month, you will probably find tenants who are grateful and will also keep the house in excellent shape.

After you have established that this house is a business property, you then sell it for $500,000. Take the $500,000 and buy other rental properties. Let's say you buy one for $150,000 and the other for $350,000, then rent both of them. Meanwhile, you move into a house and rent it from someone else. You could conceivably set up a dummy corporation and rent your house from it, but the IRS might very well nix that deal.

After another year has passed, you decide to move into the $150,000 house. You now have your smaller house without having paid one nickel of capital-gains taxes. Furthermore, you continue to rent out the $350,000 property, earning a handsome rate of return on that property as well (more about that later). You did suffer some minor inconvenience from the one extra move, but in return you've saved up to $100,000 in capital-gains taxes. Real estate permits you to capture all your gains without paying any tax.

No other type of investment can make this claim. Even if you follow all the rules for IRAs, Keoghs, 401(k)s, SEPs, or other retirement plans, you must pay taxes on the money when you take it out. The only way you can avoid payment of capital-gains taxes on stocks is to hold them until your death, in which case you don't get the benefit. But with the investment rollover rule, you can avoid the capital-gains taxes when you sell your real estate—and use 100 instead of 67 percent of the money for retirement income.

To review: No investment is risk-free. From time to time, real estate prices do decline. However, if you hold a house for seven or eight years, 99 percent of the time the price will rise. If inflation remains near 5 percent, real estate prices will, on average, increase at least 7 percent per year. If you leverage your real estate with a fairly conservative 20 percent down payment, and either move to a bigger house or refinance with home equity every 10 years, you will earn an average rate of almost 20 percent per year, even if you only pick houses that appreciate at the average rate. Finally, when you are ready to downsize your residence, you can avoid all capital-gains taxes either by swapping housing at the same value or by first converting to a rental unit. No other type of investment offers all these advantages.

RENTING RESIDENTIAL REAL ESTATE

If investing in your own home is such a great idea, isn't investing in other real estate an equally lucrative idea?

For many people it is. But read the caveats first.

I'm assuming that you get some real enjoyment—psychic income—out of living in a beautiful house in a wonderful neighborhood with lots of space where the family can spread out. With real estate purchased for investment purposes, there isn't any positive psychic income—instead, there's grief. Tenants don't always pay on time, and even those who do complain about the leaky roof, the broken pipes, or the dishwasher that short-circuited. Of course all of these things can happen to your own home, but it's a lot more annoying when your tenants call you late in the evening and let loose with a barrage of grievances and demands.

But setting aside the question of psychic gain or loss for a moment, let's look at the straight dollars and cents differences between owning and renting.

1. I said earlier that the cost of renting and buying was about the same on an after-tax basis. That means if you pay $1,000 per month for the mortgage payments and real estate taxes, you could rent the place for about $700 per month. The tax benefits to you on rental property are severely diluted in this case, because the $700 a month is income. Of course, if you have expenses you can deduct them, but that cuts down on your cash flow and hence your rate of return.

2. Hardly anyone has their rental property occupied 100 percent of the time. A normal vacancy rate would be about 1 month out of 12; you might do better or worse. But on an average basis, you have to take those vacancies into account when determining the rate of return.

3. Most tenants don't treat the house with the same loving care you lavish on your own house. That's one reason repairs are usually higher with tenants than with owners.

4. If you don't want to be bothered by all those late-night calls—and if you don't enjoy pounding on the door when the rent is late and hearing about how both kids are sick and the husband just got laid off—you can hire an agent to collect the rent and handle the grief, for which he will charge 6 percent. Since my disutility for grief is fairly high, I always pay the 6 percent, and that's included in my calculations. If you are the sort who can turn a deaf ear to these complaints, and be ready to call the sheriff when the rent becomes delinquent, you can save the 6 percent and boost the rate of return accordingly.

However, there is one big plus in the rental deal that once again is tied to inflation. Over time, you can boost the rental payments to keep pace with other prices, while your mortgage payment remains the same—although taxes, insurance, and repair costs will all rise proportionately with inflation. And, most of the time you'll get to sell the building for a good deal more than you paid for it. Without the inflation-based escalation, you won't make much money renting because the market forces that determine rental prices reflect the fact that inflation is forever. That's fine; just so you understand the reasons you are or are not making money by renting property.

Now let's do the arithmetic. Assume you bought a house for $125,000 for purposes of renting it out. You paid 20 percent down, so the monthly payments plus real estate taxes are about $1,000 a month. The rental income, however, is only $700 less 8 percent for the vacancy and 6 percent for the agent, so you are out of pocket (after including the tax advantages) about $300 a month. For the moment I'm assuming there are no more repairs than there would be on your own home, which is the most favorable case. As the rent increases, the $300 a month shortfall diminishes, so with 5 percent inflation, the rent will be greater than the monthly payment by the ninth year. In the meantime, however, your cash-flow drain significantly reduces the rate of return.

To see how much of a drain this is, suppose the value of the house rises from $125,000 to $250,000 after 10 years. Assuming an investment of a $25,000 down payment and $7,500 closing costs, your average rate of return on equity before deducting settlement costs would be 15.9 percent per year if you didn't have to pay that extra $300 a month. However, with the $300 a month shortfall—assuming the money would otherwise earn 10 percent per year—the rate of return drops to 12.6 percent. That would be a very favorable rate of return on your money during your retirement years, when you will have less to do in any case, especially if the investment rollover rule saved you the capital-gains taxes. However, it's not a particularly exciting gain for accumulating wealth, considering all the extra time it entails. So my conclusion is that renting out property is more for retirement years than for accumulating wealth.

Sometimes it appears that those who have owned buildings for years are earning a rate of return that is absurdly high. Suppose the buildings have been in the family for two generations; what now has a market value of $150,000 was originally bought for $15,000, and it's renting for $1,250 a month. Since the annual rentals are equal to the original cost, it might appear that the annual rate of return is 100 percent. However, if the building were sold for $150,000 and the assets reinvested elsewhere, the annual income would still be $15,000 per year. Renting property provides moderate but not exceptional rates of return.

If you have lived in a house for a long time and decide to move out for any of several reasons, but still want to hang on to the old homestead, you probably won't be able to get the accumulated equity out with a home-equity loan because you aren't an owner-occupant. In that case, renting is not only the best use of the asset but will bring in a very high rate of return. However, that's a special case.

COMMERCIAL REAL ESTATE

Anyone who drove through Houston, Texas, during the mid-1980s could readily see the disadvantages of investing in commercial real estate in a formerly booming region that becomes temporarily depressed. The same scenario was reinforced in any major Northeastern city in 1990.

For that matter, residential real estate in Houston didn't do so well during the 1980s either. But a house has some rental value; if the price is too high, it can be adjusted down until tenants are found. Furthermore, if you live in the house you get some utility from the space, even if the asset is not appreciating at the moment. Besides, even in the worst of the 1980s, the national vacancy rate for homes—as opposed to apartment buildings—was only about 1 percent. However, a commercial building can remain vacant for many years and return zero rent. For that reason, my rules on investing in commercial real estate are a bit different.

Unlike the situation in major cities, where rental vacancy rates have remained low for decades, a tight commercial market invariably leads to overbuilding and high vacancy rates. Even in Washington, D.C., which suffered virtually no letdown at all during the severe 1981–82 recession, the office vacancy rate went from a virtually invisible 0.1 percent in 1979 to over 15 percent during the late 1980s. The 0.1 percent rate was an irresistible target for too many builders, resulting in severe overbuilding.

Occasionally renters default on their payments by moving out of town, but unless you are dealing with low-income families, most people would rather pay their rent than be evicted. However, businesses often go bankrupt on short notice, and unless the tenants have personally signed for the lease, the building owners are out of luck.

Many of the *Forbes* 400 have made their billions primarily or exclusively in real estate—including A. Alfred Taubman ($2 billion), Donald Bren ($1.8 billion), Harry Helmsley ($1.7 billion), Samuel LeFrak ($1.7 billion), and Edward DeBartolo ($1.4 billion). Before he let Atlantic City go to his head, Donald Trump was also on this list, although it's not clear he ever belonged there. So I'm hardly about to suggest that commercial real estate isn't a high-powered route to great wealth. However, these great fortunes came from *building* massive projects in prime locations, not just from *managing* existing buildings. Even during the early 1980s, with all the favorable tax laws, operating strip shopping centers was not the best way to get rich. And with the change in tax laws after 1986, many of these projects went bankrupt, so commercial real estate is now an entirely different ball game.

None of this means you can't make money at commercial real estate. What it does mean is that unlike residential real estate, which will appreciate in price 99 percent of the time, you could get stuck with some real turkeys for years. To avoid this, here are my guidelines.

1. Only consider buildings that are 90 percent or better occupied. If a building is mostly vacant, it may be offered to you on a "bargain" basis. Usually the only bargain will be for the seller. Don't assume that a vacant building will soon be occupied.
2. If one key tenant occupies a substantial portion of the building, check the lease very carefully to make sure that the tenant is fully liable. Mobil Oil, for example, might occupy three floors of a building, but the lease could be drawn with a subsidiary of Mobil Oil that has no assets. If they decide to break the lease, the subsidiary goes bankrupt and there's nothing you can do about it.

3. Check neighboring properties. Even if the building you are considering is almost full, if others nearby are empty and offering much lower rents, you can assume that some of your tenants will switch when their leases expire—or you will have to reduce the rates to keep them from moving out.

4. Assuming you've identified an almost fully rented property with honest tenants in a good location—and there are still such opportunities in most communities—it's time to check the books to examine income and expenses in recent years. Both of these should be fairly steady. If income is way up this year, or expenses are way down, that should sound an alarm.

5. Calculate what your mortgage payments will be for the new purchase price, factor in current revenues and expenses, and *only buy buildings that have a positive cash flow*. If the figures turn out to be negative at the current asking price, lower your bid to the point where cash flow is positive. If the seller isn't interested, move on to the next building. (Before 1986, it sometimes made sense to buy properties with a negative cash flow because of the tax breaks, but those days are gone forever.)

   By the way, that doesn't mean you should automatically assume that a building with a positive cash flow is a good investment. Commercial real estate is a riskier investment than the stock market because there's less liquidity. If a stock goes down, you can always sell it on the spot. If it turns around and comes back, you can repurchase it; if not, you're well rid of it.

   With commercial real estate, however, if something goes wrong, you may never get your money out. I'm not talking only about a temporary decline in the occupancy rates—what could be called "market risk." Your major tenant may go bankrupt or not renew the lease; maintenance costs skyrocket; liability costs soar. Some costs, such as higher taxes, routine maintenance, and utility bills can be passed along, but what happens if there's a fire in one of the units and your remaining tenants move out? Insurance usually covers only your direct out-of-pocket losses. Suppose a drug dealer sets up shop in one of your units but pays the rent on time; evicting him may be a time-consuming and expensive proposition.

Because of all these factors, I'm not interested in commercial real estate deals unless under normal circumstances the overall rate of return—including capital gains—is 20 percent or more per year, based on holding the building ten years or more. By normal circumstances, I mean that if the occupancy rate is 90 percent at the time of purchase, it stays near 90 percent. Also, new rents should keep pace with the rate of inflation, although in many cases multiyear leases generally do not. If the area is overbuilt and rents have been stagnant for several years, I'd pass.

As with residential rental property, commercial rents can be raised in future years except for tenants with long leases. Of course, expenses other than mortgage interest also rise over time, but they represent only about one-third of the total costs. If you can raise rents only 3 percent per year but can also pass through all increases in costs, the building may still be worth purchasing. But make sure you have watertight cost-pass-through clauses.

I've only nibbled at the surface of commercial real estate here. Most master leases run into the hundreds of pages, and unlike most of the other investment strategies discussed in this book, you can't do it yourself. In this case, you should always work with a competent real estate lawyer and tax adviser.

REITs AND RELPs

Because large commercial real estate deals are so complicated, many smaller investors have been tempted to buy into real estate investment trusts or real estate limited partnerships. Someone else buys the property, hires the lawyer and accountant, does all the paperwork—and takes 15 to 20 percent off the top for his troubles. They then turn around and offer equity shares in these properties to individual investors.

Before 1986, the tax laws were structured so that most of these deals produced some very lucrative tax benefits, even if the investments themselves generated little or no actual return. Thus they were worthwhile even though profits were nil. However, the Tax Reform Act of 1986 annihilated these tax shelters to the point where no new ones will ever grow, much as the ancient Romans sowed salt on the site of Carthage so no city could ever arise there again. If you buy such a security now, it should be strictly for current yield and capital gains, not for tax advantages.

The financial pages regularly carry articles touting the advantages of investing in some derivative instrument based on real estate—whether it is a limited partnership, real estate investment trust, or real estate annuity. I wouldn't bite at any of them, and here's why.

In most of these derived instruments, you are doing nothing more than participating in the income from mortgages. The deals are usually structured in such a way that the individual investor gets very little of the capital gains. You can earn an average rate of return of 12 percent per year in the stock market with the proverbial dart board. Over the long run, few if any mortgages earn more than 12 percent—and certainly not after the syndicators have taken their share off the top. The arithmetic simply doesn't add up.

If some hotshot tries to tell you that in addition to the mortgage interest you will also get capital gains, remember you can't have your cake and eat it too. When you buy commercial real estate, the first few years generate little if any cash flow; the rent is approximately equal to the mortgage payments plus expenses. The profits come in later years, when (a) the rents appreciate and (b) the building is sold at a gain.

The only way the investor gets a better deal by purchasing a derived instrument than buying real estate on his own is if the organizers can pick better properties than individuals can. However, over the past 10 years the record has been just the opposite: The syndicates have picked properties that appreciated very little, mainly because they overpaid for them in order to earn their up-front fees. This caused a conflict of interest: Up-front fees were more important than long-term gains. If you want to invest in commercial real estate, pick your properties yourself and watch them carefully. If that isn't your style, stick to residential real estate or the stock market.

Since the changes in the tax laws in 1986, I've avoided all derivative real estate products, and suggest you do the same.

Chapter 10

Life Insurance

SAVINGS OR SCAM?

Buying life insurance is one of the most controversial aspects of financial planning and wealth creation. The unctuous life-insurance salesman does his best to convince you that, but for him, your loved ones would be left penniless. Yet most independent financial planners claim that except for term insurance, it's a scam, not much different from throwing your money down the proverbial rat hole.

Who is right?

If we strip the argument of all the emotional overtones surrounding family responsibilities, the fear of dying, and the personalities of most insurance salespeople, the argument simply reduces to another straight-forward calculation based on alternative yields. Although hundreds of variants of life insurance policies are currently available, the decision all boils down to the same question. Who can earn a higher rate of return on your invested funds—you or the insurance company with its tax benefits?

Separating Death Benefits and Savings Plans

First, the one basic distinction in life insurance. *Term insurance* is a strict insurance premium against premature death. If you live out your life to a ripe old age, you get nothing. It's just like fire insurance for your house: if it never burns down, you never get a penny of those premiums back— and you're pretty happy it worked out that way, too. Normal people don't buy fire insurance hoping they can collect. Since term insurance is a policy against premature death, it should really be called death insurance—just as other policies are called fire insurance or theft insurance—but the industry probably wouldn't sell as many policies under that name. Or at least that's what they think. But *you* know what it is.

Whole life insurance and its successors combine term insurance with a savings plan; the main varieties are discussed in this chapter. No matter what the name, they all consist of two separate parts: the actual insurance premium against premature death, plus a method of savings. That savings can be used either for your retirement years or passed along to your heirs. The amount you pay over and above the term premium is a form of saving. Either the insurance company can do a better job of investing your assets than you could, or it can't. No need to complicate the argument with emotional overtones.

Just remember that these are two different goals—death benefits and savings plans—and you will understand much of the mystery about life insurance that baffles most policyholders and not a few agents.

Term Insurance: The True Cost of Death Insurance Rises Every Year

The key factor to remember about death-benefit premiums—as opposed to savings—is that as you get older, the probability of your death during the following year increases. So don't be fooled. Even if your premium payments don't rise as you get older, the *true* cost of death insurance rises each year.

When you're 35, the cost of death insurance for nonsmokers is only about $100 per year for a $100,000 policy—odds of 1 in a 1,000. By the time you have reached 65, the odds have risen to 1 in 100, and by the time you're 80, to 1 in 20. The odds are about double for smokers, by the way.

The true death-insurance premium increases every year, even if you have a fully paid-up policy and are paying no premiums at all. You might wonder how the premium can be increasing if you are not paying anything at all. The answer is that the cash value accumulated in your policy earns interest each year. That amount is offset by the true cost of death insurance. When the cost of death insurance exceeds the increase due to investment income, your death benefit remains in force at the stated policy amount, but the cash value—the amount you would receive if you cashed in the policy— begins to diminish.

Deciding when to cash in your life insurance policy is a complicated decision that depends on how much value has been built up in the policy, your needs for cash during retirement years, your desire to pass along assets to your heirs, whether you are likely to live more or less years than the mortality tables say, and—most important of all—the tax situation. I'll explore all of these issues later. The key factor to recognize at the start is that even with a fixed annual premium or a fully paid-up policy, the true cost of death insurance rises every year.

The amount of the increase can be determined quite easily. One way is simply to look at any standard mortality table that the insurance industry uses—or that the IRS prepares for annuities. If the table says the chances of someone your age and sex dying next year is 0.015, then your true death-insurance premium will be $15 per $1,000 face amount of the policy. If you don't have one of these tables handy, ask your insurance agent to provide you with rates for term and whole life insurance for each age. The term rate is the cost of death insurance; the difference is what you are setting aside for savings, less sales commissions and the cost of managing your money.

Whole Life and Its Successors: "New" Types of Life Insurance

Before 1980, life insurance was fairly simple. You either purchased term or you bought what was called whole life insurance, which combined death benefits with a savings plan. In general, whole life was quite unsatisfactory because it paid an abysmally low rate of return and was very inflexible. Since 1980, however, the industry has changed significantly. Now you can choose from a variety of policies, which are often known as *universal life* or *variable life*, with the following features.

- Rates of return are tied to market interest rates.
- Your money can be invested in stocks instead of bonds, or switched back and forth.
- Commission costs and expenses are clearly stated in the policy.
- Payments can be increased, decreased, or even skipped.
- Death benefits are increased if you live longer.

I'll discuss all of these in detail later. The point to note here is that the life insurance industry is now quite different from the way it was in 1980.

So don't make the mistake of basing your decision about life insurance on some outmoded source that was written many years ago.

Buy Term and Invest the Difference?

Most financial planners outside the industry will tell you, as an inviolate rule, to "buy term and invest the difference." For any given age and risk category, the premiums per $1,000 of life insurance will be substantially higher for whole life than for term. Suppose, for example, the premiums at age 35 were $1,000 for a $100,000 whole life policy and $100 for a term policy. If you opted for term, you could then take the remaining $900 and invest it in a money market account, real estate, bonds, stocks, or other types of assets. As you got older, your term premium would rise to $200, $300, and so on, until by the time you reached age 65, the term premium would rise almost to the $1,000 you paid for whole life.

Now ask yourself: Will the interest, dividends, and capital gains you accumulated on the difference you invested on your own equal or exceed the $100,000 you would have accumulated in your policy by age 65 if you had purchased a whole life policy? If they will, you're better off buying the term policy and dropping it when you turn 65.

Using the average premiums charged by most life insurance companies, it turns out that you would reach the $100,000 goal by investing the difference between term and whole life and earning an average yield of 8.5 percent per year. Since that's roughly equivalent to current money market rates, it might seem you would do just as well by investing your own money.

However, there's one catch that is so large it makes all the difference, which is—not too surprisingly—taxes. Remember the 8.5 percent would have to be an after-tax rate of return, which means the funds would have to be in an IRA or a similar tax-deferred savings plan. But not everyone can avail themselves of such a plan. Even if you can, there are maximum limits on the annual amount that can be invested on a tax-deferred basis, limits that do not apply to life insurance. That doesn't mean life insurance is necessarily a good investment. Often it isn't. Nonetheless, it does enjoy certain tax advantages that are not available for other forms of savings, so just make sure you're not comparing apples and bicycles.

The Triple Tax-Free Advantage of Life Insurance

The school of thought that recommends only term insurance points out, with some justification, that the insurance industry has had a very poor track record at investing its funds, and your accumulation is severely diluted by excessive sales commissions and operating costs. Neither of these is false. However, the trouble with this just-say-no-to-whole-life approach is that it completely disregards the tax angle. The life insurance industry survived the Tax Reform Act of 1986 almost unscathed, one of the very few industries to do so. As a result, life insurance is one of the very few investments that is triple tax-free—the buildup of assets is tax-deferred, the death benefits are exempt from income tax, and with proper planning, those benefits can also be exempted from estate tax. All of these factors must be considered when making an intelligent decision about financial planning.

Here's how tax advantages benefit holders of life insurance.

1. **Inside buildup.** This term refers to the fact that the interest, dividends, and capital gains on your investment are not taxed. If you have a money market fund earning, say, 9 percent, your after-tax rate of return is usually about 6 percent. If the same funds were invested in an insurance policy, you would earn the entire 9 percent, less commissions and expenses.

   IRAs used to have the same advantage, but it was stripped away after 1986 except for the self-employed, those who work for companies without a retirement plan, or low-income wage earners. Other retirement plans carry greater tax-deferral benefits, but all of them have some limit. There is none on most forms of life insurance.

   Inside buildup also works for assets that you hold for a long time and appreciate in value, such as real estate, or stocks that you never sell. However, these types of investments have no flexibility.

2. **Proceeds can sometimes be received tax-free.** Suppose you paid $10,000 for a piece of real estate that was later worth $100,000. If you didn't buy another piece of real estate that cost at least that much, you would have to pay taxes on some or all of the $90,000 in profits. But suppose you paid $10,000 in premiums for an insurance policy that was later worth $100,000. You would owe no tax on any of the proceeds if they were paid as a death benefit. If you use the proceeds for retirement income, they are usually taxed, but even here you may be able to take advantage of a tax-free switch to an annuity. I'll discuss that in the next chapter.

3. **Avoid estate taxes.** The policy can be owned by your wife or children, and as long as they pay the premiums, the payoff of the policy at your death will pass to them without any estate taxes (this is discussed in more detail in Chapter 13). This setup is particularly valuable for relatively large estates that exceed the $1.2 million tax-free transfer.

It's true that almost any asset can be placed in trust to escape estate taxes. You can turn over your stocks and bonds, real estate, or even the family business to the children early in life, before these assets appreciate very much. However, that means relinquishing control over the assets, which may be disadvantageous for other reasons. Life insurance policies are one of the better ways of avoiding estate taxes—and since marginal tax rates run as high as 55 percent, compared with the maximum 33 percent on personal income taxes, that is definitely not a trivial consideration.

Thus the basic question about the relative merits of life insurance must be rephrased: Will your investment performance on an *after-tax* basis be better than the insurance company's investment on a *pretax* basis? For example, you may be able to earn 12 percent per year, whereas the insurance company can earn only 8 percent per year. However, after considering the 33 percent tax bite on the incremental earnings each year *and* the 55 percent estate tax bite, your rate of return could actually be as low as 4 percent. That's an extreme case, because insurance isn't the only way to avoid estate taxes. However, even without any estate taxes, your 12 percent rate would be pulled down to the 8 percent generated by the insurance company.

Whole life insurance payments have one other feature that some would consider to be a plus: They force you to save. In a totally rational world, this would be irrelevant; but for many people it's far too easy to spend whatever money is left over in the bank at the end of each month. If you have that type of personality, making regular life insurance payments will help build up the savings account. On the other hand, if you don't have any trouble saving a certain amount of your income every month, disregard this paragraph.

WHAT RATE OF RETURN DOES THE INSURANCE COMPANY EARN ON YOUR MONEY?

For many years, the rate of return that insurance companies earned was a well-kept secret; they wouldn't tell you, and figuring it out entailed a lot of complicated calculations involving logarithms. Since most people would rather get ripped off by insurance salesmen than relearn logarithms, policyholders invested in the dark, although they had some vague feeling that their investments were not doing very well.

The cover was lifted from this secrecy in 1979, when the Federal Trade

Commission (FTC) published a study showing that, believe it or not, the average annual rate of return earned by insurance companies on your money was a paltry 1.3 percent! The insurance industry, of course, chose not to believe it; ten years later it still claimed the whole thing was just one big mistake. In fact, the average rate of return was actually around 4 percent; the FTC had chosen the worst-case scenario. Nonetheless, that still stinks. Whether or not the FTC slanted the numbers in its study, there was no question that during the 1970s, the rate of return earned by the insurance industry was so far below the market rate that your money was indeed being squandered. A 4 percent return is a dereliction of fiduciary responsibility when riskless Treasury bills are paying 14 percent.

Even though the industry cried foul, insurance personnel knew in their hearts there was enough truth in the report to necessitate a complete remolding of the concept of life insurance. They first introduced an option generally known as universal life, which states the precise amount the policyholder is paying for death benefits and the remaining amount that is invested. They introduced tables that showed how much the cash value of the policy would be worth at different ages under the assumption of various interest rates. In most cases, the tables were constructed on a rate that was equivalent to current credit-market rates—i.e., what could be earned on the highest-quality (Aaa) corporate bond or a short-term CD, whichever was higher. The industry later introduced variable life, which means you can choose to have your money invested in stocks instead of bonds.

While this truth-in-investing approach was certainly welcome, two clouds still partially obscure the sunshine. First, the posted rate earned is based only on the actual amount of money invested, which is equal to the total premiums minus the death benefit *minus* the sales commissions and operating expenses. The amount the agent gets up front is pretty hefty— often it's more than the full first year's commission—so it never pays to buy whole life insurance for only a short time. If you have reason to believe the policy will remain in force for only a few years, term is the only sensible option. However, as I'll show later, if you hold the policy for most of your adult life, the sales commissions won't make much difference on the overall rate of return.

The second problem is that the current rate is not guaranteed for very long. A close examination of the policies reveals that after the first year or two, the guaranteed rate drops from the current market rate, which is usually in the 8 to 10 percent range, down to 4 or 4½ percent, an unethically low yield and reminiscent of the bad old days. That's allegedly to protect the insurance companies in case market rates ever drop that low again, so they won't be operating at a loss.

This is one of the last remaining scams in life insurance, and yet I know of no company that guarantees market rates indefinitely. The reason it's a scam is that anyone can buy a 40-year bond guaranteed by an agency of the U.S. government and lock in today's rate of interest for the next 40 years. And if that isn't good enough, one can buy a perpetual British bond with no maturity date that locks in the current rate forever. Yet no insurance company does this.

So it is always possible that the insurance company, after getting your signature on the dotted line and locking you in by charging those hefty initial sales commissions, will then tell you, "Sorry, we're only paying 4½ percent instead of 9 percent." As I noted in Chapter 7, even banks that "guarantee" above-market rates of interest mean no such thing. Except for those companies that had gone bankrupt, though, no insurance company has dropped such a bombshell, since it would lose most of its policyholders if it did. Furthermore, with variable life you can require your assets to be invested in bonds or stocks rather than the asset mix chosen by the insurance companies. That way, you won't be sandbagged.

I don't think any major insurance company would run the risk of alienating its entire client base by paying below-market rates. If you don't believe that, then do buy term and invest the difference. But in a risky world, the chances of the rates dropping all the way to the guaranteed minimum are pretty small. You're more likely to be hit by a car on the way to the agent's office.

Thus the general approach that determines what kind of insurance policy you should buy is fairly straightforward. First, find out the cost of the death insurance benefits. Then calculate whether the rate of return the insurance company is offering at current market rates is better than you think you could do on your own. Don't forget to take tax considerations into account.

WHICH TERM INSURANCE POLICY TO BUY

Term insurance rates can be calculated very easily, providing you are healthy and not in an excessively high-risk occupation, such as professional skydiving or alligator wrestling. Take your age, check the standard mortality tables to determine the average chance you'll die in the next year, and adjust for differences in mortality rates due to health conditions. You will find that rates are quite competitive, and the insurance companies charge relatively little for administration and sales commissions on term insurance.

Shopping for the Best Rate

Of course in real life nothing is ever quite that simple, because there are actually several different mortality tables: males and females, smokers and nonsmokers, and something called a "preferred risk," which means that your health is better than average and the insurance agent likes you. But in principle, the premiums are based on straightforward actuarial calculations, adjusted for your personal health and lifestyle. For example, according to the 1980 Life Insurance Commissioners Standard Ordinary Mortality Table, if you are 30 years old and male, the chance of dying in the next year is 1.73 in 1,000; for 30-year-old females, it's 1.35 in 1,000. Now don't get all charged up about males and females being treated differently; these figures are based on actual experience for the 1970–75 period.

These figures seem to suggest that if a 30-year-old male bought term insurance for the next year, he would pay about $1.73 per $1,000 coverage, or $173 per year for a $100,000 policy. That could be a one-year policy, automatically renewable next year at your option, but more often policies are written for five-year intervals, with the rate fixed for the first five years. When you are young, the difference in premiums between a one- and five-year policy is minuscule.

Yet if you are a nonsmoker and paid $173, you would be overpaying by at least a factor of two. Checking the rates charged by major insurance companies reveals that for nonsmokers, the average annual premium on a $100,000 policy for a 30-year-old is about $80, not $173. Only for smokers is it $173 or more. Those who still smoke might want to think about that for a minute.

The point is that while the mortality tables cover everyone—those who are already sick, addicted to drugs, live in high-crime slums, etc.—the insurance companies naturally try to screen out the bad risks. As a result, you pay a much lower premium, providing of course you don't smoke.

No matter what your rating, the premiums rise as you get older because the chance of mortality increases. Using the standard tables—which include the bad as well as the good risks—the mortality rate for males rises from 1.73 per 1,000 at age 30 to 3.02 at age 40, 6.71 at age 50, 16.08 at age 60, and 39.51 at age 70. Nonsmokers can expect to pay about half these rates all the way up the age scale. As I already pointed out, your *true* insurance premium will rise proportionately with increasing age no matter what premium you are actually paying.

Virtually all term insurance policies are renewable indefinitely, but check the fine print just to make sure. Also, some term insurance policies will allow you to increase your coverage by a certain amount every time you renew; that could be important if your health suddenly deteriorates.

One word of caution: Don't get suckered in by what turns out to be an artificially low introductory rate. Ask to see the entire rate schedule over the years, if in fact you are planning to keep the policy for more than a few years. If the rate jumps, you will always have the opportunity to switch to a different company. However, that means another medical exam and the increasing possibility that, as you grow older, at some point you may be turned down or "rated," which means charged a much higher than normal premium because of some health problem, such as obesity, high blood pressure, or diabetes. You are better off getting a so-called "preferred" rating—i.e., the lowest rate offered—when you're young and healthy, then staying with that company. So it does pay to check the complete schedule of annual or five-year increases in the premiums.

The Best Age Span for Holding Term Insurance

There are no hard-and-fast rules that tell you when to stop buying term insurance. For strictly insurance purposes—as opposed to estate planning purposes, as discussed in chapter 13—term insurance usually makes more economic sense if you are under 50. If you are over 50 and apply for term insurance—particularly if it is a large amount—the insurance company will go over the application with a fine-tooth comb, especially the parts about when your parents died and your current health record. And, you won't be able to beat the system by lying about these things—the courts have consistently ruled that if you lie on your insurance form, the insurance company doesn't owe you a nickel when you die, even if the cause of death (e.g., accident) has no relationship to the statement you answered falsely (e.g., diabetes). Naturally, the industry only wants to insure those risks who are likely to outperform the mortality tables.

Except for estate planning purposes, most people don't consider buying a new term insurance policy after age 50. Occasionally, there might be a legitimate reason. The major cause outside of estate planning purposes would be a change in economic status. You might have been fired or resigned from a company that had provided you with a generous life insurance policy; or you might be starting your own company and the investors had demanded a so-called key man policy. In that case, shop around for the best deal—and keep your blood pressure low, at least in the doctor's office.

Most of the time, however, term insurance is a young person's product, designed to be purchased before your assets have appreciated enough to leave your family comfortably provided for in the event of your untimely demise. Once you have reached that point, particularly if it is later in life, term insurance usually becomes uneconomic because it becomes so much more expensive. In general, I think it makes the most sense to have term from age 25 to 50, with a gray area from 50 to 65. After that, the rates just don't make sense unless you're about to die but the insurance company doesn't know and can't find out, or you need to insure against a large estate tax bill.

Owning term insurance is a lifestyle decision, like auto or fire insurance, and not an investment decision. Unless you hate your spouse and children, you will want to provide them with some sort of financial security during your younger years. But as you grow older, savings should take the place of life insurance. Those savings could be through the insurance company in the form of whole life insurance, although that need not be the case.

By the time you are ready to retire at 65, you should have saved enough money to allow your heirs to live comfortably even without life insurance. That can easily be accomplished, as I have already shown, by investing 10 percent of your after-tax income at an annual rate of 12 percent. But let's face it; not everyone starts saving in their youth when they should. Your income may have been quite meager then, you may have come into wealth later in life, or perhaps you just don't have the discipline to save on your own. Whatever the reason, you would prefer to use life insurance to provide a substantial retirement income or a bequest to your heirs. What is the best way to accomplish this?

LIFE INSURANCE BENEFITS OTHER THAN DEATH PAYMENTS

To answer this question, we now return to the question of who can invest your money better after considering all the tax angles—you or the insurance company.

In all policies, the amount left over after paying current death-benefit premiums, sales commissions, money-management fees, and administrative expenses is invested on your behalf. This investment builds up over time; the longer you have held the policy, the larger the value of the total investment, up to the point where the death-benefit premium rate exceeds the rate of return. Usually this doesn't happen until you're in your mid-eighties.

It used to be that you could receive *either* the death benefit, which is the face amount of the policy, or the accumulated cash value, but not both. That was unfair to those who lived longer; the insurance company had the use of their money for more years, but their heirs received no additional insurance benefits. With the advent of universal life, that has now changed. You can choose one of two types of death-benefit plans: one that pays the face amount regardless of when you die, and one that pays a somewhat smaller amount initially but increases over time, so that if you outlive the mortality tables you eventually get more than the face amount.

Which policy is better for you depends on whether you think you will outlive the mortality tables, since the benefits are based strictly on actuarial calculations. Most people, I assume, think they will outlive their compeers. However, if you believe your health is failing, or your family has a history of short life spans, or even if you are feeling morbid, you might opt for the full face-value option. The point is that the insurance companies now provide this option and don't steal the extra goodies from those who enjoy a particularly long life.

However, many people do not buy life insurance primarily for the death benefits, but for the retirement benefits. They could have purchased term insurance and invested the difference but chose not to. We will assume the decision to purchase whole life was a rational choice—that is, these people were not bamboozled by an insurance agent. The rational reasons for doing so, including the tax advantages, are the following.

1. You don't think you are very good at managing money and believe the insurance company can earn a higher rate of return than you can. In my opinion, once you've read this book, that's no longer a very good reason. However, there are better ones.
2. You have good and sufficient reason to believe your life span is shorter than average. Hopefully, that doesn't apply to anyone who is reading this.
3. You have a closely held business that is valuable enough to be subject to estate taxes, and you don't want to pass it on to your heirs prematurely because you are still actively involved in man-

agement. The proceeds from the insurance policy will satisfy the requirement for estate taxes instead of your heirs having to sell the company at a fire-sale price.

4. You use life insurance to reduce or totally avoid estate taxes even if you do not own a closely-held business. Since the maximum rate is 55 percent, this is not a trivial consideration.

5. Your income and expenses have increased dramatically at a relatively advanced age where term insurance would already be expensive and investing the difference would not generate the necessary income for your family if you were to die shortly after retirement age. Under our standard assumptions, you could match the face amount of the life insurance policy at 65 by investing the difference at 8½ percent if you started at age 35. If you started at age 55, you would have to earn a 17 percent after-tax rate of return, which is much more difficult.

Many people have bought life insurance in the past, and will buy it in the future, because they like the savings feature of it and the security of having a retirement income. With universal life and its spinoffs, you can see what part of your premium is being used for each function, and what your retirement benefits will be under various alternative assumptions about interest rates. With variable life, you can earn the higher long-term rate of return generated by the stock market.

THE GALLERY OF LIFE INSURANCE PRODUCTS

There are almost as many types of life insurance as there are mortgages, and I'm not going to run through all of them. However, for practical purposes, all policies offered fall into one of the following five categories.

1. *Old-style whole life.* It pays only about 4 percent per year. While this was the industry standard before 1979, virtually no one offers it anymore.

2. *Interest-sensitive whole life.* Many of the same features as old-style whole life are offered—fixed annual payments, fixed death benefits, high sales commissions—but the rate of return earned on your money is tied to market interest rates. The higher the rate of interest the insurance company can earn, the better the deal for the policyholder; either the cash value is higher or the premiums are lower. Of course, if the rate of return was pushed up by investing in real estate or junk bonds that crash, the cash value

would be revised downward. Remember, only a 4 percent rate of return is actually guaranteed. The entire class of life-insurance policies has been brought into question by the collapse of the First Executive Corp., which in its heyday had written over $60 billion worth of policies.

3. *Universal life.* The premiums are flexible, and so is the death benefit. You can skip paying premiums as long as there is enough cash buildup in the policy to cover the premium. Naturally, the cash value and death benefit will be lower the less you pay into the policy. The money is usually invested at market interest rates. The expenses are listed separately so you can see precisely what they are; in general they are much more moderate than other types of life insurance.

    Some people have claimed this flexibility is the cat's meow, but it seems to me one of the reasons for buying life insurance is the discipline it imposes to save regularly; universal life removes that benefit. Universal life is valuable for its relatively low cost, not for its greater flexibility.

4. *Variable life.* The premiums are fixed, but your money is invested in the stock market. That means your cash value or death benefit could be much higher than the face amount of the policy—but the death benefit cannot be lower. As a trade-off for this flexibility, the premiums are a little higher than for policies that are tied to interest rates, but the chances for greater accumulation are substantial. Considering that over the long run the stock market returns an average of 12 percent per year while the bond market returns 8 percent per year, this is probably your best bet in life insurance. Death benefits as well as cash value are flexible—the better the stock market does, the more money is accumulated in your policy.

5. *Variable universal life.* This combines the stock market feature of variable life with the flexible payment and relatively low cost features of universal life.

In addition, almost all policies offer you flexibility in payment schedules to suit your lifetime flow of income and expenses.

Which is best for you?

If you're the kind of person who has no trouble paying your premiums every year, variable universal life is the best deal because (a) the funds are invested in stocks instead of bonds and (b) the costs are lower. On the other hand, if you are inclined to skip a payment every now and then, just use the straight variable life version so you won't be tempted.

Many variable life policies will allow you to switch your investment among stocks, bonds, and money market funds. Suppose, for example, that inflation suddenly surged to double-digit rates again, as it did in 1973–74 and in 1979–80 because of a tripling in crude oil prices. Oil prices could rise very rapidly again, food prices could soar, the dollar could plummet because of international considerations, or the president could appoint an easy-money Fed chairman who would goose the economy during an election campaign. Just because these things have happened in the past, of course, is no particular reason to expect them to crop up again, but they could recur. If inflation rises above 10 percent, batten down the storm hatches, because the stock market will go into a tailspin and your investments should be shifted into money market funds until the siege of double-digit inflation, tight money, and recession has ended. Most variable life policies permit you to do precisely that.

How Much Do Commissions and Expenses Hurt?

This is a vitally important question—and one that all *honest* insurance salesmen will answer candidly. Since the world's not perfect, I'll try to answer it for you here.

Excluding the term insurance portion, the economics of life insurance, regardless of the particular flavor, is quite simple. Insurance companies will charge you certain fees, which are called commissions and expenses, to manage your money. We know, of course, that except for the tax angles, they can't do a better job than you could on your own—not because they're necessarily stupid, although of course some of them are, but because you could find out what investment management firm they use and send the money there yourself. Offsetting those fees, the insurance company can accumulate your assets on a tax-deferred basis, so that you pay tax only when you withdraw the difference between the cash value and the premiums; no income taxes at all are paid on death benefits.

So the question boils down to a simple one: Are the fees charged larger or smaller than the advantage from tax-deferred buildup?

At this point we are talking only about the comparison with the value you can withdraw at retirement, paying taxes on the profits; these are known as surrender values. Most policies are cashed out instead of held for death benefits. For those who hold policies for death benefits, the effect of estate taxes must also be considered; this makes the entire calculation more complicated.

Universal life policies spell out what the expenses are, as opposed to whole life, where they are still a secret. However, these policies neglect to tell you how much the sales commissions are; you have to work back and figure that out yourself. This is not the place to give the precise calculations for the thousands of firms that offer variable life policies. However, I will provide some guidelines, using a specific numerical example.

Consider a universal life insurance policy, face amount of $100,000, for a male nonsmoker aged 35. He would pay about $1,000 per year for this insurance. A certain amount of that goes toward the death-benefit premium—the term insurance part. It starts at about $90 and rises to about $950 by age 65. The rest is invested in the policyholder's choice of money market funds, bonds, or stocks. If you bought term insurance, you would invest all the remaining funds. The insurance company invests the remaining funds less commissions and expenses.

Because the term insurance premiums remain low for many years, and because of the way compound interest works, we can assume that approximately 90 percent of the premium—i.e., $900 of the $1,000 premium—is invested for appreciation. If you could earn 12 percent per year in the stock market, $900 each year would cumulate to $243,000. After paying the 33 percent tax on the profits, you would have $172,000. Taking the more conservative route and earning 8 percent per year in bonds or a money market fund means the $900 annual payments would cumulate to $110,000, or $83,000 after taxes.

These figures assume buildup on a tax-deferred basis. On an after-tax basis, assuming a 37½ percent marginal rate (33 percent federal plus 4½ percent state/local average), the sums would be vastly less impressive: $100,000 and $63,000 respectively. Can the insurance company do better than that?

In almost every case, yes. A typical high-cost company would charge the entire first-year commissions, excluding the term insurance costs (i.e., the $910), and 7½ percent of the premium every year thereafter. That would be equivalent to putting in $825 instead of $900 for 29 years instead of 30 years. At a 12 percent rate for the stock market, the sum would be $198,000, or $141,000 after taxes; for the 8 percent bond yield, it would be $93,000, or $71,000 after taxes.

A typical low-cost company would charge one-half of the first-year commissions and 4 percent of the premiums thereafter. In that case, the 12 percent return would yield $219,000, or $154,000 after taxes, while the 8 percent return would yield $101,000, or $76,000 after taxes. These figures are summarized in the following table.

	Stock Market 12%	Bond Market 8%
Invest yourself on tax-deferred basis	$172,000	$83,000
Life insurance company, low-cost	154,000	76,000
Life insurance company, high-cost	141,000	71,000
Invest yourself, no tax deferral	100,000	63,000

All these calculations assume you hold the policy for 30 years; if you hold it for a much shorter time, the commissions take a much bigger bite—but that's not the point of life insurance.

These results are surprisingly clear-cut, considering all the brouhaha among financial advisers about the justification for saving through life insurance. If you can put aside funds in a tax-deferred account you are obviously better off, but in many cases those amounts are capped. Also, if you can outperform the market averages you will also do better than the insurance companies, and the final section of this book is devoted to explaining precisely how to go about doing that. But if you don't feel you can beat the averages, *and* you don't have a way to set aside tax-deferred funds, the tax advantages offered by the life insurance industry are dominant—provided you don't pick a company that has invested your money in assets that are now worthless. Since that has happened to a number of the "big names" lately, I'll next discuss how to choose the right company.

CHOOSING YOUR INSURANCE COMPANY

Assuming you decide to invest in a non-term life policy, the odyssey to find the best insurance company then begins. In theory, it's easy. You want a company that is financially solid, charges the lowest costs, and at least matches if it does not outperform the market averages. I will assume here that you don't have health problems or other disabilities that will preclude you from getting coverage at the normal rates. If you do, you'll probably have to work with an agent to find out which companies are most likely to insure high-risk people with various illnesses.

In the past, would-be purchasers of life insurance policies used to rely on the rankings prepared by A. M. Best Company, whose book was known as the "Bible" of the insurance industry. But that was before the collapse of the First Executive Corporation.

Its demise was headline news—literally. Both *The New York Times* and *The Wall Street Journal* ran that story as their page one right-hand column on April 12, 1991, the day after it happened. But the problems of First

Executive had been well publicized earlier; its stock had plummeted from 16 in late 1989 to 3 by the beginning of 1990.

And how did A. M. Best adjust its rating when First Executive stock was sliding by over 80 percent? Why, not at all. It kept its rating at A+, the highest level, until it was far too late. Not too surprisingly, this brought forth a blizzard of stories about how Best was handing out A+ ratings too freely—and apparently it was, since some of its other A+ ratings don't look so hot these days either.

What's an individual investor to do? After all, you can't really expect your local real estate agent to give you the lowdown on which companies are in financial difficulty if a rating service the size of A. M. Best can't keep up.

The day after First Executive collapsed, the *Wall Street Journal* ran a lengthy article addressing this very issue, and here is essentially what it said:

Don't rely only on A. M. Best. Better yet, don't rely on Best at all. Instead, check the ratings prepared by S&P, Moody's, and Duff & Phelps. Maybe you've never heard of the latter; it is smaller, but it is also stingier in handing out the top ratings.

According to *The Wall Street Journal*, these three companies will give you their ratings for any insurance company free of charge, although whenever I've called S&P, it always charged me two dollars per piece of information. Even though that's annoying, it's still not very much to find out that your insurance company of choice is likely to remain solvent.

Indeed, even before the news of their junk bond portfolio was reflected in the stock price, Moody's gave Executive Life only its fifth highest rating, while Duff & Phelps gave it their eighth highest. For that matter, I spoke at a First Executive conference in 1986, and even then, some rating services had negative comments on the company. So policyholders could have been forewarned.

Several financial ratios can also help determine whether an insurance company is likely to be solvent in the future, such as the ratio of total capital to invested assets, and the ratio of high-risk assets to total capital. However, the rating services (except Best) take these into account, so if a company earns the top rating from all services, it is likely to remain in business for the indefinite future.

But suppose you didn't check carefully enough, and thought the rates offered by First Executive were for real instead of just some cruel joke, and went ahead and bought their policy. Or suppose your employer purchased one of their annuities without giving you any choice. How bad off are you?

As this went to press, the issue was far from being resolved, but the experts who follow the insurance industry were virtually unanimous in their opinions that (a) all death benefits will be paid in full, (b) so-called "guaranteed" investment contracts and annuities, which stated they would pay at a certain rate of return, will pay a much lower rate of return, and (c) all redemptions of cash value and loans against the policy will be prohibited for an indefinite time period.

In other words, death benefit claims will be honored, but retirement benefit claims will be slashed. And you're locked in.

This would follow the pattern set when Baldwin-United went bankrupt in the early 1980s. They offered primarily annuities, and the upshot of the settlement was that policyholders received some payout, but at a lower rate than had been originally "guaranteed". I think the same arrangement will be reached with First Executive policyholders.

If you were one of these policyholders, you are not alone. First Executive wrote $60 billion worth of policies, and many celebrated stock pickers, such as Peter Lynch, included First Executive stock in their portfolios. But all that is water over the dam. How can you avoid a similar mistake next time—since there will always be a "next time"?

1. Check all the ratings, particularly Moody's and Duff & Phelps. If there is even a whiff of doubt that the company you are considering has invested heavily in junk bonds or doubtful real estate mortgages, be glad you found out early.

As of April, 1991, 9 of the top 12 companies received high ratings all around. Obviously First Executive didn't, and neither did Equitable or Travelers. I seriously doubt that either of those companies will be able to attract much new business over the next few years no matter how high a rate of interest they offer—and in spite of the meaningless pap offered by their chief executives that both companies are "financially strong".

2. Unfortunately, there is no escaping the trade-off between risk and return in life insurance policies, any more than would be the case for other financial instruments. A little common sense helps here: If you find some company that pays a higher rate of return than any other life insurer, it may be nothing more than a ticking time bomb, about to head into bankruptcy. The First Executive experience has brought this into bold relief, but we all should have remembered it anyhow.

Whenever you buy an interest-sensitive whole-life policy, you are at the mercy of the insurance company's investment committee, which often feels no obligation to tell you how they are investing your money. The problem is that you can't withdraw your money without paying a huge financial penalty. If your mutual fund manager goes haywire and flushes your money down the drain on junk bonds, you can sell your shares and reinvest the money elsewhere without paying too much of a penalty. But life insurance isn't designed that way; when you buy a policy, you essentially must place your bets on the long run.

Since predicting next year's economy is hard enough without trying to contemplate what will happen 10, 20, or 30 years down the road, here's my conclusion: Buy life insurance because of the tax benefits, but invest the money yourself. Choose a universal or variable life policy, where you get to direct your money to stocks or high-quality bonds. You don't have to be a genius—you can choose an index fund—but that way you won't be ripped off by having some "investment" manager destroy your wealth by sinking it in worthless junk bonds or mortgages on bankrupt real estate.

Some say it is unfair to tar and feather the entire industry for the sins of Fred Carr. If so, I plead guilty. Besides, as I'll show you in the following chapters, virtually none of the big-name money managers can beat the stock market indexes, so you aren't losing anything by investing the money yourself.

If you are the thrifty sort who doesn't like to waste money, it may gall you to have to give hundreds of thousands of dollars over your lifetime to unsavory salesmen and incompetent professionals who mismanage your money. Unfortunately, the only other choice is worse, which is to pay more in taxes. So swallow your pride and let the insurance companies have the money many of them don't deserve. Just don't let them misdirect it to worthless assets—choose a policy where *you* make the investment choices. Then you can at least bask in the satisfaction that you have withheld some tribute from the tax man.

FLEXIBILITY WITH YOUR POLICY

Once the initial sales commission is paid, the cash value of your policy starts to accumulate. Along with the policy, your insurance agent will probably provide a table with two sets of figures. One is the current accumulated value, which is the amount you can borrow against, and the other is the current surrender value, which is the amount you could take out if you were to cancel the policy. While most people will want to hold the policy until retirement or death, there are several interim options.

Borrowing Against the Policy

You can borrow against the cash value at the rate stated in the policy, which is usually close to the current money market rate, now about 8 percent. Thus if you turned around and reinvested the money, it would be a wash. Furthermore, if you die without repaying the loan, your heirs receive only the face amount of the policy minus the amount you have borrowed.

Back in the early 1980s, when the rate of return on insurance policies was abnormally low, so was the policy loan rate. Thus in many cases, people could borrow money at 4 or 5 percent and reinvest it at 15 to 18 percent. That took much of the sting out of the abominable rates of return the insurance industry was earning. No policy currently written has that option. You will essentially be borrowing at the same rate at which you could reinvest the money, so it's usually not worth it.

The only reason to borrow against your policy, short of being in desperate straits, is if you would otherwise have to borrow the money at a much higher rate of interest to fund some worthwhile purpose such as a house or college education for the children. Since the policy borrowing rate is the lowest in town, this method does have some advantages. But don't forget that (a) your death benefit is reduced by the amount you borrow and (b) in almost all cases you could have bought term and invested the difference, so you would have had the money without having to borrow at all. While your insurance policy can be a useful source of cash if you are strapped, you shouldn't buy a life insurance policy because of this benefit. All you are doing is borrowing back your own money, which could have been invested elsewhere. This option should be used only in extreme conditions.

Other Options

1. You can withdraw the surrender value. If you do, though, the policy is canceled, and if you do that during the first few years, your rate of return is reduced almost to zero. Most insurance companies will charge you a hefty premium if you take out the surrender value ahead of time. If you do choose to buy a life policy other than term, it should generally remain in force at least until retirement.
2. You can convert your policy to an annuity. I'll cover this in the next chapter.
3. If you are terminally ill, some companies will permit you to draw virtually the full death benefit ahead of time to pay for hospital or nursing care. Not a very pleasant subject, but something you might want to consider if you are concerned about being a drain on your relatives near the end of your lifetime.

FLEXIBILITY IN PAYMENT SCHEDULES

In the old days—i.e., before 1979—the attitude of the life insurance industry was basically take it or leave it. If you didn't like their plain vanilla policies with an unconscionably low 4 percent rate of return, you could leave it. By the early 1980s, that's precisely what most people did. As a result of the reformation of the industry, one of the new wrinkles permits you to have virtually any combination of payment schedules you want, providing only that you have enough buildup in your policy to cover the term insurance premium. You can pay more earlier, more later, nothing later, or some combination in between. In all cases, you are insured for the same death benefit. The difference is the amount of cash value at retirement age.

These options are not the same as those in universal life, where you can skip a payment and have your death benefit and surrender value reduced accordingly. These are preplanned schedules, where your benefits are decided in advance but are tailored to fit your particular life and income situation. The major choices can be grouped into the following categories.

Pay Less Now, More Later

One common variety allows you to start off slowly, for example, paying 50 percent of the normal premium for the first five years. After that, you pay the regular amounts for as long as the policy is in force. That policy might be useful for someone whose income is relatively modest now but is expected to rise rapidly.

Another common variety of policy has a sliding scale for as long as 20 years. The premiums start out at some very low level, usually one-fourth to one-third of the regular whole life premiums, and then increase gradually but do not catch up with the regular premiums for 20 years. This option is actually quite similar to term insurance, since the cost of the premium rises more or less in line with the true cost of insuring against death.

In both of these options, the cash value is far less than for the normal nonterm life policies. That makes sense: Less in means less out. These policies are recommended for those who will do most of their retirement savings in forms other than life insurance.

Pay More Now, Less Later

One kind of life insurance that grew by leaps and bounds after the Tax Reform Act of 1986 is called single-premium life insurance, which is exactly what it sounds like. You pay one premium, and that's it.

That hardly seems like insurance at all—and to a large extent, it isn't. After all, if you die soon after the policy is issued, you have paid far too much in premiums. And the accumulated cash value of such a policy is only moderate. Yet this became one of the hottest sellers, including multimillion-dollar policies to some of the savviest investors around. There had to be a reason.

As you may have guessed, the reason was taxes. First, the insurance company has the benefits of investing without paying taxes on the earned income. Second, and even more critical, it was possible to borrow against these policies on an interest-free basis—but not have the loans count as income.

This sounded too good to be true—and Congress thought so, too. In 1988, it abruptly yanked the juiciest parts of the tax benefits, presumably never to be replaced. Sales of single-premium life insurance promptly plunged, although they are still offered—perhaps to those reading last year's tax manual.

Another possibility is that you pay the usual premium for whole life for 5 or 6 years; after that you pay nothing. In other words, instead of paying premiums for 20, 30, or 40 years, you only pay them for 5 or 6 years, yet you still get covered for the same amount. For example, if you are age 35, you pay $1,000 for 5 years for a $100,000 policy and never a penny more. This is used mainly for estate planning tactics, since the cash value remains low for many years. There are also paid-up life insurance policies after 20 years, after 30 years, at age 65, and at age 85. Tell the insurance agent what option you have in mind, and it's probably available.

Decreasing Death Benefit

The third major type of option is one where your premium remains stable, but it has been set at a much lower level than the normal whole life premium. You start out with the full death benefit, but then the amount decreases over time. This would make sense if, for example, you had virtually no savings at first but over time built up a substantial nest egg, so you wouldn't need so much insurance later on.

WHICH POLICY FOR YOU?

The policy you choose depends in large part on your goals and aspirations, and whether you want to save for your retirement through a life insurance policy or on your own. It also depends in part on whether your income stream is likely to be steady or erratic, and how much you have when you first get started in your career. Some people have trust funds and gifts from relatives; others don't.

All right, that's a mealy-mouthed answer. So I'll give you my guidelines.

1. If you plan your life right—save right from the start, increase your income steadily over your working life, are astute at managing your own financial affairs, can take advantage of tax-deferred retirement plans, and can beat the market averages regularly—then the choice is easy. The old dictum of "buy term and invest the difference" holds. But not everyone plans his life that well, and not everyone is an astute money manager.

2. The insurance companies have come out of the Dark Ages, and most of them now pay market rates of interest. In the vast majority of cases, the insurance companies will reduce your yield by 1 to 2 percent per year to cover the costs of selling and managing your assets. In most cases, the tax bite will reduce the yield by about 3 percent. So if your own investment strategy can't beat the market, life insurance will probably increase your rate of return—provided you invest in high-grade stocks and bonds, and not junk.

3. Under certain circumstances, life insurance is a major way to reduce or completely eliminate estate taxes.

4. If the idea of term insurance disappearing bothers you, buy the kind of life insurance where you pay less now and more later. That is similar to term insurance as far as the true costs are concerned, but your policy doesn't evaporate later in life.

5. The premiums will be somewhat better for larger policies no matter which insurance company you use, since the cost of administrating a $10,000 policy is the same as the cost for administrating a $1 million policy. However, many of the smaller companies reinsure a policy above a certain amount. If you purchased a $1 million policy, some insurance companies would reinsure $500,000 of that amount with another company, so you wouldn't get the benefits of smaller administration costs. Thus if you are going for the jumbo policies, your best rates will generally be with the very biggest companies.

CONCLUSION

As a general rule term insurance is really all you need, providing you have the discipline to save on your own. However, life insurance is far from being the rotten deal it was a decade ago; rates are now competitive with money market, bond, or stock-market mutual funds. Life insurance also has some attractive tax angles, although some of them could be whittled away during the 1990s. Finally, while you won't get rich by accumulating life insurance, if you're one of those people who have trouble saving, it will help to assure financial stability in later years.

Chapter 11

Those Golden Retirement Years

You may hope to live forever, but you certainly don't want to work forever. Even if forced retirement and boredom are not your game, as you approach retirement age you are better off with the flexibility of choosing your own time and place for work instead of being at the whim of some employer who will probably dump you anyway. Which simply means that planning for retirement is required, not optional.

START TO SAVE EARLY—AND USE TAX DEFERRALS

The two chief guidelines for your retirement planning are succinct and easy to remember.

1. Start early. For every $1 you invest at age 25, you will get the same retirement benefit as for every $10 you invest at age 45.
2. Use tax deferrals. Starting at age 25, every $1 you invest on a tax-deferred basis during your working life will be worth $4 invested on an after-tax basis.

All these figures are based on a 12 percent annual rate of return, which is the average long-term return in the stock market.

Let's put some flesh and blood behind these figures. Suppose you invested $1,000 per year from age 25 to 65 at 12 percent per year. After paying taxes on the accumulated amount at a 33 percent rate, you would have $588,825. On the other hand, if you had to pay taxes at a 37.5 percent marginal rate on the $1,000 before you invested it and also had to pay taxes on the dividends and capital gains at the same rate, you would have only $152,688. Even if that sounds like a fair amount for investing $1,000 for 40 years, it certainly isn't enough to live on after you've retired.

Some aspects of financial planning—predicting the stock market, choosing hot stocks, forecasting interest rates—are very difficult; even the experts don't have a very good track record. But other aspects are so straightforward that there is really no argument at all. This isn't a matter of being psychic or having a sixth sense for the market; it's just plain, commonsense arithmetic. Start early. And use tax-deferred accounts. Period.

Good. I've convinced you. What kind of tax-deferred savings plan should you choose?

YOUR CHOICE OF RETIREMENT PLANS

Now we take a few steps away from simplicity and toward reality. Your choices, until Congress mucks up the works the next time, are the following.

- *Individual retirement accounts (IRAs)*.
- *Employee-funded pensions*, usually known as 401(k) plans, named after that section of the tax code. Simplified employee pension plans (SEPs) have many basic similarities and are discussed in the same section. In some cases, employers can also contribute to these plans.
- *Self-employed retirement plans*, usually known as Keogh plans, after Vincent Keogh, who sponsored the legislation in what was the tenth bill introduced in the House of Representatives that year; hence Keoghs are sometimes known as H. R. 10 plans.
- *Tax-deferred annuities*, which are retirement plans that also contain some death benefits and share certain similarities with life insurance. In fact, they used to be sold exclusively by the life insurance industry but are now actively offered by the brokerage industry and by money management firms as well.

These are plans in which you, the employee, make some or all of the contribution. Some of you have pension plans where the employer makes all the contributions and does all the investing, in which case you have no discretion over how the assets are managed. If you are covered by an employer-funded pension plan, ordinarily you won't be able to have a separate retirement plan, although there are some exceptions. But this chapter is devoted primarily to plans to which you contribute and for which you make the investment decisions.

All these plans have something in common. You invest now and deduct the amount invested from your taxable income. Your funds accumulate on a tax-deferred basis. And when you start to use the funds for retirement, you pay tax on the accumulated earnings at the then-current tax rate. The differences stem from the maximum amount you can invest each year, how much is contributed by the employer as well as the employee, and the terms under which you can take your money out of the plan.

All the calculations in this chapter, as well as throughout the book, are based on the most recent tax laws passed near the end of 1990. Congress may very well raise income tax rates again in future years, so the tax bite on your profits will be higher than I have calculated. Nonetheless, the tax benefits are so overwhelming that within any reasonable range of tax rates, it still pays to save now and pay your tax bills later. For that matter, as tax rates rise further, tax-deferred forms of saving become even more important.

IRAs

Like the old gray mare, IRAs aren't what they used to be. From 1982 through 1986, everyone who had wage and salary income was permitted to take a tax deduction for their contribution to an IRA, regardless of whether they were also covered by another pension plan.

IRAs are the most common type of employee-funded retirement plan, and for that reason the one with which you are probably most familiar. However, while an IRA is a lot better than nothing, it is inferior to all the other types of retirement plans discussed in this chapter for several reasons.

1. Your contributions are much smaller. Furthermore, as the law currently stands, the maximum annual contribution doesn't rise proportionately with inflation, whereas it does for most other pension plans.
2. You can't borrow from the plan.
3. Early-retirement and medical-expense exceptions do not apply unless you convert to an annuity.

4. In some circumstances you may be taxed more heavily on the withdrawals.

So while a properly managed IRA started early in life can still provide a modest amount of money for your retirement, it is not an appropriate vehicle for accumulating substantial wealth, by which I mean at least $3 million in today's dollars over your working lifetime. To do that, you will need to save $8,000 to $10,000 per year, adjusted upward for inflation, on a tax-deferred basis, and earn 12 percent per year. This can be done under the existing tax laws, but either your employer has to set up a pension plan, you must have self-employed income, you must use the inside-buildup provisions offered by some group such as the life insurance industry, or you must start your own company.

If your employer doesn't have a pension plan, you can deduct up to $2,000 per year of earned income for your IRA. If both you and your spouse work for companies that don't have plans, you can each contribute up to $2,000. If only one of you works, the total deductible amount is $2,250. If your spouse is covered by a pension plan but you are not, you can still contribute to an IRA by filing separate tax returns. However, in some cases the tax rates are higher, so you have to balance that against the benefits of the IRA deduction.

Suppose your employer does have a pension plan. If you earn more than $35,000, or if you and your spouse earn more than $50,000, none of the principal invested in an IRA is deductible. However, you can still contribute to a nondeductible IRA and let the earnings accumulate on a tax-deferred basis. This is not necessarily a bad idea, it's just not as good as full deductibility.

To go back to the example given at the beginning of the chapter, after 40 years you had $588,825 on a fully tax-deferred basis and $152,688 on an after-tax basis. Now suppose the principal were not tax-deductible but the buildup was, and you paid a 33 percent rate on the profits. You would then have $372,966 after 40 years. So half a loaf is clearly better than none. Unfortunately, that $372,966 will be worth less than $60,000 40 years from now, which doesn't even begin to approach the principal you will need for a retirement income.

The actual tax laws, of course, are more complicated; I'm just painting the broad outlines here. Most, but not all, of the details are in J. K. Lasser and similar handbooks, and you should consult them or your tax adviser before actually filing your taxes.

So IRAs are a good start, but they won't pay many bills at retirement time. Because the maximum tax-deferred contribution is limited to $2,000 per person, the eventual accumulation will be quite modest once inflation takes its bite. Furthermore, at least as the law is written today, there is no provision for increasing the amount as inflation rises. That means in 40 years, the real value of your $2,000 contribution will be less than $300. Maybe Congress will get around to rectifying that oversight, and maybe it won't. But other forms of tax-deferred retirement plans do have an inflation factor built in, which automatically makes them superior.

401(K) AND SEP PLANS

These plans can be funded by you, the employee, or by both you and your employer. The maximum allowable annual contribution rises with inflation; it started at $7,000 in 1987 and has so far moved up to $7,313 in 1988, $7,627 in 1989, and $7,979 in 1990. If my forecast of 5 percent inflation is correct, the ceiling would be lifted to $56,376 by 2030. If your employer chooses to contribute to these plans, the two of you together can currently contribute up to $30,000 per year; that amount is not currently indexed, although I expect it will be sometime in the future.

That $30,000, indexed for inflation over your working lifetime and invested at an annual rate of 12 percent, is a tremendous amount. It works out to $5.9 million in constant dollars before taxes, or a fantastic $41 million before adjusting for higher prices. These amounts would then be subject to income tax when you start to withdraw the money. This may sound unbelievable, even with the miracle of compound interest, but just remember that the first year's investment of $30,000 alone, if invested at 12 percent, would be worth almost $3 million in 40 years.

Admittedly, most people don't have $30,000 to set aside each year, and I'm not suggesting that you do. I am making a different point, one that is fairly important: The advantages in the tax laws, in spite of having been emasculated in the Tax Reform Act of 1986, are still written so that you can accumulate a very sizable fortune completely on a tax-deferred basis if you are willing to start early. Furthermore, even if you don't start your $30,000 annual retirement fund until you are 45, and save for only 20 years, the accumulated amount will still be almost $1.3 million in today's dollars. The tax benefits are still substantial in spite of the 1986 cutbacks.

In order to take advantage of a retirement plan of this size, though, either you must be self-employed or your employer must have a 401(k) or SEP set up. If he does not, perhaps you could talk him into the idea;

it needn't cost him anything. If he doesn't want to be bothered, you have several choices: Move back to the little-league IRA plans, quit your job and join a company that does have such a plan, or start your own company.

Assuming that you are now, or soon will be, working for a firm that has a retirement plan, you merely have to notify your employer that you wish to have a certain amount of your salary deducted up to the $7,979 plus inflation limit. That amount will be deducted from your salary and is not subject to income tax. There is one odd glitch in the law, which is that the income *is* subject to Social Security tax. However, if your remaining salary is over the ceiling amount anyway, that becomes a moot point.

Your employer may decide, out of the goodness of his heart, or for other reasons, to make an additional contribution to your retirement fund—up to the aforementioned $30,000 limit. Why would he want to do that?

1. His contribution may actually be in lieu of a salary hike. You and your employer agree that your pay hike will take the form of higher contribution benefits instead of a boost in salary. This is all quite legal, and it does save on taxes—although it also cuts down on your current income, so not everyone can afford to do that.
2. Many firms offer profit-sharing plans to provide incentives, and the money from that plan could go into a 401(k); that way it doesn't bite into your base salary.
3. If you work for a large organization, a pension plan has probably already been set up as a method of attracting and retaining skilled and valuable employees.
4. If you work for a small organization, a 401(k) plan may be just another way for the owners to reduce their tax burden by having the company contribute to *their* retirement plan. Of course, the IRS saw through this one very quickly and decided that if an owner/employee offers the plan to himself, or perhaps himself and spouse, he has to offer the plan to almost all employees (there are lots of twists to the law, but that's the gist of it). Also, if the organization has less than 25 employees, it will probably set up a SEP because the paperwork is easier; except for that, the terms are about the same.

That's not to say that an owner/employee couldn't legitimately create a 401(k) plan as a tool for retaining key employees, but in most cases this is better done through an employee stock ownership plan (ESOP), which is discussed in the next chapter. So for now we'll assume that a 401(k) plan is already in place and that it isn't designed merely as a tax shelter for owner/employees.

If you can spring for it, $7,979 plus inflation over your working lifetime adds up to a hefty sum. It's equivalent to paying about $5,000 per year after taxes, or just over $400 a month.

What is a "hefty sum"? Using the standard 12 percent rate of return calculations—and adjusting your annual investment up by 5 percent per year for inflation—it yields a total of $15.6 million after forty years; after paying the 33 percent tax, you still have about $11 million. That's about $1.6 million in today's prices—enough to retire on comfortably, assuming you also have some equity built up in your house.

I don't have to remind you that if you can somehow talk your employer into contributing the remaining $22,021, so a total of $30,000 per year is contributed to your plan, you will retire very wealthy, with about $6 million after taxes in today's prices. But it would be a rare employer that would be so generous—unless you, the employee, also happen to be the employer. Which brings us to the next section.

SELF-EMPLOYMENT RETIREMENT PLANS (KEOGHS)

The tax advantages of starting your own company are so substantial that I've devoted the entire next chapter to them. Apart from the retirement plans I've covered and home-mortgage interest, this is really the only remaining tax shelter. Municipal bonds are still a possibility, but they pay only an average of about 7½ percent per year, which is less than what you would earn from the stock market even on an after-tax basis.

Of course, starting a company is not for everyone, and I'll go through the pros and cons of that. But for the moment, let's assume that you have substantial self-employment income that you want to set aside for retirement. Providing your income is high enough, you can save up to $30,000 per year on a tax-deferred basis. The only other parties who have to agree are the other members of your family, who might prefer to spend the money now instead of later. But you don't have to get your boss to agree to set up a pension program.

There are two kinds of Keogh plans, known as *defined benefit* and *defined contribution* plans. The latter in turn has two varieties. A *money-purchase* plan requries you to put in the same percentage of your income each year, while a *profit-sharing* plan allows greater flexibility; some years you could put in nothing at all. In return for that greater flexibility, however, the ceiling contribution is smaller. As it turns out, however, that isn't much of a restriction, because you can set up *two* Keogh plans.

The money-purchase plan works as follows. Take your Schedule C income after all deductions other than the Keogh plan; assume that was $100,000. The IRS says you can contribute up to 25 percent of your earned income, or $30,000, to the plan each year, whichever is less. It sounds as if with an income of $100,000, your maximum contribution would be $25,000. It isn't. The way the law reads, you can contribute 25 percent of your income only *after* deducting the Keogh amount. As a result, you can only take 25 percent of $80,000. So for purposes of simplicity, just think of the maximum Keogh contribution under a money-purchase plan as 20 percent of net Schedule C income.

Once you've committed yourself to the money-purchase plan, you *must* contribute 20 percent of your income each year, even if you had a bad year. Otherwise, you are engaging in what the IRS calls "prohibited transactions," just as you would be if you didn't pay enough in taxes and you must pay a 10 percent penalty on the earnings you didn't contribute. I find it ironic that, whereas the vast majority of people who get into trouble with the IRS do so for underpaying their taxes, it is also possible to run afoul of the tax authorities by overpaying your taxes if you deduct too little for your Keogh percentage. If you don't want to break the law but don't have the money, you will have to borrow it, just as would be the case if you didn't have enough money to pay the IRS. While the moral dimension of paying more rather than less to the IRS may be entirely different, the legal dimension turns out to be similar.

To avoid this dilemma, many self-employed people consider a profit-sharing plan. Under this plan, you can put up to 15 percent of your Schedule C earnings before the Keogh deduction—i.e., approximately 13.0435 percent after the deduction—into the retirement fund, but you need not put in anything at all. So if you really need the money for something else that year, your Keogh deduction could be zero.

This choice in the regulations introduces the possibility of proceeding as follows, based on the assumption that most years you will want the maximum 20 percent deduction, but also want to retain some flexibility for bad years. First, set up a money-purchase plan with a stated rate of 6.9565 percent each year. In other words, you must pay 6.9565 percent of your net income into that particular Keogh plan every year. Second, set up a profit-sharing plan, which entitles you to put up to 13.0435 percent of your net income, so that the two plans together total 20 percent—*if* you choose to contribute the maximum amount each year. But if you don't, you won't run afoul of the law. That's the most common—and in most cases the most sensible—option.

Earn $209,200 a Year—Tax-Free

However, there is one granddaddy of a deduction left that, believe it or not in this day and age, could conceivably allow you to deduct your entire income up to $209,200 per year—this amount also rises by the inflation rate—and pay no taxes whatsoever. There's only one catch—you couldn't spend it either. Nonetheless, it's a tax break that dwarfs all the others. As you might expect, it works only in special situations.

This tax break goes under the name of a *defined-benefit plan*; it is also available for smaller sums. It is based on the part of the tax law that permits you, as a self-employed person, to set aside enough money so that you can receive an annual retirement benefit of up to $102,582 plus the inflation adjustment. The actual calculations are based on actuarial tables provided by the IRS. If you are already near retirement age, that would require a principal amount of about $1 million, based on government actuarial tables and assumptions about rates of return.

Ordinarily, people can't afford to forgo all their current income for purposes of retirement planning, but in the case of retired politicians, performers, or best-selling authors, the tax breaks can be very attractive indeed. Suppose, for example, someone had a comfortable but not luxurious income of $100,000 per year from his normal job, and in addition, happened to earn $209,200 or more per year for several years, after which his income returned to normal. He could then contribute the entire additional $209,200 per year to the defined-benefit Keogh plan, providing the total amount didn't exceed the principal necessary to provide the annual retirement benefit of $102,582 plus inflation. No other method still exists that can reduce your taxes on earned income that much and not run afoul of the alternative minimum tax.

Admittedly, this is a somewhat unusual case, but I mention it here because the defined-benefit plan is primarily designed for unusual cases, or for those who began to earn substantial self-employed income only in their later years. In almost every other case, the maximum $30,000 annual contribution will far more than take care of your retirement and investment needs. Nonetheless, it's good to know that if you do suddenly strike it rich, it's possible to defer taxes on up to $209,200 of income per year.

ACCEPTABLE ASSETS FOR YOUR
RETIREMENT PLAN

One other advantage of an IRA or Keogh is that, within certain broad limits, you can invest in any type of investment—money market funds, bonds, stocks, most real estate, and some collectibles. There are, however, a few restrictions. It seems that the IRS doesn't want you decorating your house with your retirement fund, so that rules out such items as objets d'art, antiques, and Oriental rugs. You are also prohibited from investing your money in stamps or coins, with one exception—gold and silver eagles minted by the U.S. Treasury, or any coins minted by a state, are acceptable. But if you think gold and silver are good long-term investments—which they aren't—you could just buy bullion.

As noted above, IRAs have one big disadvantage: You can't borrow against them to buy a house. In the case of the other plans, you can borrow up to $50,000 to purchase a principal mortgage, providing that amount is less than half of the total value of the retirement fund. Furthermore, you don't have to pay it back at any specified time.

Except for this one big loophole of borrowing against the plan for your house, I would invest your retirement plan funds in the stock market, using an index mutual fund if you don't fancy yourself much of a stock picker. If you can manage to move to the sidelines during recessions and get back in at the beginning of stock market booms, you will be even further ahead. (I'll show you how to do this in the next part of the book.) I don't recommend wild speculation—options or futures—for retirement accounts, although they are legal.

Except for IRAs, you can generally borrow against your retirement plan to pay deductible medical expenses (i.e., those over 7½ percent of your income), and for certain hardship cases, including staving off eviction or foreclosure. The laws are not very clear on these; "hardship" can mean different things to you and to the tax assessor. In any case, these are cases of financial distress, not wealth accumulation. Nonetheless, they do provide some flexibility that could come in handy during periods of temporary disruption of income or other family disasters.

PAYING TAXES ON YOUR RETIREMENT BENEFITS

This is one of the most complicated areas of the entire tax code. Every year *Money* magazine asks 50 tax advisers and attorneys to compute the taxes on a hypothetical return. In 1989, according to the magazine, only 2 of the 50 participants got it right. Of course, maybe *Money* didn't get it right either; several of the preparers said their way was better than the "correct" solution proposed by the experts at *Money*.

The sad fact is, *nobody knows*. This part of the tax code has become so arcane that nobody—Congress, the IRS, or tax experts—really understands what it says. The law itself is riddled with internal inconsistencies and contradictions. It is indeed a sad commentary on our so-called voluntary tax system when even taxpayers who wish to be 100 percent honest cannot tell how much tax they are supposed to pay.

Maybe these problems will be straightened out, but don't bet on it. The trend in tax "simplification" is to make the code even more complicated. If George Orwell were alive today, he would be writing satires on the IRS bureaucracy, not Communism.

I can tell you what the *intent* of the tax code is. I can also suggest that for the wealthy there are ambiguities in the law that probably deserve a court test; but in these areas, there are absolutely no guarantees about which way the courts would rule. For that matter, there are no guarantees about when the case would even be decided. Tax litigation that stretches out 10 or even 15 years is, unfortunately, no longer uncommon. I was recently involved in a tax court ruling, based on a 1981 deduction, that wasn't settled until 1990. And the only reason it got decided that "quickly" was because it was settled out of court.

At any rate, here's the general outline of what the IRS wants you to believe. Please note that in each and every case, the tax code has dangling qualifiers, so *Money* magazine notwithstanding, you're probably still better off using a tax adviser when you first start to unwind your retirement account.

Before 59½

1. It is not illegal to take your money out of the plans at any time, but those who do so before retirement age must usually pay the IRS a penalty, which is 10 percent of the premature distribution plus the income taxes owed in any case. However, if you are really strapped, that might not be a bad solution, and in many cases it's cheaper than borrowing the money. A 10 percent penalty is not particularly onerous if it provides what could be a substantial improvement in financial flexibility.
2. In most cases, money cannot be withdrawn from the retirement account without penalty until you are 59½. However, there are quite a few exceptions: you are dead, you take early retirement at

55 and have a retirement account other than an IRA, you annuitize your IRA, your employer goes out of business, you are fired, you become disabled, or you are divorced and the judge orders you to give some of your retirement money to your spouse. In legal lexicon, this last rule is known as a "qualified domestic relations order."

59½ to 70½

3. Between 59½ and 70½, you have a choice. On the one hand, you could start spending the money you have accumulated while you're still young enough to enjoy it. On the other hand, if you spend it now, you won't have it later. If you are 59½, the actuaries at the IRS say you will live an average of 26 more years. What may seem like plenty of money now may dwindle rapidly in 20 years when, with 5 percent inflation, things will cost an average of 2.65 times as much.

Until you are 70½, you can take out the whole amount, nothing at all, or a certain amount every year. In certain cases, you may have to pay a penalty excise tax. You can keep contributing to the retirement plan on a tax-deferred basis.

Over 70½

4. Once you are 70½, the rules change, and the IRS becomes very nasty if you don't start taking the minimum required benefits based on actuarial tables. You could be penalized a whopping 50 percent on the amount that you were supposed to withdraw but did not. If you can show that you made an honest mistake, the IRS is permitted to relent and will usually give you an extra year to correct the error, but why bother with all that hassle?

The amount you are required to withdraw is based on the number of years left in your life, and is calculated by dividing the total amount that has been accumulated by your remaining actuarial life. Note that for every year you don't die, your actuarial life increases, so if you really want to take out as little as possible, the withdrawal requirement has to be recalculated every year. In many cases, these plans are set up in such a way that you or your beneficiary will continue to receive funds as long as either of you is alive. That requires using something called a "joint life and last survivor life expectancy" table, which the IRS will also provide.

The general idea behind all these complicated regulations is that you should eventually use up all the funds in your tax-deferred retirement plan. This is *not* a vehicle for bequeathing money to the next generation, unless it so happens that your life span is shorter than average. The IRS provides tax benefits to permit you to save for retirement; you are not supposed to continue using these benefits once you have retired.

5. You will generally be required to pay income tax, at the then-prevailing rate, on the amount of money you take out of the fund, less any nondeductible contributions you put in. In many cases, all your contributions have been deductible. However, if you contributed to a nondeductible IRA, your tax payments will be lower. If you have saved consistently throughout your life and have retired to a state that doesn't have any income tax, you'll pay a maximum rate of 33 percent tax on this amount. If you choose to remain in New York, California, or some other high-tax state after retirement, of course your tax burden will be greater.

The 15% Excise Tax on the "Wealthy"

You have a choice of drawing the money out of your retirement fund in a lump sum or on an annual basis. You pay the normal income tax either way—but in addition, the IRS demands its additional pound of flesh by imposing a surtax, which it calls an excise tax although it's plainly on your income, for the "wealthy." In particular, you must pay a 15 percent excise tax if you withdraw more than $150,000 per year, or a lump sum of more than $750,000. There are some exceptions, but most of them are tricky. In general, you are stuck paying this additional tax unless you die, in which case your heirs generally don't have to pay the excise tax. That's really quite big of the IRS, considering that they already nicked the estate for up to 55 percent.

Unless you need the money all at once, and most retired people don't, it obviously makes more sense to collect $150,000 per year without paying the excise tax rather than collect the lump sum and pay the penalty tax. Furthermore, the remaining funds can continue to build up on a tax-deferred basis.

However, while $150,000 per year sounds like a reasonable amount to live on right now, particularly if you own your house outright and there are no college tuition bills to pay, inflation will eat away at the real value, and one day it won't be worth very much. I suppose by that time Congress and the IRS will get around to indexing that figure, but so far they haven't.

The IRS states that you can't contribute more than $30,000 per year to your retirement under a defined contribution plan no matter how many companies you have. That closes an obvious loophole that would otherwise allow an independent entrepreneur to set up several companies and deduct $30,000 per year for retirement from each one. However, the regulations are silent about someone who sets up a Keogh plan and funds it up to

$750,000, then stops funding that plan but starts another company and funds *that* pension plan up to $750,000, continuing the chain indefinitely. Under such a scheme, no single pension plan would have more than $750,000, and hence the crafty tax planner could unwind one $750,000 plan each year without having to pay the 15 percent excise tax. Or could he?

The IRS doesn't know, the courts don't know, and therefore your tax adviser probably doesn't know either. Most conservative advisers would rule out such a scheme, and it does carry the risks of backfiring. Many will choose to pay the extra 15 percent and sit back and enjoy life instead of battling in the tax courts for the rest of their lives. It depends on how aggressively you want to interpret the tax code, and how much psychic income you might get out of beating the IRS.

Besides, if you happen to be at this income level, the key tax factor isn't the 15 percent excise tax on lump-sum distributions but the far more onerous 55 percent tax rate on estates. This is complicated enough to merit a separate chapter. But before moving on to that subject, let's have a look at annuities, which provide a tax-deferred method of accumulating funds even for those who don't have a company-sponsored pension plan or their own company.

MAXIMIZING YOUR VALUES FROM ANNUITIES

If you have your own company, or if your employer offers a pension plan, the tax benefits will permit you to build up a very substantial tax-deferred retirement income. However, suppose you don't fall into either of these categories. Are you stuck with a little-league IRA plan?

Fortunately not. The tax laws also permit you to purchase an annuity where the funds can accumulate on a tax-deferred basis. Just as is the case for variable life insurance policies, you can direct that the money be invested in a mutual fund in order to benefit from the greater longer-term rewards generated by the stock market. Also, you can have both an annuity and an IRA. You have to pay taxes on the money that is initially invested in an annuity, so it isn't nearly as good a deal as other retirement plans. However, for many people it is the only remaining game in town.

The original idea of an annuity was to provide a method of generating a high rate of return on your investment for your retirement years. In return for that higher rate of return, your principal would gradually be diminished and there would be nothing left to pass along to your heirs.

Maybe some of you who are reading this either have no heirs, don't like any of them, or think they should make it on their own. In that case, an annuity may be for you. But the entire concept of this book is built around wealth creation, not dissolution. If that were the extent of the benefits of annuities, that's all the space it would rate here. However, because of the tax-deferred buildup, annuities rate more respect—and space.

Before the Tax Reform Act of 1986, annuities were hardly worth discussing. However, their tax advantages remained intact while many others folded. Annuities still provide a way to accumulate wealth without paying taxes on the income earned by your capital. In other words, they permit inside buildup, just the way life insurance does. Indeed, annuities used to be sold almost exclusively by life insurance companies, but that's all changed now. Many of the big money-management firms such as Fidelity, Keystone, Putnam, and others now offer annuities.

Naturally the insurance companies and investment firms don't manage your money for free. They charge you a sales commission, management fees, and other expenses. Also, some of the money goes for a form of death benefits, which I'll explain below. So the question once again becomes: Are the fees you pay for management more or less than the amount you would pay the government in taxes?

As it turns out, most of the time it's a fairly close call. Annuities are definitely not for everyone. And in my opinion, they are a waste of money if the money is invested in bonds. With stocks, on the other hand, you have a fighting chance of doing better with an annuity than on your own. But since there are several different twists and turns with annuities, I'll go through some of the nuts and bolts before presenting any definitive conclusions.

THREE "SIMPLE" STEPS TO ANNUITIES

1. CHOOSING THE COMPANY AND TYPE OF ACCOUNT

Once upon a time, annuities were invested in stodgy things like bonds. After sales commissions, maintenance charges, and expenses, you were better off investing the money yourself. Like the dismal returns on life insurance policies of the 1970s, annuities were only for losers.

As happened with life insurance companies, would-be investors eventually got tired of that game. Variable annuities were born, and investment companies switched from bonds to stocks. Now you can send your money to companies like Fidelity, and they will invest it in the same type of stocks that they choose for mutual funds. In fact, the investment procedure is virtually indistinguishable—except that you are getting the inside buildup. It's like a nondeductible IRA, except the annual amounts invested can be unlimited.

2. INVESTING THE MONEY

You have almost complete flexibility here. Some plans require you to invest a certain amount each month. However, you can vary the amount each month or year (subject to some very small minimum investment, often $25 a year) or you can pay one lump sum all at once. Unlike life insurance, there's no such thing as "falling behind" in your payments, because you aren't actually buying life insurance. Also, unlike a Keogh, you aren't in violation of any tax laws if you miss a payment. It's a savings account, and you invest whatever amount you want to invest.

3. GETTING THE MONEY OUT

Since in general you don't get any death benefit with an annuity—except that payments are usually guaranteed for a certain number of years even if you pass away the day after the payments start—the entire point of investing your money is to have adequate financial reserves for retirement. Technically, annuity companies give you two choices: a lump sum withdrawal or monthly payments. But in my book, there's only one choice—take the lump sum payment. Never annuitize. I'll explain why below.

Now let's go back over each of these three steps in more detail.

Always Choose a Variable Annuity

In the first place, I assume you're sold on the idea that over the long run, stocks give a much better rate of return than bonds. So what you want is called a variable annuity, meaning the amount of money you will eventually receive is not fixed or guaranteed, since no one knows how much the stock market will rise. The alternative would be a guaranteed annuity, based on current and projected future interest rates, but in general those returns are nothing to write home about.

At this point it's time to bring out the *past performance is no guarantee of future returns* banner, since you don't know who is going to be the best money manager in the long run. This is a potential stumbling block. In the case of mutual funds, assuming you have purchased a no-load or low-load fund, you can always switch to some other fund manager if your current manager turns out to be a turkey. However, annuities not only have a sales commission but high redemption or surrender fees. If you take your money out after only a few years, you don't get all of it back. Just like life insurance, signing up for an annuity should mean making a long-term commitment.

Thus when choosing a variable annuity, the process is essentially the same as shopping for a mutual-fund adviser, except that long-term performance is more important. However, this is somewhat of a Catch-22 situation because most variable annuities have only been on the market a short time and therefore don't have long track records. That isn't quite as serious as it sounds, since any reputable company selling annuities will tell you which organization is managing its money. In many cases, particularly with life insurance companies, it's not their own people. Nonetheless, you're not only putting your money on the horse for this race but for many races in the future.

This information is available in several places, including *Standard and Poor's Stock Guide*, which provides the name of the organization, the fund manager, the size and type of fund, and the total return over each of the past four years—providing it has been in business that long; most have not. In fact, many have records for only one or two years, so comparisons are dicey.

Given that long-term records are generally not available, we're back to choosing based on the performance the investment managers racked up in other types of performance. Even that's no guarantee, since a Fidelity name does not mean, for example, that you would be getting the talents of a Peter Lynch.

Enough caveats. Here's my list of do's and don'ts.

1. Since this is an investment for the long haul, I would be suspicious of any fund that invests primarily in small growth stocks, even if the performance record is superior. Here's why. In many cases, these big investment managers will take a very sizable stake in a small company and in buying it boost the price substantially. That will artificially skew the performance record, because when they go to sell those stocks, prices will probably be correspondingly depressed.

   Furthermore, over the long run small growth stocks don't really outperform the giants.
2. Most big brokerage houses don't have an above-average trade record. So I would not invest my money in a fund run by Merrill Lynch or Shearson Lehman Hutton, or whatever it is called by the time you read this book.

3. I would also be careful of any fund that has only a few million dollars in assets. Management fees are liable to be so large they will severely dilute any of the profits.
4. Since this is for the long haul, you're interested in funds whose stated goal is growth—as opposed to income or so-called "balanced" funds.

Most Annuities Don't Beat the Dart Board

Given these criteria, here are the performance rates for growth funds during 1988, 1989 and 1990 as taken from *Standard and Poor's Stock Guide* at the end of that year. I've actually given the names of the investment managers rather than the offerees, since that's the information you'll need to make your decision. In some cases they're the same. All funds with records for at least two years are listed here; when one company had two or more growth funds, I picked the one with the best performance.

Performance for 1988, 1989 and 1990, Total Return

	1988	1989	1990	2/3-Yr Avg
AMEV	N/A	34.7%	−4.6%	15.1%
Aetna Life Insurance	13.2%	27.5%	+2.0%	14.2%
Neuberger & Berman	24.4%	27.7%	−9.4%	14.2%
Fred Alger	N/A	22.4%	+2.7%	12.6%
Capital Research	14.4%	35.8%	−5.2%	15.0%
Fidelity	14.3%	29.7%	−12.9%	10.4%
Shearson Lehman Hutton	6.1%	28.6%	−3.7%	10.3%
General American Life Ins.	N/A	29.9%	−4.0%	13.0%
Sun America/Wellington	20.0%	23.4%	−18.5%	8.3%
Sun Life of Canada	5.7%	45.3%	−10.8%	13.4%
J&W Seligman	N/A	27.0%	−4.8%	8.6%
American Capital Asset	N/A	32.5%	−8.1%	12.2%
Twentieth Century Mgmt.	−3.6%	27.7%	−9.4%	4.9%
Sass Investors	19.2%	25.9%	−13.0%	10.7%
Dean Witter	8.8%	17.7%	−4.6%	7.3%
Ohio National Life	13.8%	21.9%	−4.9%	10.3%
Phoenix Mutual Life	2.6%	34.5%	2.8%	13.3%
Nationwide	24.4%	27.7%	−9.4%	14.2%
Security Benefit Life	8.8%	33.3%	−10.9%	10.4%
Carillon Advisers	29.8%	10.2%	−17.0%	7.7%
Value Line	6.6%	30.2%	6.4%	14.4%
Guardian	19.2%	22.2%	−11.4%	10.0%
Hartford/Wellington	17.5%	24.5%	−5.1%	12.3%
Putnam	N/A	30.5%	−3.4%	13.6%
S&P 500	16.6%	31.7%	−3.1%	15.1%

Considering the management fees and expenses, you would have to do at least 2 percent per year better than the S&P to come out ahead. But even if there were 0 percent expenses—guess what? *None* of the 24 variable annuity growth funds were able to beat the S&P average over the past three years.

Does this mean I'm trying to talk you out of buying annuities, even those that are fully invested in growth stocks?

Sort of. You can do better yourself by buying a no-load index fund *if* it's tax-deferred. Which is precisely where the tax angle comes in. If you can indeed invest your own funds so that the inside buildup is tax-deferred—in 401(k)s, SEPs, or Keoghs—you can forget all about annuities. Period.

However, for those who can invest only a small proportion of their assets in the tax-free sector, annuities should remain in the picture. Even if the investment managers do 1 to 2 percent worse than the S&P, inside buildup will raise the rate of return above the S&P on a taxable basis.

So if you need to purchase an annuity for tax reasons, I'd suggest you pick one that (a) has a three-year track record almost as good as the S&P average, (b) is close to the S&P gains every year, and (c) has at least $100 million under management. At least for the past three years, variable annuity managers satisfying these criteria include Capital Research and Aetna.

Other Hidden Charges of Annuities

Now that we've established that you will be entrusting your money to those highly paid superstars who, year in and year out, do worse than the dart board, what other hidden charges should be expected?

Sales charges are commissions to the broker or life insurance agent who sells you the annuity in the first place. Just as is the case for life insurance or mutual funds, the fees can range anywhere from no load at all up to the 8½ percent maximum charged by some mutual funds. Neither *Best's* nor the various ranking services disclose what the fees are, so you will simply have to ask.

Naturally you will do better if 100 percent of your money, rather than 91.5 percent of your money, is put to work, but don't get too hysterical over the front-end fee if in fact you plan to hold the annuity for a long time. If the annuity is held for 30 years, during which the average rate of return is 10 percent per year, and you invest $1,000 every year for 30 years, the no-load fund would be worth $180,943, while the maximum 8½ percent load would be worth $165,563. But suppose that the high-load fund actually performs somewhat better, with an average rate of return of 11 instead of 10 percent per year, your annuity would grow to $202,136.

Of course, there is no guarantee that funds with high loads will generate higher rates of return. On the other hand, if you do identify a stellar performer, and it turns out to have a front-end load, balance the higher cost against the higher return. As indicated in my example above, most of the time the benefits will outweigh the extra costs.

However, it isn't the commission charges that usually take the biggest bite out of your dollar—it's the management fees. These run from 1½ to 3 percent of the amount in your annuity. At first glance it might seem as if 1½ to 3 percent is much less than 8½ percent. Not so. The 8½ percent applies only to the *initial* amount. The 1½ to 3 percent applies to the *total* amount. That initial $1,000 will be worth $17,445 in 30 years, which means the annuity company or fund manager could pick your pocket for $262 to $524 of your money per original $1,000 invested—much more than the maximum $85 initial commission.

Arthur Lipper and Company calculates the total return including the management fees, so with a little arithmetic you can work back and see how much you are being charged by these investment gurus who fail to beat the S&P. An easier and somewhat more reliable way for the arithmetically impaired to determine these fees is to purchase *Best's Retirement Income Guide*, which lists the maintenance and asset management fees for most of the individual variable annuities that are currently available. Most companies are fairly honest and spell out precisely what you are paying. However, some companies, when asked for their "maintenance and asset management fees," replied "annually." I wouldn't touch those annuities with a ten-foot pole.

Please note: Maintenance and asset management fees do *not* include expenses, which are on top of all other fees. After all, someone has to pay for all those advertisements. Usually these run another 1 to 1½ percent of your investment, and as far as I know, there's no escaping them. Just keep them in mind when you do the arithmetic.

Most annuities, like other life insurance products, have so-called surrender costs, which means if you withdraw your money before the first 10 years, you don't get all of it back. Usually these redemption fees start at 10 percent for the first year and then decline 1 percent per year until they disappear. That may seem like a harsh penalty; but as I've said, these are long-term investments. If you think you will need your money in a few years, put it in a mutual fund and live with the tax consequences.

Tax Deferral Gains Overcome Inept Management Decisions

In order to see how important the inside buildup is, consider the 30-year total returns under the following alternative investment strategies.

1. Invest funds in the stock market and earn the average rate of 12 percent per year before tax and 7½ percent after tax.
2. Purchase an annuity that earns 12 percent per year and has low costs: no front-load commission and 1½ percent annual fees for maintenance and expenses. The figures are also shown for the meatball investment company that underperforms the market by an average of 2 percent each year.
3. Purchase an annuity that earns 12 percent per year but has high costs: 8½ percent front-load commission and 3 percent annual fees for maintenance and expenses. Figures are also shown for the sluggards.

All these calculations are based on the assumption of investing $1,000 per year for 30 years. All figures are before paying any tax on the proceeds, since with an annuity the amounts are paid out annually and are therefore spread over many years.

1a.	Pretax 12% rate of return	$270,293
1b.	After-tax 7½% rate of return	$111,154
2a.	Low-cost annuity, 12% rate of return	$199,874
2b.	Low-cost annuity, 10% rate of return	$134,773
3a.	High-cost annuity, 12% rate of return	$135,946
3b.	High-cost annuity, 10% rate of return	$92,482

Take a minute to look at these figures; they are very revealing. Even though the insurance company or mutual fund does no better than the dart board and rips you off for unconscionable sales commissions and management fees, the tax bite—even at a relatively moderate 37½ percent marginal rate—is so important that over the long run you still come out ahead if you buy an annuity. And if you live in a state with a high income tax rate—or if the federal government raises the top marginal rate further in the future, which is far from unlikely—the advantages of inside buildup will be just that much more significant. Only if you have the worst possible combination of high load, high expenses, and meatball performance will your money accumulate at a slower rate than it would on an after-tax basis.

If you can follow the tips in this book and outperform the market averages, that's another story entirely. But it's not easy. None of the "experts" managed to accomplish this over the past three years. If you have only average skills at outguessing the market, the message here is to take advantage of the inside buildup.

An Oversupply of Investment Managers

In the examples above you invest a total of $30,000 at 12 percent, and if you could invest it on your own the total gain would be $240,000. If you hire the "experts," taking the median case, you get $106,000 for supplying all the capital, and the thieves at the other end get $134,000 for doing nothing more than sitting at the dart board, taking their big fees, and investing your money with no more acumen that the proverbial chimpanzee. Those managers get paid more for sitting on your assets than you do for working hard and saving.

If that's your view as well as mine, we are clearly not the only ones who have reached that conclusion. As a result, there are a tremendous number of no-brainers who have decided to go into business as investment advisers and start mutual funds or annuity programs to relieve you of your excess cash. Many of them were previously fired from the brokerage industry for nonperformance. The result is what an economist would call oversupply. Because thousands of organizations are more than willing to take your money, they have to advertise heavily to attract your investment dollar. Thus many of their firms don't make any money either. The net result is what I call a negative-sum game, a powerful example of the distortions of the tax system. You are worse off, but the investment advisers and funds are not better off.

By now you've probably guessed that I don't own any annuities and never will. That's because between the companies I own and my activities as an author and lecturer, I have plenty of opportunity to fund a Keogh plan to the maximum. And by now I have probably convinced you that annuities should only be second choice for you as well. Nonetheless, that's not the end of the story. *If* you're willing to invest in stocks, and *if* you buy a low-load fund, and *if* you do business with a fund that has a reasonable expense ratio, and *if* you retain the annuity for a long time—by which I mean 20 years or more—then you'll end up with more money investing on your own without the tax-deferred buildup. Damning with faint praise, to be sure, but take whatever opportunities the tax code provides.

IRA Conversion to Annuities: Getting Your Money Before 59½

There's one more important reason for discussing annuities in some detail. In many cases, as retirement age approaches and taxes would otherwise be due, you can undertake a tax-free rollover to an annuity. This is a particularly useful device for getting some of your IRA funds out before you reach the age of 59½.

Specifically, to withdraw funds from your IRA before 59½, simply set up an annuity based on the IRS tables and start paying yourself the alloted sums. If you are still fairly young, the maximum annual amount you can receive without penalty ranges from 6 to 8 percent of the principal—e.g., $30,000 to $40,000 on a principal of $500,000. Of course, you will have to pay taxes on that income. But the key here is to set up *your own* annuity instead of buying one from an insurance company or investment management firm. I'll explain why in the final section of this chapter.

LUMP SUM OR ANNUAL PAYMENT: THE CRITICAL DECISION

Let's assume you have faithfully invested in an annuity for at least 20 years, are about to retire, and are faced with a major decision that will affect the rest of your life. Perhaps you will have built up $250,000 in an annuity, and can either take the $250,000 all at once or receive a certain amount for the rest of your life—or in many cases, for the remaining lifetimes of you and your spouse, whomever lives longer.

One reason this strikes many people as a hard decision is that they don't know how much longer they will live. Of course, the insurance company or mutual fund doesn't know either, but it has the law of large numbers on its side. The actuarial and mortality tables will tell it how long you— or you and your spouse—can be expected to live on average.

Of course, if you have some reason to believe that your life span will be shorter than the average, take the lump sum. But that doesn't really solve the problem. My guess is that unless you have cancer or a history of heart attacks, if you (a) have a sizable annuity and (b) are reading this book, you will probably outlive the mortality tables. After all, those tables are based on everyone—the poor, those who do not receive adequate medical care, those who have lived a hard life, and those who have been alcohol or drug abusers. You probably don't fit into any of these categories, and may you enjoy your old age. In that case, what should you do with the annuity?

WHY YOU SHOULD NEVER ANNUITIZE

I will show you how it is possible for you to take the lump sum at the beginning, get larger annual payments than you would from the average annuity even if you live *forever*, and yet have the *full amount* left to pass on to your heirs.

That's important enough for you to slow down, stop, and read it again. By taking the lump-sum payment, you will not only get larger annual payments than any annuity company will pay, but the entire sum can be passed along intact to your heirs.

How could that possibly be the case? The difference is that once you reach retirement age, the tax advantages change completely. Read on, and using my typical "simple example," I'll show you how this "miracle" is accomplished.

Once again, I'll assume you invest $1,000 per year in a low-expense annuity at age 35, so by age 65 you will have a lump sum of approximately $200,000. Taxes are due on $170,000, since the original $30,000 investment was money on which you had already paid taxes.

As it turns out, the IRS permits some advantageous choices here. First, you can calculate the tax rate on that $170,000 as if it were received over 10 years. If you don't have any other taxable income, your income would only be subject to the marginal tax rate effective at $17,000. That could reduce your marginal tax rate from 33 percent to 15 percent, although if you have substantial other income, it won't make any difference.

The second possibility is to roll over the annuity to an IRA for the next 5½ years, thereby earning tax-deferred interest until you are 70½. Most of the time, because of other penalties, it's not worth it, so I don't recommend that option.

Let's assume, however, that you are fairly well off, so income-averaging or IRA rollovers don't matter. Even then, my statement holds. You then have $200,000 pretax, or $143,900 after tax, assuming that you've retired to some location that doesn't have a state or municipal income tax and you are in the 33 percent bracket. Investing that at 12 percent would yield $17,268 per year, subject up to 33 percent income tax, or $11,570 after tax. The big, mean IRS has reduced your 12 percent rate to a measly 5.78 percent by double-dipping out of both the principal and the interest. Even though you get to keep your $200,000 and eventually pass it along to your heirs, that's a pretty hefty price to pay.

Now suppose you let the insurance company or mutual fund keep your $200,000 and receive your monthly payments. These may or may not be larger than $17,268 per year. But when you or your spouse dies, there will be nothing left to pass along to your heirs. All annuities work that way.

The precise amount of the annual payments depends on what sort of payout you choose. It certainly would be a shame if, after faithfully saving $1,000 per year for 30 years, on the day after you retire you have a heart attack and expire. You would get precisely nothing. The insurance company or investment fund would get to keep every penny.

Most people who buy annuities obviously don't want to take that risk, so most annuities are structured so that even if you die, your designatee gets payments for a certain number of years. Most of these are written for a guaranteed payment of 10, 15, or 20 years, known as 10 (or 15 or 20) years certain. Naturally, the guarantee means your monthly payments are somewhat less, although the penalty isn't very large. Changes from straight life payments to 10 years certain reduces the payments by about 6 percent, while changing to 20 years certain reduces them by about 15 percent.

Another popular option guarantees the payments each month until either you or your spouse dies. That provides some financial security for your partner as long as he or she lives. That option also reduces the monthly payments by about 15 percent.

By their very nature, most people who buy annuities are not gamblers. So I will assume here that anyone who has an annuity would choose either 20 years certain or joint survivorship, which reduces the payments 15 percent from what you would otherwise receive.

Here again, I'll assume a 12 percent average annual return from the stock market. The question then becomes: How much do you receive each year from a $200,000 lump sum if the principal is completely exhausted in 20 years?

If the financial organization holding your annuity took no charges out for maintenance or investment fees, the answer would simply be $26,426 per year. You have to pay taxes at the 33 percent rate on 94.3 percent of this, because the tax rate is based on your *total* expected payments minus your initial $30,000 investment. Thus the after-tax payment is $18,200, assuming there are no charges or fees at all.

However, the annuity company is not doing this just for recreation; it charges you something extra. Total fees are generally about 2 percent of the total amount, which would reduce the yield from 12 to 10 percent, or $15,167. That figure then has to be reduced by 15 percent because you opted for 20 years certain or joint survivorship, which takes it down to $12,892.

That is admittedly better than the $11,570 you would get if you took the money and invested it on your own. But remember, if you did that, the $200,000 would remain intact, whereas if you receive the higher annual payment, none of the principal is left. Furthermore, we're not finished yet.

You could, of course, save the 2 percent annual fee and set up your own annuity, in which the principal would be exhausted after 20 years. The only problem with that is if you lived beyond 85, you wouldn't have any annuity funds coming in at all, whereas the annuity you purchase will continue to pay off until you die. So I'm not recommending that option either. But I do have a better idea.

THE EVANS PLAN FOR SELF-ANNUITIES

Here's the Evans plan, which amounts to self-insuring against being impoverished at a ripe old age *and* passing the entire principal on to your heirs. Of the $143,900 you have after taxes from the lump-sum $200,000 distribution, take $20,000 and buy a single-premium annuity that you plan to use starting at age 85. At 12 percent per year, the value will grow to $200,000 in 20 years. That leaves $123,900 to invest at 12 percent and draw down the principal as well as interest.

Since much of your payment will be a drawdown of principal, you won't have to pay taxes on that part—just on the dividends and capital gains you earn. Your annual pretax payment will be $16,372 per year, which works out to $13,016 per year after taxes, assuming a 33 percent tax bracket. Please note: That compares favorably with the $12,892 per year from the annuity issuer, and your $200,000 principal remains intact forever.

You might wonder how (a) investing $123,900 at 12 percent can yield $13,016 per year, while (b) investing $143,900 at 12 percent yields only $12,892 per year. It's the tax structure at work again. You pay the full 33 percent tax in the first case. In the second case, though, you draw down your principal—which is not taxed—at the same time you're building up future funds on a tax-deferred basis. You can take advantage of this feature of annuities no matter what your age.

So the $13,016 per year beats the insurance company's payment of $12,892. Furthermore, at age 85 you'll have your $200,000 left, either to pass on to your heirs, spend in your truly golden years, or start the game all over again, if you think you'll live another 20 years—and more power to you!

Let's stop and review this for a minute. Note what has been accomplished here, because this is the investment equivalent of the famed "free lunch." You take the lump-sum distribution. Your annual payments are *more* than you would get from an annuity, *and in addition*, your principal will always remain intact, to be passed on to the beneficiary of your choice.

In two words: *never annuitize*. Take the money and invest it yourself.

As you can see, once you don't get the tax break differential, it doesn't make any sense to have someone manage your money for you unless they can earn a better than average market return. But as I've shown you—and there's lots more evidence to follow in the next section—the vast majority of investment funds cannot match the market averages. Once you've retired, the tax breaks disappear, and now it's the investment managers who are running uphill.

Furthermore, you can invest your funds with one of the very few mutual funds that has consistently outperformed the averages and be money ahead. Even without that added incentive, though, annuitizing never makes sense unless you are incompetent and can't even match the market averages— which can easily be done by investing in an index fund.

Finally, even if you have no heirs or favorite charities, it just seems to be human nature that you would rather pass along your life savings to some person or organization you name personally than donate it to some impersonal insurance company or investment fund. The life insurance companies and investment firms don't show any charity toward you—so I wouldn't make them a gift in return.

Chapter 12

Advantages of Your Own Business

If there's one thing I ought to be an expert on, it's starting your own business. At latest count, I've started 10 companies, beginning with the M&M Coin Company, when I was 16, to my latest creation, Electronic Information Systems. This tally includes only those companies that actually generated business revenues; it omits all those that were on the drawing board but never brought in any dollars. Some were multimillion-dollar successes; some were fiascos. But it's clear enough that I like to start companies; it's almost a hobby. So what do I enjoy about it?

1. It's more fun working for yourself. As one eminently successful entrepreneur said, it's like getting a report card every day. In a large corporation you can be doing a whale of a job but often no one notices and no one cares—and it may not even affect the bottom line.
2. The tax breaks are quite considerable, although they used to be even better. If you do lose money, at least you can claim the government as a partner.
3. If you are really good at what you do, few companies will pay you what you are worth. Mike Milken, with his $550 million annual compensation, was a notable exception—although a lot of good it did him in the long run. But the more likely case is someone like Andy Krieger, a foreign-exchange trading whiz who used to

work for Bankers Trust and made $300 million trading one year. The chairman of the bank offered what he thought was an exceedingly generous bonus—$3 million ("More than I make," he said). A few weeks later, Krieger left and set up his own shop.

Steve Jobs and Steve Wozniak would hardly have received upwards of $70 million apiece if they had invented the PC while working for IBM. They would probably have received a $5,000 bonus and a year's supply of crisp white shirts.

And how about Bill Gates, the founder of Microsoft, at age 34 the world's youngest billionaire? You have to do it on your own.

Of course, not all of us are Bill Gates, or even Steve Jobs or Wozniak. But you don't have to make your fortune in high-tech. In fact, looking at the *Forbes* 400, I'm struck by how few made their fortunes in high-tech. The 1989 edition of the *Forbes* 400 even included an article by George Gilder entitled "Where are the Microchip Billionaires?" The list includes plenty of people in real estate, construction, publishing, investment, and old-line manufacturing (like textiles); quite a few oil scions were on the list, too. You certainly don't have to be a technical genius to start out on your own.

The hardest decision is the one to give up a secure paycheck and head out into the world where, if you fail, you receive nothing and may lose a sizable proportion of your total assets. You have to be in the right frame of mind to take those risks.

ONE STEP AT A TIME

That's why it's often best to take the plunge one step at a time. Try a little part-time business on your own. If you like it better than your regular job, it may very well be time to make the big decision. But if not, you've lost very little—and probably gained some tax breaks.

Here's how I see the logical progression.

1. Getting your feet wet: starting a small business on the side.
2. Plunging in on a full-time basis—possibly just you and the spouse.
3. Growing the business—alternatives for raising money.
4. Decision time, now that you're successful: expanding or selling.
5. Passing your company along to future generations.

ONE BOSS—OR HUNDREDS?

Not everyone has the temperament or personality to start a business. Sure, at one time or another all of us have said how nice it would be to tell the boss precisely where to go and do everything the right way—our way.

Let me reiterate something you probably know. If you go into business for yourself, you won't have one boss anymore. You'll have hundreds, or—if you're lucky—thousands. Each customer is the boss, telling you how they want it done and when they want it. If you don't enjoy selling— if you don't get a certain satisfaction out of making the customer happy— you're better off sticking with the one-boss situation.

Customer-bosses can be a royal pain. They don't buy what they said they wanted, they think it's too expensive, and when they do agree to buy, they don't pay on time. Even if the product or service is perfect, they complain it doesn't do what you promised. Not all customers behave like boors. But enough of them do to make it imperative that you have at least some rhinoceros in your skin.

Of course, some one-boss situations are like that too, but in most cases you have the option of finding another job. If you've sunk your life savings into your pet project only to find that no one else is impressed, it's tough luck, Charlie.

That's why you probably should try a little enterprise on the side to make sure the inevitable heartaches of owning and running your own business don't disagree with you. It could be a business that's related to your primary job. In the case of lawyers, doctors, attorneys, accountants, investment advisers, teachers, musicians, etc., it's fairly straightforward to do a little extra work out of your home. But it doesn't have to be a busman's holiday, so to speak. You could try nibbling at something different to see if you enjoy it. Depending on your lifestyle and predilections, it could be a pet-sitting service, a travel agency, a repair shop, a part-time sales job, renting real estate, or a hundred other small business services that fill the gap in your neighborhood.

If you can't think of any part-time activity where you'd like to earn a few extra bucks on the side, or if you're so caught up in your present job that you can't carve out a few extra hours, that's fine. Don't start your own business, and skip to the next chapter. But if you are entrepreneurially minded—and given the 11 million small businesses and independent professional practices in the United States, obviously quite a few of us are—the best idea is probably to start small and get the flavor of what it's like to be your own boss, beholden to no one. Except all the customers.

BUSINESS ON THE SIDE, TAX ADVANTAGES TO GO

One of the main advantages of having a nice little business on the side, besides opening up the possibility of becoming a full-scale entrepreneur, is that up to some fairly reasonable limits, the income it brings in can in effect be tax-free. Not tax-deferred, like retirement savings, but tax-free. Because you can deduct expenses up to the limit of your earnings.

Of course, it doesn't start out that way. You have to declare all your gross receipts on Schedule C of your income tax return. But every business has some legitimate expenses, and they can be deducted up to the limit of that income.

Back in the 1960s, an IRS agent—in the first of my many audits—told me the general rule of thumb they follow. Expenses are deductible up to the amount of income. That's a very sound rule, and in my case one that has held up for 25 years. The IRS has gotten progressively stricter and nastier to the point where expenses are almost automatically disallowed if you don't have any income to show for it. But if you do, the write-offs flow naturally.

Your Home is Your Office

The standard rule of thumb for the office at home is to deduct the proportion of your home that is used as the place of business. If you have an eight-room house and use one room for the office or business headquarters, write off one-eighth of the house. Technically this is supposed to be based on square feet, and maybe somewhere there really does exist an IRS agent who comes to the house and measures the size of your office compared with that of the living room, bedroom, and kitchen. In my opinion, you can use a small room and still treat it as equal to all other rooms.

The most straightforward way to calculate the deduction is to sum up all your housing-related expenses—mortgage, property taxes, utilities, repairs, and any maintenance fees for a condominium or similar structure—and divide by eight. If you rent, the one-eighth factor holds just the same. By the way, major repairs don't count; they have to be capitalized over their taxable lifetime. If you have two or more phone lines, one can be "exclusively" for business; to be kosher about it, you should list this number in the phone book under the business name.

Alternatively, you could do an "arm's length" deal with yourself and deduct a rental payment equivalent to what the square footage would cost if you rented from someone else. Usually, though, the difference isn't worth having to explain to the IRS what you thought you were doing.

Those Entertaining Tax Deductions

Next we turn to the gray area of entertainment. Presumably every so often you hold cocktail parties or dinners and invite your clients, both present and prospective, and have them sign the guest book. You also note in your own records what business deals were discussed.

Either 80 or 100 percent of the cost of the dinner is deductible—depending on some arcane rules that you should discuss with your tax adviser, providing he can understand them—but after that the law is even less clear. Can you deduct the part of the rest of the house—besides the one-eighth that is your office—because you used it for entertainment? I'd say no to that one unless you can prove that you used one or more rooms in the house exclusively for entertainment, which sounds like a waste of money just to save a few tax dollars.

On the other hand, don't overlook the legitimate costs of household care, cleaning services, window washers, and yard and pool maintenance to spruce up your place so that clients don't think you live in a dump. Some entrepreneurs deduct the entire cost of a maid on the grounds that they wouldn't clean up the house but for their clients; I don't go that far. Depending on how much you entertain—according to those records mentioned above—and what your total costs are, you can deduct some reasonable proportion, which is probably somewhere between one-fourth and one-half.

Will the IRS object? I can't speak for all agents. As noted previously, I generally take these deductions, even though a number of tax advisers have told me not to try. In the course of several audits, no agent has ever questioned them. If the rest of your return is in tip-top shape, my guess is they won't pick on these items.

Every Company Needs a Car—If It's Deductible

Next is the company car. If your office is at home and your clients come to see you, no dice. If you drive it only to and from the office or store, that doesn't count either. However, if you use it in the company business—delivering goods, chauffeuring people around (as real estate agents do), or calling on clients at their residence or place of business—then you have a legitimate deduction. If some of your clients also happen to be personal friends, you probably discussed some business when you were visiting them on a social occasion. All of these are legitimate business uses of your car, providing you don't overdo it.

The company car used to be such an obvious perquisite of a self-owned business that the IRS finally clamped down with its usual sledgehammer approach and decided that everyone who claimed that deduction had to keep a log of which trips were business and which were personal, complete with mileage records. Again, be reasonable about it and most of your automobile expenses can be deductible—providing, of course, you have the income to cover them.

In my opinion, the best way to handle this is to have two cars, which you probably do anyway if you're married. You should be able to convince the IRS agent that one is used strictly for business purposes, providing you really do take some business trips in it.

Taking an (Un)Taxing Vacation

Another key perquisite of owning your own business is that at least some of your vacations can be tax-deductible. You won't be too surprised to hear that the IRS is not very happy about this and has worked to whittle these deductions down, but some advantages do remain. The standard ploy is attending a convention sponsored by the industry in which you work, and while you're there, taking a few extra days for vacation. Some people who sign up for the convention aren't too compulsive about going to all those boring meetings and hearing speeches by long-winded economists. Often when I address a convention there are 600 people at dinner and 200 people at the business session the next morning. Naturally the host tells me how surprised he is that more people didn't show up. Sure he is.

Most of the time you can take your spouse along on a deductible basis, too. The general idea is that you "entertain" at these conventions, and your spouse is obviously essential to keep the cocktail-party chatter vibrant and stimulating. But don't try the old ploy of having your wife take "notes" at the meetings. It's been tried, and it's been defeated—even if she is an expert at shorthand. It seems that some years ago the IRS figured out that if you really wanted a record of what that long-winded economist said, you could tape it yourself—or have the association tape it, which they usually do anyway.

Several years ago the IRS also decided that while domestic junketing was still hunky-dory, foreign meetings weren't. So for those exotic international locations, the deductions are now mighty slim. Unless you go for less than one week, you can only deduct those parts of the expenses that are directly germane to the business part of the meeting. That means an unsatisfactorily small proportion of the airfare; in this case, the game is hardly worth the candle.

This ruling has affected me directly, not because I do much junketing but because of where I speak. In the old days, when fully deductible meetings could be held anywhere in the world, it used to be Acapulco, Rio, and the Riviera. Now I'm asked to speak in Birmingham, Alabama, McAllen, Texas, and Pierre (pronounced Peer, which proves I've actually been there), South Dakota. I still get to go to Hawaii every now and then, but it's just not the same.

Pushing the IRS Too Far

Some wise guys try to stretch the outside income concept beyond all reasonable limits. In one notable court case, an imaginative would-be tax avoider claimed he had his own business as a money manager because he received interest and dividends on his investment. He had maybe $250,000 in assets and earned perhaps $20,000 a year in income—and for that he'd tried to deduct the cost of his study, his investment magazines, any dinners where he discussed stocks, and so forth.

Naturally the IRS disallowed this, but in doing so it came up with an interesting ruling that I wouldn't have expected. If the notorious Mr. M had actually been a *trader*, said the IRS, and made money trading in and out of stocks, options, or futures, instead of just sitting on his assets all year long, he would indeed have been in the business of trading and could actually have taken all those deductions.

I'm obviously not suggesting that you churn your account just to get a few tax breaks, thereby transferring your hard-earned dollars from yourself to the broker. That's a small tail wagging a very big dog. However, if it just so happens you are the type of investor who trades frequently *and can make money at it*, then you may be eligible for the home office, company car, entertainment, and vacation deduction sweepstakes. In that case, you could deduct all your trips to those so-called investment seminars, which the IRS won't allow anymore for most people. Sometimes the tax court rules in wondrous ways.

Leaving aside the more exotic types of businesses, such as trying to trade for a living, let's consider a fairly typical situation. You might have outside income of $10,000 per year, "office" expenses of $4,000, entertainment of $2,000, company car expenses of $2,000, and vacation—make that meeting—expenses of $2,000. We're not talking huge bucks here, but you do save the taxes on the $10,000, plus bringing in a little extra income on the side. Admittedly, when marginal tax rates were 50 to 70 percent, this made even more sense, but even at a top rate of 33 percent plus state and local income tax in many localities, you're still getting almost two bucks for the price of one.

At least that's how I got started on my own.

TAKING THE BIG PLUNGE: TOTAL IMMERSION

Quitting your job to start your own company qualifies as one of the biggest decisions of your life. It isn't totally irrevocable, because you could always fold your tent, go hat in hand back to your former employer or to a headhunter and say, I failed, please forgive me and find me another job. However, you will have lost much of your savings and more of your self-esteem. So I assume that like Caesar, once you've crossed the Rubicon to work for yourself full-time, there's no turning back.

If you take this step, be prepared to live on a much lower income, or quite possibly on no income at all, for the first year. Unless you've discovered a legal way to make dollar bills at half price, or a bust enhancer that works with no side effects, it will take you a while to market your product or service and collect the revenues. Ask yourself whether you are prepared to live without any salary for the first year. If the answer is no, don't make the move.

That's what I did when I started my econometric consulting firm, which later became Chase Econometrics. I gave up my none-too-princely salary of $13,750 per year as an associate professor at the Wharton School, dug into my savings, and 10 years later I sold my shares of the company for $2.5 million, which isn't a bad annual rate of return.

Raising Money to Get Started

Depending on the type of business you start, you may be able to convince someone else to fund the new company in return for part ownership. Of course, you can always try to borrow money without having to give up any equity. Notice I said *try*.

Among the revelations that came out of the S&L bailout scandal, it appears that during the 1980s, there were indeed bankers who would lend you all the money you asked for without requiring any collateral. All I can say is that I must travel in the wrong circles, because I never met any such lending officers. In my experience, banks will lend money on so-called bankable assets, which could be your home or other real estate, personal assets that have been adequately appraised (jewelry, objets d'art, etc.), or equipment you buy for the business, and I have from time to time borrowed against such assets. But I have never met a banker who was willing to lend me money just to meet the payroll without getting something extra in return.

Whether to relinquish part of the company to obtain needed funds is a difficult call; I have seen successes and failures both ways. If it is mainly a personal services business and you are the only employee, then it's silly to borrow money for what in effect would be paying your own salary, even providing you have valuable collateral. But if you need money to purchase assets or meet a payroll, someone else's money may be essential to get the company off the ground. Then the question becomes whether the money should be in the form of a loan, equity in the company, or a hybrid that usually takes the form of a *convertible debenture*. This is really a loan, but interest and principal payments are ordinarily deferred until the company becomes profitable; in return you give up some of the equity.

One size doesn't fit all, and in starting my various companies I have used all three methods. If you have substantial assets, even if they are illiquid—such as your house—it's easy to borrow against them, and that is the obvious first place to raise money. However, you may not have that option; you're young, highly motivated, and have a fantastic new idea— but you're not yet rich.

Those Unfriendly Bankers

Borrowing from the banks works only if you are buying a specific capital asset, such as a computer or a certain type of machine that is necessary to produce the new product. In that case, you can obtain a loan similar to a car loan; the money is secured by a depreciating asset. You don't have to start your own business to get that kind of a loan, and for that matter the bank would prefer you have a steady job rather than zero income when it makes the loan. In fact, telling the loan officer you have zero income is definitely not recommended under any circumstances.

Most banks won't lend you money just to meet the payroll in a service business, since there are no collectible assets, slavery having been outlawed some years ago. One of the old clichés I heard many times in my initial requests for capital is that the assets go down the elevator every night. So if you need money to hire people to develop and market your new product or service, a bank loan won't cut it.

Venture Capitalists: A Disappearing Breed

When I started out on my own, venture-capital deals were the vehicle of choice. I was young, had no experience at running my own company, and had no tangible assets, yet several organizations said they were willing to put up the money in return for a sizable chunk of the company's stock.

Today, though, venture-capital deals for start-up situations are much more difficult to find. So many venture-capital deals haven't worked out over the past 20 years that the venue has all but disappeared. You still read stories about "venture-capital" firms, and some people will gladly take your money to send you lists of such firms, but in fact most of them now provide expansion money for companies that are already established.

Thus the purely venture-capital option for start-up firms is no longer a practical one. On my last foray into this area I was told by someone who claimed he did venture-capital deals that the three quickest ways to lose his money were vintage wines, loose women, and start-up venture-capital deals. You won't be too surprised to hear that he turned me down, too.

Using Convertible Debentures

In a convertible debenture situation, the lender provides the money up front in the form of a loan and also takes part of the equity in the company. Of course deals vary, but in general a pure venture-capital firm will take more than half of the company, while the lender who provides a convertible debenture usually takes 15 to 25 percent. Unlike a loan, you don't have to start paying interest for some stated period of time, usually two to three years, which at least theoretically gives the company time to get on its feet. After that, the interest and principal are usually repaid over some fairly short period of time, which could range anywhere from two to five years.

In many cases, banks have set up what they call venture-capital subsidiaries but are actually small business investment corporations, or SBICs. The government guarantees most of the principal, so if the fledgling firm goes under, the bank's losses are minimized. Under an SBIC, the bank or other lending institution is much more likely to advance you some capital.

Nonetheless, raising capital for a true start-up situation is much more difficult today than it was 10 or 20 years ago. Your best bet nowadays is to use your own savings, borrow as much as you can from the bank on your existing assets, and try to raise fairly small amounts of money from each of a number of friends and relatives. Dealing with the venture-capital sharks is generally not a rewarding experience.

Yes, you could lose everything. And desiccated old bankers will mutter into their green eyeshades that only one out of every five small businesses ever makes it. Even if you aren't ruined financially, you'll have to pick up the pieces of your life and put them back together. So I'm not minimizing the risks involved. The decision is best taken only if you are quite convinced that your new ventures will be a smashing success. This is not for the fainthearted.

CHOOSING THE RIGHT TYPE OF BUSINESS . . .

What kind of businesses have the best chance of survival and success?

1. START WITH AN EXISTING CLIENT BASE.
In most cases you'll be starting some sort of service business; this also includes high-tech start-ups which depend largely on developing new products or services. You'll fare better if you managed to build up a small client base when you were running the new company on a part-time basis. Sometimes your previous employer will assist you with the switch and graciously permit you to take some of your clients when you leave; he might even become your first client. Of course, you might also be given 20 minutes to clean out your desk with an armed guard standing by.

The key here is that unless you have specifically signed a noncompete clause, there is no law in the country that says you can't call up your friends and ask if you can continue to work with them, regardless of what some unfriendly lawyer may tell you. The line is drawn at possession of tangible articles that belong to your former employer; for example, you probably can't take any actual lists with you.

In either case, having a stable client base, even if it's a small one, should get you through the difficult first year.

2. USE VENDOR CAPITAL.
If you're starting a manufacturing or retailing business, you run the risk of ordering supplies and then finding you can't sell the product quickly—or even if you can, not getting paid promptly. That's where many firms use what has become known as vendor capital; you borrow from suppliers by not paying on time. This practice doesn't work in the long run, but if

you are just getting started, sometimes other companies will be generous in how long they will leave bills pending. I said *sometimes*.

3. STICK TO WHAT YOU KNOW WELL.

This point should be too obvious to rate even a brief mention, but go into a business in which you have knowledge, experience, and aptitude. Some people are mathematical whizzes; others never mastered the arcane art of balancing their checkbook correctly. Some are natural-born sales-people; others prefer to work behind the scenes. Some are natural tinkerers and inventors; others can't change a light bulb without losing their balance or getting an electrical shock. The kind of business that will work best for you is one that you know well, in which you have some experience, and where you enjoy putting in those long hours. If you think a particular type of business is exciting or glamorous, try it out on a part-time basis, or by working for someone else, before plunging into the maelstrom.

. . . AND AVOIDING THE WRONG TYPE

I'm always surprised by the number of people, including many of my friends, who start businesses they know absolutely nothing about. At the top of that list is restaurants.

It has probably crossed your mind, too. After returning home from a lousy meal and worse service, you're convinced that you can do better. And indeed, new neighborhood restaurants open—and close—almost every week.

Very few restaurants make money initially, and there's a good reason for that. If you have a clothing shop, or a bookstore, or sell various types of services, your inventory doesn't spoil. But if the special of the day is fresh Dover sole or Norwegian salmon and no one orders it, you're out a bundle. You can try fish chowder the next day or feed it to stray kittens, but you won't make money that way.

Restaurants sound glamorous—to those who haven't tried it. Most people who do soon come to the conclusion that the business consists mainly of drudgery, hard work, employees who don't show up on the busiest night of the year, spoiled food, and losses. In my opinion the only people who consistently make money from the restaurant business are the construction firms, the interior decorators, and the restaurant equipment-supply firms. Next to starting your own airline, restaurants are generally the worst business investment.

At this point I can hear a voice from the balcony asking, And how much did you lose on *your* restaurant, Evans?

Not very much, but that's only because we never opened it. We were going to start a seafood restaurant on Cape Cod. A brilliant idea, I'm sure you'll agree, considering there are already more seafood restaurants than people on the Cape. It must have been after that two-hour wait for greasy, inedible food at three-star prices. Anyway, we bought the land. Then we dealt with a long line of local elected officials who had their hands out for payments for checking the soil (to make sure we weren't in the wetlands), testing the water, agreeing to the curb cuts, approving the construction, ruling on the height of the sign, and so on. But the coup de grace, as far as I was concerned, was the state's requirement that we install a bathroom for the handicapped big enough to drive a truck through. Meanwhile, I had finally managed to find out enough about the economics of a restaurant to wonder what had ever possessed me. So we sold the land at a profit and I returned to my other phantasmagorical business schemes.

It is, of course, possible to sign up for a franchise restaurant; you deliver the dollars and get a standard building, operating format, and at least some initial name recognition. Many of the early franchisees of McDonald's, Burger King, Wendy's, and the other big-name companies have done very well.

However, I wouldn't stray into that area these days. The prime locations for the big names have already been taken, and your chance of attracting a profitable market share is much smaller now. Many of the new franchises that currently advertise in the *Wall Street Journal* and other eminently respectable publications are little more than outright scams; they take your money and give very little in return. Most of the time you can't resell these franchises for your initial investment.

If you want to go into business on your own, be extremely careful about any franchise opportunity. Make sure that a reasonable proportion of the fee you pay is earmarked to advertise the chain, that you don't get stuck buying products from the franchiser at above-market prices, and in particular, that someone else can't come along and put up a similar store across the street.

Finally, there's the adorable country inn where you and your spouse had such a refreshing weekend years ago; you just found out that it's on the market and the price is so reasonable. Of course, you might ask yourself why if it's a proven moneymaker, but at this point I'll assume that emotions briefly bested logic and you just forgot to inquire.

By this time you can probably imagine what to expect. In addition to all the problems of the restaurant on site, there are the pipes breaking at 3:00 A.M., the furnace or air-conditioning unit that dies at the same time, the no-shows—both guests and employees—on the busiest weekends. Sure, you can get their credit-card number and bill them for not showing up. But don't forget that the credit-card companies generally won't pay you if the customers claim they never signed up in the first place—or they did sign up but have a cancellation number, which they may have obtained from an unscrupulous desk clerk. The people who try this are scum, of course, but that's precisely who welshes out on reservations anyway. If you're Hilton or Sheraton, you send the lawyers after them, but if you're Itsy-Bitsy-Cutesy Hideaway, you count your losses. Just ask onetime presidential candidate George McGovern how his lodge in Connecticut went bankrupt.

I hope I've convinced you not to open your own restaurant or buy a country inn, and to stick to what you know best. Now let's get back to the nuts and bolts of actually organizing the company.

To C or Not to C

Let's say the business of your dreams hasn't yet turned into nightmares, you have managed to scrape together enough capital, and are open for business. Are you better off as an individual or as a corporation?

Many of the reasons often given for choosing one form of organization over the other are specious. On one hand, it is claimed that incorporating will protect you from lawsuits. Maybe that was once true, but not in today's litigation-happy society. On the other hand, it is often said that incorporating subjects your income to double taxation. That's true for a regular corporation, but can be avoided by forming what is known as a subchapter S corporation. So before deciding which is best for you, let's first clear away the underbrush.

Some people will claim a corporate entity is better because you can't be sued individually, or because the bank can't come after your personal assets if the company goes bankrupt. Don't believe it. If you're just starting up, the bank will probably make you sign personally for any loans. Nowadays ambitious lawyers will pierce the corporate shell to sue any individual owners who are believed to have assets, and even a top corporate executive will go to jail if 12 honest men and women think he did something wrong. If you're worried about being sued, get excess liability insurance, which gives you $1–$5 million in peace of mind for only a few hundred dollars a year.

Avoiding Double or Triple Taxation: The S Corporation Advantage

In terms of taxes, the major distinction is not between a sole proprietorship and a corporation but between a regular corporation, known as a *C corporation*, and a so-called *subchapter S corporation*, in which all the profits—and losses—automatically flow through to the personal income tax returns of the owners. If you made $50,000 last year, that sum gets added to your other income and you have to pay taxes on it. If you lost $50,000—providing you really did lose it and it's not just a phantom transaction—the loss is subtracted from your other income before taxes.

You will have to pay taxes on any profit earned, whether you report it as an individual, a partnership, an S corporation, or a regular C corporation. The major disadvantage of a C corporation is that in certain cases you can be taxed up to three times—once when you earn the income, a second time after it is declared as a dividend, and possibly even a third time if the IRS deems you have accumulated "too much" money. That's a mistake to be avoided at almost all costs.

You might think all this can be avoided by paying yourself a salary equal to the profits and therefore avoiding double taxation. In many cases, however, this is disallowed by the IRS, and here's why. Suppose you previously had a salary of $50,000 a year and a new corporation that you form turns out to be relatively successful and earns $250,000 a year. You decide to pay that all in salary to yourself. However, in a C corporation, the IRS has the right to declare that your salary cannot exceed what you could have earned elsewhere, and all the rest is really a dividend. Whammo—you pay taxes twice. With an S corporation, you never take that risk.

Some Advantages of a C Corporation

Since an S corporation always avoids double or triple taxation, it might seem like the ideal solution. However, where the tax laws are involved nothing is ever that simple. As it turns out, there are certain circumstances where a C corporation is superior to an S corporation. Here are the main ones:

1. Suppose you have profits of $50,000 one year but spend it all on computer equipment that will sharply increase your profits in future years. That means your cash flow for the year is zero—yet you could owe taxes of up to $16,500 on the profit, in an S corporation, which means you will have to borrow the money to

pay your taxes. This usually isn't critical—you can ordinarily borrow at least half of the value of the equipment—but it's something that shouldn't be overlooked if the company regularly requires new equipment.

2. In most cases, the first $50,000 of corporate income is taxed at only 15 percent, compared with the 33 percent rate for personal income, so you could save an extra $5,000 per year at the lower corporate tax rate. After that, the rate jumps to 34 percent, so this advantage soon disappears—unless you never have profits of more than $50,000 per year.

   However, this initial low bracket does not apply to people in certain types of service professions. If you are in legal, medical, engineering, architectural, accounting, actuarial, performing, or consulting work, you must pay the flat 34 percent tax rate starting on the first dollar of profit. Authors and lecturers are not penalized in this way—fine with me, although I really can't tell you why we're exempt. Maybe it's because we'd write and say terrible things about the IRS if we didn't have extra tax breaks to keep us quiet. (No, that couldn't be it.)

3. Fringe benefits—particularly those expensive health-care policies—are deductible for C but not for S corporations. You can also deduct the premiums on up to $50,000 of group term life insurance per employee, but that's chicken feed. However, with health-care costs approaching $10,000 per family per year, deducting that item is not negligible.

4. You can borrow from your corporate pension plan—e.g., for a down payment on a house—in a C corporation but not in an S corporation.

5. Finally, in one of the biggest remaining tax breaks, a C corporation allows you to put 15 percent of your salary into an employee stock ownership program (ESOP) and deduct that amount from your profits. In a one-person company, that means you're simply transferring the stock to yourself. In effect, you get a tax deduction without laying out any cash—one of the very few such cases to survive the Tax Reform Act of 1986. In almost every other situation, you must have real expenses or real losses in order to take deductions. Nonetheless, there are some questionable aspects to this arrangement, which I'll discuss below.

By now you may be wondering whether it is worth bothering to incorporate at all. Under a C corporation, you are subject to double or even triple taxation, while under an S corporation, you can't deduct some of your ordinary business expenses, such as medical-care premiums. Is there a way around this dilemma?

If you are the sole employee of your business, the truth of the matter is it doesn't make much difference. The Keogh plan can be applied to accumulate generous pension benefits, and the saving on the medical-care benefit deduction nets you only about $2,000 per year—not much more than the cost of hiring an accountant and lawyer to file your taxes and annual report forms.

Once you start to expand, though, I think incorporation makes more sense for several reasons.

1. It is easier to deal with banks and other financial institutions in obtaining lines of credit and other sources of capital.
2. Most corporate customers would rather do business with another corporation. It gives an aura of stability and prosperity.
3. One of the best ways to reward key employees in a growing, profitable corporation is to award them shares of the company. Obviously that's impossible if you're the sole owner.

Thus as a practical business matter, once the company has grown beyond two or three people, it pays to incorporate. Which leads right back to our previous question—a C or an S corporation?

Having Your C and Eating It Too

As it turns out, the dilemma can be neatly solved by having *two* corporations, one C and one S. Pay yourself a normal salary—what someone in your profession with your experience, education, and abilities would earn if you worked for someone else—in the C corporation, and take all those deductions and benefits to which you are legally entitled: fringe benefits, pension benefits, and lower tax rates on the first $50,000 of profits. Buy most of your equipment through that corporation as well.

Then move your funds around so the rest of your profits show up in the S corporation. You can arrange this by cross-billing for services, providing they are at market rates and you can convince the IRS that these are for real services provided—such as rent, secretarial service, etc.—and not just a sham for tax purposes. Then pay a maximum rate of 33 percent on the remaining profits through your S corporation.

Do I do it this way? Of course.

There are a few limitations that you should keep in mind, however.

1. No matter how many corporations you form, your pension plans are limited by the overall amount that can be set aside in a Keogh. The IRS definitely will not permit you to have two pension plans just because you have two corporations. However, if you and your spouse file income tax returns separately, you can set up a pension

plan for each of you, effectively doubling the deduction.

One problem here is that in most cases if you deduct the pension benefit payments for you and your spouse, you have to offer similar benefits to other employees of the corporation. However, you can, under certain circumstances, set up a separate corporation with only two employees, while running the larger corporation without a pension plan. I've discussed how to set up your pension plan in the previous chapter.

2. You can only use the 15 percent marginal tax rate on the first $50,000 once, no matter how many corporations you set up. Otherwise some hotshot entrepreneur would set up a whole raft of dummy corporations and pay only 15 percent on his total profits. The IRS outlawed this one way back in 1953.
3. Make sure you have a foolproof paper trail. Don't just switch $20,000 from one bank account to the other to make the balance come out right at the end of the year; the IRS will see right through that one. Plan ahead. Issue invoices between your two companies, treating them as two entirely separate entities. And make sure services are always billed at market rates.
4. It helps if there is some distinguishing feature between the two companies; you don't want to name Corporation A Amalgamated Milkshakes for the First $50,000 of Profits and Corporation B Amalgamated Milkshakes for Profits Over $50,000. I keep my economic forecasting services and my investment advisory services in separate companies; that's not only legal, it makes sense to the IRS auditors.

Pros and Cons of an ESOP

I mentioned earlier that you can also reduce your tax burden by forming an *employee stock ownership program* (ESOP). However, that's not the main reason for taking this step. This concept was originally developed by Louis Kelso and championed in the U.S. Senate by Russell Long, son and originally namesake of Huey Long, who ran on a "share the wealth" program during the 1930s. The original idea was one of "people's capitalism"; let employees own stock in the company where they work. They will boost productivity and profitability, and the fruits of capital will be shared by labor.

As it turns out, most employees aren't so interested in the burdens of ownership. The difference between profitable and unprofitable firms is largely good management rather than profit sharing, so the original concept has faded. To encourage companies to consider this option, however, Russell Long persuaded Congress to vote certain tax benefits for those that set up ESOPs, and they survived the Tax Reform Act of 1986.

The basic idea is that a corporation can put stock valued at up to 15 percent of the employee's annual compensation into his or her pension plan—and take a tax deduction for that contribution, even though it represents no cash outlay on the part of the firm. This is the main added inducement to sharing the wealth with your employees, although there are a few smaller tax benefits as well.

Kelso and Long thought their "share the wealth" program would apply mainly to large industrial complexes, but the way the law is written, it could also apply to very small corporations—all the way down to single-owner companies. In that case, however, you would merely be transferring stock from yourself to yourself. Is it worth it?

The answer lies in the possible tax breaks. Suppose your corporation—of which you are the sole owner and employee—has gross revenues of $150,000, expenses of $50,000, and pays you a salary of $75,000. Ordinarily this would mean pretax profits of $25,000 and an income tax bill of $3,750.

However, suppose you put 15 percent of your salary, or $11,250, into your corporate pension plan in the form of corporate stock. The corporation's pretax income would drop to $13,750 and its income tax to $2,062.50—for a savings of $1,087.50. As the corporation grew, the savings would rise more than proportionately because the corporate tax rate rises to 25 percent from $50,000 to $75,000 of net income and to 34 percent above $75,000. Thus if the corporation had pretax profits of $350,000 and your salary was $200,000, the annual tax benefit would be $10,200. Meanwhile, since you're merely transferring the stock to yourself, you're not diluting your control.

What are the disadvantages to this scheme, which appears to reduce your tax bill at no addition cost?

1. The IRS is still testing the concept of one-person ESOPs in the courts—so far to no avail. However the ruling could still be overturned—retroactively.
2. In a large, publicly traded corporation, the value of the stock is easily determined. But in a one-person corporation, someone has to place a value on the stock, and in general it can't be you. The CPA's fee may equal or exceed the tax savings for small corporations.
3. If you do add employees, pension plans cannot discriminate against them, so they too will be entitled to stock equivalent to 15 percent of their compensation. In spite of the fact that the original idea of ESOPs was to widen ownership of the corporation, you may not want to do that.

My view of ESOPs is that they are an extremely useful tool for those who really do want to distribute their stock to valued employees. But strictly as a tax gimmick, I'd say the pluses and minuses were fairly evenly weighted, and I wouldn't rush into one just to save the tax dollars.

GROWING THE COMPANY

At this point I'll assume that you have started on your own, incorporated the business, and after some initial rocky years, are now solidly profitable. Now comes the next major step: To expand the company, you need capital in addition to what can be generated internally.

This is a completely different proposition from the venture-capital start-up situation, where the few firms still in business require both arms and legs and most of your teeth before they will fork over more than a dime. I wouldn't say you can cut your own deal, but many of these so-called venture-capital firms will show great interest in providing additional growth capital in return for a fairly modest proportion of the company, by which I generally mean somewhere between one-fourth and one-third.

Three "Offers" Equals One Deal

Remember one useful rule of thumb: Three offers equals one deal. If you talk to a number of venture-capital firms for second-stage financing and only one of them produces an offer, the chances are very high that you'll never see the money. Most of the time they'll find some reason to back out at the end.

Here again I speak from personal experience. Once I was trying to raise second-stage financing for one of my companies, and the deal on the table was $2 million for 40 percent of the company. I thought the percentage was a bit steep, but we had the deal all worked out and I had stayed late on a Tuesday evening to go over all the details with the company's lawyers. The closing was set for Friday morning. At 9:00 A.M., the deal was still on. At 10:00 A.M., when I was just about to leave for the airport, they called back and said it was off. No reason; they had just changed their minds.

The name of the company that pulled this little stunt was American Express, and the deal was far enough along that later that day a reporter from the *Wall Street Journal*, working from independent sources, called me to verify that it had gone through. So it wasn't just my imagination.

I still carry my American Express card. I actually tried a Diner's Club card for a while, but I took some important clients out to dinner and there was a barely suppressed snicker when I paid the bill, so I decided not to be a sore loser and went back to the standard method of payment. Although I wasn't overjoyed about the way the deal worked out, I ignored my own rule of thumb—three offers equals one deal. In this case the American Express offer was the only one I had received for this particular deal. As it turned out, I was probably better off without American Express, because a friend managed to round up $750,000 for me in a complicated tax-shelter deal without my having to give up any of the company, and I borrowed the rest. But when I did this deal, I was fairly well known. In general, these rescue operations can't be counted on. Besides, those types of tax-shelter deals don't exist anymore.

I mention this episode not to show what ogres they are at American Express—well, not entirely anyway—but to stress to any would-be entrepreneur that the money becomes yours precisely at the instant when their check is deposited, and not one second sooner. I have known several promising companies that were wrecked by failing to observe this most basic rule: Don't spend it until you have it.

The other possibility is an initial public offering (IPO)—raising money through the stock market. Unfortunately, this isn't cheap. Legal bills can easily run $250,000 to $500,000, and you have to spend days of your valuable time dotting every *i* and crossing every *t* for the SEC. Even more important, the underwriter has the absolute authority to abort the offering the day before it is scheduled if in his sole wisdom market conditions are not appropriate. If this happens, you're out the quarter or half million, and it's your tough luck.

Of course, many companies have gone public and become spectacular successes. Generally, however, that's the *next* stage of development. In fact, the investors who supply additional capital once you have reached profitability can help an IPO go more smoothly later on. They are familiar with the IPO process and are much less likely to be sandbagged because their money is at stake, too. But trying to raise capital when you first become profitable through an IPO is a very risky step, and not one that I recommend.

This sounds more like a list of don'ts than of do's, but that's because raising money for a small, growing company is a delicate operation. It would be a terrible shame to work hard for several years, nurse the company to profitability, and then see your efforts go down the drain simply because you miscalculated new sources of funding.

Thus my advice in this second stage of the company's life cycle is to postpone IPOs and work with the venture-capital firms—but negotiate with several of them, and always have two backup offers in case your first choice has a change of heart. If you don't have any backup offers, my guess is that you don't have a deal.

Valuing the Company for Further Expansion

Let's assume that you're fortunate enough to have several offers. How much of your company should you offer for the additional capital you receive?

There are two ways to figure this, based on the current status of the company or its expected growth rate.

Let's take an example. Suppose your little company has sales of $1 million and profits of $100,000. For a company whose earnings are not growing, most buyers would assign a value of $1 million. However, I assume that at this stage the company is growing rapidly or there would be no point in raising money for expansion.

Suppose you can reasonably expect the company to grow at 25 percent per year for the next decade. That means the company increases 10-fold in 10 years. In my opinion that is the maximum reasonable growth rate to put in the business plan. One usual rule of thumb in the stock market, which I'll discuss in greater detail in the next part of this book, is that for rapidly growing companies, the growth rate is approximately equal to the P/E ratio. So assuming you can get the prospective investor to agree on the likelihood of a 25 percent growth rate, your company should currently be valued at $2.5 million.

The amount of money you need to raise will then determine how much of the company you should give up. If you need $500,000 in capital, be prepared to hand over at least 20 percent of the stock—and, as I'll explain below, up to 33⅓ percent. If the investor wants a substantially larger proportion, he doesn't really think the company will grow that fast. Either he's right, and you need to do some retooling of your own plans, or he takes you for a sucker, in which case you're clearly better off with another investor.

To look at it from the investor's viewpoint, suppose profits do increase 10-fold in ten years so the company is then earning $1 million. If earnings are flat after that point, the total value of the company would be $10 million. However, it's more likely that although growth will have eased, the company will still be expanding at a normal rate, in which case the

P/E multiple would be about 15. That is a standard number used by many venture capitalists. It means the company would be worth $15 million, and the 20 percent share owned by the investors is worth $3 million. Under those assumptions, they have received an annual rate of return of 20 percent.

In fact, that would be a very superior rate of return judged against most other assets, but many venture capitalists will tell you they require a 25 percent annual rate of return, which means their share would be worth $5 million. In that case they would need to start with one-third of the company for their $500,000. I think that's a little piggy, but it's not outside the range of what reputable venture capitalists demand.

Of course, the actual proportion of your company that you hand over depends on the actual profits, sales, expected growth rate, and amount of capital needed. However, these numbers can be plugged into the formula given below to see whether the offers you receive are in the ballpark. Remember, these are for financing when the company is already solidly profitable but too small to take public without a great deal of risk.

A. The minimum fraction of the company you should offer would be: Amount of financing required divideed by (current profits × expected growth rate), where the growth rate is expressed in percent.

B. The maximum amount to give up should be: Amount of financing required divided by (current profit × average P/E ratio of stock market).

In our example above:

$$\text{A.} \quad \frac{500,000}{100,000 \times 25} = \frac{1}{5}$$

$$\text{B} \quad \frac{500,000}{100,000 \times 15} = \frac{1}{3}$$

Unless you expect your company to grow at a below-average rate—in which case you shouldn't be trying to raise financing at all—the share you give up will be larger under the second formula than under the first.

CASHING IN SOME OF YOUR CHIPS

Up to this point you have not really enjoyed the monetary benefits of your own company. Yes, you have received an adequate salary and some very pleasant fringe benefits, and have earned the psychic income from seeing your own creation grow and prosper, but have not cashed in on the big time yet. However, the company is now earning $1 million or more per year after taxes, and it is time to convert some of that earning power into your own personal income. Maybe you would like to enjoy some of the finer things in life, or would simply feel more comfortable with some diversification. In any case, you would like to sell some or all of your stock.

If the company has grown to the point where it is generating at least $1 million per year after taxes, that usually implies sales of over $10 million—the threshold at which there starts to be real interest buying in your company, either for an IPO or a sale to a much larger company.

In many cases the standard opening offer you receive will be one times sales, or 5 times cash flow, or 10 times after-tax profits. There are a lot of sharks around who figure that you may be tired of running the business and want to cash out, and are not shy about offering you bottom dollar for it. Tell those guys to go stuff it.

If you can play the part of the reluctant seller, so much the better, whether you are dealing with a small entrepreneur or the mightiest bank. You could do far worse than emulate what one entrepreneur allegedly told J. P. Morgan: "I did not come to sell. I heard that you wished to buy."

Most of the time, assuming your company is peaking and is no longer in the red-hot growth phase, a good price would be 2 times sales, or 10 times cash flow, or 20 times earnings. Once in a great while, someone who apparently flunked elementary finance will offer 30 times earnings. While still pretending to play the reluctant seller, don't let that guy get out the door.

All these rules of thumb hold for what I would call low-tech, or at least medium-tech companies. For truly exciting new discoveries, there are no set rules. Genentech went public at a price that was about 500 times earnings. It was considered so awesome that the Massachusetts state commissioner would not sanction the stock for sale in that state. Always looking out for the welfare of the citizens in Massachusetts, yes they are.

Admittedly, the chance to take your company public at 500 times earnings—or even 100 times earnings—is almost like getting money for free, and it would be a foolish entrepreneur to turn down that kind of financing. But most of the time the deals are much more prosaic and going public is a mixed blessing. Your paperwork burden increases geometrically, you are subject to all sorts of crank stockholder suits, and in many cases, the cost of the capital you raise, including paying the lawyers and the brokerage houses that sell the issue, may well be higher than the cost of borrowing funds.

I never took a company public, so maybe I'm slighting the advantages it offers. However, I know a number of people who have gone this route, and most of them are dissatisfied with the results. In fact, many of them end up going private again after a few years. Some who didn't got taken over by an unfriendly monster, and while the value of their stock rose, they were unceremoniously ousted from the company after the buyout and left on the sidelines to watch their life's work go down the tubes.

You have several options apart from going public. First, if you want to continue expanding your company, and you already have a solidly profitable firm, it is usually possible to raise equity capital without having to go public. Second, if you want to get your money out to launch another career or simply retire, that's fine, too. Sell the company to someone else and enjoy spending or reinvesting your hard-earned assets. Third, if you want to diversify by cashing out some of your assets, you can sell a minority interest to one or a small group of investors. However, going public while retaining ownership and control seldom works. Especially in this day and age of hostile takeovers, the founder far too often ends up embittered by the results.

PASSING THE COMPANY ALONG TO THE NEXT GENERATION

We're now at the final stage of the life cycle, assuming you have retained control of the corporation. You have carefully nurtured the company for many years but are now near retirement age—and know you can't take it with you.

The worst possible thing is to do nothing. Uncle Sam will come along, after you've spent a lifetime building up these assets, and put his grubby paws in the pot for 55 percent of everything you've accomplished. Just because you happen to have passed away.

Assuming that your estate planning is in order, you still have to make a basic decision: Do you want to pass the company along to the children, or would you rather sell the company at its peak value and turn over the maximum value to them while you're still alive to see it?

This is often the most difficult question of all for many longtime owners and entrepreneurs, but it cannot be answered intelligently without a thorough understanding of the estate tax law. That is not only the most complicated but the most important part of the tax code to understand, lest you forfeit over half your lifetime earnings to your natural adversary—the IRS. Before turning to this issue, it is first necessary to review the basic structure of wills, trusts, and estate planning.

Chapter 13

You Can't Take It with You—
But You Don't Have to
Leave Half of It to Uncle Sam

ESTATE TAX RATES ARE TOO HIGH—
BUT YOU CAN AVOID THEM

Throughout this book I have repeatedly stressed the benefits of using the tax laws to your advantage, pointing out how you can soften the blow of marginal tax rates ranging from 31 to 43 percent by using tax-free or tax-deferred methods. However, the biggest tax bite could still await you from the grave—an estate tax that could rob you of 55 percent of everything you have managed to save and accumulate during your lifetime.

Fortunately, with adequate planning you don't have to pay anything near that rate. For unlike the Tax Reform Act of 1986, which closed most of the important loopholes for income taxes, the estate tax code still has holes big enough to drive a truck through. But this can't be left to chance. You must plan well ahead of time.

The theory behind having an estate tax rate that is almost twice the maximum tax rate on personal income is something like this. If tax rates on earned income are too high, people will evade their tax responsibilities by using tax-deferred or tax-free sources of income; as a last resort, such as is currently the case in Sweden, they simply won't work as hard. If tax rates are too high, the fabric of society eventually falls apart. Massive cheating becomes commonplace, and the underground economy becomes larger than reported income, as has happened in Italy and Greece.

However, dead people have already made all their decisions, so no matter how much you tax them it won't affect incentives or tax evasion. Since executors and trustees are personally liable if the estate doesn't pay all its taxes, they usually pony up whatever the IRS demands. Furthermore, everyone knows, or thinks they know, some nincompoop children of some fabulously wealthy industrialist or investment banker, sitting at the poolside, martini in hand, frittering away their lives on the money Daddy left them. So when the top personal income tax rate was cut from 50 to 28 percent, no one bothered to reduce estate tax rates.

At least in my opinion this "logic" is seriously flawed in a number of places. In the first place, few of us would work to accumulate a fortune if we really thought the government was going to take it all when we passed away. Second, if the aim of taxpayers is really to punish the sybarites who live off inherited income, then tax consumption—don't tax savings. After all, these heirs might put the money to work investing in a better America; why prejudge them?

However, there is not too much point in working up a lather over the tax inequities visited upon the rich because you can still avoid paying them. In this chapter you will learn how the very rich manage to pass their fortunes down from one generation to another with very little tax penalty—in spite of tax rates that on the surface are designed precisely to ensure this doesn't happen.

First Things First: Writing Your Will

Since this book is about wealth accumulation and preservation, I will assume that everyone who has gotten this far knows that it is essential to have a will. So I won't spend much time on the details. Furthermore, if I have to convince you of the benefits of having a lawyer write your will at this point in the book, I'm reaching the wrong audience.

A will can be binding even if it is not drawn up by a lawyer. There is nothing legally incorrect about a document that says, in its entirety, "Being of sound mind and body, I leave all my worldly possessions to my wife," or, for that matter, "to my cat, Kippers."

But before even considering this option, ask yourself: How many times in my life have you given someone what were perceived as clear, unmistakable instructions, only to find out later that person had no idea what he was supposed to do. Well, it's that way when you die, only worse, because you can't come back and explain what you *really* meant. That's why, even if your beneficiaries and heirs are a model family that never squabbles about anything, it pays to have a disinterested party explain your last wishes to the court.

Of course, many families do squabble. If they didn't, most of the soap-opera industry would have to find gainful employment. But just because TV exploits these quarrels doesn't mean they don't really happen. Even if the will is worded unambiguously, relatives who are not included as beneficiaries often sue to overturn its provisions. You can specifically exclude them by name, saying they are otherwise adequately provided for, but that doesn't always work either.

Of course, your putative heirs can sue your estate even if your will was drawn by a competent lawyer, but the difference lies in having a person, not just a mute piece of paper, to represent your point of view. Most judges, who were lawyers in their former lives, are more likely to believe a lawyer than your voice from the grave. Look at it from the judge's (former lawyer's) point of view: What kind of jerk couldn't be bothered to use a lawyer, and why should I believe what he said?

You probably have a will drawn up already. If you don't, set up an appointment with your lawyer before you go on to the next section.

The Benefits of Trusts

Wills are only a necessary first step in planning the disposition of your assets in the manner you would have desired. The key to intelligent estate planning is to set up one or more trusts to distribute your assets after your demise.

Some people think trusts are only for the "rich." It's true that if you are rich, trusts are a requirement. However, they are also quite useful for those with more modest assets. The estate tax kicks in as soon as your total assets exceed $600,000, and with the value of your house and pension plan, it is surprisingly easy to exceed that limit. You may not think that a pension plan that pays a moderate $20,000 per year puts you in the upper brackets, but that could mask a principal amount ranging anywhere from $150,000 to $300,000. These days, a house worth in excess of $300,000 is far from being a mansion. Furthermore, with the inexorable movement of inflation, the real value of that $600,000 exemption will shrink significantly in the years ahead, as it is not currently indexed to inflation.

Even if estate taxes are not a concern, setting up a trust provides three major advantages for you and your beneficiaries.

1. Trusts are much harder to overturn than wills. Your last wishes have a much better chance of being honored. This is particularly true in the case of second marriages and other family complications.
2. Trusts provide for an orderly transition of your financial affairs if you become incapacitated. It could happen—a serious accident, a stroke, even Alzheimer's disease. When these tragedies overtake you, it is unfortunately all too common for unscrupulous relatives or "friends" to claim that you could not have been in sound mind when you wrote your last will and testament. Trusts also reduce the chances of an inept, court-appointed guardian squandering the money you left to your children.
3. Trusts avoid probate court, which has several benefits: you save probate fees, the money is available to your beneficiaries after a much shorter waiting period, and the terms of your will are not disclosed in public.

You are well advised to pay enough to hire a competent lawyer to work on your trusts; remember, if he or she makes a mistake, it is irrevocable. If the IRS claims your estate owes $2 million in taxes instead of $2,000, you're not around to argue your own case—and if the lawyer goofed, he'll never admit it, but will instead claim that was the way *you* wanted it.

Of course, that's not to say that the IRS won't challenge your estate; it does challenge most of the big ones. However, if your trust agreements are written correctly, you can win every time. That's because most of the fights revolve around the valuation of assets, which is one "expert" opinion against another. But you don't stand much of a chance unless the wording of the trust agreement is precisely correct.

CHOOSING THE RIGHT LAWYER

Lawyers are like people in any other profession—cab drivers, brain surgeons, baseball players, Mafia hit men, schoolteachers, etc.—in that some are better than others. That being the case, it logically follows that some are worse than others. Don't get stuck with a worse one.

Perhaps that's easier said than done. How can you tell in advance—and since you won't be around, that's the only way—that the attorney you hire is competent?

1. Perhaps most obvious, the lawyer you choose should be experienced and spend most of his time working on estates and trusts.

He (or she, but I'll use he for simplicity) should have seen hundreds of similar documents and know precisely how the IRS has ruled on key cases. No "all-purpose" lawyers need apply.

2. Before selecting the lawyer for your trust, use him for some other similar work—it could very well be drawing up a will—to determine whether he's competent, returns your phone calls, and finishes the job on time. That will tell you whether he considers you a valuable client or just someone who's brought in one more piece of paper to be processed—namely, your check.

3. If possible, I would choose a lawyer who is younger than you are so that with any luck he'll be around to administer your trust in the manner that you would have wanted.

4. Married men should have their wives meet with the lawyer. After all, statistically speaking, she will be the one to deal with him after your demise. If he treats her in a patronizing or antagonistic fashion, I'd say forget it.*

5. Don't be afraid to ask "stupid" questions. If you don't understand some clause, please ask the lawyer to explain it. Most of the time he will respond appropriately; but occasionally you will get some dimbulb who just copied the relevant sections out of the tax code, or found them in the word processor, and doesn't understand what he's doing.

6. My personal preference is to ask the lawyer, in a polite, businesslike fashion, how much it will cost to draw up the documents—then expect him to honor that fee. It's an even better sign if he volunteers the information, but if not, don't be afraid to pop the question. Lawyers ought to be able to tell you in advance approximately what their services on a trust agreement will cost.

Now that you have selected the right lawyer, let's go through how trust agreements work.

INTRODUCTION TO TRUSTS

There are so many different types of trusts that no two standard reference books agree on precisely how many there are. However, I've grouped the relevant trusts into the following major categories:

1. Trusts that do *not* reduce your estate taxes but are set up to permit you to manage your affairs better. These are usually known as

---

* Statistically, women outlive men, so throughout this section I've used the example of a man leaving his estate to his wife; obviously, the same advice holds for a married woman planning her estate.

revocable living trusts, or by the legal name, *inter vivos* trusts.
2. Trusts that take advantage of the estate tax deductions for married couples. The main types in this category are the bypass trust, marital deduction trust, and qualified terminated interest property (QTIP) trust. If the value of your estate is over $600,000, you should almost always use one or more of these trusts.
3. Life insurance trusts, where the beneficiaries own your policy. These take the face value of your life insurance policy out of your estate, while the maximum charge to the estate is only the premiums—and is often zero.
4. Trusts that arise from gifts to your family. These keep your children from squandering the gifts before they have reached the age at which, in your opinion, they will be mature enough to use the funds wisely. If you don't mind them spending the money right away, you don't need a trust. Just make a gift.
5. Remainder trusts, in which you sell someone a future interest in some asset, but you retain control of this asset until your death. This is particularly useful for passing along family businesses but can also be used for other assets.
6. Gifts to charitable organizations, in which you nonetheless retain the right to either the interest or the principal. If you simply want to bestow money on some deserving organization with no strings attached, go right ahead; you don't need any fancy legal work for that good deed.

LIVING TRUSTS DO NOT REDUCE YOUR TAXES BUT AVOID PROBATE

Just because the tax-avoidance angle is the most important aspect of estate planning doesn't mean it is the only angle. Many trusts do not remove assets from your estate at all. They are set up for other purposes, primarily to ensure that your assets go to the people who are supposed to get them.

The advantages of a revocable living trust are substantial even though it saves nothing on taxes. The principal benefits of such trusts, some of which have already been mentioned, are:

1. You are totally in control of your assets while still alive and competent. Thus your stock or bond portfolio, real estate, or other assets can be managed according to your wishes.
2. The trust provides for an immediate transition to a trustee whom you know and respect should you become incompetent. You might have a stroke that would immediately render you incapable of

making such decisions; that's the problem with putting off these decisions until it's too late.

3. Your explicit wishes are more likely to be followed after your death.
4. As the name implies, you can change your mind whenever you want, as long as you are mentally competent. Since you retain control over the assets, they remain in your estate and are subject to taxes—but as I'll show you, there are several other kinds of trusts that can be set up to avoid taxes. In general, if your estate is over $600,000, you are best off with *both* a revocable living trust and an additional trust that does reduce your taxes.
5. Your estate avoids probate court. But why is that a good thing?

The Trouble with Probate

Perhaps it seems perverse in this day and age of profuse litigation, but probate court was originally set up to benefit the estate of the deceased. The general idea was that the probate court would announce your death by public notices, at which point any alleged creditors of the estate would be required to come forth in a reasonably prompt manner and identify themselves to the court. If they didn't, no further claims against the estate would be allowed. This would save your heirs from nuisance suits by long-lost relatives with nothing better to do, or from someone claiming to have discovered only yesterday that the decedent had somehow injured him 10 years ago.

However, our court system has turned into an almost total morass, and probate court is no different. It often takes two to three years for a relatively simple estate to move through probate. In addition, there are two other major disadvantages. Because the original idea of the probate court was to publish notices of your death, your entire estate becomes a matter of public record, so all the snoops in town can find out how much you were worth and who your beneficiaries are.

Furthermore, it is not cheap. Of course, as I have stressed repeatedly throughout this book, no one performs their services for free, but in most cases probate fees are much higher than the cost of drawing up a trust agreement. The table below probate fees for California; most states have a similar schedule.

There is no way to avoid these fees; they come off the top, before your heirs get a nickel.

Thus for most people who have any more than the bare minimum of assets, avoiding probate court is a clear plus, and an excellent reason for setting up a revocable living trust even if your estate is under $600,000.

The Cost of Probate

Assets	Minimum Fees
$200,000	$10,300
$300,000	$14,300
$400,000	$18,300
$500,000	$22,300
$750,000	$32,300
$1,000,000	$42,300
$2,000,000	$62,300
$3,000,000	$82,300
$5,000,000	$122,300

Possible Disadvantages of a Living Trust

Are there any disadvantages to a living trust?

A few. First, you will have to pay a lawyer to draw up such a trust. Considering that you are *not* saving anything on taxes, that may appear to be an unwarranted expense when you are young.

Second, most states will allow you to be the trustee; if not, a close relative will often serve without pay. But if neither of these options is available, you will have to pay trustee fees, which will reduce the value of your estate.

Third, many people do not realize that any assets in a revocable living trust must be signed over to the trust. Any bank accounts, or securities accounts holding stocks, bonds, or money market funds, must also be transferred from your name to that of the trust. If you own real estate, someone must create a deed that will transfer that real estate from you to the living trust. If you have a mortgage, the lender must be notified. The title insurance company must also be informed, so it will continue to provide that insurance for the trust.

In the olden days, when you signed up for a mortgage with your neighborhood bank and it stayed there, this would not have presented a problem. However, these days, with the proliferation of mortgage-backed securities, your mortgage probably will be sold to another financial institution. Here's the rub. Many institutions won't purchase mortgages held in trust because, in the case of an irrevocable trust, the funds might not be there to service the mortgage payments, or the trust might have some stipulation against selling the property. You and I know the difference between a revocable living trust and an irrevocable trust, but some of the clerks at financial institutions don't know or don't care. As a result, it may be necessary to switch the house back from the trust to your own name and then, after the mortgage sale has taken place, switch it back again. In a similar vein, you might have trouble getting a second mortgage or home-equity loan if the house is held in trust.

So while revocable living trusts are extremely useful, they aren't perfect. My own view is that while you are still young, your estate is still relatively moderate, and your home is likely to be subject to new mortgages, you probably don't need to rush to set up a living trust. By the time you start to think about retirement, however, it should be an accomplished fact. But it isn't necessary to take this step right away. Unlike other forms of estate planning, where switching assets at an earlier age reduces your taxes, delaying the formation of a living trust won't make any difference unless you die or become mentally incompetent at an unusually early age.

A BRIEF OUTLINE OF THE ESTATE TAX CODE

1. No matter how much your estate is worth, you can always take an unlimited marital deduction. If you leave your entire estate to your spouse, no taxes are due upon your death. However, that's just avoiding responsibility, because then the entire burden of paying taxes falls on your spouse. So in my view, as well as that of tax advisers and estate planners, that's no solution at all.
2. If your total estate—equity in your home, life insurance policies, and any remaining value in annuities you might have—is less than $600,000, you will owe no estate taxes. Even in that case, probate fees could be as much as $25,000, as shown above, so it would pay to set up a trust.
3. If the value of your estate is between $600,000 and $1.2 million, the standard ploy is to set up a bypass trust, sometimes known as a credit shelter trust or family trust. This essentially boosts the estate tax deduction to $1.2 million without your having to worry about other, more complicated kinds of trusts.
4. You can give any beneficiary you choose a gift of up to $10,000 per year without its being subject to any estate or gift tax. That means if you are married, you and your spouse can give a total of $20,000 per year in gifts to each child or grandchild. This is independent of your lifetime exemption of $600,000.

If you decide to increase the size of the annual gift beyond that limit, you don't have to pay any tax then, but you are required to file Form 706 stating you have given a gift exceeding the maximum annual amount permitted. The IRS keeps track of all these forms, and after your death, will subtract all these excessive gifts from your $600,000 lifetime exemption. For that reason, few people exceed the annual gift allowance. If you want to give your heirs or beneficiaries a much bigger gift—such as a house—there are several ways to accomplish this without exceeding the annual gift allowance.

Based on this outline, it is clear that the very first order of business, providing your estate is likely to be $1.2 million or larger, is to make sure that both you and your spouse take advantage of the maximum $600,000 deduction available to each of you.

TRUSTS TO TAKE ADVANTAGE OF THE MARITAL DEDUCTION

If the total value of your estate is under $600,000, you will owe no estate taxes. Period.

Hopefully, however, that won't apply to most people who are reading this book. If your estate will be over $1.2 million, you will either have to pay some estate taxes or plan carefully to avoid those taxes. For married couples with estates worth between $600,000 and $1.2 million, though, the method of avoiding taxes is so straightforward that no one should miss it. Furthermore, there are trusts to suit every domestic scenario, from the husband who loves and trusts his wife after all these years to the one who thinks he and his spouse have grown apart but doesn't want her to starve. A separate type of trust is designed specifically for second marriages, to make sure the "wrong" set of children doesn't end up with your hard-earned money.

The basic mechanics of the law are very simple. Suppose you are married and have assets of $1.2 million. You get only a $600,000 deduction—but as noted above, an unlimited marital deduction.

In other words, even if you had $20 million, you could leave it all to your spouse without paying any taxes. That wouldn't accomplish very much, of course, because your spouse would have to pay the tax at his or her death. So the marital deduction should always be used in conjunction with setting up one of several trusts.

Consider an elderly man with a $1.2 million estate. He leaves $600,000 to his heirs—let's say, the children—and $600,000 to his wife. The money left to the children is *his* exemption. When his wife dies, she will leave the remaining $600,000 to the children; that's *her* exemption. Neither husband nor wife will pay any estate tax. Why complicate a very simple arrangement with trusts?

In fact, there are several good reasons.

First, while $600,000 may sound like a fair amount of cash if someone were to write you a check tomorrow, it's not much to live on over the next 20 or 30 years with inflation at 5 percent per year. The husband and wife may both want the surviving spouse to be able to draw on the income—and, if necessary, even the principal—of the entire $1.2 million. But not at the cost of having to pay $192,800 in federal estate taxes for the privilege. A bypass trust would permit the old man's wife to receive the benefits from the entire $1.2 million without any of it being taxed to her estate.

Bypass Trusts

In a bypass trust you put up to $600,000 of your assets in a trust that bypasses the estate, hence the name. You name the beneficiaries of the trust—quite possibly your children—but your spouse (again, it's statistically likely to be the wife) receives the income from the trust as long as she lives. She can also receive the principal in emergencies, such as extensive medical care, if the trustee deems that advisable. After your spouse dies, the principal goes to whomever you have named as the beneficiary.

If you desire, you can give your spouse almost unlimited flexibility with a bypass trust—but you don't have to. You can make her the sole trustee, permit her to make all the investment decisions, and pay herself all the income, plus the principal as needed for health care, education, maintenance, and support. Just about everything except a sable coat or Lamborghini. Furthermore, if you leave instructions, she can even redivide the money among the children, just in case one of them gets uppity after Dad has passed away.

You don't have to be that generous, though. It's also possible to set up a bypass trust that has an outside trustee with strict instructions to pass along only the income from the trust without any exceptions. It's entirely up to you.

Thus a bypass trust offers almost unlimited flexibility, yet avoids estate taxes. Unless you really think the children need the money right away, or you don't want your wife to get her hands on that much income, there is very little reason for not creating a bypass trust if your estate is over $600,000.

That $600,000 represents *your* lifetime deduction from the estate tax laws. The remainder of your $1.2 million estate, which would in any case pass to your spouse tax-free as long as she lives, is *her* $600,000 deduction. That is how you move the extra $600,000 out of the reach of the IRS at the time of death.

Now let's talk about the $600,000 you left your spouse outright. If you trust your wife's judgment and discretion about how to distribute your funds after you die, you can simply leave her the additional $600,000 without any strings attached. If you do this, just make sure her assets are placed in a revocable living trust, so they won't have to go through probate when she dies.

Many husbands, however—and wives, for that matter—choose not to leave their partners that much flexibility for a variety of reasons. If you fall into this category, you have two main choices.

1. Set up a marital deduction trust. Essentially that means your spouse gets the income from the trust and gets to name the beneficiaries but doesn't manage the money.
2. Set up a QTIP trust. The big difference here is that while your spouse gets the income from the trust, she does *not* get to name the beneficiaries. You do that before your death. QTIP trusts were essentially designed for second marriages, where you want your spouse to be well taken care of during her lifetime but also want to make sure the money goes to your children rather than hers.

Marital Deduction Trust

This type of trust is used if you want to leave your spouse enough assets to let her enjoy the rest of her life, but don't want her to be bothered with the management of those assets. That decision might be made for one of two reasons. First, your spouse may not enjoy managing money; that may have been your department. Some widows are not anxious to take a flyer in the stock market if they have never done so before. Second, it protects her from pesky relatives. If Junior wants some of the trust money so he can buy a house or take his girlfriend on a round-the-world cruise, your spouse can always say sweetly that such decisions are out of her hands.

The spouse does retain one important decision. She can name the beneficiaries of the principal of the trust when she dies. She can leave it to the children, grandchildren, charities, or any other person or organization she chooses. After all, these are now *her* assets.

Many people don't want to leave that much control in the hands of the surviving spouse—especially when it's a second marriage, or when one spouse fears the financial consequences of remarriage by the other. A special type of trust has been developed to handle precisely that situation; which is the QTIP trust.

QTIP Trusts

As noted above, QTIP stands for qualified terminable interest property. The general idea here is that your spouse gets the interest from your assets as long as she is alive, after which the principal passes to your heirs. This is different from leaving your spouse all your assets and letting her dispose of them as she wishes.

A QTIP trust therefore implies you don't trust your spouse to follow your wishes. You might have good reason for doing so; after all, not all marriages are perfect. However, QTIP trusts are most commonly used in remarriages. Let's say you got married, raised a family, became divorced, and then remarried late in life. After your death, you want your spouse to be well provided for as long as she lives, but you want the principal to pass to your children rather than hers. You set up the trust to do precisely that. If you left your second wife all your assets, she might very well pass them on to her children.

Here's a similar example from the woman's point of view. You have substantial assets, your husband dies, and you remarry a man who is considerably younger than you are. He may or may not be after your money, but why take a chance. On the other hand, you like the man well enough not to want to cut him off without a cent after you die. So you set up a trust in which he gets the income from your assets while he is still alive; after his death, the principal of the trust is distributed to your children. That way he can't squander the money, and his children, whom you can't stand, won't get anything.

REDUCING ESTATE TAXES ON STATES OVER $1.2 MILLION

For the first $1.2 million of your estate, I've shown how avoiding estate taxes is quite simple. Your $600,000 exemption is available automatically. The spouse's can be fulfilled with the bypass trust. Those who want to have control over the $600,000 left to their spouses that is not in the bypass trust can set up a marital deduction or QTIP trust. Just remember that if you leave your spouse the money with no strings attached, also leave her instructions to put these assets in a revocable living trust, so they won't have to go through probate after her death.

We now turn to the heart of protecting the bulk of your estate from the clutches of the tax man. So far these have just been preliminary skirmishes.

The game now becomes craftier—and more complicated. You must start making trade-offs: how much to transfer now, and how much to retain now and transfer later—at a higher tax rate. The object is to permit you to have maximum control over your assets and the income they provide during your lifetime but nonetheless reduce taxes to the minimum. If you simply want to give your money away with no strings attached, you don't need much tax advice.

One inviolate rule of estate planning is to transfer to your heirs those assets that are most likely to appreciate in price. That way, you pay the tax only on the value at time of transfer, while the heirs enjoy the full appreciated value. This general rule applies to growth stocks and real estate, of course, but it also applies to something you might not have thought of as an appreciating asset—life insurance.

If you take out a policy at 50, for example, it can become fully paid up with premiums of only 15 or 20 percent of the face amount. In other words, $150,000 or $200,000 will buy a policy worth $1 million at death, since actuarially you are likely to live to be about 80.

Since we covered life insurance in Chapter 10, this probably isn't much of a surprise: if you invested $150,000 or $200,000 on your own, it would also be worth at least $1 million in 30 years. But the difference here is that it escapes the 55 percent estate tax, which makes a tremendous difference.

Life Insurance Trusts

One common way to pass assets on to your heirs tax-free is through a life insurance trust. This is quite simple; all that is required is that the policy be owned by your beneficiaries. There are almost no catches. The only restrictions are that since you don't own the policy, you can't change the named beneficiary and you can't borrow against the cash value in the policy. But as explained in Chapter 11, since the borrowing rate is generally the money market rate these days, that's no longer a big deal.

It is possible that you originally owned the policy and then gave it to someone else. However, the tax regulations say that you could not have given it away "in anticipation of death." That turns out to be a totally meaningless phrase. After all, who other than Bob Woodward is going to ask the dead man what was on his mind before he died? Thus the courts have taken this phrase to mean "within three years of death." Some lawyers will claim there are ways around the three-year restriction, but it almost always involves a hassle with the IRS—why bother. Just don't own the policy in the first place. This is a common arrangement that your insurance salesman will be delighted to explain to you, and it doesn't cost any more this way.

Recall from Chapter 11 that a variable life policy permits you to invest your premiums in the stock market instead of in bonds or money market funds. You can earn an average of 12 percent per year without having to pay taxes on the inside buildup. Furthermore, insurance proceeds are exempt from income tax if they are paid as death benefits (as opposed to retirement benefits). If the policy is placed in a trust, and the total amount of premiums are under $10,000 per year—$20,000 per year per couple—they will fall under the annual gift exclusion. As a result, the funds transferred in this manner will *completely* escape the 55 percent estate tax rate.

You can either pay the premiums yourself or your beneficiaries can pay them. Since the premiums may be quite hefty, that may be an undue burden on them. It usually doesn't matter, because you and your wife can each give each child or grandchild $10,000 a year free of all estate and gift taxes; they could, if you wanted, use that money to pay the premiums.

This would allow you to escape tax on the inside buildup, tax on the death benefits, and tax on your estate. To see how much you would save, let's assume you started the policy at age 35, paid $10,000 in premiums every year from 35 to 65, earned the average 12 percent annual rate in the stock market, and you lived until 80.

If you invested the funds on your own, paid income tax on capital gains and dividends, and then paid the 55 percent estate tax, your heirs would end up with $1.73 million. If you buy a life insurance policy with the proceeds, even if you pay the entire first year's premium as a sales commission and an unreasonably high 7 ½ percent of the premium thereafter—both of these are near the top end of the scale—your heirs would end up with $9.94 million. Triple taxation has taken 82.5 percent of your money.

You might question this arithmetic, wondering how life insurance could be such a wonderful deal. It isn't that life insurance per se is so wonderful, but that triple taxation is almost confiscatory. By the time you are 65, the tax-free inside buildup means your accumulated savings are worth $2.2

million instead of $1.1 million, even with the sales commissions and management fees. Inside buildup then continues to work in your favor until you are over 80. But the biggest difference occurs at the end, when the dead hand of the IRS scoops in and takes 55 percent of the proceeds.

And now you know why rich people buy life insurance.

In spite of this tremendous difference in after-tax returns, many of the best-selling books on financial planning will tell you to avoid non-term life insurance. I don't know why. My guess is that most of these books were originally written in the 1970s, before variable life existed and when policies earned only 4 percent per year, and the material has never been properly updated to reflect the changes in both the life insurance industry and the tax laws. However, after the Tax Reform Act of 1986, virtually all of the tax shelters fell, yet the life insurance industry emerged almost unscathed.

Maybe you just don't like life insurance salesmen, but in my experience they are no more dishonest than bankers, attorneys, tax accountants, or other financial professionals—or, for that matter, authors who write out-of-date guides to financial planning.

To summarize the reasons for buying life insurance, there's nothing wrong with buying enough insurance to let your loved ones continue to live comfortably if you die prematurely. Also, carrying some life insurance to pay estate taxes on illiquid assets is often a good idea if you are holding such assets at your death. But the main reason that wealthy people buy life insurance is to reduce their estate taxes. It's as simple as that.

If your estate is so small that you will pay little or no estate taxes, buying life insurance is a marginal decision. But once you throw in the 55 percent estate tax rate, the differential is insurmountable.

Gift Trusts

The government, in its infinite largesse, allows you to give anyone you choose $10,000 per year free of any additional tax. After that, you must file a gift tax return, as noted above.

One might think gifts would not require a trust. Usually they don't. The trust aspect comes into play only when you don't want the children to spend the money right away.

In the case of minors—children under 21—the law makes it easy. You put the money in a Minor's Section 2503(c) trust, and they can't get their hands on it until they're 21, at which point they get it all.

Now you and I were quite mature at age 21 and didn't squander money recklessly, but we're not so sure about our children. We would like to dole it out to them piecemeal until they reach some more advanced age. That requires you to set up a different kind of trust, known as a Crummey trust.

No, that is not an aphorism hung on it by a disgruntled IRS ex-commissioner. That is the name of the party who sued in tax court and won.

A Crummey trust is actually an odd hybrid. It stipulates that whenever you put money in the trust, you must give the beneficiaries the option of withdrawing that money within some reasonable period of time, usually 30 days.

If your children have the option of withdrawing it, why bother to go through the trust arrangement at all? Just hand them the cash and hope they say thank you.

In spite of the legal language of the Crummey doctrine, you can certainly make it known to your children that you expect them to leave the money intact for a while. Also, it may well be that you are a better money manager than your children, and while they are busy following 20something pursuits, you are astutely building their asset base. Many children can accept that logic; if they don't, you could drop a hint or two that you won't be so generous next year.

Nonetheless, a Crummey trust is of limited usefulness. For one thing, it is limited by the $10,000 annual contribution, which is not exactly small change but will not provide much help in avoiding taxes on estates of $5 million or more. Finally, once the money has been bestowed, you get no further monetary benefits from the transaction. All of these drawbacks, however, can be finessed with other types of trusts.

Remainder Trusts

We now come to an extremely important concept in estate tax law known as, "remaindered interest." There are several types of trusts that use remainders, including standard remainder trusts, charitable remainder trusts, and the colorfully named GRIT—grantor retained interest trust. But the basic concept is the same in all cases.

A remaindered interest is the part of the asset that will remain after your death. What happened to the rest of it? From a tax-law viewpoint, you spent it.

Suppose you are 50 years old and have $100,000. You make an agreement with one of your beneficiaries that you will pay yourself 8 percent of the principal each year until you die. How much of the principal will be left, assuming you live for the standard number of years?

The first year you would take $8,000; the next year, 8 percent of

$92,000, the third year 8 percent of $84,640, and so on. By the (average) time of your death, the principal would have dwindled to $15,257. That amount is known as the remaindered interest. That is what you give or sell to your beneficiary.

However, you continue to receive the income from that asset for a number of years, perhaps as long as you and your spouse live. In figuring out the value of that asset for estate tax purposes, the IRS *subtracts* its estimate of the income you will have received and only levies the tax on what they calculate as the remaining principal. Meanwhile, it is usually the case that the asset you have transferred has significantly increased in value; the IRS tables do not take appreciation into account. The earlier you transfer the asset, the more you save on estate taxes. As a result, your estate taxes can be reduced to almost nothing.

There are various types of remaindered interest trusts, but just to give you a flavor of the saving, consider the following example. Suppose you have already struck it rich by the time you reach 50 and would like to transfer assets worth $5 million. According to the IRS tables, the estate will be subject to tax on only 15.3 percent of the total cost, which would be $763,000. Assuming you haven't already diluted your lifetime exemption of $600,000, that means only $163,000 is taxable, with a total tax bill of just under $43,000.

Now let's assume the gift was in stock, which appreciates at the average rate of 12 percent per year. According to the mortality tables, you should live about 30 more years, so the $5 million will be worth an even $30 million. You have transferred $30 million worth of assets to your children at a total estate tax of $43,000—or a tax rate of 0.00143. Congratulations!

That's not the end of the good news. In addition, you are entitled to receive all the income from that $5 million as it appreciates over time. So in this case you can eat your cake and your heirs can have it, too. The only loser is the IRS, which probably will not upset too many readers.

You can use a remaindered trust to your advantage at any age, although obviously the benefits decrease with advancing age. But even after retirement, the benefits are substantial, as seen from the below table.

This doesn't have to be a young person's game, although being young helps. Even if you don't get around to setting up a remainder trust until you are 60, you'll still protect three-fourths of the principal from estate taxes, plus all of the appreciation. Remember, you will still get all the interest, dividends, or profits until you die. Assuming you plan carefully, transferring a remaindered interest almost completely wipes out your estate tax.

Your age	Proportion you are assumed to receive during the rest of your life	Value of remainder (subject to estate tax)
20	97.4%	2.6%
30	95.5%	4.5%
40	91.6%	8.4%
50	84.7%	15.3%
60	74.5%	25.5%
70	60.5%	39.5%
80	43.7%	56.3%
90	28.2%	71.8%

Of course, any time you have whisked almost $16.5 million—55 percent of $30 million—out from under the eyes of the IRS, they will go over the transaction with the finest-tooth comb they have. If you take a questionable deduction that costs the IRS $800, they might decide not to waste too much manpower if the offense wasn't blatant. But $16.5 million is bound to attract their attention. So while I have called this method to your attention and described the basic principles in this book, I haven't included the myriad of details that vary in almost every case. You really need the high-powered legal talent team on this one—if you are fortunate enough to be in the $5 million-and-up bracket. But even at a cost of several thousand in legal fees, it's clearly much too good an opportunity to pass up.

Making $5 million isn't easy for most of us. But once you have reached that milestone, at least you can keep it from the further clutches of the estate tax man. You can fully enjoy the benefits of the income from those assets, knowing that your heirs will receive virtually 100 cents on the dollar.

Charitable Trusts

Some people enjoy giving away their assets to charitable institutions. The world is a better place because of these people, and the generous instincts are appreciated by the beneficiaries. But not everyone is motivated purely by altruism. You will not be surprised to hear that in most cases, tax considerations are the major motivating force behind these generous bequests.

Many charities have bemoaned the fact that people became less generous with donations from their current income after 1986, when the top marginal rate dropped from 50 to 28 percent. But since the top estate tax rate stayed at 55 percent, there has been no drop-off in death bequests. Besides, if you play your cards right, you can get both an income tax deduction and an estate tax deduction, and yet retain control over either the income or the principal from that gift.

There are two major kinds of charitable trusts, providing you want to retain some beneficial interest; if you want to give your money away with no strings attached, you don't need me or anyone else to tell you how to do it. One kind is called a charitable lead (or income) trust, in which you disburse the income to your favorite charity for a period of up to 20 years and your heirs then get the principal back. The other kind is called a charitable remainder trust, in which the beneficiaries get the income and the charity eventually gets the principal. That is similar to the remainder trusts we just discussed, although in this case it is the charity, rather than your heirs, that eventually winds up with the principal.

I don't think much of charitable lead trusts; they seem to be neither fish nor fowl. Even if your estate gets a full deduction, the income over 20 years' time would come to much more than the tax savings. And as far as the charitable institution is concerned, while it will presumably be grateful for a while, having the income yanked out from under its feet after 20 years is not the sort of gesture that makes a lasting impression. So I wouldn't spring for this type of setup.

The charitable remainder trust, on the other hand, has a great deal to recommend it. In the first place, you can make the bequest while you are alive and well, enjoying many years of both tax benefits and gratitude from the organization. Under most circumstances, you get both an income tax deduction in the year you originally make the bequest, a further income tax deduction if you split the income with the institution during your remaining years, and an estate tax deduction when you die. Furthermore, you and your spouse can receive part or even all of the income from this trust until your deaths. An ideal time to initiate such a trust might be if you had just sold your company and had received a very large amount of income within one year. (No, I didn't do this, but I have friends who did.)

Of course the downside is that after your death the assets don't go to your heirs. But that may not be such a bad solution. If you want to leave Junior enough to keep him comfortable but not so much that he can play the ponies for the rest of his life, you might very well consider splitting your wealth up this way. You get plenty of income during your lifetime, roughly equivalent to what you would have if you invested the money yourself; the charitable organization receives the money after your death and, if you are into such things, names a building or institute after you; the government gets little or nothing. It's a three-way triumph.

If you form a charitable remainder trust, it is clear enough that you are giving away the principal, and you receive an income tax deduction for that beneficence. However, if you set up a remaindered trust in which the beneficiary is not a charity, the rules become more complicated.

If you *give* your heirs a remaindered interest in some assets, the IRS will only allow you to set up a trust for 10 years; otherwise rich families could simply pass wealth from one generation to the next by mandating that their children pass along the remaindered interest early in life. Alternatively, you can *sell* your heirs a remaindered interest, providing they can afford to buy it. This could almost completely wipe out your tax bill.

Remaindered Interest of Gifts

Grits may be something you eat with your bacon and eggs in the South, but in the context of this chapter GRIT stands for a grantor retained income trust. Furthermore, this strategy is particularly appropriate for those who are in their later years; it doesn't require planning way in advance.

Suppose both you and your wife are 65. You take $1 million in securities and place them in a trust for your children, but your wife receives the income from the trust for 10 years. The trick here is you don't have to pay any estate or gift tax on this particular transaction because the IRS requires you to pay taxes only on the remaindered interest. Like other types of remaindered trusts, the IRS will calculate the split for you. Its calculations are based on recent interest rates plus the assumption that the trust would be used up in 10 years, which you don't actually have to do at all. Using an interest rate of 8 percent, that means that about 60 percent of the amount is deductible and you pay taxes on only 40 percent. In the case of the $1 million GRIT, if there had been no other distributions to heirs, the entire amount of $400,000 would be free of estate taxes.

In fact this would be a reasonable way to provide income for your wife during your retirement years, but in some cases the two of you have other sources of income and won't need additional funds, so you can use this purely as a tax device. Let's do the arithmetic and see how it comes out.

We'll think big here, and talk about creating a GRIT for $10 million.

Let's also assume it's invested in stocks earning the usual 12 percent market rate. Of course, you have to pay income tax of up to 33 percent on capital gains and dividends. Here's the trade-off: Pay your gift tax now on a portion of that $10 million, and let the rest grow free of estate taxes, or let the whole amount accumulate and pay a 55 percent tax on the total amount 10 years from now.

Under Plan A, you pay 55 percent of $4 million, or $2.2 million. That leaves $7.8 million to invest, which earns 8 percent per year after income taxes. So you end up paying a $5.6 million estate tax on $16.8 million capital, or a rate of 33 percent, instead of 55 percent. The arithmetic would be just the same for $25, $50, or $100 million. That's some relief but not much.

The 1990 tax laws lessened the advantages of GRITs, saying the trust—owned by your heirs—has to pay you an annuity. That provides you with some income for the next 10 years, but if you don't need the money, it ends up back in your estate, subject to the 55 percent tax rate again. An 8 percent annuity would total $6.24 million over 10 years, on which $3.43 million of the estate taxes will be due.

Are there any other disadvantages to GRITs?

Yes—two, and they both depend on when you die. Suppose you live into your eighties or nineties. Then the bulk of your assets are gone, and you can't retrieve them unless you ask your children for charity. Of course, you can always set aside a reasonable amount and place only part of your assets into a GRIT.

The second disadvantage is more serious. Suppose your spouse dies before the 10-year trust has expired. Even if it's only one day earlier, the *total amount* will be included in her taxable estate. That's not usually what is meant by the "high cost of dying," although in that case it would be quite expensive.

About the only way to insure against this happening is to buy a 10-year term insurance policy for your spouse. Assuming she is in good health, it will cost about $10,000 per year per $1 million of insurance, or in the case of a $10 million fund, $1 million for the 10 years. In other words, the insurance premium against a possible $7.1 million in tax savings is about $1 million. You'll have to make that decision yourself, based on the health of your spouse and on family histories. I'm just pointing out the options that exist.

PASSING ALONG THE FAMILY BUSINESS

This is one of the toughest decisions of all. First, it often involves deciding whether or not to perpetuate a business that you built from scratch. You have to decide in advance whether your heirs will turn it into General Electric, General Motors, or General Collapse. Second, in many cases, the amounts are much bigger than any of your other bequests. Third, the IRS just cannot sit still on the matter, and keeps changing the laws every year. Indeed, the relevant part of the tax code, known as section 2036(c), was completely written in the 1990 tax revisions. So while what follows here is the latest information, bear in mind that the IRS usually needs a couple of tax decisions to clarify what Congress meant to say. So check with your tax attorney before doing anything definitive based on the latest legislation.

Because each situation is different, even an entire book couldn't describe all of the various possibilities. However, I will assume the following ground rules. You started a business many years ago, it became quite successful, and you are now ready to retire. You would like to pass the business on to your children—if that's not the case I would advise selling it, paying the capital-gains tax, and bestowing most of the proceeds through GRITs or other remaindered trusts. Assuming you're 60 when you make this decision, and the assets appreciate by 12 percent per year over the next decade, that will cut your estate tax rate from 55 to about 10 percent. This is neat and clean, and the IRS will never come after your estate and say your company was undervalued because by definition you sold it at its current market value and paid your taxes on the gain.

However, if you want to pass the company along to future generations, you will have to take your chances with the IRS. You may win, although recent cases suggest that a fight is almost guaranteed. But to understand the pitfalls, first let me explain how it used to be done in the old days. Your company issued two classes of stock, common and preferred. You retained ownership of the preferred stock and gave the common stock to your heirs.

Let's suppose at the time of this stock disbursement that your company was earning $500,000 per year after corporate income taxes. You issued 100,000 shares of preferred stock, each of which paid a $5 annual dividend, and 100,000 shares of common stock. Since the preferred stock dividend used up all of the profits, you told the IRS the common stock was worth nothing. That way you could pass it along to your heirs without paying any gift tax. After thus distributing the stock, the company decided it needed money for expansion, so it stopped the payment of dividends; the preferred stock then became almost worthless, since it provided neither income nor capital gains.

Many years later, at the time of your death, the company is prospering and now earning $3 million per year. The preferred stock is almost worthless—and the common stock has long been transferred to your heirs. Your estate tax bill for the entire company is essentially zero.

That was a great idea, but naturally the IRS didn't care for it. So the Tax Reform Act of 1986 decreed in effect that every attempt to split stock into preferred and common shares was abusive. The act became widely known as the Section 2036(c) "freeze," with lobbyists working furiously to undo the damage from the day it was passed.

Because the 1986 IRS ruling seemed so harsh, Congress relented and undid some of the damage in the 1990 tax legislation—but not all. They continued to prohibit what many considered the principal tax-dodging element, namely that the dividends on the preferred stock could conveniently vanish as soon as you distributed the common stock to your heirs. Now any dividend on the preferred must be guaranteed over your lifetime, or your estate loses the tax advantages.

Some advisers are up in arms about this revision, claiming it defeats the ability of small family businesses to be passed from one generation to the next. I'm not overjoyed about it, but considering the options facing Congress and the IRS, it seems like a fair compromise. Some owners claim they can't afford to pay any preferred dividend because all the funds are needed for growth. If that's really the problem, borrow the money from the bank, using the preferred dividends as collateral. Or if your snotty banker turns up his nose at the idea, borrow the dividends from yourself and reinvest in the company. The courts haven't tested this newest wrinkle yet, but it seems a viable alternative to me. After all, virtually any arrangement is better than turning over 55 percent of the value of your company to the IRS after you have toiled for decades to build something worthwhile.

The current tax code still permits you to set up a remaindered interest trust and sell that part of your business to your heirs, providing you are willing to guarantee the dividend on the preferred stock. As I've shown above, this can reduce your estate tax to 10 percent or less. But there are still several risks.

1. You will naturally put as low a value on the company as you can. Since it is privately held, no one—including you or the IRS—

actually knows what its value would be if it were sold to others. You can argue that if you or your family were not running the business, it would be worth a lot less.

The IRS will *not* accept that argument, but they may be wrong. In one recent spectacular case, the Newhouse family—media scions who own Condé Nast magazines and many other entities in a far-flung publishing empire, including Random House, the publisher of this book—claimed their privately traded stock was worth about $60 million. The IRS begged to differ, claiming it was over $1 billion and wanted $609 million more in taxes and another $305 million in penalties. So the matter went to court.

Most of us who were following this case realized the IRS didn't have a leg to stand on but thought the judge would reach some compromise amount. Nosiree. He ruled that the Newhouse valuation was correct without further adjustment, and the IRS retreated with egg all over its face. So it can be done, but not without a struggle.

2. Unless it's currently worthless, your heirs have to pay for the business; in the case of a substantial business, that isn't peanuts. Even 25 percent of $5 million is $1.25 million, which your children probably don't have yet. If you make the remainder a gift, the entire business could end up back in your estate, subject to the 55 percent tax rate. So don't even consider that option unless the laws change again.

One way to resolve this dilemma is to let your heirs pay for the remaindered interest over 20 years. If you have two children, that amounts to 40 payments, or slightly over $30,000 per year. You and your wife could give them gifts of $20,000 per year, which would cover most of the expense.

However, that may not be quite kosher. The problem is that you cannot give away the remainder of the business; otherwise it's a GRIT and the trust can only last for 10 years. You must sell it to them.

You—or your lawyer, since you won't be here—could try arguing that the annual gifts had nothing to do with the remaindered interest, and you would have been just as generous even if you had not just sold the children a remaindered interest (and even though you had not previously given them gifts). Your estate might or might not win.

If your children actually do work for the company, which is a reasonable assumption if you are indeed planning to pass it along to them, the dilemma vanishes. Give them a big enough raise to allow them to pay for the remaindered interest out of that money. Of course, the IRS will take its 33 percent bite of their income, but that is a relatively minor cost.

I wouldn't advise putting your children on the payroll as "consultants" if they already have full-time jobs in other fields. The IRS will see right through that.

3. If you sell a remaindered interest in the company that's valued at $5 million, and the children later sell it at $15 million, they will have to pay 28 percent capital-gains taxes on the $10 million profit. The more you reduce the value of your company now in order to save estate taxes, the more capital-gains taxes the children may have to pay in the future. But since money is time, and since the capital-gains tax rate is only half the estate tax rate, the trade-off is well worth it.

4. Under the remaindered interest provisions, you still retain control of the business and are entitled to all the profits; I'm assuming a subchapter S corporation here, as explained in the previous chapter. However, if you do sell your children a remaindered interest, it then becomes much more difficult to change your mind and later sell the business to someone else. It can be done, but the paperwork gets very messy. You really should make an irrevocable decision to pass the business along to your heirs before selling them a remaindered interest.

5. Suppose you agree your heirs can pay for their remaindered interest over the next 20 years, but unfortunately you die soon afterward. Unless you have made alternative arrangements, the unpaid balance ends up back in your taxable estate. However, there is also a way to avoid this; it's called, not too unreasonably, a self-canceling installment note. There is also a similar instrument called a sale of a private annuity, but in my view that is inferior because if you live longer than the mortality tables indicate, your heirs will have to continue to pay you indefinitely. So we'll stick with the former option.

Essentially, the agreement works the way its name suggests. If you die, the installment note, which your heirs have signed and which requires them to pay you a certain amount for a 20-year period, is canceled. They don't have to pay you, and since they're not paying you, the money cannot be counted in your estate. The liability just vanishes. And guess who's left holding the bag? Why, it's the IRS.

Naturally the IRS doesn't think much of this arrangement and will try to overturn it if possible. Its main grounds for attack are that you knew, or had good reason to know, that you were going to die. If you signed such an agreement on your deathbed in the hospital, it simply isn't going to work. But on the other hand, if you were reasonably robust and healthy and died of causes that were not known at the time, your estate will probably prevail in court.

To review, in order to transfer your family business to the children with a minimum of estate taxes:

1. Sell them a remaindered interest—the sooner the better. You retain control until the day you die, so there is very little reason to postpone.
2. Get a low but fair valuation of the company. The IRS has gone berserk in this area and will probably challenge *any* valuation you choose, so don't think you can escape its wrath just by picking a higher valuation. However, as was shown in the Newhouse case, the IRS's methodology is suspect. As long as you pick a valuation that is supportable by generally accepted accounting principles, your estate should prevail.
3. If your children work for the company, raise their salaries to cover the costs of buying the remainder; the only penalty is the 33 percent income tax. If the children don't work for you, ask your lawyer whether the current IRS regulations are likely to permit a gift of $10,000 per year per parent to each child if it is used to buy a remaindered interest.
4. Sign a self-canceling installment note so that the unpaid balance won't return, uninvited, to your taxable estate.

If you follow these four steps carefully, make the move no later than age 60, and enlist the aid of a competent attorney, you should be able to reduce your estate tax rate from 55 to 10 percent or less, *no matter how large the estate*. The only stumbling block is having the children pay you back. If the amount is large enough, it would be worthwhile to have them work for the company. Alternatively, you can sell the remaindered interest to a larger number of grandchildren and make them a gift, although you will need several grandchildren because of the generation-skipping estate tax.

Thus unlike the income tax, where the loopholes were drastically curtailed in 1986, the estate tax can almost completely be avoided, assuming you plan carefully well in advance. However, since most of us like to save on income taxes too, I'll discuss some of the ways to minimize that burden in the final chapter of this section.

Chapter 14

Minimizing Your Income Taxes

THE DEMISE OF TAX SHELTERS

Before 1964, the top marginal income tax rate was a whopping 91 percent. As was point out at the time, if that were really true, capitalism could not have survived. In fact, that rate was mainly for show; hardly anyone paid 91 percent of their income in taxes. It did mean, though, that a knowledge of tax shelters was absolutely essential to avoid having the government confiscate virtually all of your income.

That still remained the case when the top rate dropped to 70 and even to 50 percent. However, the Tax Reform Act of 1986 was a watershed. Not only was the top marginal rate dropped to 28 percent, but virtually all major tax shelters were permanently dismantled.

As a result, most firms offering tax shelters went out of business, and the emphasis shifted from trying to avoid taxes to trying to increase your income. Of course, minimizing the distortions on work effort and investments should be one of the proper functions of any tax system. For the next three years, federal income tax receipts rose much more than the "experts" had predicted; supply-side economists were partially vindicated, although by that time no one cared. Today tax shelters are almost a dead issue, and I spend very little time on them. Indeed, sheltering your estate from the 55 percent tax rate is an order of magnitude more important than trying to beat the 28 percent marginal rate on income.

That's true for two reasons. First, 28 percent—now raised to 33 percent—isn't a particularly onerous burden, although like most people I would rather pay no taxes if given the choice.* But second, as a trade-off for lowering top rates, Congress clamped down so hard on tax shelters that virtually nothing remains. Even if you do find one to your liking, you'll probably be skewered by the 24 percent alternative minimum tax. Furthermore, many of the remaining shelters are phased out as income rises above $100,000. So if you are relatively wealthy, you end up paying a 33 percent tax rate anyway, meanwhile tying up your assets with a subpar return. It's just not worth trying to beat the system.

Not all tax shelters were mere scams; some did serve useful purposes. It is the poor and lower-middle-income people who won't be able to afford housing because of changes in the tax laws; not the rich. And while some people may feel the oil industry falls into the category of the undeserving rich, by the end of the decade we will all be paying more money for gasoline because domestic drilling and exploration declined sharply after 1986 and has never recovered. The ratio of capital spending to GNP also fell after 1986 in spite of a generally robust economy, bringing productivity growth to a standstill and hampering those who wanted to raise their meager living standards. Yes, Congress did use a meat-ax on the tax code. But that's the way it happened, and the energy used getting mad at the IRS is better spent getting ahead.

You may still get a call every now and then from one of the few surviving tax-shelter salesmen. It is just barely possible that the program you are being offered has some merit. But judge it *entirely* on the economic return; tax considerations should have a weight of precisely zero.

Losses Now Mean Losses

Since tax shelters are a dead issue, I don't want to spend much time on them; but since some people may be tempted into a sucker deal, they're worth a page or two.

One of the major accomplishments of the Tax Reform Act of 1986 was the decision that passive losses could be offset only by passive income. Before then, it was quite common for doctors or attorneys—or, for that matter, authors and lecturers—to offset their earned income from passive

* Throughout this book I have used 33 percent as the top rate. The 1991 tax tables say 31 percent. However, considering that part of your exemptions and deductions gradually disappear as your income increases at higher levels, I have calculated that a 33 percent marginal rate is a more realistic estimate.

losses in real estate, agriculture, or oil and gas shelters. I certainly did my share of investing in such "assets," as did many others.

The deals were usually structured so that you got a 2½-to-1 or 3-to-1 write-off. In other words, for every dollar of "investment" in this tax shelter, you got $2.50 or $3 of tax losses. At a 50 percent marginal tax rate, that made good sense. At a 33 percent rate, it is nonsense. So to a large extent, economics alone killed the tax-shelter business.

But just to make sure, Congress determined that those tax-loss dollars could only be offset by equivalent income from passive activities—such as rental income or income from a business you owned but didn't actively manage. The two major types of income—earned income and portfolio income (interest, dividends, and capital gains) became strictly off limits for offsetting passive losses.

Another tax benefit Congress outlawed was phantom losses. These are "paper" losses for which you never actually put up any money; often they were caused by rapid depreciation. But no more. Except on rare occasions, the only loss you can take is actual dollars out of your own pocket.

If you sign up for some deal where actual losses really do mount up, you can still get a full deduction only if you are personally at risk for these losses. That provision turned out to bite a lot of well-known economists and financiers in the neck. They had to shell out two, three, and even four times the original amount they had "invested" in a tax shelter. Nowadays you generally don't get to deduct the loss unless you actually shelled out the cash, in which case you're only getting back 33 tax cents on every dollar you lose. You'll never get rich that way.

The Four Biggies

That doesn't mean there are no ways left to reduce your tax burdens. The three big ones previously discussed are mortgage interest and property taxes on your home, your retirement plan, and the benefits of owning your own business. But I have covered each of these in detail, and there's not much to add here.

The fourth key tax deduction is one you probably won't even think about—until Congress tries to take it away, too. That is the health-care premiums paid by your employer, which are tax-free.

These four types of deductions cost the government a lot of money. In 1990, according to the Office of Management and Budget, tax collections were reduced by $51 billion because of the deduction of home-mortgage interest and property taxes; $30 billion because of the tax-free status of health-care premiums; and $61 billion because of tax deferrals of retirement plans, including life insurance. These three items total over $140 billion, or about 30 percent of all the federal personal income taxes that were collected. However, the remaining tax-avoidance schemes hardly generated any savings.

Are There Any Tax Shelters Left?

Sort of.

Low-income housing. Restoration of old buildings. A few oil and gas deals. But all other construction deals are dead. And nothing on the list is very exciting.

Here's how low-income housing works. You, or a partnership you join, agree to build some low-income housing units. Let's say they cost $100,000. You get a tax credit of approximately 9 percent, or $9,000 per year for a 10-year period. Is that a good deal or not?

Unless you have more facts and figures to work with, it is impossible to tell. I'll assume you borrowed the money; otherwise you are getting a 9 percent rate of return, which is pretty puny. The question then boils down to whether the rent you receive is enough to cover the mortgage and other expenses.

Most of the time, I would caution against such a deal. Low-income people, by definition, do not have very much money, and in most cases they are unlikely to improve their lot in life. If they don't pay, you will probably have trouble evicting them because of political pressures. If their rent is being paid by the local government, you may get your money whenever the bureaucrats feel like it. I think there are too many risks involved to earn that 9 percent tax credit—and remember, you are personally liable for any losses incurred on the project. Then, too, the credit phases out if your income is over $200,000 per year, and you get nothing if it is over $250,000 per year.

The same general comments apply to rehabilitations, except there the tax credit is only 4 percent. Under ordinary circumstances, this is a nonstarter.

Donating the Facade on Your Old House

There is, however, one curious loophole left in the tax laws—at least it existed at press time. It applies to those who happen to live in an old house in a historic district. I came across this one because we used to live in Georgetown, where many houses qualify. You donate the facade of your house to some charity, and you take the deduction for that facade. It doesn't cost you a penny, except for the costs of filing a few papers and some legal advice.

Many houses in Georgetown are in the $500,000 to $1 million range. The facade is usually valued at 10 percent of the total price of the house, or $50,000 to $100,000. You donate the facade and take a whopping tax deduction that year. Of course, you can pull this stunt only once. But it's like found money.

If you have a mortgage, check to make sure the lender approves. That's usually quite straightforward. When you sell the house, the donation gets deducted from the basis, so you would have to pay capital-gains tax on that incremental amount—unless you moved into a house of similar or higher value. Even so, delaying the tax for several years, and investing the difference in the meantime, is still money in your pocket. Unfortunately, this sort of benefit is now a rarity.

Because the oil and gas industry still enjoys some additional tax deductions for depletion allowances and intangible drilling costs—although they, too, were nicked in 1986—some advisers suggest considering investing in that industry. In this case, the economics are with you, because oil and gas prices will rise faster than inflation over the next decade. Nonetheless, there are several caveats to heed before going into one of these deals. The main two are:

1. Most depletion allowances and intangible drilling costs are *not* deductible under the alternative minimum tax, so you end up paying 24 instead of 33 percent. Hardly worth the aggravation.
2. That can be sidestepped if you buy a *working interest* in an oil and gas drilling venture instead of a *limited partnership*. Since you are now actually in the oil and gas business, it can be treated as a business deduction. But then you are subject to unlimited risk. If your partner drills a 10,000-foot hole and finds only sand and water at the bottom, you may rue the day you ever considered the investment.

Every year someone dreams up a new tax-shelter gimmick, the Congress carpet bombs it the next year, rescinding the deductions retroactively. So for the most part, the search for the elusive tax shelter these days is a waste of time and money.

Do Tax-Free Municipal Bonds Boost After-Tax Income?

It might seem that I've left out one major tax shelter: The interest on most municipal bonds—"munis"—is totally free from federal taxes. Of course, munis still exist—but here again, the advantages were reduced by economics in 1986.

Historically the yield on munis has been between 70 and 75 percent of taxable corporate bonds for comparable risk classifications; at press time, the ratio was about 80 percent. When marginal tax rates were 91, 70, or even 50 percent, munis were worth holding by the wealthy. But at 33 percent, the advantages are marginal. Also, bonds are not a good long-term investment. So why bother?

In some states and cities the marginal tax rate is considerably higher, so it might seem like a good deal in those locations. As it turns out, however, the yield on municipal bonds issued by those localities is reduced proportionately with the tax savings. No bargains there either.

I think you should avoid bonds because over the long run stocks provide an annual rate of return that's about 4 percent higher. You shouldn't penalize yourself by buying bonds for the long term.

EE Savings Bonds

Some financial advisers try to make a big deal out of U.S. government savings bonds, or EE savings bonds. If you have more than a touch of gray in your hair, you may remember buying these at school during World War II.

One of the greatest sucker plays ever perpetrated on the unaware public was the issuance of savings bonds by the government. If a private-sector institution had tried a similar stunt, the SEC would probably have sued them and asked for jail sentences. They offered a measly return of 3 percent per year if held to maturity, while at the same time the government let inflation soar to an average rate of 10.3 percent in the three years following the war. That works out to a negative return of 7.3 percent per year.

After only about 30 years of gypping the public, the rocket scientists at the Treasury woke up to the fact that hardly anyone was buying their savings bonds anymore. This wasn't a stroke of moral rectitude; it was a question of economics. As a result, they gradually raised the interest rate paid by EE savings bonds close to, but slightly below, the rates on other Treasury bonds.

Taxes are not due on the interest on EE bonds until they are cashed in, which in many cases is at the date of maturity or even beyond. That gives them the same sort of inside buildup that makes life insurance policies and retirement funds worthwhile. Furthermore, the Treasury also decreed that those who use EE savings bonds for their children's college education would not have to pay any income tax on the earned interest even at maturity. Suddenly these bonds started to look attractive, and sales picked up.

But wait a minute. The tax benefits at maturity start to be phased out once your income exceeds $60,000 per year, and they completely disappear when it's over $90,000 per year. Since this is the amount senior civil servants and congressional representatives earned until 1990, maybe they thought anyone with an income above that figure was "rich." Whatever the reason, the tax advantages are available mainly to those who can't afford to save very much. So if your income is above $60,000—or will be in future years—don't start salivating at the tax advantages of holding EE savings bonds.

SENDING YOUR CHILDREN TO COLLEGE

Before 1986, this section would have been called Sending Your Children to College at Government Expense. There were lots of clever ways of using tax shelters to shift at least half the burden of college tuition and other costs to the government. The sad news is that none of them survived 1986.

So once again, the main purpose of this section is to steer you away from scams and other money-squandering schemes.

Let me start out by saying that many financial advisers will tell you that if you put aside a relatively modest amount of money when the child is born, paying for college won't seem so painful. That's exactly right, but it's also a nonissue. Of course, you will have enough money if you save early and often. The real question is whether any savings plans that permit you to defer taxes on the buildup apply specifically to colleges. The rest is all blather.

Baccalaureate Bonds: Pay Now, Learn Later

The hot item these days is to buy what are generally called baccalaureate bonds. You invest your money in them when the children are born, and all you have to do is pay today's tuition rate and not worry about inflation. Because the money goes directly to a university or its agent, the interest accumulates tax-free. Or maybe it doesn't.

The problem, you see, is that while sending your children to college may be a noble gesture on your part, and may increase the aggregate skills and productivity of this country, even permitting us to keep up with the Japanese, there is nothing in the tax code that says saving for worthy causes entitles you to a tax break. Saving for your retirement, yes. Contributing to a charity, yes. But saving for a college education—probably not.

Some colleges and universities have claimed they should be treated as charities on the grounds they are nonprofit organizations. They have some reason for doing so; if you donate money or property to a nonprofit educational institution, you are entitled to take the income tax deduction. The problem here seems to be that if you want to donate $20,000, all well and good, but if you are using that donation as a thinly disguised substitute for a tuition payment, then it is really a payment for services received and isn't subject to any deduction. After all, if you give money to the National Gallery of Art, that's a donation; if you buy lunch at the cafeteria or a calendar at their bookstore, it isn't.

Of course the tax law is never that clear, since if a rich relative of yours chooses to make a donation to the college your children are attending equal to the amount of tuition (although not room or board), it won't count against either their $10,000 annual gift exemption or the $600,000 lifetime exemption. This helps reduce their estate tax, as well as educating your children. It does not, however, reduce the amount of income tax paid by your rich relatives that year. You see, it's not *that* type of a deduction.

That is where the matter stands. The IRS has cracked down vigorously on these schemes, including one offered by the state of Michigan, and my guess is that it has a pretty good chance of winning. If Congress thinks higher education is a worthwhile goal, then it should enact, as has often been suggested, some sort of tuition credit for the income tax. But the IRS is at least theoretically supposed to enforce the law as it is written; as it currently stands, saving for college tuition is not on the list of items that receive the benefit of inside buildup.

I'm not trying to give the IRS brownie points here. What I am trying to point out is in this case the Service has logic on its side and will probably prevail in court. As a result, I really would advise against investing your money in one of these schemes, since I don't think the tax abatements will hold up. Besides, there are several other things wrong with the plans as well.

To see what I mean, let's just suppose for the moment that the IRS lost in court and tax-free accumulation was allowed for baccalaureate bonds— a doubtful hypothesis. As these programs are now designed, you pay the current tuition fee now and you'll never have to pay another penny. The interest on the bonds will cover the increased costs of tuition as inflation soars over the next 20 years. Even with the tax advantages, they're *still* a bad deal.

Suppose you want the very best for your child—Harvard, Yale, Brown, or other schools in that elite group—and suppose your child was just born. Annual costs at these institutions are now $20,000 per year and will continue to rise at about 8 percent per year. As I showed earlier in the book, that means the four-year bill will be a neck-snapping $360,000. If you start saving now, using inside buildup at an average 12 percent rate of return in the stock market, you will have to put away $4,500 per year, or $375 a month if that sounds any better. Of course, that's per child.

Now let's compare that with what the colleges are offering. Pay us the current tuition *now*, they say, and lock in the benefits. If the IRS goes along with the tax deductibility of this scheme and doesn't question it, you fork over $80,000 when your child is born and forget all about college tuition costs in the future.

I don't know about you, but when we had our first child, being relatively young and having all those additional expenses associated with the new arrival, to say nothing of dropping from two incomes to one, the last thing I wanted to do at that particular moment was hand over an enormous chunk of cash to some university. But maybe you feel differently.

Those who don't have $80,000 lying around in ready cash might be able to borrow the money. I realize often that isn't possible either, but bear with me while we run through the arithmetic—trying to make the best possible case for these prepaid tuition schemes.

> Case A: You invest $80,000 of your spare cash, and 18 to 22 years later you use it to pay tuition. At 12 percent annual appreciation, you would have $800,000—but college tuition payments come to "only" $360,000. By transferring your money to the college at the time of your child's birth, you would be squandering more than half of what you would otherwise have earned.
>
> Case B: You borrow the $80,000, transfer the money to the college immediately, and then pay down the loan as if it were a 22-year mortgage. At a 10 percent mortgage rate—assuming you can get a home-equity loan, otherwise the arithmetic is much less favorable— your monthly payments would be approximately $8,000 per year. That's $5,760 per year after taxes if you qualify for the tax deduction, which would be the case for a home-equity mortgage that didn't exceed $100,000. However, even that $5,760 is substantially higher than the $4,500 you would set aside on your own.

It's an open-and-shut case. Because you invest in the stock market— while the college or university invests in the bond market—you are better off doing your own investing. Case closed.

I've picked numbers at the high end of the tuition scale, but if you have your eyes on a less expensive private school, or a state or municipal college or university, the arithmetic is precisely the same. It still doesn't pay.

Some people fret that the stock market won't yield an average return of 12 percent per year over the next 20 years. Maybe the economy will head into a period of much higher interest rates and inflation, which would kill the stock market for a while—such as occurred from 1968 through 1974. In that case, you could shift your assets into bonds or money market funds until inflation is beaten back, maintaining a flexibility over your investments that the university prepayment schemes don't offer. Or suppose inflation and interest rates decline and the stock market soars. You could also take full advantage of this, putting aside less than you originally figured was necessary instead of tying up your funds in bonds. Either way, you are better off managing your own assets than you would be under the inflexible pay-now learn-later plan.

Even if the tax savings were genuine, there are several other negative complications. First, suppose you have saved for years but at age 18 your ungrateful offspring informs you that he or she has no intention of going to college. Such things have happened in the past. Do you get your money back?

Don't be silly. What you get back is the original amount of your investment. You will have saved for 18 years at a 0 percent rate of interest.

Then again, your child may go to college but drop out before graduating. The problems could be academic, or they could be social. I can hardly wait for the first lawsuit from the parent of a child with prepaid tuition who gets thrown out on his ear.

A more likely scenario is that Junior doesn't get into Harvard but has to settle for Horsechester College for the Very Liberal Arts, specializing in majors in Frisbee-throwing. Harvard will transfer the money; that's not the issue. The tuition at Horsechester is much lower, so how much of your money will you get back? If you guessed a pro-rata portion based on the original investment only, instead of the accumulated interest, you guessed right.

Even if you knew where your newborn son or daughter would want to go to college and that he or she would get in and stay all four years and enjoy it, and even if you happened to have that kind of cash lying around when your child was born, baccalaureate bonds would *still* be a bad deal, because you can earn a lot more in the stock market than in the bond market, and so far, none of these schemes invests in stocks.

Other Ways to Reduce the Cost of a College Education

Presumably I have convinced you of how *not* to save for your children's college education. But are there any ways to use the tax code to reduce college expenses?

Yes, there are several ways. But most of them don't amount to much anymore.

When top marginal tax rates were 50 percent or more, managing to pay college tuitions with pretax instead of after-tax dollars lopped 50 percent or more off the total cost, although never 100 percent, as some financial quacks claimed. Now, however, the maximum you can save is 33 percent. And unlike the estate tax reductions, it doesn't come right off the top; you have to put some money aside in order to make these schemes work. So in effect, you are saving very little.

To see this, consider the two polar extremes of financing. One family has plenty of money for college education but would naturally prefer to use the tax code to transfer as much of the cost as possible to the government. The other family is strapped for funds at college time, so it has to borrow the money and would like to keep interest costs as low as possible. Most parents of college-aged children are somewhere between these two extremes, so you can mix and match the examples to fit your own situation.

CASE NO. 1. YOU HAVE THE MONEY

Consider some form of investment that provides tax-deferred inside buildup. Both variable life insurance policies and 401(k) and Keogh plans fit into this category, although generally not IRAs. You can save, and then withdraw, some of the money when the tuition bills come due. In the case of variable life, you can withdraw the cash value. In the case of 401(k) and Keogh plans, you are limited to $50,000. Unless your spouse also happens to have one of these plans, that only covers about half the bill for the "prestigious" Ivy League schools.

However, you can save using these methods in any case; there is nothing special about a college education in these plans. It's true you will have to put less aside if you start early, but that's nothing more or less than the miracle of compound interest dressed in academic robes.

Before 1986, many people shifted income to their children's trust funds, since they were taxed at a much lower rate. That hardly works anymore for several reasons. First, if your child is under 14, the income is taxed at your rate no matter who receives it. Second, for children over 14, the difference is only between 15 and 33 percent, and that applies only to the first $18,550, so you're saving no more than $3,339 per year in any case. And if you don't want your children to spend the money recklessly, you will probably have to put it in a trust and have the legal papers drawn, which is not without cost. So your savings are quite modest and hardly worth the fuss.

CASE No. 2. YOU BORROW THE MONEY
By college time you should have some equity built up in your house, for which the interest is tax-deductible up to a mortgage of $100,000. Don't go for those "low-cost" student loans unless the rate is in fact lower than the *after-tax* rate on a mortgage. Presumably you can also borrow from your 401(k) or Keogh plan at low interest rates, probably 6 to 8 percent, but that interest is not tax-deductible. The tax-deductible interest on a mortgage generally makes that the best deal.

Buying a House for Joe College

If you buy a house or condominium for your children while they are at college and claim it is their principal residence, they can rent out the other rooms and reap some small tax advantages. However, while real estate is certainly a good investment for the long run, it can be fairly risky over a four-year period; you could end up losing a bundle or having to hold the property much longer than you anticipated in order to turn a profit.

Some financial advisers tout this as a way to "free" college tuition, but you know better than that. Suppose you buy a modest condominium for $100,000 and your child and three roommates live there for four years. Assuming a normal 7 percent annual appreciation, the value has risen to $131,000, but you will probably pay about $6,000 in closing costs when you buy and $8,000 when you sell, assuming you have a normal 80 percent mortgage. That means your $26,000 investment will grow to $43,000 in four years, providing you don't get caught in a real estate recession. But your child doesn't need to go to college in order for you to make that type of investment. What are the other benefits?

You have two choices. You could treat it as *your* second residence on the grounds that a member of your family lives there. In that case you get to deduct the mortgage payments and your child lives rent-free because the roommates pay you the going market rate, which is enough to cover the difference.

Or you could simply rent it out to your child and his or her friends.

Many children don't want to be bothered with collecting rent, taking care of repairs, etc., when they're busy with college; but if they do, you can pay up to $3,100 per year in tax-free management fees, saving you a whopping $1,023 per year in taxes for bugging your offspring to collect the rent and fix the heat. And that's all the extra benefits you get outside of the normal ones you would earn from owning or renting real estate in any case. It would be a lot simpler to take the $26,000 needed for the down payment and closing costs and apply it toward tuition instead.

Deducting Tuition—Forget It

The IRS has clamped down very severely on the practice of company owners deducting their children's tuition, even if they really do work for you. An employer can set up an employee-benefit plan that allows the company to deduct tuition payments, but it's not even close. The cap is $5,250 per year and, much worse, only 5 percent of the benefits can be directed to offspring of owners and shareholders. You would have to spend 19 times as much money educating other people's children to get this measly tax benefit.

Furthermore, the IRS routinely disallows deduction of tuition payments by undergraduates who are studying for a career or profession. You would have to convince the IRS that (a) having worked for you since he was 16, Junior is already established in a career, (b) he is continuing to work for you while he is a full-time student at college, and (c) whatever he is learning will merely enable him to keep up his existing skills, not learn new ones. I think you'll agree it's not worth the effort.

I realize how college tuition and related costs can cut into your budget, particularly if your children attend the top-ranked private schools. However, the IRS has no intention of giving you any help. Except for penny-ante suggestions that will generally save you less than $1,000 a year, the only recommendations I can make are:

1. If you have wealthy relatives who plan to leave you some money anyway, pitch them on the advantages of contributing the tuition payment directly to the college or university. If you don't . . .
2. Start saving early in a tax-deferred savings plan so you can withdraw some of the money at tuition time. Under most circumstances, this can be your retirement plan unless you have an IRA.
3. If you must borrow, make sure the interest is deductible by using a home-equity loan.
4. Don't bite for prepayment plans or baccalaureate bonds. In almost all cases, the educational institution or management firm will invest

your money in bonds and earn a far worse rate of return than you could do on your own. Furthermore, it is unlikely the IRS will allow the tax deduction for inside buildup.

PAYING YOUR TAXES WITH THE MINIMUM AMOUNT OF GRIEF

The Christmas-Club Mentality

Almost everyone I know complains that their taxes are too high and the money is being squandered on all sorts of useless programs *they* would never vote for. That could very well be the case. But what puzzles me is that, at the same time, many of these people give the government an interest-free loan.

My daughter, who is (I believe) reasonably intelligent about most other money matters, routinely calls me every April or May to say, "Good news, Dad. I got my tax refund check."

Most people like the idea of getting something for nothing, but that's hardly the case with your tax refund. It just means you overpaid the government and got nothing in return all year. Except for very unusual circumstances where you are starting your own business and have a net operating loss carry-forward, you should *never* get a tax refund from the IRS. You should not pay the Service a penny more than you owe it, and you should not pay it a day sooner than is required.

Many years ago, before Congress outlawed the whole scheme, many banks used to have what they called Christmas clubs. You saved a certain amount each pay period, whether it was weekly, biweekly, or monthly. Plans varied slightly, but you started paying into your own fund at the beginning of the year and built up your savings until Thanksgiving, at which point you got to withdraw your own money and spend it for Christmas presents. For the privilege of letting you save at their institution, the banks paid depositors a *zero* rate of interest. Of course there's nothing wrong with saving your money ahead of time to buy presents; in fact, it's a pretty good idea. But why deposit it someplace that won't pay you any interest?

It's the same idea with tax refunds. Many people purposely have their taxes overwithheld so that in April or May they will receive some lump sum from the government. They claim that is the only way they can "afford" to take that summer vacation, or buy a new refrigerator or washing machine, or even put a down payment on the car. Once again, it's a great idea to put aside a little money every month so you won't always be running into debt. But why let the government hold it at a zero rate of interest? If you are worried about stock market fluctuations and may need the money quickly, why not put it into a money market fund and earn 7 or 8 percent interest?

The usual responses to this suggestion are (a) I can't save any of my paycheck, but this way I don't see it so I can't spend it, and (b) the IRS will get mad at me if the number of withholding deductions is larger than the number of actual deductions in my family.

If (a) is really the problem, talk to your employer. Explain that you have trouble saving any of your take-home pay and ask whether the company has some sort of payroll-deduction scheme that automatically debits part of your paycheck and puts it into a savings account. Most employers will be happy to oblige. If they don't, open a separate savings account and each payday, write your *first* check to that savings account—before you start paying any of the other bills. I'm not even asking you to cut down on your spending; this is just the amount of money that would otherwise go to the government and earn a zero rate of interest.

As far as (b) is concerned, it is indeed the case that the IRS has cracked down on tax protesters who try to undermine the system. In a so-called taxpayers' revolt in Flint, Michigan, some employees banded together and decided to take 99 deductions—which means, of course, that no tax would be withheld at all for anyone earning less than $198,000 per year, which does indeed apply to almost everyone in Flint. The IRS was not amused and quickly promulgated two regulations. One said that the employer had to vouch for any person who wanted to take more than nine deductions, and the second imposed penalties for anyone who took excess deductions.

However, these laws are aimed at tax protesters, not at honest taxpayers who find the tax tables withhold too much. The IRS will never object to your raising your number of deductions to the point where the amount of tax withheld is equal to the amount you owe. The Service's only beef is when you have too little taken out, in which case you have to file quarterly and are subject to penalties if you don't meet these payments on a timely basis. But if you routinely get a refund every spring, I strongly advise you to increase the number of deductions to the point where you come out even—and save the difference in an interest-bearing account.

Be Honest

With the IRS auditing only about 1 percent of all tax returns each year, the chance to take a few extra deductions, or not declare some of that extra income, is very tempting. In my opinion, it's not worth it.

You should, of course, continue to be very aggressive in taking all the deductions to which you might reasonably be entitled. The sad truth of the matter is that no one in America understands precisely what the income tax code is supposed to say. The congressional staff who wrote the bill doesn't know, the elected representatives who voted on it certainly don't know, IRS employees don't know, and (if *Money* magazine is to be believed), most tax preparers don't know either. Over the past 30 years I too have made mistakes that were later flagged by the IRS; they had to do with interpretations of the alternative minimum tax and the Social Security tax on self-employment income.

So here's my brief list of do's and don'ts.

1. Always declare all of your income. If the IRS feels like it, it has the unchallenged right to run through all your bank accounts and question any deposit or withdrawal. The only funds the Service won't catch are relatively small amounts of cash that you received and then spent without ever having deposited them; the same thing applies to checks made out to "cash." However, if someone *writes* too many of these, the IRS may begin to wonder who got them, press for further information—and in so doing turn up on your doorstep.

   Be sure to declare all your income that is received by check. Former Agriculture Secretary Earl Butz didn't declare all of the income from his speaking engagements, and he went to jail for it.
2. Always take all legitimate deductions. That sounds almost too obvious to mention, but in the rush to get their tax forms in the mail by April 15, many people overlook deductions during the year. Start out with a checklist of deductibles at the beginning of each year, and every time you make a deductible payment, put a little mark next to it in your checkbook, or if you paid with a credit card, start a separate accounting sheet. That way you are far less likely to overlook minor deductions at year end.
3. Consistent with the guidelines given in this book and in standard tax manuals, be aggressive in taking marginal deductions. In spite of what the IRS will tell you, different agents treat deductions differently. However, don't fabricate deductions that don't exist and have no basis, any more than you would omit income earned. Skitch Henderson, former band director on *The Tonight Show*, took a whopping deduction for giving away what he claimed was

a music library but upon closer examination turned out to be mainly miscellaneous notes—and not of the musical variety either. He too went to jail.

4. Document each deduction thoroughly. That means a canceled check or a credit-card receipt, plus a notation indicating what the expense was for if it's not obvious. Do these notations on the day you make the purchase instead of filling in all the blanks on April 14. People's handwriting changes from day to day, so if all the notations look the same, the IRS may become suspicious. Besides, if you're rushing at the last minute, you are likely to write down something extremely stupid, such as that the magazine subscription on *Investment Advice* was for lunch at Le Haut Prix.

5. You probably haven't heard this one since grade school, but be neat. With the IRS, neatness counts. Apparently the Service thinks a sloppy tax return means sloppy bookkeeping.

6. Some advisers will tell you to avoid certain types or sizes of deductions on the grounds they will increase the odds of the IRS flagging your return. I've never believed that; providing you didn't cheat, you have nothing to fear from an audit. In my opinion you should take all the deductions to which the law entitles you, even if they are outside someone's "guidelines."

7. Most important, don't do anything that will purposely annoy the IRS. If you do, the Service will not only flag your return but will be especially nasty in the audit as well. Don't file frivolous returns, don't cross out the "under perjury" line where you sign your name, don't omit your Social Security number, and certainly don't unilaterally reduce your tax bill by a certain percentage because you don't agree with the government budget for defense, food stamps, abortions, or anything else. If you don't like the way the government is being run, contact your congressman. Don't take it out on the IRS.

Should You Be Your Own Preparer?

First, my own experience. I used to do my own tax forms, but one year I sold one business, started a new one, and had several tax shelters. Everything was so complicated that I went to a big-name (i.e., expensive) law firm. As a result, I hardly paid any taxes.

The IRS apparently figured they had me dead to rights. The Service sent in someone who was later identified to me by another IRS employee as its top agent. His name was Walter Strzgowski, and his name appeared on the front page of the *Wall Street Journal* not once but twice. I gave Walt a vacant office at Evans Economics, and he sat there for six months going through all my records. When the entire affair was wrapped up, the IRS sent me a check for $12,000. I fired the lawyers and I've done all my own returns ever since.

All right, I'll concede that I've studied the tax code more thoroughly than the average filer and I'm better prepared to do my own taxes. And many people, who are very good at what they do for a living, draw a blank when it comes to filling out their tax forms. Nonetheless, I generally advise against using a tax preparer. Here's why.

1. No matter who your tax preparer is, he can't do a competent job unless you bring him all your records for income and deductions. In other words, you must go through your own records first. So you have to do more than half of the job yourself in any case. Theoretically, you could bring in the proverbial "brown bag" of receipts and tell him to pick out the relevant ones, but come on. First, that will triple the amount of time he has to spend on your case, and second, he'll have to ask you for verification.

2. The storefront tax preparers are not supposed to use any imagination. They go down the checklist and ask if you have deductions for taxes, interest, charities, etc., and then fill in the blanks. Nothing wrong with this approach, but you could do it yourself.

3. Some evidence has come to light suggesting that (a) tax preparers make more mistakes than individuals and (b) the IRS is more likely to flag a return signed by a preparer than one signed by an individual. The IRS is officially mum on all such matters, of course—but if you were thinking about using a tax preparer to reduce your chance of audit, forget it.

4. If you have only wages and salaries, interest, and dividends I can see very little reason to use a tax preparer. Capital gains are now more complicated again in 1991, so if you have more than a few transactions, a preparer may be worth it.

On the other hand, if you have your own sole proprietorship (file a Schedule C), still use tax shelters, think you're subject to the alternative minimum tax, or are starting to take your retirement benefits from an IRA, 401(k), SEP, or Keogh, you may need expert advice. Note I said *expert*, which you won't find at a storefront. We're talking a minimum of $500 for tax advice, closer to $1,000 and up in a big city. So don't walk in the door unless you think your tax adviser can save you that much.

Suppose you don't use a tax preparer and then happen to find out on April 17—or for that matter, May 30, or July 12—that you goofed and overpaid your taxes. You always have the option of filing an amended return, Form 1040X, up to three years after the date of the original return.

Of course, if you don't use a tax preparer, you might never find out you overpaid your taxes. However, with (a) top rates down to 33 percent and (b) far fewer deductions available, most of the time these professionals aren't worth the money. It's more a matter of personal choice about how bamboozled you get after a few hours of reading the tax form and the various "easy-to-follow" tax guides.

Just remember, as I have pointed out so often in these pages, most "experts" are not geniuses. Most tax preparers are honest, many of them are hardworking, and some of them are competent. But only a few of them are geniuses, and most of us can't afford them anyway.

Surviving an Audit

It happens to the best of us. Months after filing our tax returns, we receive a computerized notice in the mail from the IRS. There are three degrees of severity.

1. We went over the arithmetic on your return and you made a mistake. If you send us $2,608.39, we will consider the matter closed. If you think we are wrong, write us and tell us why, although we probably won't agree with you.

    That is not an audit. Nor does it preclude an audit later on. But outside of having to cough up some more money, it isn't that bad. No one is accusing you of being a criminal, and no one is threatening to tie up days of your valuable time going through all your records.
2. We would like to audit your return. Please contact us for a convenient time and date.
3. You have been selected for a TCMP audit, which stands for Taxpayer Compliance and Measurement Program. In plainer English, you have crapped out in the lottery. Only 50,000 of these are performed each year, and the auditor goes over every single transaction you had all year. The idea is not to catch criminals per se, but to draw a bead on precisely how much income is being underreported and how many expenses are overstated from a small sample, and then expand these to reach nationwide estimates.

If you are selected for an audit in Class 2, the IRS thinks it found something wrong, although it hardly ever tells you where at the beginning, figuring there may be other bodies buried as well. But if you are selected for a TCMP audit, the Service doesn't necessarily expect any skullduggery, it's just that the law permits it to perform these in-depth audits on 50,000 unlucky citizens each year.

Apparently the TCMP operation usually doesn't net very much money. Of course some people are caught in the net, but a surprisingly large number—perhaps one-fourth to one-third—actually receive slight refund checks because they didn't bother to take every possible legitimate deduction. I've never fallen into the TCMP audit file, but evidently those who have understand the tax code very well once they're finished. The main problem is it cuts into your spare time for weeks.

But let's go back to the 1-million-plus audits IRS personnel perform every year when they think you have done something wrong. How should you react?

First, remember that IRS auditors are not policemen. It's true that when they audit you they expect to collect some more of your money. Bland assurances that you were selected at random, unless it's a TCMP audit, are garbage; in virtually all cases something triggered the audit. The auditors know what that was, but they won't tell you at first, because they hope to find something else too—which they probably don't know about in advance. The IRS does have "policemen," but they are sent around only after it has been determined that you do owe more money; they are the ones who tell you how much.

Every IRS official I have ever dealt with was unfailingly polite—as was I. Only the mentally defective would gratuitously insult an agent. On the other hand, don't be obsequious; it looks phony. Don't go overboard to ingratiate yourself, but treat the agent as if he's some business acquaintance you don't know very well. Chitchat about the weather or the local sports team is the right level of conversation; comments about the family aren't.

Where should the meeting take place? Since I don't think it makes any difference, the answer is, wherever the agent suggests. Trying to talk the agent out of visiting you at home, if that's what he proposes, is bound to arouse suspicion. So take his suggestion; usually it's the IRS office, but it could be either your home or, if you have your own business, your office.

I've usually been audited at my office, presumably because it is more convenient for the agent. Also, there is more room to spread out. I let the agent take whatever office happens to be vacant and let him work away, examining all the documents. I also tell him there are no secrets, and to feel free to look through the files. Some advisers will tell you not to do that, but unless you are hiding some deep, dark secret—which has absolutely no business in the files anyway—the auditor will probably be more inclined to believe your honesty on other matters if you don't pretend the files are off limits.

Agents have a rigid code of ethics about what they can and cannot accept. Coffee and tea, being "free," are all right, but don't offer to buy the agent a soda out of the machine—and, of course, don't even think about offering him a sandwich. Copying unlimited numbers of documents on the copy machine, which certainly isn't free, is considered necessary as well as acceptable. However, agents are apparently not supposed to take any other office supplies, such as pencils or paper. I don't make up these rules; I am just passing them along so you will be apprised of proper deportment.

So you establish rapport with the agent, determine the meeting place, and turn over your records. Depending on your status, these may include business as well as personal records. Of course, you will bring canceled checks or receipts for any deductions that are being questioned.

Any tax attorney or preparer will remind you always to have meticulously documented records for every deduction, and that's impeccable advice. But not all of us are that well organized. That's where your rapport with the agent could pay off. If you have an honest demeanor and have not attempted to hide anything—but concede you are less than a perfect book-keeper—you won't be the first one. Hence the auditor has the authority to accept deductions based on oral testimony. *But he doesn't have to*, because he also has the sole authority to reconstruct the records in his own fashion, in which case you'll have to fight the IRS's claims on its own territory. That's when you find out in a hurry whether you have annoyed the agent.

The last time an IRS agent audited my company, we got to the inevitable point where he asked to see the company's travel and entertainment expense records. With a broad smile, I said, "I've been waiting for you to ask," and opened file drawer after file drawer containing all the records neatly categorized by date and employee. Perhaps that was not the reaction he had been expecting, because he looked at them for about 10 seconds, closed the drawers, and that was that.

This represents absolutely no guarantee, by the way, that some other IRS auditor will spend only 10 seconds on your expense accounts; the odds are against it. In fact, a previous auditor some years earlier closely questioned me about the number of trips I took to Los Angeles until I was able to produce announcements of our company's seminars, which were deemed satisfactory. The point is to be aboveboard; once you retreat into a region of uncertainty, they can smell the kill and it's open season.

We're now at the point where the auditor has worked through all your records and now comes back to you. He either wants more information that you don't have (because you already gave him everything) or more of your money. It's time to be on your toes.

First, consider the situation in which the IRS agent is right, and he and you both know it. You wrote off your child's birthday party on the grounds that it was a business expense and you don't even have a child. Or you "failed to understand" the alternative minimum tax requirements, so you didn't file the form. In that case, don't compound an already untenable situation. Explain, with a faint air of bemusement, that these tax laws sure are complicated and somehow in the press of business you made an honest mistake and want to do the right thing. This may sound like a cop-out, but oftentimes it will save you from having to pay penalties in addition to the disputed amount plus interest. There is a time for standing up to the IRS agent, but this isn't it.

Occasionally the IRS agent is wrong and you know it. Admittedly that doesn't happen very often, but you may have a written IRS ruling on an identical case, or you may have firsthand knowledge of a case that was decided in what would be your favor. To permit the agent to save face, suggest that he might want to review his conclusions with his immediate supervisor. Remember that no IRS auditor really knows all the laws, although he probably knows more than you do. But the tax code is so intricate, and is changing so rapidly, that the courts are still interpreting revisions that occurred two reform acts ago. Which brings me to the third, and most common, situation.

The IRS questions some of your deductions or methods of tax calculation. You did it that way intentionally, thinking you were right—or perhaps your tax preparer thought he was right—but now you aren't sure. This calls for a subtle but unmistakable change in tactics. Remain polite, but no more Mister Nice Guy. Request that the agent show you the section of the tax code on which he is basing his ruling. Because the tax code is apparently written in ancient Sumerian, neither you nor he will actually be able to comprehend it, but that leads to the first appeal procedure, which is to the agent's immediate supervisor.

The supervisor probably won't understand the precise nuances of the law either, but unless your case is really off the wall, he will have seen similar cases and will be able to indicate with more authority what the law is really supposed to mean. If he says that 20 out of 20 recent cases similar to yours were decided against your position—and if you think he is telling the truth—it may be best to give in. But if you have some grounds for defense, the supervisor may agree with you. This has happened to me several times, and in my opinion it's the best way to resolve the dispute.

However, you may get no satisfaction, which leads to the next step: filing a protest with the regional director of appeals. This must be in writing, giving the director some time to look over the regulations before your next meeting. To win here, there must be some arcane point of law the supervisor didn't understand—unless he was just having a bad day, or took umbrage at the color of your tie.

If you lose here, you're usually better off calling it a day unless the amount in dispute is (a) in the six-figure range or (b) part of a major tax-shelter syndicate, which is becoming less and less common these days. You can take the case to court, but the odds there are stacked against you. The judge—and certainly the jury, if there is one—won't understand the tax law as well as either you or the IRS agent, so the outcome is a crapshoot.

Generally the public doesn't like "tax cheats," so your clever lawyer will have to convince either the judge or jury that the IRS clearly overstepped both its legal and ethical boundaries to mount a vendetta against an honest citizen. Some lawyers are very good at that but, as you can imagine, they're not cheap.

Short of actually going to court, should you have your attorney present when you meet with the IRS? Naturally your lawyer will say yes—but that may not be a good idea because bringing counsel may create the impression you have something to hide. However, some normally stable people go blank when IRS agents ask them difficult questions, such as what day it is, and can't bring themselves to give anything resembling a coherent answer. In that case, you'd better have someone do the talking for you. But the IRS auditor will not be impressed.

An audit is never a pleasant experience—even if you receive a refund at the end of the process. On the other hand, it's not nearly as serious as the two givens in life, Death and Taxes. If you are selected for an audit, your best mental strategy is to put it behind you as soon as you can, and get on with your financial life—which means investing your assets wisely and profitably. Since the best place to do that is in the stock market, we'll proceed there next.

UNDERSTANDING THE
STOCK MARKET

Chapter 15

Choosing an Investment Strategy

They asked Alan (Ace) Greenberg, head of Bear Stearns, why the Dow Jones Industrial Average dropped 508 points on Black Monday, October 19, 1987, and his entire answer was, "Stocks fluctuate. Next question."

Most of us can't toss off the loss of one-fourth of our net worth in one day as cavalierly as Ace did, but his point is well worth remembering. Stock prices do fluctuate. But that's no reason to avoid the stock market. As I keep stressing, you've got to take real risks in order to make real money. If you sleep better at night by leaving your money in the bank, that's your choice—but don't complain later on that you never got rich.

Let's get one thing straight right away. No one—and I mean *no one*— picks all the right stocks all the time. Not even the handful of geniuses who have actually become billionaires by playing the market. Just consider these two vignettes.

Story No. 1. Suppose you knew, at the beginning of every month, in which direction the stock market would move—up or down. That's all. You don't know how much it will go up or down, nor which stocks to buy. You simply buy a random assortment of stocks in months during which the market rises and sell short a random selection in months when the market declines. This strategy will net you an average return of 60 percent per year.

By now you may be expecting another miracle of compound interest conclusion, but hold on to your seats anyway. Someone who started with

$10,000 would have $120 million after 20 years, $13.3 billion after 30 years, and $1.46 trillion after 40 years, or almost half the capitalized value of all stocks on all exchanges.

You say that's impossible, that no one can do it? Of course not. No one ever has, and presumably no one ever will.

Story No. 2. This one is about the mythical investor in 1947 who also had $10,000 to invest. Each year he picked stocks in the industry that rose the most—airlines, housing, computer software, or whatever group had the biggest gain that year. In this case the experiment had to be called off by 1968, because his net worth was more than the entire capitalized value of all stocks. And if the investor had picked the individual *stock* that went up the most each year, the results would have been even more ridiculous.

Keep these anecdotes in mind when the stock you buy goes down, or the market declines while you're fully invested. Don't expect to be a genius—be satisfied with a 25 percent rate of return each year and you'll do quite handsomely over your lifetime. Very few have done better. And don't get discouraged when stocks other than the ones you pick rise faster. You don't have to kiss everyone at the dance.

BUY AND HOLD VS. MARKET TIMING

The two *principal investment strategies* for the stock market are:

1. Stay in all the time. That doesn't mean holding the same stock forever, but it does mean staying in the market—specifically, not getting in at the top and out at the bottom. Investors who try that are known as TIBOs—top in, bottom out. Unfortunately, they are the majority.
2. Try to time the market cycles. Just the opposite of No. 1, this requires nerves of jelly. Notice I didn't say nerves of steel. People with nerves of steel don't let anything bother them and usually end up poorer because of it. You have to be willing to jump in and out of the market. Admittedly this strategy isn't for everyone, and no one can time market cycles perfectly. But I will show you how to stay fully invested during the major upswings and watch the major downswings from the sidelines.

Both of these choices will work—*if* you stick with them. The problem is that most small investors—"amateurs" as they are called on Wall Street and in the commodity pits—don't follow either of these methods. Instead, their timing is almost always wrong, as they frantically bounce from one method to the other at precisely the worst time.

When the market first starts to advance after a major setback, they're skeptical that the improvement can last. They remember, all too well, how they lost a large percentage of their investment during the previous decline. So they hesitate. The market keeps rising, but they remain skeptical; it's bound to turn around any day now. After several months or even years of watching the market head higher, they finally decide they have been too cautious; they phone their broker and take the plunge again. About three months later—or three weeks if they are really star-crossed—the market heads down again.

Yet that's not even the worst of it. Suppose you were so unfortunate as to buy stocks precisely at every major market peak over the past 40 years—including August 25, 1987, when the Dow closed at 2722. As it turns out, you would *still* have made more money than if you'd left your savings in the bank, *providing* you followed a buy-and-hold strategy. In the vast majority of cases, however, that's not what small investors do. After their pet stocks fall 20 or 30 percent, they decide to "cut their losses" and sell out—just before the next rally is ready to begin.

Pick your approach and stick to it. A buy-and-hold strategy is fine; it's the one used by Peter Lynch, who was the No. 1 money manager in the United States. A market-timing strategy is also fine—providing you're consistent and exercise discipline. (In Chapter 17 I'll give you my methods for making money using that strategy.) What is bound to fail is the scattershot approach of getting into the market because someone at the bar or on the golf course told you "now is the time." It seldom is.

Later on I'll discuss the pros and cons of each basic method of investing in more detail. But first, a few basics about buying and selling stock.

HOW TO CHOOSE THE RIGHT BROKER

For openers, there are no good brokers.

Now that I got your attention, let me explain what that means.

Most full-service brokers I know are friendly, courteous, come to the telephone right away when you call, and give good execution. Some brokers can't even do that, but I don't use them and you shouldn't either. Let's assume that the broker you do choose is up to snuff in these areas of elementary politeness and competence.

What I mean is that over the long run, no broker you use will be able to recommend stocks that go up faster than the market. There are a few blessed individuals who have this gift, and they're all very rich. Some of them work 90 hours a week and talk to their wives only on anniversaries, while others spend most of their time on the ski slopes or their yachts. But none of them talk to the average investor, and there's no point in pretending they do.

Of course, your broker will have plenty of suggestions every day. He gets paid to push stocks that are recommended by the research department of his firm. Some years ago I tracked the recommendations of all the major brokerage houses, and the results were just what you might expect: They were equal to, but did not exceed, the market averages. That doesn't mean there aren't some real winners on the list; it's just that there are also plenty of losers. So the next time your broker recommends a stock, if you are a naturally polite person and don't like to upset people, listen carefully, nod agreeably, and smile during the appropriate pauses. But don't expect to outperform the market if you take his or her advice.

In other words, don't choose a broker by the quality of advice you can expect to get. It's all the same, and it's all average.

In that case, how do you choose a broker?

What this question really boils down to is the difference between choosing a full-service and a discount broker. By full-service I mean the retail giants of the industry—Merrill Lynch, Dean Witter, Kidder Peabody, Paine Webber, and so forth. You will be assigned an account executive who will take a personal interest in your account, providing it's of decent size, and see that you get efficient execution with a minimum of back-office snafus. They're usually expensive.

Discount brokers actually come in two flavors: French vanilla and plain vanilla. Some of the larger discount brokers, such as Charles Schwab and Quick and Reilly, have many of the same ancillary services that the "full-service" firms have. There are, of course, major differences. Most of the time your call will be routed to whoever is working the phones, and you won't have an individual account executive. Discount brokers are not permitted to give advice on what stocks you should buy or sell, but as I've explained, that kind of advice isn't worth much anyway. These brokers will put your funds into a money market account while you're on the sidelines, and some discount brokers will provide other firms' research reports at a nominal cost. Further down the list are the plain-vanilla operators, such as Waterhouse Securities, Cross & Brown, and others who give even lower rates and no services whatsoever except execution. They're inexpensive.

However, that isn't the end of the story. Discount brokers have one major disadvantage that virtually all of them share: When the market gets busy, they put you on hold. Most of the time that probably doesn't matter if you don't trade very much and can do something else while you're waiting on the phone. But October 19, 1987, wasn't most of the time. In several well-documented instances, clients could not get through to their discount brokers the entire day. Worse than that, many of these brokers then sold out their margin positions without notifying their clients, thereby dumping stocks at the bottom of the plunge. When some clients fought back and went to binding arbitration, which is part of every standard contract, Quick and Reilly said (as reported in the *Wall Street Journal*) they would not honor the finding of the arbitrator. If you have a dispute with a discount broker, you can't really expect to get satisfaction.

My personal experience is that in some cases the execution at the discount brokers isn't so hot either. I'm not saying they cheat, which is a very serious charge; besides, all orders are presumably time-stamped. But orders to buy "at the market" sometimes get mangled by the discount brokers and you get a worse price. It's happened to me. Unbeknownst to these discount brokers (I assume), I have a quote screen in my office, so I would occasionally see my own purchases cross the screen—at a higher price than any of the other surrounding trades. It didn't take too many of these trades before I decided it was time to switch brokers.

Bare-bones brokerage fees at the discount houses are usually as much as 70 percent below the full-service houses. That's a substantial difference, providing the level of execution is comparable. But what I usually end up doing is negotiating with full-service brokerage houses to give me a discount of 40 to 50 percent, and then trading with them. It costs a little more, but the execution is earlier and cleaner.

Naturally, most brokerage houses won't offer you discount rates if you don't ask. And to get these kinds of discounts, you have to be an active trader. If you're the sort of cautious investor who buys 100 shares of AT&T twice a year, you certainly won't get any discount—although the commissions won't amount to much either. But if you have an active account of $100,000 or more and turn it over twice a year or more on average, don't be bashful about asking for discounts. You'll get them.

MECHANICS OF BUYING AND SELLING STOCKS

Let's assume that you have chosen the type of broker that fits your individual situation best, and now you're ready to trade. You have selected the stock of your choice—let's say it's Compaq Computer (CPQ)—and you are ready to place your order.

Some people like to be very efficient. They go home in the evening or on the weekend, study their possible stock selections, make their choice, and then place the order early the next morning to be executed at the open so they can go ahead and concentrate on their real business of the day. The problem with this approach is that liquidity is often missing on the open, and you could get stuck with too high a price if you execute a "market order."

If you are able to call your broker during the day, it's best to let the stock settle down and not place your order before about 10:15 in the morning. That gives the specialists time to balance the order books. It also allows you to see which way your prospective stock is heading, on the outside chance that it went down even though you were sure it would rise. The disadvantage may be the disruption in your other morning's work; you'll have to balance out the costs and benefits of this one on an individual basis. The same general caveats apply to orders placed at the close. Avoid them.

One way to get around the problem of being stiffed on the open is to put in a limit instead of a market order. A market order means just what the name implies; you place an order to buy, but not at any specific price. Most of the time we're talking small differences. If CPQ is trading at, say, 82½, and you don't have a huge order, it should be executed at not more than 82¾. However, even those ¼-point gaps can add up over time if you're an active trader. In that case, you can enter an order with a specific limit: buy CPQ at 82½ or less. If someone else buys it and it jumps to 82¾ on the next trade, most of the time it will come back to 82½ and you will get the better price.

Most of the time, of course, is not the same thing as all of the time. Occasionally a stock will get away from you, and CPQ will rise to 87 without your ever having bought a single share. In trying to save ¼ point, you'll have lost the opportunity to make 4¼ points. So the question boils down to the old risk/reward ratio: What proportion of the time does the stock get away from you, and what are the potential gains and losses?

I don't have any set rules on this particular issue. Sometimes I use market orders, and sometimes I use limit orders. The major considerations are whether the stock has been volatile in recent days and how big the order is. If a stock has been meandering lazily between 53⅝ and 53⅞, the probability is very high that I can get it at the lower price. But if the stock has been climbing steadily, I am probably better off with a market order.

A compromise position is to put in a limit order, but at ⅛ or ¼ above the current price, which allows you a little extra flexibility. The problem is that, human nature being what it is, if you put in your order for CPQ at 82¾ or better and the stock is currently trading at 82½, don't be too surprised if it gets filled at the higher level.

The larger the order, the more important it is to specify some limits. An order of 200 shares probably would not move the market; 2,000 might have a much bigger effect. Most of the time I use some limits unless it's a very fast market and the stock is rising rapidly. If I don't get a fill after about an hour, it is time to call back and raise the limit slightly. Of course, that means you have to follow the market closely, which isn't always possible.

One other thing to remember about a limit order. You have to specify whether it is a "day order" or "good until canceled." You might think that the latter is a better idea—if you don't get the stock one day, you'll get it the next day when it temporarily dips back to your specified level.

Here's what can happen, though. Suppose you wanted to buy CPQ at 82½ and it got away from you; the lowest price that day was 82¾. You keep your buy order active indefinitely. The stock rises to 87; then it turns around and heads back down in a hurry. Maybe the earnings weren't up to snuff that quarter, or the market is in a slump, or the top 10 officers and directors sold some of their stock, or big traders decided to take profits. Whatever the reason, the price plunges back to 76. Somewhere in that range it will cross 82½, and you will be stuck riding the stock down to the bottom.

If you don't get the stock one day, think about it again the next day, but don't let those buy orders remain active indefinitely. More often than not, just when you've forgotten all about them you will end up buying a stock that is heading south.

Some people use "buy stops" in placing their orders. There are advantages and disadvantages to this method, but as the saying goes, it's like giving the floor trader a free gift.

A buy stop works like this. To take CPQ again, suppose you look at the charts and determine there is a major resistance level at 83; the stock has risen to 83 three times and turned back each time. Now it's at 82½, so it might very well hit 83 and turn down a fourth time. On the other hand, if it can break 83, it might rise to 100 or more. So you put in an order to buy at 83¼.

Not everyone agrees on this one, but most active traders admit that putting a buy stop on the specialist's books is an incentive for him to take advantage of the extra ¼ or ½ point. Sure, he'll buy your CPQ at 83¼— and then watch it go back to 82½ for all those buyers who didn't put in a buy stop. Most of the time this is a sucker's play. The few times it really does work will be overwhelmed by the times you'll pick up the paper the next morning and find out that, by golly, you bought at the high of the day.

In spite of these pitfalls, buying a stock is often the easier half of the transaction. How do you know when to sell?

Later on I'll discuss some of the technical patterns that should alert you that your stock is about to head south. But in terms of execution strategy, the usual plan is to put what are known as trailing stops on your stock, which are often 5 percent or so below the current price. Suppose you bought CPQ at 82 and it quickly rises to 91. You might then put a "sell stop" 5 percent below the market price, which in this case would be 86½. The broker will then automatically sell your stock if CPQ touches down at this level.

You can't lose very much on any given stock this way, and if you are busy with real work during the day, this will ensure that a small loss never turns into a big one. Even so, I don't recommend this method, especially on automatic pilot. In the first place, if the price declines near your sell-stop limit, the specialist will take that last ¼ or ½ point as a gift, just as he is likely to do on the upside. But whenever a stock price declines 5 percent, you ought to ask yourself whether that decline was due to a weakening in the overall position of the stock or was just the result of a temporarily declining market or a consolidation before bigger gains. Often a stock will drop 5 percent on a bad earnings report—and then, once the news has been digested, resume its upward pattern. Think it over and take a look at the factors that caused the stock to decline before you decide to sell.

I'm not saying, of course, that you shouldn't cut your losses. Later on I'll discuss the strategies of how to know when to bail out of a stock that's going down. My point here is that there's no point in giving the specialist a free ride by in effect authorizing him to sell your stock ¼ or ½ point lower than any other price that day.

To review the basics of choosing a broker and buying and selling stocks:

1. Don't expect world-record-beating ideas from anyone who sits in his office all day and takes orders on the phone.
2. If you use a discount broker, don't expect good service on busy days.

3. Don't use market orders to buy or sell stock near the open or the close.
4. Market orders are usually better for stodgy stocks, limit orders for volatile ones. The bigger the order, the more important it is to set some limit.
5. If you do use limit orders, make them "day only" orders.
6. Don't use buy stops and sell stops automatically. Use them only as a monitoring device that causes you to take a second look at how the stock has been doing recently.

CASH OR MARGIN

Everything I've said so far implies that you are buying stocks for cash. Most brokers will encourage you to buy on margin. They make money on the funds they lend you, and if you buy twice as much stock the commissions are obviously larger as well.

Here's how margins work. There are actually two parts to margin requirements. The first is set by the Fed, and indicates the percentage of the stock price that you must plunk down with your order. This has been 50 percent since 1974, although in the past it has moved as high as 100 percent. If margin requirements are at 50 percent, you can buy twice as many shares with your initial investment.

Suppose you buy 200 shares of CPQ at $80 on margin, or $16,000 worth of shares for a total investment of $8,000. The price then rises to 120; you sell your shares for $24,000, pay the broker back the $8,000 you borrowed, and have a net profit of $8,000 less interest payments and commissions—almost a 100 percent profit instead of the 50 percent you would otherwise have earned.

Of course, the stock could go down. If it fell to 40, that would be the end of your $8,000 investment. But long before that happened, your broker would ask you for more money, which is the second part of the margin requirements. New York Stock Exchange (NYSE) requirements say you must maintain 25 percent of the equity, but many brokerage houses, to be on the safe side, will require that you maintain a 35 percent equity. Since you borrowed half the money in the first place, that means you will get a margin call if the stock price falls below 70 percent of the original value.

Margin calls are very unpleasant experiences. You must either put up more money immediately or the broker will sell all your shares at the current low price. That's a choice most people would rather avoid.

Here's my rule on margin. If the market has given the signal that a major bull market has just started, buying on margin is probably a good idea. However, if the bull market is in an advanced stage, or has shown signs of choppiness, I'd stick to 100 percent cash investing.

SELLING SHORT

He who sells what isn't hiz'n
Buys it back or goes to prison

Most people think there is something vaguely un-American about selling something they don't own. And it is true that the majority of the time, the market goes up. Over the past 40 years, it has risen an average of 8 percent per year. So it stands to reason that buying stock will make you more money in the long run then selling it short. Including the positive effect of dividends, the total return in the stock market has been negative in only 9 of the past 42 years.

Nonetheless, the market has been known to decline from time to time, and when that happens most investors are happy just to reach the sidelines in time. But those who are willing to go short can earn money in bad as well as good markets.

Selling short simply means, in the words of the ditty, that you sell something you don't own, which you do by borrowing the stock from the broker. That means you must buy it back someday. If you buy it back at a price that's lower than it was on the day you borrowed it, you made money on the deal. In practice, when you sell a stock short, the broker borrows someone else's shares and sells them; you then owe the lender these shares until the broker is instructed to buy them back.

Let's take a specific example. Suppose CPQ did indeed hit a resistance level at 83 and will be heading down to 66. You sell the stock short at 81, and you buy it back at 66. In other words, you bought it back for $15 less than you sold it for, so you made a profit of $15 on every share you sold.

This may look like precisely the reverse of buying at $66 and selling at $81 and making a $15/share profit when the price is rising. However, buying (long) and selling short are not asymmetrical. There are four fundamental differences.

1. Most of the time the market is rising. So over the longer run, if buying is like running downhill, selling short is like running uphill.

I have an ironclad rule not to sell an individual stock short unless the overall market is heading down. Once in a while I will miss some really nifty opportunity to short a stock that is heading toward bankruptcy, but on balance I'm almost sure to come out ahead by following this rule.

2. For NYSE stocks, you, as an individual investor, can't sell short unless there is an uptick in the market. If CPQ is at 82 and you want to sell short, you have to wait until it moves to 82¼ before shorting it. They waived that exemption for the big boys on program trading, which is one of the reasons so many people are upset by this particular scam. Over-the-counter (OTC) stocks can be sold short without waiting for an uptick, no matter how small you are.

3. You can lose an unlimited amount of money selling short. When you buy a stock, your maximum loss is limited by the amount of money you paid for the stock (except for buying on margin, but even there the broker will sell you out before you lose your entire investment). Suppose you have reason to believe that Amalgamated Xygots, now selling at 4, is about to declare bankruptcy. You figure the stock will be worth zero next month, so you sell short. Instead, some leveraged takeover artists pounce on the stock, sell off the overvalued assets, reorganize the company, renegotiate contracts with the unions, and a year later it's selling for 20. This could happen, by the way—Penn Central stock was at 6 when it declared bankruptcy, and it later rose to 72.

   In this case, you would not only have lost your original investment of $4/share, but would have to buy it back at $20/share, which means a loss of 500 percent of your initial investment. That's a very skewed risk/reward ratio.

4. You earn dividends on stock you own; you have to pay the dividends to the owner of the stock for those shares you sell short. As a practical matter, however, this isn't as important as the other three factors, since most of the stocks anyone would want to sell short are volatile stocks with a very low dividend yield, or stocks of companies that are in trouble and don't pay any dividend.

Yes, you could have become wealthy very quickly during October 1987 if you had sold short—and not just the dogs either. Perfectly respectable stocks fell one-half to two-thirds their value within less than a month. On the other hand, if you knew the market was about to crash, you could have made—and this is no exaggeration—up to 1,000 times your money by judiciously timed purchases of put options, which are discussed next.

Here's my general opinion on selling short. Don't. Even if you know "for sure" that either a particular stock or the overall market is going down, the risk/reward ratio is usually much better buying put options than going short. If a particular stock is too small to have options, then you are playing with fire, because one small group of investors can whipsaw you out of the money. Remember, selling a stock short is one of the very few ways to lose more than 100 percent of your investment in the market.

BUYING OR SELLING OPTIONS
INSTEAD OF STOCKS

Buying or selling options is a very high-risk occupation for anyone who tries; it is a high-reward occupation for only a few. This strategy is suitable only for those who can follow the market very closely and enjoy jumping in and out of positions on a moment's notice. On the other hand, options can be very profitable, and they involve less risk than selling short.

Call and put options are symmetrical, but since the market rises most of the time, we'll start with call options. Suppose CPQ is currently selling at 82 and you think it will rise to 94 within the next two weeks. Buying the stock with cash will net you a 14.6 percent gain, minus commissions, which is not at all bad for a two-week investment. Buying on margin will net you almost twice as much, or about 30 percent. But buying a call option could mean the chance to triple your money during the two-week period. That's enough to get the adrenaline pumping.

A stock option bears some similarity to other types of options in that it provides you with a choice of whether to buy something in the future, and you are paying some premium for this flexibility. For example, you might take out an option on a piece of real estate, offering the seller $5,000 if he agrees to hold it off the market for 30 days while you try to obtain financing. If you decide to purchase it, you can do so at the agreed-on sales price; if not, you lose your $5,000 and the seller is free to put the property back on the market.

Call options have the same basic underlying characteristic; the investor pays some premium for the opportunity to buy the stock at a later date for a certain price. If the option is not exercised, the premium is forfeited.

Every option that is purchased must have been written by some other investor. This means someone else is betting that the option will expire worthless and he will be able to pocket the premium for writing the option. If you make money, someone else loses. As a result, if option writers as a group start losing money, the price of options increases sharply—just as insurance rates go up in a war zone. This often happens in volatile markets caused by a major shock.

Options are regularly traded for about 400 stocks, and also for the S&P 100 and 500 and other stock market indexes—although not for the Dow Jones Industrial Average. They are also traded for futures; the principle is the same, although since futures contracts are often more volatile than stocks, the roller-coaster effect is amplified.

The theoretical value of any option is determined by a formula that incorporates the current value of the underlying instrument, the strike price, the current interest rate, dividend yield of the underlying stock, the time to expiration, and the volatility of the stock. This last factor causes most of the change in the difference between the price of the option and the price of the underlying stock.

Most of the time, the quoted price will hew fairly closely to the theoretical values. Occasionally, a major disparity appears. Various computer programs enable traders to skim quickly through thousands of options to find those few that are "overvalued" and "undervalued" according to the standard formulas.

However, for all but the most dedicated traders who spend their day doing little else, this method won't work very well, since most of the profit will be eaten up by commissions and the percentage spread between the bid and asked prices, which is generally much larger than for the underlying stock. If you play the options market at all, it should be on a stock or index whose price you think will make a large move up or down in the near future.

The "strike price" means the price at which you have the right to buy the underlying stock. Options are written for a variety of prices near the current market price, usually in increments of $5. For low-priced stocks, the increment is usually $2.50, and for high-priced stocks, it is generally $10.

Options are actually written so that the investor has the right to buy 100 shares of the underlying stock, not 1. To see how this works, let's take a real-life of CPQ selling at $82, with the investor interested in buying a call option for 100 shares at various strike prices. We also have to pick a date, so let's assume this is January 1st. Options always expire on the third Friday of every month, so the investor has the choice of purchasing a January option, which expires in less than three weeks; or a February option, which expires in a month and a half. Occasionally options are offered for more than three months as well. The longer the time until expiration, the greater the price of the option. The investor will also have a choice of strike prices that are both above and below the current price of $82. The available choices might be summarized as follows:

Strike	Expiration Month		
Price	Jan	Feb	Mar
75	8	9½	11
80	4	6	7½
85	2	3¼	4

Remember, you must multiply these figures by 100 to find out what you actually pay—an 80–strike price February option would cost $600, plus commissions.

Now let's see what happens. Suppose the price of CPQ stays at 82 indefinitely. When the options written at the strike price of 75 expire, they will all be worth 7. Thus anyone buying these options would lose money. That's always the case; you never make money on a call option unless the price rises. The options written at the strike price of 80 would be worth 2 at expiration, and those written at the strike price of 85 would expire worthless.

If the price of CPQ rises to 84 before the third Friday in January, you would make a little money on the 75s, break even on the 80s, and lose money on the 85s. If the price rose to 86 by the January expiration date, you would still lose money on the 85s, even though the price had increased from 82 to 86 in less than three weeks.

Options at strike prices above the current value of the stock are known as "out-of-the-money" options. As someone once remarked when I was explaining this, "It sounds like out-of-the-money investors to me." That's not a bad rule of thumb to remember. If you do buy call options, buy them at strike prices below the current level of the stock. That way you will generally make money if the stock moves in the direction you expect.

Options hucksters will invariably tell you that they offer "limited risk with unlimited opportunity." By "limited risk," they mean that you can't lose more than your original investment, which might happen by selling short, writing options, or trading in futures. What they obviously don't tell you is that much of the time you do lose most if not all of your investment.

The major drawback with options is that, as noted above, they are a deteriorating asset. Consider again the case of the CPQ option with a strike price of $80 that expires in a month. If the stock itself is currently selling for $82, the option probably will be priced at 4 to 5. Thus if you bought the option and the stock stayed right at $82, your option would only be worth 2 on expiration day. You would have lost more than half your money even though the stock did not decline at all.

Options are very risky, but they can also provide magnificent returns. Our investment advisory service gave a signal to buy UAL at 128 on June 20, 1989, just before the takeover rumors started to fly; three months later it was at 280. That would have meant a gain of over 100 percent on the stock within a period of only two months, which isn't too shabby. Yet those who bought August 125 call options that day at 6½ would have made more than 25 times their original investment. Furthermore, if they had pyramided their profits by moving to successively higher-priced options with greater leverage, the gains would have been even more phenomenal.

In order to minimize the risk of buying options, I suggest the following rules.

1. Buy only in-the-money options; i.e., options at a strike price that is at or below the current market price. In the case of the CPQ example above, where the stock was selling for 82, that means buying an option with a strike price of 80, not 85. The 85 option will be much cheaper, but the stock would have to rise at least 4 points before you have any chance of making money.
2. Don't buy options that are close to the expiration date. Give yourself a minimum of one month; two to three months is even better. Options on most stocks are generally offered one, two, and three months into the future, although sometimes one of these months will be skipped, and options four to six months in the future will be available. In my book, that's going out too far because the premiums become too expensive.
3. Trading options is not like trading stocks, which will generally fall a few points and consolidate even in the middle of a major rally, but should be held for the duration of the upturn. If the stock on which you hold an option starts to decline even slightly, sell the option. Generally you'll be able to buy it back cheaper within a few days; but if it continues to drop, forget about it entirely. There is one major exception to this rule, however, which applies to stocks that are known to be takeover candidates. Often the price of the stock will decline just before the next major offer is made, so unless the bidding process is near exhaustion, you will probably be better off holding the option in that circumstance.
4. Stay away from writing naked options, since that offers you the opposite mix from buying options—limited gain but unlimited risk. The most you can make is the premium, but if the stock skyrockets, you could lose many times your original investment.

I don't even discuss writing naked options in this book because I don't think they have an acceptable risk/reward ratio. On the other hand, writing covered options—i.e., options on stock you already own—is a conservative strategy that can enhance your rate of return. In that case, you would want to write out-of-the-money options, since they have the least chance of making money for the buyer.

5. The rules are symmetrical for buying put options if you expect the price of the stock to decline in the near future. The mechanics are exactly the same in either direction. But I would strongly advise against buying put options in a rising market, just as I wouldn't sell short in a rising market, even if it looks as if some particular stock is headed for the doghouse.

However, buying stock-option puts and calls are just the icing on the cake. We have a lot of fundamentals to cover before then—how to tell when the market will go up or down, and which stocks to select. This is really the heart of stock market investing.

I started this chapter by saying that no one can predict every twist and turn of the market on a monthly basis. On the other hand, there are some key factors that will identify major turns in the market almost every time—and every serious investor should follow these closely. I'll discuss them in the next chapter.

Chapter 16

How to Predict the Stock Market

I know of no surer way to accumulate wealth than by using the methods of cyclical investing in the stock market—buying in near the beginning of bull markets, getting out near the top, and then moving into cash—or even going short—in bear markets. Anyone who followed this strategy faithfully for the past 40 years would have earned the golden 25 percent annual rate of return on investment. That's why I picked that number as a difficult but achievable goal. That's almost a 10,000-fold appreciation over 40 years. The few people who have done it became both rich and famous.

A 40,000 Dow by 2030?

From 1949 to 1989, the Dow increased from 175 to 2750. If the stock market were to duplicate that performance during the next 40 years, the Dow would be above 40,000 by the year 2030. Many people can't imagine the Dow rising to such heights, and they dismiss such claims as ridiculous. However, all that represents is an extrapolation of the past 40 years. So if the Dow won't rise to these levels, then it must be that the 1949–89 period had some special features that won't be repeated. However, although there were some unusually large gains during part of that period, I expect the stock market to do just as well over the next 40 years.

The long-term arithmetic of stock market growth is quite straightforward. In the long run, stock prices should rise at the same rate as profits, which in turn should rise at the same rate as GNP. Over the long run, I expect GNP in constant prices to rise about 3 percent per year, while inflation should average 5 percent per year. If that's indeed the case, then over the next 40 years the economy, corporate profits, and stock prices will all rise about 8 percent per year. With the miracle of compound interest, that means an 18-fold gain.

Viewed in this perspective, the last 40 years were not so unusual. However, since not everyone sees it that way, I'll respond briefly to some of the main objections.

Objection No. 1. The growth in the stock market shortly after World War II reflected the return to normalcy from levels depressed by the crash, the Depression, and the war, so at least until 1957, gains were larger than usual.

Only a little. From 1949 to 1989, the stock market has risen an average of 7.8 percent per year. During the same period, GNP has risen precisely the same amount—7.8 percent. That's no coincidence. It is true that from 1949 to 1957, the stock market did rise faster than the economy as P/E ratios returned from depressed levels to normal, but during the 1970s stock prices were depressed by a onetime rise in interest rates that probably won't be repeated again.

Objection No. 2. The market has become more volatile with all those program traders and computerized models, to the point where it can decline 22 percent in one day. That doesn't leave us little guys any time to get out of the way.

Over the long run, the market has generally been quite volatile. In fact, it was much wilder during the 1920s and 1930s. The period from 1949 through 1961 was unusually placid, and that's the era that probably won't be repeated. But don't get overly spooked by the October 1987 crash; unlike some previous bear markets, there were plenty of warnings to get out earlier, and I'll point them out later. Far from brewing up a storm overnight, the market had already declined 20 percent before the crash.

Even more important, if you had bought a random selection of stocks on January 1, 1987, failed to sell anything before the crash but held on to all your selections, your portfolio would still have been up 40 percent by the end of 1989. Once the crash was over, prices soon rebounded.

Objection No. 3. These calculations don't include brokerage fees.

True. But on the other hand, these calculations don't include dividends either, which average about 4 percent per year. Unless you really churn the account, brokerage fees should be less than 4 percent per year. And unless you're trading options, I don't recommend turning your entire portfolio over more than twice a year.

These calculations don't take capital-gains taxes or income taxes into account. That's why it's always best to build up your nest egg in a tax-deferred account. But it doesn't take millions to start. Even that $2,000 per year IRA will do most of the job—if you can react to stock market cycles as soon as they develop.

Objection No. 4. No one can be expected to call each and every market turn on the nose.

Quite true. But on the other hand, the 25 percent rate assumes that you picked a random selection of stocks. I'll show you how to do better than that and pick stocks that are most likely to beat the averages.

Furthermore, suppose you had no idea when the next major turning point in the market would occur and you used the following very simple rule of thumb: Wait until the market has turned up 5 percent before buying, and wait until the market had declined 5 percent before selling. If you follow this rule faithfully, once in a while you will get whipsawed—but not very often. And as long as you catch the major swings, it hardly reduces your long-term rate of return at all.

To demonstrate this, I recalculated the long-term (1949–89) average rate of return assuming that an investor always missed the first 5 percent of each major upturn and the first 5 percent of each major downturn but was otherwise in tune with market cycles. There have been 15 major turning points, which are listed later in the book. Missing that initial 5 percent after each turning point slices the annual rate of return by 3 percent, from 25 to 22 percent. I can offer you several hints on individual stock selection that will more than make up that 3 percent difference.

Here's the outline of my game plan to maximize your investment performance in the stock market.

First, track the fundamental, or economic, factors that determine the long-term swings in the market: profits, interest rates and inflation, and tax rates.

Second, develop a series of trading rules that identify when stock market cycles are about to begin and end. This may sound difficult, but I'll show you which ones have worked best in the past.

Third, identify the key factors that indicate which stocks are most likely to outperform the market. In the long run, of course, stocks with the greatest percentage increase in profits are always the big winners. But in the short run, the key is to identify stocks that are undervalued, which isn't always the same thing.

Fourth, learn how to "read the tape" and use technical patterns to get in and out of those winning stocks. Most of the time—except when some takeover artist springs a surprise on everyone—the telltale signs are there to monitor.

FUNDAMENTAL FACTORS THAT DETERMINE STOCK MARKET BEHAVIOR

The major swings in the market are governed by three main variables: profits, interest rates and inflation, and tax rates. Because these all relate to economic conditions, they are usually known as fundamental factors.

The minor, or secondary, swings depend on a host of individual factors that are too many and diverse to mention here. Fortunately, however, they can be summarized by a few key technical indicators that measure the short-term optimism or pessimism of the market. These timing adjustments are quite important, and those who don't use them have to be geniuses in picking individual stocks to maintain an average of 25 percent per year with a buy-and-hold strategy. But before worrying about timing adjustments, you need a good sense of where the fundamental factors are leading the market.

THE IMPORTANCE OF EARNINGS

In the long run, the single most important determinant of both the overall stock market and individual stocks is profits—total corporate profits for the aggregate market, company profits for individual stocks. The usual way to express the relationship of profits to the stock market is by the price/earnings (P/E) ratio, the ratio of the price of a stock to its annual earnings per share.

For the market as a whole, the P/E ratio is calculated as a weighted average of the P/E ratio for each stock. For most indexes, the larger the company, the bigger the weight. Thus, for example, IBM is more important than, say, King World Products. However, in the case of the most widely used average—the Dow Jones Industrial Average (DJIA)—unweighted values of earnings and prices are used. This sometimes leads to bizarre results. For example, in 1982, when the P/E ratios of broad-based market averages were about 12, the DJIA P/E ratio briefly zoomed to 114 because a couple of firms had losses for the year. That's why most empirical stock-market research, including that of my own firm, is based on the S&P 500.

The major problem here is that the concept of earnings is a very slippery one. Some firms routinely overstate their earnings; others routinely under-state them. I'll discuss some of these problems in Chapter 18, on individual stock selection. But a few key guidelines also apply to earnings for the overall market.

The basic measure of earnings that should be used is the sum of the earnings of the most recent four quarters. Since the earnings for most firms have some seasonal pattern, it makes more sense to use the figures for the entire year. Earnings usually decline during the third quarter because most people take their vacation in summer and production levels are lower—but you certainly wouldn't want to get out of the market just because of vacation schedules, nor would you want to buy retail-store stocks because most of their sales and earnings come during the fourth quarter. For this reason, analysts generally compare earnings with levels of the same quarter a year ago.

Don't be seduced into buying a stock because of exceptional growth in expected future earnings. Future earnings would be valuable information if you were sure of them, but predicting earnings accurately is a task that has eluded even the best and the brightest—and one that often causes more problems than ignoring future earnings completely. Some brokers, in order to hype a stock, will tell you that while it is selling at a very high P/E multiple based on *this* year's earnings, *next* year's earnings will rise so much that it is actually very reasonably priced. The same lame logic is often used to justify an overbought market. Usually it's just so much hot air, since even the best analysts can't predict changes in earnings trends very well. In fact, earnings generally rise rapidly at the beginning of up-turns, not at the end. But many investors ignore the obvious warning signs of impending slowdowns or recessions by listening to such siren songs. This happened in 1987 and again in 1990.

You won't make many investment mistakes in the overall market using current instead of future earnings, although for individual stocks you have to be more careful. My firm uses the lower of current and expected earnings to justify the purchase of any stock. Fundamental analysis works well even if it's restricted to using past rather than expected future earnings because even the best stock market analysts, while extremely adept and nimble at adjusting to the latest actual information, can't predict the economy better than anyone else.

While earnings are important, they clearly are not the only factor that influences stock market prices. If they were, the P/E ratio wouldn't fluctuate very much over time. However, that's clearly not the case. Over the past 40 years, the annual P/E ratio for the S&P 500 has ranged all the way from 7 to 21.4, as shown in Table 19. Other major factors that affect stock prices were obviously at work. Most of these fluctuations in the P/E ratios are determined by changes in interest rates, inflation, and tax rates—both corporate income and capital-gains tax rates.

THE IMPORTANCE OF INTEREST RATES

Interest rates are one of the most important determinants of the P/E ratio, although they are not, as the financial press might have its readers believe, the only one.

It's important to remember that predicting stock prices by looking at interest rates without also considering what is happening to profits is a serious error. Over the long run, that's obvious. Stock prices have risen 18-fold over the past 40 years. Profits have risen 10-fold over the same period. But interest rates have also risen. They are almost three times as high now as they were in 1949, yet interest rates and stock prices are inversely related. In the long run, profits dominate stock market behavior.

Even in the short run, interest rates don't explain all the movement in stock prices. Bond yields were at almost the same level in early 1983 as in mid-1987, yet over that period stock prices more than doubled, as did profits. So the key to understanding major swings in the stock market is to compare interest rates with the P/E ratio, not just with stock prices.

That leads to one of my fundamental rules for determining long-term swings in the stock market. If profits are rising faster than interest rates, the market will continue to improve. That's precisely what happened during the first half of 1987; it also occurred in 1988 and the first half of 1989. So the key factor is the relationship between the P/E ratio and interest rates, not just between stock prices and interest rates.

Different interest rates don't move in the same direction all the time either. On an annual basis, short-term and long-term rates have moved in different directions in 8 of the past 37 years, and fluctuations in short-term rates explain less than half the variance in long-term rates.

Long-term interest rates depend more on the expected rate of inflation than do short-term rates. Thus, for example, if the Fed were tightening monetary policy to ensure that inflation would not accelerate, long-term rates might decline at the same time that short-term rates were increasing.

That is precisely what happened in early 1989. In that circumstance, the P/E ratio would be more likely to increase than decrease. On the other hand, if investors thought the Fed were artificially trying to keep the recovery alive by reducing short-term rates when inflation was accelerating, long-term rates would rise and the P/E ratio would decline.

Thus to see where the stock market is heading, investors need to look at the rate of inflation as well as interest rates to determine whether the P/E ratio will move in the opposite direction of rates, as it usually does, or whether short- and long-term rates themselves are diverging.

It makes sense that when both short- and long-term interest rates rise, the P/E ratio will decline. The more interest rates rise, the more attractive liquid investments such as money market funds and bonds become. As a result, investors will generally pay less for stocks per dollar of earnings. Thus when all interest rates are moving in the same direction the yield on debt is closely correlated with the yield on stocks—which is the amount of earnings per share, or the inverse of the P/E ratio.

When short- and long-term interest rates are diverging, though, the old rules go out the window. From April 1988 to April 1989, short-term interest rates rose a full 3 percentage points; the prime rate, for example, rose from 8½ to 11½ percent. Ordinarily that would be enough to knock the stuffings out of the stock market. But this time stock prices astounded the experts and rose over 20 percent. That disparity caught many of the biggest and most sophisticated money managers completely off guard. So don't make the mistake of thinking stock prices follow short-term interest rates slavishly.

This is important. Please remember it the next time you pick up some best-seller on the stock market or money management that blandly assures you that the prime rate and stock prices always move in opposite directions. You would have lost a bundle in early 1989 following this hackneyed advice. Furthermore, when interest rates don't all move in the same direction, long-term interest rates (bond yields) are now a more important determinant of stock prices than short-term interest rates.* Knowing that would have made you a bundle in the 1988–89 market.

From mid-1988 to mid-1989, the P/E ratio of the S&P 500 rose 10 percent. Over the same period, bond yields fell 4 percent, while short-term interest rates rose almost 20 percent. In this case, the P/E rose more

* Before 1980, short-term rates used to be more important. However, with the increasing globalization of securities markets, a decline in short-term rates is usually accompanied by a decline in the dollar, which makes foreign investors less eager to buy both bonds and stocks.

than long-term interest rates fell because the market was still undervalued in early 1988 in the aftermath of the shock from the October 1987 crash. By the end of 1989, the stock market was no longer undervalued, so it leveled off.

Remember: The key interest-rate indicator of stock market behavior is *bond yields* rather than short-term rates, such as the discount rate or prime rate. Particularly over the past 10 years, bond yields have been a much better predictor of stock market prices than the prime rate. Bond rates are tied more closely to changes in the expected rate of inflation, and higher inflation depresses the P/E ratio for several reasons. First, when inflation rises, the quality of earnings deteriorates. Profits are artificially overstated when inflation rises, but firms must pay higher taxes on their book profits, even though they are not really better off. In other words, firms pay real taxes on phony profits. Second, revenues that are puffed up by price increases will eventually be offset by cost increases, so the gains are only temporary. Third, higher inflation means higher interest rates, which makes stocks less attractive than alternative liquid investments. Fourth, if inflation intensifies, the Fed will eventually tighten enough to cause a recession, which will bring down both profits and stock prices.

So far we have seen that:

1. The most important long-run determinant of stock prices is profits.
2. The P/E ratio is inversely related to long-term interest rates. Short-term interest rates aren't as important.
3. The P/E ratio is inversely related to the expected rate of inflation.

THE RULE OF 20

While they are helpful, these rules don't tell you when to buy or sell stocks; that also depends on whether the market is over- or undervalued. While no single factor will tell you which phase the market is in all the time, the Rule of 20 is a very useful rule of thumb to gauge the relative position of the stock market.

Here's how the Rule of 20 works.

Add the current P/E ratio to the rate of inflation. If the sum is under 20 and the market is still rising, stay in the market. If it is over 20, the market is overvalued and will suffer a major setback in the near future. This rule by itself doesn't tell you when to sell—that's covered in the next chapter—but it does serve as a warning signal that stock prices are over-valued and the peak is near.

As a corollary, when the P/E of the market itself approaches 20, watch out. Even if inflation is zero, which it hasn't been since 1955, a major bear market is lurking around the corner.

The market very seldom sports a P/E ratio of over 20. But when it does, the results are spectacular—on the downside. The P/E ratio has exceeded 20 only three times during the past 60 years. The first was in late 1961 and early 1962. Suddenly and without warning—the economy didn't soften and interest rates did not rise—stock prices plunged over 30 percent in three months. Some people associated that sharp decline with John F. Kennedy's battle with the steel industry. However, the market decline was well advanced by the time that debacle took place; all it did was accelerate what was already the sharpest stock market decline in 25 years.

The second time the P/E ratio exceeded 20 was in early 1972. The market didn't crash right away then either, because profits were distorted by the wage and price controls. As soon as they were loosened in January 1973, the market started to decline, and ultimately fell almost 50 percent—a far more serious debacle than the 1962 shakeup. Interest rates and inflation both rose sharply, and the economy headed into a recession—the worst possible combination for stock prices.

The third time the P/E ratio exceeded 20 was even more ominous: the summer of 1987. In this case, some of the market decline could have been attributed to a rise in interest rates, but that was not the major factor. The market was severely overvalued and overripe for a correction. When the time came, it was swift and without recourse.

Shortly before all three of these crashes, gurus came out of the wood-work to explain to us mere mortals that a new age was dawning, and stocks could no longer be valued by the old methods—like P/E ratios or interest rates. In short, stock market prosperity was assured forever. The mystery is not that these clowns surfaced but that so many people listened to them.

It will probably be several years before the stock market P/E ratio exceeds 20 again; after all, it has happened only three times in the past 60 years. But if it does, please don't listen to any siren songs about how all the rules of the game have changed. Count your money, and at the first sign of weakness, head for the sidelines—or, if you're more aggressive, go short.

Table 19 shows the annual P/E ratio from 1950 through 1990. As described above, the three times the P/E ratio moved above 20 were followed by serious market crashes. However, a great deal more useful

Table 19
The Rule of 20

Average P/E Ratio		Inflation Rate	Sum	Average P/E Ratio		Inflation‡ Rate	Sum
1950	7.0	5.9	12.9	1970	18.7	5.6	24.3*
1951	8.5	6.0	14.5	1971	15.1	3.3	18.4
1952	10.3	0.8	11.1	1972*	18.9	3.4	22.3*
1953	9.9	0.7	10.6	1973	15.9	8.7	24.6*
1954	11.2	−0.7	10.5	1974	10.0	12.3	22.3*
1955	12.2	0.4	12.6	1975	10.2	6.9	17.1
1956	13.2	3.0	16.2	1976	12.2	4.9	17.1
1957	13.0	2.9	15.9	1977	9.8	6.7	16.7
1958	15.6	1.8	17.4	1978	8.7	9.0	17.7
1959	17.3	1.7	19.0	1979	7.9	13.3	21.2*
1960	16.9	1.4	18.3	1980	8.0	12.5	20.5*
1961	21.4	0.7	22.1*	1981	8.7	8.9	17.6
1962	17.8	1.3	19.1	1982	8.1	3.8	11.9
1963	18.0	1.6	19.6	1983	12.6	3.8	16.4
1964	18.6	1.0	19.6	1984	10.8	3.9	14.7
1965	17.9	1.9	19.8	1985	11.5	3.8	15.3
1966	15.6	3.5	19.1	1986	16.0	1.1	17.1
1967	17.2	3.0	20.2*	1987†	19.3	4.4	23.7*
1968	17.6	4.7	22.3*	1988	11.2	4.4	15.6
1969	16.8	6.2	23.0*	1989	13.5	4.6	18.1
				1990	15.3	6.1	21.4*

* Reached peak of 20.1 in March 1972.
† Average 21.6 July–September 1987.
‡ On a monthly average basis.
† Indicates years of severely overbought market.

information can be drawn from this table. Twice during this period, the P/E ratio plus inflation declined below 12—during the early 1950s and again in 1982. Both of these were followed by spectacular bull markets: prices tripled from late 1953 to late 1961, and tripled again from mid-1982 to mid-1987, for an average annual gain of 20 percent during those periods. During the rest of the postwar period, stock prices advanced only an average of 4 percent per year. For that matter, the decline in the sum of the P/E ratio plus inflation to 14 at the beginning of 1988, while not quite in the same league, did lead to a 60 percent run-up in stock prices during the next two years.

The years during which the sum of the P/E ratio plus inflation was more than 20, but the P/E ratio itself was below 20, were followed by poor stock performance. This sum exceeded 20 in 1967; stock prices declined 20 percent over the next three years. It then exceeded 20 again in 1979; stock prices rose briefly in 1980, but then fell in the 1981–82 recession and did not regain their footing until August 1982.

Also note what happened in 1990. By mid-year, with the P/E up to 16, and the sum at 21½, it was once again clear the market was overvalued. The oil shock made the decline more severe than would have otherwise been the case—but according to the Rule of 20, the market was set for a correction in any case.

Moving out of the market whenever the sum of the P/E ratio and inflation exceeded 20, and staying in the rest of the time, would have been a very profitable investment strategy over the past 40 years. Investors who followed this strategy would have remained in the market during the mild downturns of 1953 and 1957 but would have avoided all major bear markets.

THE IMPORTANCE OF CHANGES IN THE TAX RATES

The sum of the P/E ratio and inflation was low during most of the 1950s, which featured a roaring bull market. However, it was also low during the 1975–78 period as well, and that was not a particularly good time for stocks—for a specific reason. During these years the maximum rate on capital-gains tax, which had been 25 percent for many years, rose to 49⅛ percent. Since investors in stocks were penalized, many of them switched into other types of assets where returns were less heavily taxed. In November 1978, the maximum capital-gains tax rate was lowered to 28 percent, which was followed by a substantial market rally, even though interest rates and inflation increased the following year.

This isn't just some after-the-fact explanation, as the *Wall Street Journal* was kind enough to remind its readers on its October 21, 1980, editorial page:

> The claims made in 1978 on behalf of the Steiger amendment [to reduce capital gains taxes] have been uncannily accurate. Economist

Michael K. Evans predicted that a reduction in the maximum capital gains tax rate from 49.1% to 25% [the original Steiger proposal] would raise stock prices about 40% . . . The New York Stock Exchange Composite stock average closed last week 44% above its level of November 1978.

Although it usually isn't mentioned, the increase in the capital-gains tax from 20 to 28 percent in 1987 was one of the factors that contributed to the crash, although it doesn't explain the exact timing. The effect of changes in capital-gains tax rates doesn't occur all at once; it is spread over two years. A lowering of the tax rate unlocks more capital gains, which generates more profits to be reinvested, and this ripple effect gradually spreads through the market. Indeed, should the capital-gains tax rate on stock market sales be lowered in the future, it would have a similarly bullish effect on stock prices over the following two years.

The other caveat on using the Rule of 20 reflects how profits are calculated. The Tax Reform Act of 1986 lengthened the tax life for many types of capital expenditures, which meant that many firms could write off plant and equipment only about half as fast as before. The reason for doing so was to make corporations pay higher taxes. If depreciation write-offs are smaller in any given year, book profits will be higher and therefore tax payments will also be higher, so firms are not really better off.

In order to work best, then, the Rule of 20 should be adjusted for major changes in the corporate income and capital-gains tax rates. With these adjustments, stock prices should continue to rise when the P/E ratio plus inflation is less than 20 and decline when this sum is more than 20. Because the P/E ratio plus inflation was so much below 20 during the first decade following World War II, there were virtually no declines in stock prices even during the recessions of 1949 and 1954. When the market finally did become overvalued in 1961, it was ripe for a sharp setback the following year.

The overvaluation of the market that began in 1967 led to a prolonged period of virtually no gain. Stock prices retreated relative to other liquid assets until yields moved back into equilibrium. This was not finally accomplished until the massive plunge in 1973 and 1974 that sliced stock prices almost in half. From 1975 through 1989, though, the return on stocks has been above average, although the market has become more volatile.

FUNDAMENTAL RULES OF MARKET TIMING

My major rules for buying and selling stocks based on *fundamental* factors are:

1. Buy stocks whenever long-term interest rates are declining.
2. When long-term interest rates start to increase, stay in the market as long as profits are rising faster than interest rates and the P/E ratio plus inflation is less than 20. In the past, that sum has always risen above 20 near the end of bull markets.
3. When the Rule of 20 is violated, get out of the market as soon as long-term interest rates start to rise, profit growth slows down, or—if neither of these occurs—when stock prices drop more than 5 percent.
4. Get back into the market once the Rule of 20 is reinstated, long-term interest rates start to decline, or, if they do not, after stock prices have risen 5 percent.

Remember, the Rule of 20 is affected by major changes in tax rates. A lower capital-gains tax rate could mean stocks would keep rising above the levels indicated by the Rule of 20. Since 1986, changes in the tax laws have led to an overstatement of profits, so the market should start to decline before the Rule of 20 would indicate.

Using these simple rules would have generated superior stock market performance throughout the past 40 years. As a long-term investor, you would have remained in the bull market all through the postwar period, then sold out in 1962. You would have moved back into the market shortly after the nasty 1962 break and stayed there until interest rates started to rise near the end of 1968, thus avoiding the decline during the 1969–70 recession. This method would have flashed another buy signal when the economy emerged from recession in late 1970, moving you back in the market during 1971 and 1972, but it flashed a sell signal early in 1973, thus completely avoiding the 1973–74 debacle when the market declined almost 50 percent. These rules generated another buy signal in 1975 and a sell signal in 1979. They would have moved you back into the market during the spring of 1980, when interest rates plummeted, but out again by the end of that year.

Finally, this rule would have put you back into the market a few months ahead of the great bull market that began in August 1982. It would have flashed a sell signal in 1987, when the P/E ratio moved above 20— although that was before the August peak—but then, when most investors were fleeing the market after the crash, would have reinstated a buy signal. For by the end of 1987, the P/E declined to a modest 14, inflation and interest rates were steady, and profits were still rising rapidly. Ordinarily that's a perfect time to get back into the market, but most investors were so spooked by the thought of another 1929 that they avoided stocks like the plague. In retrospect, though, it's no surprise that the market zoomed again in 1988 and most of 1989.

USING TECHNICAL ANALYSIS TO FINE-TUNE BUY AND SELL SIGNALS

I've shown that the Rule of 20 is a very useful guideline for gauging the overall tenor of the market and determining whether it's still in a bull or bear phase. However, it does not pinpoint the precise times major market moves begin and end. This rule needs some fine-tuning before it can be used for optimal stock market investing.

Furthermore, often it's not immediately obvious when profits and interest rates are changing direction; small squiggles may give false signals. Sometimes it takes two to three months to find out what is really happening, in which case the market has left you far behind. This is where *technical analysis* can be very useful to active investors.

Technical analysis, in contrast to fundamental analysis, has nothing to do with the economy. It is based on the branch of stock market forecasting that assumes all known information is already reflected in market prices and can be uncovered by the appropriate reading of the available statistics. This doesn't mean there are no surprises—in fact, surprises occur every day, if not every minute. But because the stock market is a very efficient market with thousands of intelligent, highly motivated players, all this information immediately gets translated into the movements of the market itself.

If, for example, the Fed decides to ease, dedicated Fed-watchers will know it less than five minutes after it happens and start switching their asset allocation toward stocks, so you may as well join the bandwagon, too. On the other hand, if the major traders *don't* think the Fed has eased yet, the market will probably continue to stagnate or decline until this information becomes known.

To a certain extent, the argument for using technical indicators is unassailable. If the vast majority of traders and investors are bullish on the market, you and I would be foolish to bet against the collective wisdom. Don't try to be a smart aleck. This means don't sell when everyone else is buying. Even if they're wrong, *your* investment portfolio is no match for the $3 trillion the big boys are investing. You're just throwing your money away if you sell short in a bull market because it "might" turn soon. Wait for the evidence.

The value of all the stocks on the various markets is in excess of $3 trillion, and most stocks in the Dow have a capitalization of over $10 billion. Unless you're prepared to invest numbers of this magnitude, your investment won't make any perceptible difference in the overall market, which will go right ahead and do precisely what it was planning to do whether or not you bought or sold that day.

I know it's easy to become paranoid. After I had bought some call options only to find out later that was the top of the market, I couldn't help thinking that they must have seen me coming. But once you've calmed down and returned to rationality, it should be obvious that your order didn't turn the market around.

This isn't to say that you couldn't move a stock that has an average trading volume of 5,000 shares, but as far as the overall market goes, it's strictly no contest. Even if you follow all the rules and end up a billionaire, you'll still be able to trade actively in the market without making much of a ripple.

The argument over technical analysis comes not from whether the collective wisdom and judgment of the market is stronger and more powerful than the individual investor but from the interpretation of the data. The problem with technical analysis isn't too little information but too much. If the stock market stutters and declines 5 percent after a steady three-month gain, is that the start of a major bear-market move, or just some overdue profit-taking? Disagreements over issues like this cause the market to career wildly from one direction to the other.

With the widespread use of PCs and the proliferation of fairly sophisticated software, anyone can purchase a computer program for a few hundred dollars, sign up for a daily data feed (or input the numbers manually), and test literally hundreds of different technical indicators. After a while, you begin to suffer from information overload, and the exercise becomes futile. Besides, anyone who has done this for a few months will admit after a few beers that his favorite "foolproof" indicator that worked so well during the previous cycle usually disintegrates the next time around. For if enough traders discover that a certain system works, they will alter their investing patterns in such a way that the system usually becomes invalid.

THE ELM AND MAIN STREET SYNDROME

Suppose some stranger stood at the corner of Elm and Main streets and announced that he would hand out $100,000 to the first person in line at 9:00 A.M. the next morning, and you just happened to be passing by at the very instant this announcement was made. Would you wait until 8:59 A.M. before putting in an appearance? Of course not. You would stand glued to the spot to make sure no one got in line ahead of you.

It's the same way with the stock market. If you or anyone else discovers a signal that has always moved just before the market changes direction, then naturally whoever finds out about it will buy into the market as soon as the signal occurs, and stocks will rise ahead of their appointed schedule. By definition, the forecast will have turned out to be wrong.

This is why I always get a chuckle out of studies that show that in the past, the market almost always rose just before holidays, or just after long weekends, or on Fridays, or at the end of the quarter, or whatever. These results really did happen on a historical basis; presumably no one invented the figures just to publish a phony index. Yet if people really believe these results, they will naturally buy ahead of whatever event is supposed to trigger the rally, and the timing will be destroyed.

I'll give you just one example out of many. Some hardworking statistician once found that the market almost always rose during the last few days of June and the first few days of July because, he said, it's the end of the quarter and just before a major holiday. These results were published, and they caused many amateur investors to buy into the market on June 23, 1989, expecting to cash in on the gains the following week. Of course, exactly the opposite happened: The market fell 100 points the next week. Once that foolishness had ended and the weak sisters were wiped out, the market then rose 9 percent in July. The only losers were the "market timers" who thought they could capitalize on a quick rally. So I assume you won't waste your money following any of these silly rules—even if they have worked perfectly in the past.

I'm not trying to trash sophisticated technical analysis. Not at all. If you're willing to spend all day following all the squiggles, have a lightning-quick mind and an iron discipline, it's possible to do fantastically well. Paul Tudor Jones has made over 100 percent each year for his clients over the past five years. Don't worry about where to find him, because he has long since stopped accepting new funds and in fact sends the profits back to the investors instead of reinvesting them. But that kind of job is like washing the windows of the Empire State Building without a safety net. Richard Dennis, who turned $400 into $200 million within 18 years—a mere 107 percent per year over that stretch—suddenly mislaid his touch and, within a few months in 1989, lost half his clients' money.

In my opinion the gist of technical analysis for the amateur—and by that I mean someone who doesn't trade for a living—is very simple. You buy when the vast majority of investors want to buy, and you sell when they want to sell.

That and 75 cents will get you a copy of the *Wall Street Journal* unless you know how to identify these points. But while they don't reveal themselves automatically, there are a number of key series to watch that have not only worked every time in the past but also have some logical basis for working in the future, so we aren't just playing *Wheel of Fortune* here.

Some forms of technical analysis are nothing but pure gibberish. I'm not going to bother to discuss those methods that are akin to tarot cards and astrology. In my book, Fibonnaci arcs and Gann cycles are out, out, out. So is Elliott Wave Theory. No one can predict the market five or ten years from now—and those who claim they did were either just plain lucky or endowed with an overabundance of chutzpah. One mental midget even claimed that his stock market theory was based on historical evidence stemming from the year 2000 B.C. These theories may be more humorous than the Saturday morning cartoons, but if you try to use them for serious investment advice, you'll find they are just about as useful.

Even among the most reliable indicators, stock market investors who have responsibilities in life other than trading full-time can't afford to look at the myriad technical indicators that are available each day. So you won't find a treatise here on Stochastic Oscillators, Moving Average Convergence Divergence, Accumulation/Distribution parameters, or Williams' R. In fact, I'm not going to recommend any complicated technical indicators in this book. The type of technical indicators I've chosen have the following virtues.

First, they are simple enough that you can use them every day without having to be a computer jockey.

Second, they relate to the basic strengths and weaknesses of the market, so they don't depend on abstruse mathematical formulas.

Third, they have been extremely accurate during the past 30 years.

This last point may not mean anything in view of what I said above, except I have tried to choose those indicators that will still be valid even if "everyone" follows them. These are self-reinforcing measures, which means if a bandwagon effect does develop, the resulting move in the stock market will just be that much stronger—not weaker.

Just because these signals are easy to understand and simple to calculate doesn't mean they don't work well. In the next chapter, I'll discuss the rationale behind each key signal and present the evidence that supports each of their track records.

Chapter 17

How to Time Stock Market Cycles

A recent survey of small investors showed that 82 percent followed a buy-and-hold strategy, while only 18 percent were market-timers. Peter Lynch, former fund manager extraordinaire of Fidelity Magellan, claims that he can't outguess the market and refuses to lose sleep nights wondering about the current phase of the cycle for stock prices.

So market timing isn't for everyone—and it may not be for you either. Yet I have a sneaking suspicion that if investors had a series of simple, understandable rules that told them when the major turning points were about to occur, they would use this information even if they didn't admit it to anyone else.

With the proliferation of inexpensive and easily accessible computer power, many economists and financial analysts have been known to "torture the data until it confesses"—trying so many different combinations and permutations of the historical data that eventually they find some formula that tracks all the previous turning points perfectly.

Of course, there is certainly nothing wrong with studying historical data. In fact, it's essential to understand how the markets have reacted to various fundamental and technical phenomena in the past. On the other hand, overdosing on past coincidences invariably results in spurious correlations that have no more than a random chance of being repeated in the future.

OLD BUT USEFUL MARKET CLICHÉS

So after years of chasing these indicators around the computer screen, I've retreated to the basic concept of KISS—Keep it Simple, Stupid. In line with this simplistic approach, let's briefly review some old but useful market clichés.

Cliché No. 1. "The trend is your friend." You don't want to sell stocks in a rising market, and you don't want to buy them in a declining market.

Obviously there has to be more to the stock market than that, or we would be reduced to the axiom Will Rogers gave when asked how to pick stocks: "Only buy stocks that go up. If they don't go up, don't buy them." On the other hand, I have seen allegedly sophisticated managers get so tangled up in their charts and computer programs that they can't wait for the turning point to occur so they can head in a new direction.

In fact, this happens often enough that it has occasioned another aphorism . . .

Cliché No. 2: "The first wave of short sellers always gets killed." (It applies to premature buying on the upside, too.) So, please don't try to be a genius. Let the other guy make the first buck. Wait until a market upturn has been established before buying, and a downturn before selling. When the really big moves start, you won't have to wait very long.

Cliché No. 3. "You can't fight the tape." This may sound like No. 1, but there are some important differences. This refers to the breadth of the market: the number of stocks whose price rose during the day compared to the number that fell, and to the volume of stocks traded that moved up and down. This advice is particularly useful near the end of bull markets, when it is often the case that a few big stocks keep pushing the averages up, but most stocks are declining.

I didn't include the most banal advice of all—"Buy low, sell high"— since that has deteriorated into a third-rate vaudeville routine. But with these three clichés firmly in mind, here's the information to watch each day.

1. Market relative to its moving average
2. Momentum of market, as measured by the rate of change of prices
3. Advance/decline ratio and the advance/decline line
4. Up/down volume
5. Net new highs (useful only at upper turning points)
6. Price and volume comparisons

As discussed in this chapter, these rules apply to moves in the overall market, and the assumption here is that you are dealing with a so-called random selection of stocks. These rules need to be modified for selecting individual stocks, as I'll discuss in the next chapter. However, unless you have solid information that a particular company is about to be taken over, or that its upcoming earnings report will be a real blockbuster, knowing whether the market is about to rise or fall is at least as important as choosing stocks that outperform the market.

MOVING AVERAGES

The first and most basic rule is to buy stocks only when they are going up and sell them only when they are going down, which means you shouldn't try to outguess turning points ahead of time.

The problem is that market fluctuations often make it difficult to tell whether the market is in an uptrend or a downtrend. Even in those fateful days before the October 1987 crash, the market would occasionally head back up for a brief time; in fact, the Dow moved up 37 points the very Tuesday before the crash. For this reason, it's useful to look at the market relative to its *moving average* over the past several days or weeks. For conservative investors, the 50-day (10-week) moving average is the best single guide. Don't buy stocks unless the market is above its 10-week average, and don't sell them unless it's below that average.

This rule may be too stodgy for active investors, many of whom prefer to use the 21-day or even the 10-day moving average. Which you use should depend on how often you like to trade in and out. But it should be clear that when the market is below any of these moving averages, it's best to wait until prices start to turn up again, or until you get an unequivocal buy signal from the breadth indicators, which I'll discuss below. Furthermore, using a moving average rule will keep you from nibbling at the first upturn, which only rarely means that the market is ready to romp.

In October 1987, the 200-day moving average briefly received quite a bit of publicity because stock prices moved below that average on Thursday, October 15; the next two days, the Dow fell 617 points. However, that was something of a fluke. Using shorter moving averages would have moved you out of the market when it was 200 points higher. Furthermore, when the market finally climbed back above its 200-day moving average in June 1988, the result was a big yawner. Nothing happened, which is the usual case. Most of the time, long-term moving averages provide a signal well after the major change has already occurred.

MEASURES OF MOMENTUM

Momentum, or rate-of-change variables, can be quite useful in gauging when to buy or sell, but they are also somewhat trickier to interpret, because the market seldom cooperates and moves in textbook fashion. For every beautiful, symmetrical graph in the technical indicator books, there are at least a dozen similar cases that didn't work out nearly as well.

The basic idea of momentum is tied to overall cyclical behavior. Assume that some particular event sends stock prices moving higher. It might be a decline in interest rates, or a series of strong profit reports, or even some political event. In any case, stocks rise that day. Word spreads about how the economic climate is now better for stocks, so more investors buy the following day. For a while, the market rises rapidly.

This buying pressure continues for a while until stock prices have risen enough that prices now fully reflect this new development, so they stop increasing. Usually, human nature being what it is, stocks overshoot their equilibrium value and decline a little. That is why bear traps exist even in the most robust bull markets. But in any case, the rate of change is sharply diminished—the momentum has died out.

Conversely, if some unexpected bad news occurs, stock prices decline until they have fallen to a level commensurate with the less favorable economic environment. Then they remain at those levels for a while or bounce back slightly until some further news starts the next market cycle.

It's therefore best to buy stocks just after a bull market has started, and to sell them just after a bear market has started. Another cliché? Perhaps. But I have consistently been surprised by the number of smaller investors who watch the market rise continuously for several months and then decide to buy stocks just before the upper turning point is reached. If you are one of those people who watch the market move higher before deciding to buy stocks, and you notice that the daily gains are becoming slimmer and slimmer, wait for a correction before calling your broker. If, on the other hand, the momentum of the market—the average daily change— seems to be holding its own, it may still be safe to buy. But be aware that your upward journey in the market may be unnervingly short.

MEASURES OF MARKET BREADTH:
ADVANCERS AND DECLINERS

Throughout this book I've tried to avoid what some writers call "financial pornography"—absolutely outrageous claims that "guarantee" instant wealth. You are probably familiar with the genre from your junk mail. This stock is *guaranteed* to rise 10-fold, you can earn 463,787.6 percent on your money, and so on.

For that reason, I'm *not* about to reveal a guaranteed method of predicting when the stock market is about to turn around. As I've said, in the long run it is the fundamental factors—profits, interest rates and inflation, and tax rates—that determine where the market is heading, but what they don't tell you is just when the market is about to reach a turning point. Nonetheless, I will go so far as to state that the careful use of the key breadth indicators of the market—the advance/decline (A/D) ratio and the ratio of up volume to down volume (up/down or U/D ratio)—will improve your accuracy in predicting major market upturns. In the world of uncertain financial markets, this is as close as you'll get to a real guarantee.

The basic idea behind these measures is that while every major-market rally ultimately depends on a favorable change in the fundamentals, the precise date when that rally starts usually occurs when the vast majority of stocks start to rise. Unlike some of the other technical signals that ultimately self-destruct—such as the seasonal patterns that fall apart as everyone tries to beat the gun—these signals are self-reinforcing. The more traders that buy based on these signals, and the larger the proportion of stocks that rise, the more likely that a rally really is under way.

The *A/D ratio* equals the number of NYSE stocks that rise on any given day divided by the number that fell. Unchanged stocks are not included in this formula. A ratio of greater than 4:1 is unusual enough to merit further attention, although by itself it is not necessarily a buy signal. A 5:1 increase is an even stronger signal.

The *U/D ratio* equals the trading volume of stocks that rise that day divided by the trading volume of stocks that fall. Here again, stocks whose price was unchanged are not included in the formula. From a theoretical point of view, this ought to be a somewhat better measure; if a stock rose 1½ points on unusually large volume, that should be more significant than the same increase on unusually small volume. A ratio of more than 8:1 for the U/D ratio deserves further attention; more than 10:1 is an even more robust indicator.

THRUST DAYS

A day in which the A/D ratio exceeds 4 *and* the U/D ratio exceeds 8 is usually called a *breadth thrust day*, or just a *thrust day*. It is a necessary but not sufficient condition for a buy signal. Sometimes unexpected events occur that send the market into a tizzy but in retrospect are not bullish. A perfect example of this occurred on August 16, 1971, right after Nixon announced the wage and price controls. The move caught most traders off guard, so the market soared, with the A/D ratio at 14.0 and the U/D ratio at 9.2. However, once analysts started to think through the ramifications of the program, they realized that controls might not be so wonderful for the stock market, so prices started to slide back down, and the market gradually moved lower until November of that year.

In order to find an unequivocal buy signal, it is necessary to have *two* thrust days within close proximity—always a month or less, but usually within a few days. The logic is that if, after a major advance, traders think the matter through and still decide the market will move higher, then a major advance is indeed in store.

There have been 15 significant stock market cycles since 1949. I define a cycle as one that includes a decline of 10 percent or more in the S&P 500 average on a closing basis (ignoring interday highs and lows), then rises to a new peak. If the market falls 15 percent and then rises only 10 percent before declining again, that's part of the same cycle.

The first four stock market cycles, which took place from 1949 through 1960, were all caused by the onset of recessions and were therefore almost entirely related to fundamental rather than technical indicators. In those days before the proliferation of computers, technical jockeys didn't cause much disruption. With the widespread use of computers, though, the precise timing of cycles has become increasingly divorced from strictly fundamental factors and more dependent on technical signals. Thus our analysis of technical indicators starts with the 1962 stock market cycle and covers the last 11 cycles. The thrust days, and their values, are given in Table 20.

If this system works as well as I have intimated, you'd probably expect me to say that in all 11 cases, the rally began with two thrust days.

Almost, but not quite. We need one more refinement. If you had bought a random assortment of stocks based on these signals and held them for six months or more, you would have made substantial gains in every case. However, you might not have had gains for shorter periods of time in certain cases. So here's the third part of the rule.

Table 20
"Thrust Days" Signals for Major Market Upturns, 1962–Present

Date of Trough	Date of Signal	A/D Ratio	U/D Ratio	% Gain Before Next Major Decline
5/28/62	5/31	5.6	n.a.	
	6/6	4.5		
				79.8
6/26/62	6/28	7.8	n.a.	
	7/10	6.5		
10/7/66	10/12	3.5	10.7	33.3
	10/18	3.2	6.2	
3/5/68	4/1	4.0	7.9	23.5
	4/8	4.0	9.3	
5/26/70	5/27	6.9	15.9	51.2
	5/28	4.5	4.3	
11/26/71	11/29	6.4	9.6	33.4
	12/1	4.2	6.1	
10/3/74	10/7	5.7	8.4	
	10/9	4.6	8.1	
	10/10	5.1	4.2	
				73.1
12/23/74	12/31	4.1	8.0	
	1/2	9.1	7.0	
	1/10	7.4	7.2	
11/14/78	12/1	6.0	7.6	28.1
	12/22	5.0	8.1	
3/27/80	3/28	5.2	10.2	43.1
	4/22	5.4	14.3	
8/12/82	8/17	10.1	44.5	
	8/20	5.0	30.3	
				68.6
(second signal)	10/11	5.2	9.2	
	11/3	6.0	12.2	

Table 20 (cont.)
"Thrust Days" Signals for Major Market Upturns, 1962–Present

Date of Trough	Date of Signal	A/D Ratio	U/D Ratio	% Gain Before Next Major Decline
7/24/84	8/1	4.4	10.2	69.1
	8/2	5.5	11.7	
	8/3	4.6	11.0	
12/31/86*	1/2/87	9.0	26.3	39.1
	1/3/87	9.4	18.2	
10/19/87	10/21	8.4	21.2	⎫
	10/30	7.2	8.3	⎬ 64.8
12/4/87	1/4/88	8.2	18.6	⎪
	1/15/88	4.8	7.9	⎭

* actually a continuation of the previous bull market

There have been three major market debacles during the postwar period: the spring of 1962, 1973–74, and the fall of 1987. In each of these three cases, the market was sufficiently traumatized that the *first* set of two thrust days turned out not to be the actual signal. The market had two thrust days on May 31 and June 6, 1962; however, it then fell back later in the month, and the actual buy signal was not given until June 28 and July 10—after which the S&P 500 rose 80 percent over the next 3½ years.

In September 1974, the market troughed on October 3 and then had *three* thrust days on October 7, 9, and 10. That's a pretty powerful indicator, and anyone buying stocks on October 10 and holding them until the peak in September 1976 would have had a very handsome gain of 73 percent. However, the market then retreated—although it didn't quite recede to its September lows—and gave another three-day buy signal on December 31, 1974, and January 2 and January 10, 1975. That one was for real.

The most striking case of this double bottom occurred after the October 19, 1987 crash. Dispelling the doomsayers, the market didn't wait very long to rebound; the first thrust day of the buy signal was only two days later, on October 21, when the A/D ratio was 8.4 and the U/D ratio was 21.2. A second signal was given on October 30.

However, the market was not yet finished licking its wounds, and it then declined gradually through November, testing the October 19 lows again on December 4. When stocks held at that level, the market gradually began to improve again. The first thrust day of the second buy signal was January 4, 1988, and the second was January 15. At that point, the market was set to rally, and anyone buying in on that date would have had a 60 percent gain through mid-1990, in spite of widespread doubt at the time that stock prices would "ever" recover.

The double-thrust-day buy signals don't necessarily have to follow a major trough in the market; they are also critical in signaling the second and third legs of a bull market. That happened at the beginning of August 1984 and January 1987, even though the market had declined only moderately over the previous several months. Since it wasn't clear at either juncture whether the bull market would continue, these were also important buy signals.

Let me reemphasize the importance of a *repeat* signal for thrust days. On May 11, 1990, the market signaled a near-thrust day with A/D of 3.8 and U/D of 21.3. The Dow closed at 2,801 that day and ultimately moved up to 3,000—but then plunged to 2,365. In the middle of the decline, another thrust day occurred on August 27. Once again there was no confirmation, and prices soon headed back down again.

HOW TO SPOT A MAJOR MARKET ADVANCE

To summarize, here's how to use technical analysis to determine that a *major market advance* is about to occur.

1. Look for a day with an A/D ratio above 4 and a U/D ratio above 8. Both conditions must occur. If they are above 5 and 10 respectively, the signal is even stronger.
2. Wait for a second day with similar market characteristics within a month. Usually it will occur within a week.
3. If the market has just finished a significant but not devastating decline, that's a buy signal.
4. If the market has recently "crashed"—a decline of 25 percent or more, culminating in a major plunge—wait for a second set of buy signals.

This set of signals predicted each of the 11 major market upturns from 1962 through 1988 within an average of 7 percent of the trough. Whenever double-thrust days have occurred in a market that's already moving up, they have signaled the next leg of a bull market. Within these parameters, this indicator has never once given a false signal.

Sometimes a single thrust day of A/D above 4 and U/D above 8 will serve as a valid buy signal. This works most of the time but is not as reliable. Here are the guidelines to follow in that case.

1. Almost half the time, the market advances strongly in one of the first five days of the year. These times are generally suspect; in early January, always wait for a second thrust day before assuming that a bull market is in progress.
2. A one-day signal is probably valid if the market is already moving up; then it indicates the next leg up of a bull market. If the market is heading down, turning points invariably require two such days. In fact, the market gave several one-day signals during the 1981– 82 decline, none of which were valid.
3. Be especially careful if the one-day signal is due to some unexpected political, as opposed to economic, event. I'd always wait for a second signal in that case.

If this signal works as well as I have suggested, why bother with any other aspects of technical analysis?

Because, as it turns out, in spite of the perfect track record of this signal from 1962 through 1988, it did not predict the market upturn following the trough on October 11, 1990. Of course, circumstances were unusual; Iraq had recently invaded Kuwait, oil prices had soared from $17 to $40/ barrel, and no one knew if or when the U.S. would enter the war, or what the casualties might be. It is not surprising that even seasoned stock market analysts had no idea where the market was heading.

The market rebounded slightly from its October 11th lows, but gave no signs—either through Thrust Days or increasing volume—that these gains were anything more than random movements. Furthermore, in the beginning days of 1991, the market reversed course and slumped sharply, almost returning to the October lows by mid-January. The January 15th deadline given to Iraq passed, and many became even more bearish. Then the U.S. attacked—and the next day the Dow rose 114 points, with A/D and U/D ratios signalling a Thrust Day.

However, as I've pointed out above, one Thrust Day is usually not sufficient to mark the beginning of a major rally. The confirmation came on February 4th and 11th, both of which were Thrust Days. However, by the close of business on the 11th, the market was 25 percent above its trough level of October 11th, and that was giving away too much of the store.

One approach, I suppose, would be to throw a pie in the face of all the technicians and write off that entire discipline. Before doing that, though, take a minute to consider the circumstances when the market turned around. Oil prices were $40/barrel and many thought they would rise even further, although in fact they did nothing of the sort. There was little doubt that if a prolonged war developed, it would worsen the recession already in place, decimating profits and sending interest rates even higher.

From October to February, the stock market followed the fundamentals: It rallied as oil prices and inflation and interest rates declined. In line with our earlier comments about fundamental factors, that makes perfect sense. The problem during this period was that no forecaster could predict what would happen in the Middle East three months in the future.

The technical signals I've recommended in this section are based on the idea that when certain economic events occur, the best and the brightest investors recognize them right away, and they all go off and buy stocks at the same time. That's still an excellent reason to join them. Yet in a world of genuine uncertainty, where the stability of the entire world economy is called into question by a war started by a megalomaniac dictator, you simply won't find this sort of consensus. For that matter, the stock market remained depressed for years after World War II, and it also failed to respond to positive economic stimuli during the Korean War.

This episode can be used to drive home an important point: You can't invest in the stock market on automatic pilot. However, having stated what is perhaps the obvious, I will reiterate my (slightly revised) position: Except during times of war, Thrust Days are still a very useful signal for the beginning of major market upturns, and I fully expect them to be helpful in the years ahead.

If you're a long-term investor who doesn't have time to follow the market very closely on a day-to-day basis, the thrust day rule should still be sufficient—for predicting upturns. However, as the Persian Gulf war incident indicates, it is still worthwhile looking at other technical indicators for the following reasons:

1. Most important, this signal predicts only bull markets, not bear markets. Another set of signals is needed to predict the upper turning point.
2. At least historically, these signals have been flashed only rarely— 11 such signals during the past 30 years. Those who like to trade

more actively may find it useful to know where the stock market cycle currently stands.

3. This method might not work as well in the future; its record is already slightly tarnished by the war. Looking at other factors—moving averages, momentum, and volume—should maximize the odds of being correct.

PREDICTING THE UPPER TURNING POINT

If unusually high levels of A/D and U/D ratios invariably predict the beginnings of bull markets, then it might seem logical to suppose that the inverse—very high levels of decline/advance and down/up ratios—would predict the beginnings of bear markets. Sorry, it doesn't work that way.

Most market upturns begin with thrust days—with banners waving and trumpets blaring, as it were. They don't ring a bell to announce the beginning of the bull market, but a double-thrust day is usually the next best thing.

By comparison, market declines usually start gradually; it is not at all apparent that the peak has been reached. In fact, more often than not it is the case that very high levels of these inverse ratios signal the *end* of the bear market, not the beginning. As pessimism starts to gain momentum, decline/advance and down/up ratios increase until, typically, they culminate in a frenzy of selling. But by then the decline is usually over.

It is important to remember that the stock market exhibits a fundamental asymmetry between buying and selling. Some of this is due to purely technical reasons. Most large institutions as well as individual investors either are not permitted or do not like to sell short, since the gains are limited but the losses are not. A stock now selling at 40 cannot go lower than zero, but it could possibly go to 200.

Most of the difference, however, is psychological. Even in a raging bear market, most investors still have a few stocks they like. In the case of brokers, the recommended list helps pay the rent. But leaving cynicism to one side for the moment, a decision to buy a stock generally carries with it a belief that this stock will outperform the market. The investor has made a decision that, at least for a while, involves some pride—*I'm smarter than the market*. On the other hand, if you sell all your stocks and don't have any holdings left, there is an undercurrent of feeling that runs, *I can't find any stocks to buy—I'm dumber than the market*. Selling doesn't carry the same panache as buying.

Of course, selling all your stocks at the peak of a bull market would turn out to be a stroke of genius rather than stupidity. But right at the top, no one knows for sure that the market has peaked, and the vast majority of investors hope it hasn't. As a result, whereas bull markets invariably start off with one or two days of outsize gains, bear markets don't begin with a major decline. In virtually all cases, the market moves sideways for a while and makes one last attempt to reach a new peak before plunging decisively.

To see this, look at the three most important market declines of the past 40 years. The stock market peaked on December 12, 1961, with the S&P at 72.64. For the next three months, however, it moved sideways. It wasn't until early April that the signs of deterioration became evident.

The market peaked on January 11, 1973 with the S&P at 120.24, and then headed down, but recovered later in the year and by October 12 was back to 111.14. Then disaster struck, as it fell more than 40 percent over the next year.

After the S&P peaked at 336.77 on August 25, 1987, the market staged a final attempt, rallying back to 328.08 on October 5 before plunging 31.5 percent in two dizzying weeks.

Even the smaller declines of 1966, 1968, and 1981 exhibited the same pattern; after reaching what ultimately turned out to be the peak values, the market rallied one more time before entering its swan dive. That means investors have some leeway in getting out even if they miss the initial signal; you will lose a little money if you wait for the second peak, but not very much.

Some of this asymmetry represents fundamental factors, notably Fed policy. The Fed generally eases as soon as a recession is under way, which is one of the reasons that the stock market rallies. However, when the economy appears to be overheating, the Fed tightens gradually at first, trying to apply just the right amount of pressure to moderate inflation without bringing the expansion to a halt. Usually the first dose isn't enough, so policy is tightened further, and the stock market responds by heading lower again. This procedure is generally repeated several times until either inflation is dampened or the economy does indeed head into recession.

TECHNICAL FACTORS THAT IDENTIFY MARKET PEAKS

Market technicians have been unable to develop any rules that predict upper turning points with the same degree of accuracy as the A/D and

U/D rules for lower turning points. As I mentioned above, these ratios aren't used at all at market peaks. Instead, we rely on what might be called cousins of these ratios: the cumulative advance/decline (A/D) line and net new highs.

The cumulative A/D line is simply the sum of advances minus declines for each day from some arbitrary origin. If 877 stocks rose in price and 454 fell, the contribution to the A/D line for that day would be +423. It doesn't matter where the series starts as long as it goes back far enough to track the market since the last peak.

When the popular market averages—the DJIA, S&P, or NYSE indexes—move to new peaks, the cumulative A/D line for the NYSE should also move above its previous peak value. In other words, the increase in the overall market averages should be mirrored by the breadth of the market; the new peaks should not just be caused by increases in a few big-cap stocks that the majority of issues fail to follow.

If the A/D ratio fails to validate the new peak, it means the broad market is not keeping up with the leading stocks, and the whole house of cards is likely to collapse. The clearest example of this lack of convergence occurred in August 1987. While the Dow and S&P 500 moved to new highs, the A/D line declined—and the rest is history. Furthermore, precisely the same pattern occurred again in October 1989—permitting us to call the 190-point decline in the Dow on the nose. It recurred for the third time in three years in July 1990 and gave a clear sell signal—which we followed—before the Iraqi invasion of Kuwait. The portfolios I manage were all moved to 100 percent cash during the week of July 23rd, and this was announced in the *Evans Report*.

Most of the time, the A/D line will mimic the market all the way up to the last peak. But the next time a divergence like this one occurs, you should know what to expect.

Another key tape indicator is the number of *net new highs*, the number of stocks making new highs that day minus the number making new lows. This indicator is useful only at peaks. When the market has been declining for a while and is just beginning to turn around, hardly any stocks will be reading new highs in the initial stages of the bull market. However, as the market advances, more and more stocks will make new highs. In the later stages of a typical bull market, 200 to 300 NYSE stocks will reach new highs every day, with hardly any of them making new lows. When net new highs then decline below 0, meaning more stocks are making new lows than new highs, it's time to turn cautious—and when it drops below – 100, it's time to get out. That signal also worked in April 1962, January 1973, early October 1987, and July 1990.

The only problem with this indicator is that it sometimes gives false signals. In particular, it indicated an exit from the market in April 1987, when the bull market still had four more months to go. But if you had looked to the cumulative A/D line for corroboration, you would have seen that it confirmed the March peak of the market, whereas it diverged at the August peak. Thus, when the number of net new highs rebounded back above 100 in May it was time to get back in the market.

CHANGE IN VOLUME

The final indicator worth monitoring is *stock market volume*. This indicator is more erratic than the others, so although it's a popular one, I don't give it as much weight. The following use of volume statistics are of some use, but keep in mind that they don't work all the time.

1. When the start of a bull market is signaled by two thrust days, volume usually picks up as well. If it does, that represents additional confirmation that a bull market is really under way. If it doesn't, it pays to wait for that second two-day signal. A thrust day is an even more convincing signal if accompanied by a rise in volume of 50 percent or more, relative to average volume of the past 30 days.
2. If the market makes new highs on decreasing volume, that is a reasonably good sign that the bulls are becoming tired and a dip is likely.
3. It used to be thought that the same theory applied in reverse on the downside: If the market moves to new lows but volume diminishes, the decline is almost ended. However, on Black Monday, when the market plunged 508 points on the Dow, volume soared to 604 million shares, almost twice the previous record— yet the market rebounded the next day. So I wouldn't try to draw any conclusions from the level of volume at the lower turning points.

HOW TO SPOT A MAJOR MARKET DECLINE

Although the signals for the upper turning points aren't as clear as those that signal the lower turning points, here's what to check.

1. Anytime the market retreats from a peak, make sure the cumulative A/D line has verified that peak by forming a peak of its own. If it has not, sell.

2. If net new highs drop below 0, the market is weak and caution is advised. If they drop below − 100, it is usually time to sell out, although this signal doesn't work all the time. I usually give the market one more day to see if it snaps back; if it does, stay in for a little longer.
3. In every bear market, stock prices have rallied at least once after the peak has passed without returning to the previous peak value. If this latest peak does not match the previous one, sell out as soon as the market starts down again. Don't stick around to see what happens; sometimes the second plunge is so steep that there isn't much time to sell.

The figures for the A/D line, up/down volume, net new highs, and the cumulative A/D line are given every day in the *Investor's Daily*. The *Wall Street Journal* doesn't yet publish the A/D line, although it's found weekly in *Barron's*. So you don't need a computer system or a data feed to plot these simple indicators.

My firm monitors more than two dozen technical indicators each day, and some analysts look at many more than that. Except for waiting for thrust days, which happen an average of only once every other year, no single indicator works best all the time, and no indicator works equally well for both buy and sell signals. Some are better for bull markets; others for bear markets. Some work better in markets with strong trends; others, such as short-term oscillators, are better suited for markets with choppy trends. Most signals can't catch sharp one-day reversals.

On the other hand, I will make this unequivocal statement. Every single indicator we follow signaled a major market weakness during the first half of October 1987. So at least in my book, the argument about which is better—technical or fundamental analysis—is a meaningless one. Both of them help to improve accuracy at calling stock market turning points.

BUY AND SELL SIGNALS ARE NOT SYMMETRICAL

When using the technical indicators I've selected, it's best to keep a few key points in mind.

1. These indicators are *not* symmetrical. The indicators that give the best buy signals are no help generally when it comes to sell signals, and vice versa.

   Bull markets start with a bang, but bear markets end with a bang. The theory that bull markets end in an excess of buying frenzy is incorrect; volume around August 25, 1987, was close to average.

2. Over the long run, the market moves up most of the time, so the key signals should be designed to keep you in the market a majority of the time. You don't want to be selling out on every little downturn.

3. In recent years, due in part to the proliferation of computers and technical analysis, downside moves have tended to be more explosive than upside moves. Sometimes these occur with little advance warning. However, the worst thing to do is panic and get out of the market just after a sharp decline, if in fact the market is headed back up.

   This comment isn't meant to apply to the October 1987 crash, which gave plenty of advance warning signals. It does, however, apply to days like January 8, 1988, when the Dow fell 140 points, or 6.7 percent, in one day; as it turned out, that was the low point for the year. We don't want a system that gives a sell signal on days like that.

4. Finally, before acting on any buy or sell signal, always consider the fundamental factors as well—the P/E ratio, recent interest rates and Fed policy, and the inflation rate.

KEYS TO TIMING MARKET CYCLES

I will now show how this blend of fundamental and technical indicators has tracked the major bull and bear markets of the past 40 years. I've separated bull and bear markets, but I've done so in such a way that the market is either in a bull or bear market phase, as shown in Table 21. It seldom goes sideways for very long.

During the post–World War II period, there have been 15 major bull markets, defined as an increase of 20 percent or more in the S&P 500. However, there have been only eight business cycles. Besides, the stock market generally turns up about four months before the recovery starts, which is actually a very good rule for predicting the economy but does nothing to explain the market. So we will have to look elsewhere.

Sticking with fundamental factors for the moment, each of the past 10 upturns was preceded by an average decline in short- and long-term interest rates of at least 1 percentage point (e.g., from 7 to 6 percent). The lag here is somewhat variable, so you would have had to use technical indicators to catch the exact turning point. However, whenever rates drop this much, be prepared for the emergence of a bull market if one hasn't already started.

Table 21
The 15 Major Stock Market Cycles

Date of Trough	Value	% Decline	Date of Peak	Value	% Increase
6/13/49	13.55	− 20.6	1/5/53	26.66	96.7
9/14/53	22.71	− 14.8	7/15/57	49.15	116.3
10/22/57	38.98	− 20.7	8/3/59	60.71	55.7
10/25/60	52.30	− 13.9	12/12/61	72.64	38.9
6/26/62	52.32	− 28.0	2/9/66	94.06	79.8
10/7/66	73.20	− 22.2	9/25/67	97.59	33.3
3/5/68	87.72	− 10.1	11/29/68	108.37	23.5
5/26/70	69.29	− 36.1	4/28/71	104.77	51.2
11/26/71	90.16	− 13.9	1/11/73	120.24	33.4
10/3/74	62.28	− 48.2	9/21/76	107.83	73.1
3/6/78	86.90	− 19.4	10/5/79	111.27	28.1
3/27/80	98.22	− 11.7	11/28/80	140.52	43.1
8/12/82	102.42	− 27.1	10/10/83	172.65	68.6
7/24/84	147.82	− 14.4	8/25/87	336.77	127.8
12/4/87	223.92	− 33.5	7/6/90	368.95	64.8
10/11/90	295.46	− 19.9			

All figures based on S&P 500, daily closing averages.
I define a "stock market cycle" as follows: The market must decline 10 percent or more, and the next peak must surpass the previous peak.

Next, check to make sure the P/E ratio plus the rate of inflation is less than 20. That is generally the case when the market has been declining, but not always. It is possible for a slight recovery in the market to start with a violation of the Rule of 20, in which case the bull market will turn out to be stunted.

Assuming that interest rate and P/E criteria are met, wait for the technical buy signal, which is two thrust days within one month; they usually occur within a few days of each other. If the market is just coming off a major decline, wait for a second signal. It won't make that much difference in the long run but it will save you the heartburn of watching all those stocks you just picked go down for another month or two.

Congratulations. You have now moved back into the market very near the beginning of a bull market. Now when do you get out?

First, bull markets have no set length. Sometimes they last less than a year, sometimes as long as four years. So simply counting the months will tell you nothing. Let the market run without worrying too much whether long-term interest rates are stable or declining. I don't get too concerned about modest gains in short-term rates, which almost always occur at the beginning of business cycles. However, substantial increases in long-term rates are a different story. A gain of 1 percentage point or more in long-term interest rates is the first caution signal. It isn't necessarily a sell signal, because the market will generally keep rising as long as profits rise faster than interest rates, but it is a first warning.

The next warning sign occurs when the P/E ratio plus inflation exceeds 20. That means stocks are overpriced unless profits increase substantially the next year, but they seldom do at an advanced stage of the cycle. The market has occasionally been known to improve for more than a year after that boundary was crossed, so it's not an immediate sell signal.

As long as stock prices keep rising, and of course I don't mean every day—even the most rampant bull markets have down days—there's no reason to sell out. However, when stock prices decline more than 5 percent, it's time to reassess the fundamental factors. If long-term interest rates have risen more than 1 percent and the P/E ratio plus inflation is greater than 20, it's time to think about moving to the sidelines.

Someday the market may drop 20 or 30 percent from its peak without even pausing for breath. However, that hasn't happened yet; prices have always moved back up somewhat in an attempt to test the old highs. It's that second peak that usually tells the tale. If the market falls short of its previous peak, or the A/D line fails to reach a new peak, that's the clearest signal I know to move out of the market. If you're not sure, wait until net new highs turn negative and then exit; but you may save a few points by moving right away.

Once stocks head into a bear market phase after failing to validate the previous peak, they usually gain downward momentum until the bear market ends in a selling frenzy. The October 19, 1987, crash was the most extreme example of this, but the bear markets of 1962, 1966, 1970, and 1974 all ended with sharp downward thrusts that were marked in large part by smaller accounts telling their brokers to "sell everything." Presumably you won't have to join that crowd because you'll have sold out near the top.

Once the bear market has come to an end, wait patiently until a thrust-day signal is given. Don't be too impatient and jump the gun; there will be plenty of gains left even if you miss the first 5 or even 10 percent of the upturn. However, if the first thrust day is accompanied by a doubling in volume, as was the case in 1982, it's probably safe to jump in right away.

SUMMARY

To briefly summarize the key points in this chapter:

RULES FOR BULL MARKETS

1. P/E plus inflation is less than 20, then wait for:
2. Two thrust days: A/D greater than 4:1, and U/D greater than 8:1. If the market is just emerging from a protracted slump, wait for a second signal. If volume jumps significantly on a thrust day, that is an even stronger buy signal.

Note: If these signals turn up when a bull market is already in progress, it is time to shift into stocks that are likely to accelerate when the market rises rapidly.

RULES FOR BEAR MARKETS

1. Warning signals: at least a 1-percentage-point rise in long-term interest rates, and P/E ratio plus inflation exceeds 20.
2. When the market starts down, check to see whether the latest peak is validated by the A/D line. If not, get out immediately.
3. If it is validated, wait for the next peak. If it is below the previous peak, or if the A/D line does not confirm, get out as soon as the market turns down again. If net new highs are negative, that intensifies the sell signal.

RULES FOR CHURNING MARKETS
These rules should cover almost all situations in the market, but occasionally stock prices will churn aimlessly for a while without fitting any of these circumstances. In particular, suppose you have sold your stocks using the above signals, but the market has started back up again without any buy signals appearing.

1. Do nothing until the market moves up 5 percent from its most recent trough (not more than one month ago).
2. Then look for a single thrust day; if the P/E ratio plus inflation

is less than 20 and interest rates have recently been declining, it's probably worth getting back in.

That happened in April 1987, when it initially appeared the bull market was over. Interest rates had been rising, the P/E ratio plus inflation was above 20 and the P/E ratio itself was approaching 20, and net new highs had suddenly dropped below −100. The market did correct briefly, then it suddenly recovered near the end of May and moved up another 20 percent before reaching its final peak. Why was August the end of the bull market instead of April?

KEY DIFFERENCES BETWEEN MAY 1987 AND SEPTEMBER 1987

1. The A/D line confirmed the March peak but did not confirm the August peak.
2. The P/E ratio was below 20 in May but above 20 in August— although P/E plus inflation was above 20 both times.
3. Probably most important, bond yields fell slightly in May, whereas they headed up steadily in August and September, and the Fed raised the discount rate in September.

One final note. Suppose you had completely misread the signals and failed to get out of the market before Black Monday, but had stayed in the market. Eventually you would have done all right, since the market did surpass its previous highs by mid-1989. The real disaster would have been riding the market all the way down and then dumping your stocks at the bottom.

As I said at the beginning, pick your system and stick to it: Either buy and hold or use market timing with technical signals. Just don't get whip-sawed by your emotions.

Chapter 18

Choosing the Right Stocks

What do Masco Screw Products, Capital Cities Broadcasting, and The Limited all have in common?

Since 1958 the prices of these stocks have all increased by 800 times or more. That's right. Every $1,000 invested in those stocks back then would be worth more than $800,000 now.

Okay, let's try again. What do The Dreyfus Corporation, Boeing Aircraft, Melville, and Nucor Steel have in common?

All of these companies were out of favor in 1974 because of temporarily depressed earnings, but since then, their stock prices have all increased at least 50 times in price. Not as spectacular a total gain, but on an annual percentage basis the rise is just as great.

And what do Chrysler, K Mart, and Toys "R" Us have in common?

All given up for dead, they managed to post gains of at least 35 times over a 10-year period.

One more time. What do Avon Products, Polaroid, and Xerox have in common?

Wrong. While they all *were* great growth companies at one point, they are currently selling for anywhere from one-half to one-fourth of their peak values back in 1973.

Which brings us to the key question of this chapter: What makes the price of an individual stock outperform the market?

There are lots of fancy reasons, but in the long run the answer is always the same: Earnings grow rapidly.

One important caveat before we start. Be sure not to overpay for earnings. If a stock is selling for a P/E of 100, even if its earnings grow 50 percent per year for the next five years, the price may not appreciate because this phenomenal growth record is already built into it. But in the long run, earnings are the key to optimal stock selection.

THE THREE TYPES OF STOCKS THAT OUTPERFORM THE MARKET

Potential gainers fall into one of three major categories: *growth stocks, cyclical stocks*, and *turnaround stocks*.

Takeover candidates are not included in this list. The chance to double or even triple your money within a few months is an exciting proposition—and with options, the gains can be astronomical. Naturally that appeals to lots of people; that's why racetracks and casinos continue to prosper in spite of the certainty that over the long run, only the owners and the tax collectors win. If I were able to identify a takeover candidate before anyone else has seen the signals, of course I would buy it. However, since insider trading became a prosecutable crime, most of the telltale technical signals have disappeared. So while there are a few hints later in this chapter about how to handle possible takeover stocks, we're going to concentrate here on long-term values rather than on the get-rich-quick schemes.

Before buying any stock for possible long-term appreciation—as opposed to short-term trading based on technical signals—you should firmly identify in your own mind the factors that will make this stock appreciate. Far too many people buy stocks on some vague hope or faith. "It's in a growth industry," or "It has top-notch management" may be admirable qualities, but unless they translate into higher stock prices, they aren't worth a nickel to you. Also, remember that you aren't the only one scrutinizing individual stocks and looking for bargains. If you discover a company whose profits really are going to double each year, chances are that other people have also discovered this jewel and that future growth is already reflected in the current stock price. In general, the great stock picks in the past have been companies that, for one reason or another, were ignored by most of the investing public. You will make the most money by finding diamonds in the rough.

THE SIREN SONG OF RAPID GROWTH

Most amateur investors are drawn to companies that are in high-growth industries. Maybe they sound more glamorous. But the record, especially over the past few years, has been far from convincing. During the 1980s—as well as the 1970s and the 1960s—computers and electronics have clearly been at the forefront of the growth parade. By comparison, investors tend to ignore the troglodytes of American industry—the steel, auto, and tobacco industries, particularly the latter, which actually has negative growth. Nonetheless, since 1982 an investor would have made more money investing in auto, steel, and tobacco companies than in computer and similar high-tech companies. Don't be swayed by the siren song of rapid growth. It is only one of the many criteria that determine the price of the stock, and generally it is not the most important one. The field is littered with promising growth-stock companies that somehow never quite delivered on their initial promise.

P/E Ratios and Growth Trends

The market generally pays a premium for growth. The general rule of thumb is that the P/E ratio is equal to the expected future growth rate in earnings. Thus, for example, if earnings are expected to rise 20 percent per year in the future, the market would generally assign a P/E of 20 to that stock; a 40 percent growth in earnings would merit a P/E of 40, and so on. This formula applies only to growth companies; a company with no expected growth in earnings would sell at book value rather than zero. But it is a useful first cut for ranking companies with P/E ratios above the market average.

Since no one can actually predict future earnings on a consistent basis, "expected future" earnings are usually similar to "recent past" earnings, with one significant exception. Even stock market analysts realize that companies can't keep growing at 100 or even 50 percent per year forever, so if a company's earnings have recently been growing at a stratospheric rate, the P/E ratio will usually be somewhat lower. Occasionally, however, a company will slip through the net and trade at 100 times earnings. I'd avoid these like the plague.

As a general rule of thumb, any company whose P/E ratio is well below its recent growth rate of earnings merits further examination. As with any general rule, though, this approach has its pitfalls.

Profits may be ready to tumble for reasons that are so obvious even the

Street knows about them. The causes might be macroeconomic (the economy is heading into a recession) or specific (fraud discovered at the company, loss of a huge lawsuit, or expiration of key patents). Finding companies whose recent growth rate is substantially higher than their P/E is obviously no guarantee of success.

Don't even consider buying high-flying companies whose P/E is greater than recent earnings growth. These are almost sure to take a tumble in the near future. It was precisely this sort of myopia that led to the collapse of the Nifty Fifty in 1973–74, as will be discussed in Chapter 19.

In addition, I would avoid almost all stocks whose underlying P/E ratio is more than twice the market average, even if that is equal to or less than recent earnings growth. By "underlying," I mean that sometimes a company suffers a temporary setback that wipes out virtually all its earnings. Analysts realize that this situation is about to be reversed, and hence the stock price does not decline proportionately to the drop in earnings. In an extreme case, the P/E ratio would be infinite if the company had no earnings at all or an actual loss. In that case, the ratio obviously becomes meaningless and other gauges, such as cash flow and book value, are substituted.

However, if a company is posting steady earnings gains and the P/E ratio is above 30 in normal markets or 40 in extreme bull markets, I would skip down to the next listing. Your chances of making money on such a stock aren't zero, but in the long run the amount you'll eventually lose on buying high-flyers will dwarf whatever gains you may accumulate.

The Fallen Virgins

The market is extremely unforgiving of high-growth companies that stumble even momentarily. As Wall Street cynics say, a company can lose its virginity only once. As long as profits rise steadily every year and every quarter, analysts are more than willing to tout the stock at 40 and 50 times earnings. Once disappointed, though, they'll move on to greener pastures as prices dive-bomb down to 10 or 15 times earnings. Even if earnings fully recover, the stock price will only be about one-third of its level during the glory days.

Most companies that have rapid growth in sales and earnings also have matching growth in costs as they add employees and expand capacity. Sales can decline on a dime, but expenses usually can't. If costs have been rising at 50 percent a year and the pace of sales modulates slightly, it takes even well-managed firms several months to bring those costs under control.

They are stuck with existing buildings and equipment, and employees cannot usually be dismissed without severance pay and other termination benefits. Thus profits may shrink drastically for a while.

Most of the great growth stocks in the high-tech area eventually fell on bad times. For many years, Wang Computers was one of the most dependable growth stocks, rising more than 10-fold from 1973 to 1983 at a time when most high-flyers were falling by the wayside. Founding father An Wang even wrote an autobiography telling the world what a marvelous job he had done. However, just as stock prices were heating up in the great bull market of the 1980s, Wang pulled a Wrong-Way Corrigan. The company ran into financial difficulties, and the price of the stock plummeted from 42 to 6 just as stock prices in general were tripling.

Even high-tech stocks whose profits have grown steadily may be so overpriced when they first come out that there is little room left for appreciation. From 1983 to 1989, profits of Genentech rose from $0.04 to $0.70 a share, but the stock price increased only from 12 to 17 (adjusted for splits), although it was higher in the 1987 bull market. With a P/E of over 400 when the company first went public, there wasn't much room for expansion. In many other cases, companies never make the transition from high-tech garage to full-line financial giant.

Occasionally a high-tech stock really will perform spectacularly. Tandy Corporation was selling at (split-adjusted) ¼ when it acquired Radio Shack in 1967. Twenty years later it was at 60, a 240-fold increase. Even those gains, however, were due to retailing rather than technology. In fact, as anyone who ever tried to use a Radio Shack computer will tell you, they're almost low-tech (for years the TRS-80 was ubiquitously known as the Trash 80). Retailing rather than electronics boosted the stock price.

The most outstanding success story in the computer field is Compaq, which rose from $3 in 1984 to $100 in 1989. Unfortunately, however, this is the exception that proves the rule. The biggest fortunes made in trading stocks—as opposed to starting a company and owning a substantial chunk of the shares—have come from undervalued companies in moderate or slow-growth industries. That doesn't mean you shouldn't own any high-tech stocks, but don't overload your portfolio with them.

10 RULES FOR PICKING GROWTH STOCKS

As the opening salvo about Avon Products, Polaroid, and Xerox made clear, you don't make money by buying growth stocks after they have finished growing. By the time these stocks were discovered by most of the investment community, their rapid growth had come to an end. For that reason as well as the points already discussed, I suggest you generally *stay away* from the areas in which the "name" growth stocks have historically appeared. Avoid most stocks in the high-tech industries. A few companies in those industries will do fantastically well, and in 10 years you'll probably be kicking yourself for not buying them way back when. But for every growth star that finally dazzles Wall Street, a hundred other companies with similar promise never make it out of the starting gate and wind up forgotten if not bankrupt.

This does *not* mean you should avoid growth stocks entirely. Just pick the right stocks, which are generally found in the right industries. Here's my list of the qualities to consider—assuming, of course, that earnings have been growing rapidly and you have no valid reason to expect them to slow down.

1. Don't Overpay for Growth. Look for companies with high growth rates but moderate P/E ratios. They don't have to be low—in fact, they probably should be at or slightly above the market P/E average—but I would be extremely wary of buying any stock with a P/E that's more than twice the market average. And although there are supposed to be no immutable laws in investing, I'm laying down one rule with no exceptions: Never buy a stock with a P/E of 100 or more.

2. Dull Companies Make Jack. Don't ignore companies that make dull products in dull industries. A company can do quite well in an industry that isn't growing fast, providing it has a niche for some product that for various reasons does not attract a horde of competitors. Masco Screw Products was, as its name suggests, just a small nuts-and-bolts firm in Detroit that was going nowhere. The stock was stagnant during most of the 1950s, which in general was an excellent decade for stock prices, and earnings declined almost to the vanishing point. Then Masco developed the one-handled bathroom faucet, and in the next four years, the stock price rose more than 30 times. Moreover, patents protected it from major competitors, and sales and profits kept rising. Eventually the company achieved fame of some sort for being one of the very few stocks whose value rose over 1,000 times. That finally attracted quite a bit of attention and, as you may have guessed, it has underperformed the market ever since.

Note that niches are not the same as fads. This year's Nintendo knockoff probably won't make a dime. Toy companies are, in general, notoriously bad investments for the long run. Remember Teddy Ruxpin? He was the guiding light behind the new issue offer of Worlds of Wonder, Inc., which came out at 27, went to 29 the first day, and then headed inexorably downward to 1 before declaring bankruptcy.

Genuine Auto Parts, another example, has risen more than 300 times since 1954 and has almost tripled since 1984, even though total auto sales have stagnated. Of course, some companies manufacturing automotive components or nuts and bolts never get off the dime, but this company had rapid earnings growth before it became a stellar growth company.

3. Secrets Are My Success. The smaller number of institutions that own the stock or follow the company, the better. Both the *Daily Graphs* from William O'Neil and Company and the weekly graphs from Mansfield provide information on how much of the stock is owned by banks and mutual funds.

When an analyst at any major brokerage house starts following a stock with an initial recommendation, that stock price generally receives a boost. As more institutions buy the shares, the P/E rises further. Eventually all major institutional investors know about the stock, and it won't receive any further boosts from new investor discoveries. Furthermore, if the earnings are lower than expected some quarter, the institutions are likely to dump the stock mercilessly, whereas individual investors tend to be more patient.

4. Monopoly, Thy Name Is Profit. Monopolies are technically illegal, but look for situations where competition is negligible if not completely absent. In Washington, D.C., right under the nose of allegedly vigilant antitrust officers, Giant Food carved out a market niche in supermarkets that sent the stock up almost 100 times; the *Washington Post* monopolized the newspaper business to send its stock from 3¾ (after splits) to 300; and GEICO dominated the low-cost auto insurance industry to rise from 2 to 146.

5. Repeat Business Means Repeat Profits. Sales should be characterized by repeat business. Tampax, Inc.—now Tambrands—was another success story from 1948 to 1973, rising over 500-fold. (Then it became large enough to become an institution stock, pushing the P/E ratio up to unsustainable levels, and it finally crashed.) Once the company has made initial sales or advertising contacts, whether by personal contact, direct mail, or mass marketing, the same customers should come back again and again. Obviously this rules out companies that produce computer software products that don't generate repeat business.

6. Goliath Won't Get Any Larger. Growth companies should be small to medium in size when you discover them. Maybe that's obvious, but it is amazing how many otherwise intelligent investors still thought IBM was a growth stock after it had become so big it would have been almost impossible for it to outperform the overall economy.

7. Steady as She Grows. The company doesn't have to be in a fast-growing industry. In many ways, it's almost better if it isn't, because a moderate- or slow-growth industry won't attract as many new entrants. As long as growth remains steady, profits won't disappear and send the stock plummeting. One classic example is retail-store chains, which in the aggregate can grow no faster than the overall economy. Sears's dominant market position was first challenged during the 1960s by S. S. Kresge, later known as K Mart, and during the 1970s and 1980s by Wal-Mart. The stock of Kresge/K Mart rose more than 50 times from 1963 to 1972. Wal-Mart stock is an even more amazing success story, increasing more than 300-fold from 1971 to 1987, a nifty 40 percent per year. In the slow-growing beer industry, where demand is increasing only about 1 percent per year, Anheuser-Busch stock rose more than 10 times since 1978 as it gobbled up market share.

In one bizarre twist, the tobacco industry, which actually has negative growth, spawned some of the fastest-appreciating stocks in the entire market during the 1980s. Investors shunned the industry for two reasons: the decline in total sales, and the threat of all those lawsuits. As a result, when the cigarette companies raised their prices about twice as fast as the rate of inflation, nothing happened. The government did not intervene, predators did not enter what they perceived to be a declining market, and consumers hardly cut back on their demand at all; those who are addicted to nicotine are very insensitive to prices. Thus Philip Morris, U.S. Tobacco, RJR Nabisco (before it went private), and Loews (Lorillard) have far outperformed the market. Philip Morris stock, for example, has risen 7-fold since 1982. I'm not saying that negative growth is a plus, of course, but if you can find a rapidly growing company in a stagnating industry that isn't attracting any competitors, so much the better.

8. No Geniuses Need Apply. Whatever the company does should be straightforward and easily duplicated as it expands. A financial services company that depends on the deal-making of a few geniuses might have a few stellar growth years, but it will probably not become a major financial powerhouse unless the same level of performance can be copied by mere mortals. The Limited, Wal-Mart, and Liz Claiborne are all retail stores that found their niche and were able to duplicate a successful store concept easily. These growth companies don't have to be in retailing; in the manufacturing sector, Crown Cork and Seal, which makes cans and cork seals— just as it says—has appreciated over 100 times since 1961. Automatic Data

Processing figured out how to do small-business payrolls more efficiently; their stock also rose almost 100 times. The stock of Food Lion Supermarkets has risen more than 200 times since 1971.

9. Avoid Wolves at the Door. This means avoiding companies that advances in technology can render obsolete overnight. That is the major problem with many high-tech companies; their xygots are quickly rendered obsolete by the next generation. Storage Technology fell from 14½ to 1 before a rare reverse 1:10 split coincided with its return to profitability. Even well-managed companies find that bigger, better-financed predators will attack. IBM certainly did not invent or market the first big computer, nor for that matter the first PC. Those distinctions go to Sperry Rand and Apple. However, when Big Blue geared up for the kill, the effect on its competitors was disastrous. Sperry Rand finally merged with Burroughs and now hides under the name of something called Unisys, which is itself now close to death's door. Apple managed to recover, but only after a long dry spell when its profits and stock price were severely depressed and even its admirers didn't know whether it would survive. Predators don't bother stodgy businesses whose total sales are flat or declining; as noted, nobody is breaking down the doors to get into the cigarette business.

10. Higher Dividends Equal Lower Growth. Look for a company that pays little or no dividends. Of course, lack of dividends can also mean lack of profits, but we're only considering companies with rapid earnings growth. When a company pays half or more of its profits in dividends, that means it's not recycling its cash flow back into expansion. When IBM started paying out more than half of its profits as dividends, it ceased being a growth company.

CYCLICAL STOCKS: WHEN TO BUY THEM

Some analysts can visit a small, unknown company, talk to management, examine the operations, read the income statement and balance sheet, visit the customers, and come back and pronounce it one of the great growth stars of the next decade. In my view, this is a rare talent and one that is extremely difficult to master. It's much simpler to analyze companies that are already known entities but are out of favor with Wall Street because their earnings have fallen—yet stand a reasonable chance of rapid growth next year.

Firms with low P/E ratios can be grouped into two principal groups. The first is cyclical stocks—companies with high capital expenses and large swings in sales. They are almost sure to have wide fluctuations in profits even if they are well managed. Wall Street invariably knocks down their P/E ratios because profits fluctuate cyclically.

The second group is firms that have been poorly managed and suffered a steep decline in profits but have the potential to return to glory. Often this is accomplished by bringing in new management. However, sometimes the old team gets religion and starts reacting vigorously to competitive pressures; labor also sees the light and becomes more productive. These descriptions probably fit the auto and steel industries the best, but similar situations have happened in soft-goods, retailing, distribution, and even financial services.

Wall Street values consistency and stability of earnings very highly. Thus, over the course of the business cycle, companies with cyclical earnings will sell at a lower P/E ratio than those with stable earnings, even taking into account any differentials in growth rates. That's why, when choosing stocks, it's important to compare the P/E ratio with an industry average as well as with the market average. For example, suppose the overall P/E market ratio is 13. A bank stock or auto stock with a P/E of 8 might be overpriced, whereas a pharmaceutical company with a P/E ratio of 17 might be underpriced.

Profits of cyclical industries invariably decline during recessions, but sometimes these sectors are also plagued with problems of overcapacity and price-cutting even if no downturn develops. For example, in 1987 and 1988, the prices of paper, industrial chemicals, plastics, and metals rose at double-digit rates even though inflation remained below 5 percent. As a result, profits zoomed and, because most stocks in those industries did not rise much more than the overall market, many P/E ratios fell to a range of 5 to 7. However, these large price increases also generated capacity expansion in all these industries, so by mid-1989 commodity prices had declined and profit margins started to collapse. When the recession started, their profits declined even further and stock prices continued to plunge in spite of unusually low P/E ratios.

Here's how I determine which cyclical issues are good buys.

First, look for cyclical stocks with P/E ratios at least one-third less than the P/E for the overall market; one-half is even better. Cyclical stocks are generally those in the following industries: transportation equipment, machinery (except computers), metals, forest products, paper, chemicals and plastics, building materials, petroleum refining and oil service, textiles, and household durables.

Second, estimate a reasonable worst-case scenario for how much profits could decline next year. There are several different approaches, but one reasonable way is to look at the percentage decline during the previous recession and apply that to the most recent four-quarters earnings figure. Often profits of cyclical companies are negative in recession years; in that case, calculate the percentage decline in cash flow.

Third, calculate the P/E ratio—or price/cash flow ratio—with next year's lower profits. If it still turns out to be less than 20 percent below the current P/E or cash-flow multiple of the overall market, the stock should at least be considered for purchase.

Turnaround Situations: A Real Potential Money-Maker

Trying to guess cyclical trends in the market is a difficult proposition, but turnaround companies can often be spotted a mile away. Yet when these companies first start to recover, they are generally despised by individuals and institutions alike. Chrysler—why they're a ward of the government. Con Edison—they lost me *thousands* of dollars of business because of their blackouts. International Harvester—imagine paying Archie McCardell a $1.8 million bonus for almost driving the company into bankruptcy.

If you have sworn to "get even" with some company because it sold you defective merchandise, refused to honor your guarantee, served you a bad meal, ruined your vacation plans, or cut off your utilities, and you're unwilling to reconsider even when new management has been put in place, that's okay. Just skip this section and you can still get rich following all the advice in the rest of the book. However, for those who didn't hold grudges and didn't mind buying companies known to have been real stinkers—even those that had caused them personal grief—turnaround situations represented some of the biggest percentage gains during the 1980s. And they're easy to spot. A change in management is hardly a secret. Furthermore, because of the negative reaction of would-be investors, in most cases profits rise for at least a year before the stock starts to move higher again. That leaves plenty of time to determine that the recovery in earnings isn't just a fluke.

One of the outstanding success stories of the 1980s was Chrysler, and it just happened to be one that I knew about in advance. In 1982, when Chrysler stock was selling at 4 (up from its low of 3⅛ the previous year), I got a call from someone at the company asking if I knew any good economists who were looking for jobs. Since it was a recession year and many erstwhile forecasters had recently gotten the ax, I replied I knew several of them, but why was he asking? "We're hiring," he told me.

Naturally I didn't believe him, and mumbled something about them being only one step away from kicking the bucket. "Yes, I know," he said, "that's what everyone else says, too. No one believes we've turned the corner."

Chrysler stock rose to 30 the next year and a high of 48 in 1987 before backing off later in the decade. So here was some valuable information, entirely in the public domain, that would have enabled me to make 12 times my money in the space of three years. And how many shares did I buy at bargain prices? If you guessed zero, you're real warm. Yet when I went back and looked at the earnings reports, I found that the turnaround had started in early 1981. Virtually everyone had missed it because of preconceptions about the old Chrysler.

This story has a moderately happy ending, at least from my own point of view, because after this happened I made up my mind that if another call like that ever materialized, I wouldn't remain on the sidelines. As it so happens, I did get a similar call about a year later from what was then International Harvester, also asking for names of economists. The stock at that time was 3½. This time I didn't hesitate to buy, and it rose to 12 the next year before fading back. Once again, the earnings turned around before the stock price did.

Unfortunately, I haven't received any similar calls since then, but the point is that most of the large-scale turnarounds and bankruptcies are adequately covered in the business and financial press, and it doesn't take much research to know who's in trouble, or who has appointed a new management team. Follow the quarterly earnings reports—available in the *Wall Street Journal* or from any standard chart service—and when you begin to see a steady upward trend, it's time to buy in. With the rest of the investment community still soured on the company, your downside risk is minimal.

Having said all this, let me emphasize one key point, which is that you should always wait until the turnaround has started. Some companies are reorganized and promptly go bankrupt and never recover. Crazy Eddie is a prime example. When the new management team took over, they found that $65 million of inventory was unaccountably missing, and the company eventually filed for bankruptcy. Wait for profits to turn up before you invest.

Here's what to look for in turnaround situations.

1. The company, after years of profitability, has recently posted huge losses.

2. The company is still viable and has sufficient assets to support substantial profits again in the future. A retailing firm that has lost the confidence of its consumers is probably a dead dodo.
3. New management has been installed and the principal cause of the losses has been removed.
4. The company has returned to profitability. This last step is particularly important—do not jump into the stock before the profits have reappeared.

IBM—WORLD'S GREATEST GROWTH STOCK?

To round out our discussion of stock selection, let's take a brief look at IBM, commonly touted as the world's greatest stock. But don't listen to anyone who tells you this unless they attach a few dates to the price increases.

IBM was actually incorporated in 1911, but it didn't really don the mantle of Quintessential Growth Company until after World War II. From 1947 to 1962, the price of the stock, adjusted for stock splits and stock dividends, rose from ½ to a peak of 34—a 68-fold increase, or about 32 percent per year in capital gains plus cash dividends, which averaged about 2 percent during this high-growth period. I mean, that's no Masco Screw Products, but on the other hand it was a much better known company and institutions could buy almost unlimited amounts without having to worry about exceeding various regulatory limits. The price then continued up to 90 in early 1973, an acceptable but certainly not a superlative performance of 10 percent per year.

Since then, however, the stock has been a walking disaster. In late 1989, it fell below 100, a total gain of only 10 percent for the past 16 years. Indeed, after 1962 IBM became just another cyclical stock; it declined 50 percent that year, another 50 percent in the 1973–74 debacle, and almost 50 percent in the 1987 crash.

Let me put it this way. If you had taken $1,000 in 1973 and put it in a CD, you would have had $3,700 at the end of 1989. If you had invested in IBM stock, including reinvestment of all dividends, you would have had $2,077 (assuming both investments were in a tax-deferred fund). That's right—you would have done much better putting your money into the bank than into IBM stock.

Here is an even more shocking statistic. Suppose, with perfect timing, you had bought IBM in August 1982, on the very day before the stock market began its greatest bull market, and had held it until mid-1989.

Also suppose that on the same day you had bought a seven-year CD from the bank. You would still have done better leaving your money in the bank than buying IBM. While the average stock was rising more than three times in price, IBM could hardly increase at all, and for the most basic reason—earnings in 1989 were just about the same as they were in 1982.

In spite of this, IBM is still the company most widely covered by stock analysts and the business press. Maybe they think it will come back some-day, or maybe they just think other people think it will. But my prediction is that over the long run, you will continue to do better by leaving your money in the bank than by buying IBM stock. Maybe it's still a great company, but it won't grow any faster than the overall economy. Management will continue to issue those encouraging broadsides about how the company's profits will now grow 15 percent per year forever. They may even reach those goals three years out of four, but in the fourth year earnings will be down 10 percent, and the average will be only 8 percent per year, which is the same growth rate as nominal GNP. When any company gets as big as most national economies, it can no longer be expected to outperform the U.S. economy.

TECHNICAL ANALYSIS OF INDIVIDUAL STOCKS

The technical signals discussed in the previous chapter were based primarily on the breadth of the overall market—advance/decline ratio, up/down ratio, net new highs, and cumulative advance/decline line. Since none of these apply to individual stocks, the technical repertoire that can be followed without fancy computer programs is more limited. Here's what I consider to be the key technical factors that affect individual stocks.

1. Patterns of buying and selling volume, also known as *accumulation* and *distribution*. In order for a stock to be considered a buy, when its price rises volume should be increasing, and when the price falls, as it inevitably will, volume should be diminishing. Also note whether the stock closes near the high of the day. For example, if a stock moved from 31½ to 32 on heavy volume but had traded as high as 34 that day, this would be considered a negative rather than a positive reaction.
2. Support and resistance levels. No stock prices go straight up; after a substantial gain, profit-taking invariably occurs and the price declines a little. This is sometimes known as the *5 percent stutter*

rule, which says that after a stock price has risen to a new peak, it usually declines 5 percent before heading higher again. (This is also known as the *3-point rule*, since many stocks trade in the 50–60 range.)

Another important rule is that the price should not fall below the level at which the most recent run-up started. If the stock can't hold above its previous support level, it probably isn't in a longer-term upward trend. If the stock has fallen sharply and is trying to stage a comeback, it's likely to stall out near its previous peak level, known as the *resistance level*. If it can pierce through that level, it may go substantially higher.

These guidelines don't work all the time. They are presented here as useful caution flags. I would be wary about buying a stock right below its resistance level; the upside potential is much smaller than the downside risk. Wait until it breaks through resistance before purchasing.

3. Identify the reason, if any, why a stock price surges on big volume. If earnings were higher than expected, all well and good. But if it's just a rumor of a takeover or buyout, be careful. Ever since the LBO craze started, high price and volume changes don't always mean what they used to. Later in this chapter, I'll explain how to hedge against being taken to the cleaners by buyout rumors.

In the days before they sent Ivan Boesky off to Lompoc to work for 11 cents an hour, arbitragers and other insiders used to get advance word of these deals, so other sharp-eyed traders could spot precisely those signs of unusual activity that technical analysis is designed to identify. This would often serve as a reliable tip-off that some major deal was in the works. The ardor for making money on inside information has cooled somewhat since it's turned out that ambitious government prosecutors will demand all your trading gains and at least one year of your life for doing so.

However, patterns will sometimes emerge in trading before the big announcement is made public. Those who are getting ready to make a takeover bid usually try to accumulate shares at relatively low prices, but less than the 5 percent minimum, so they don't have to file with the SEC. The problem is that these signals are often false alarms.

4. Don't buy a stock unless it's going up. I don't mean that as part of the old vaudeville routine. Don't bottom-fish—don't try to guess when the stock has bottomed out and buy it at its precise trough. The only time a stock price cannot go lower is when it is at zero. There is very little to be gained by trying to guess when the stock will bottom out and buying in "slightly" ahead of that event. Wait until the uptrend is established—which leads to the next rule.

5. Give the stock a little breathing room so that the occasional uptick in a declining market won't sucker you into buying a stock that

still has more room to decline. The best rule is not to buy a stock unless it's above its 21-day moving average. More conservative investors use the 50-day moving average.

6. Look for a stock that has exhibited significant movement in the past, since you aren't going to make much money on a stock that doesn't move. A stock that has traded in a certain cyclical range, recently declined to the bottom of that range, and then started higher again is a reasonably safe bet, providing the fundamentals are also sound.

Technical analysis is based on the presumption that at least some of the time, when major news is about to be announced, someone acts on it before the results are made public. This isn't necessarily illegal. An officer or director of a company could in good conscience buy stock if he had reason to believe that profits would be up sharply, as long as he didn't tell the investing public that he thought they would decline. However, analysts can occasionally be too clever for their own good, which leads us to the story of Control Data.

Ulric Weil, who used to be a top analyst for high-tech stocks for Morgan Stanley, was spotted by an acquaintance in a New York airport heading for Minneapolis. Since there was only one major computer company in that part of the country at the time, this acquaintance naturally surmised that Weil was planning to visit Control Data. In those days, it was generally believed that he was bullish on the stock, so the acquaintance put two and two together. Weil likes Control Data; he is visiting the company; he will return and write a favorable report; the stock will rise. Trying to get in ahead of a good thing, the acquaintance purchased a fair amount of Control Data and along with others, caused the stock to rise 5 points before Weil returned.

As it happened, Control Data was starting to decline, so when Weil got back to his desk, he wrote a negative report, which sent the price down almost 10 points. In this case, trying to outguess the analysts proved to be a fool's errand. And there's always the risk that a substantial one-day or even two-day rise in the stock will prove to be based on false rumors, leaving you exposed after having taken a substantial position on what appeared to be the beginning of a major move up.

USING OPTIONS ON TAKEOVER PLAYS

Suppose a stock does pop up on rumors, and also flashes a buy signal based on all the standard technical indicators. You would like to strike it rich, but you also want a safety net. Here's one way to do that using options.

Suppose the stock rose from 45 to 50, with rumors that it's really worth 75 if taken over. No one knows whether there will be a $75 offer; if there were definite information on that point, the stock would be selling for about 74½. The risk, which is not insubstantial, is that it will plop back down to 45 in another day or two. It is very unlikely, however, that it will stay at 50 for very long. Either the rumor is true, which means 75, or it is false, which means 45.

If you put a subjective probability of more than 20 percent on the rumor, then you buy the stock at 50; if not, you leave it alone. But for those who use options, there is an alternative strategy that essentially consists of buying an at-the-money put and a far out-of-the-money call. No two situations are identical, but in a typical situation, an at-the-money put option at 50 that expires in about one month would cost about $2 ($200 for 100 shares), while a call option at 65 would also probably cost about $2, since that's still way beyond the likely range if no buyout does occur.

Let's assume that you buy 10 puts, strike price 50, and 10 calls, strike price 65, for a total of $4,000. If the price falls back to 45, the call options expire worthless, but the put options rise to a value of 5, so your total net gain (excluding commissions) is $1,000. If the price does rise to 75, your put option expires worthless but the call options are worth $10,000, for a total net gain of $6,000. The only way you lose money is if the stock stays close to 50.

Naturally this doesn't work all the time. When buyout rumors surface, the prices of both put and call options often skyrocket. If, in the above example, the price for puts and calls had risen from $2 to $3, then you would still make money if the price goes to 75, but would lose money if it fell back to 45. In situations of this sort, you have to do the arithmetic each time, based on the current value of the options. But it does provide a way to hedge when the technical indicators give no clear signals.

INSIDER BUYING AND SELLING AS A GUIDE TO STOCK SELECTION

Many analysts claim that those who are closest to a given company's situation—officers, directors, or major shareholders—should know more about the future profits of the company than does the casual investor. As a result, they attach great weight to published reports on insider buying and selling.

In most situations, insiders have not bought the stock they own at anywhere near market prices. Either they received it when they started the company or they obtained it as stock options or bonuses for meeting various specified objectives. These aren't counted as insider purchases, which occur only when someone buys the stock at market prices, just as you or I would do. Thus it is invariably the case that the ratio of insider sales to insider purchases is well above unity. A ratio of 2:1 or even 3:1 does *not* mean there is something wrong with the company or that those in the know are bailing out.

Furthermore, most insider sales may have nothing to do with the state of the company's finances. The seller may need the money for retirement purposes, to pay taxes, or to finance a home or a college education. However, even if this isn't the case, insiders have to say something of the sort. If any insider actually admitted, "I sold all my shares because I knew profits would be down next quarter and I wanted to get out ahead of all you other stockholders," he would be in court for the rest of his life. So take these pious statements with the requisite amount of salt. As Alan Abelson, the perceptive editor of *Barron's*, has said, he has heard of many different reasons for insiders selling their stock, but never because they thought it was going to go up.

Nonetheless, although the logic of tracking insider purchases and sales may be compelling, the record is not. There are many cases in which insider selling has not been a reliable guide to stock market performance. For example, Marion Labs, a high-flyer during the mid-1980s, had been in the doldrums ever since the 1987 crash and never regained its previous peaks in spite of the fact that profits continued to grow at about 40 percent per year. Over that two-year period there was almost a steady stream of insider sales. However, on July 10, Dow Chemical announced that it was buying most of the shares at $38; the price at the time of the announcement was 25. We can only assume that all those insiders who had sold stock at prices in the low 20s were quite surprised by the turn of events, and the buyout was truly a well-kept secret. So I'm an agnostic on the question of insider selling. If the stock has strong earnings growth and favorable technical factors, I will overlook a record of insider sales.

While insiders should know the profit picture long before anyone else, in many cases they do not know about upcoming buyouts. It is apparently possible to be too cynical about insider motives; it may well be that they do need the cash for purchasing a home, college tuition payments, or retirement. Not all insiders are multimillionaires.

On the other hand, insider buying is relatively rare. If several insiders have purchased stock over the past few months, that is usually a clear signal they expect better news during the next quarter or two. So my general rule is that while insider selling gives mixed signals, insider buying is important. Even so, in no case will I make a decision to buy or sell based solely or even primarily on insider trading.

WHEN TO SELL

As a theoretical proposition, you want to sell stock when other investment opportunities appear to be more profitable. This means sometimes you sell a stock that will keep rising because other stock prices will increase faster. As a practical matter, though, the decision to sell is usually triggered by a drop in the price, not a mere slackening of the growth rate.

My rule for when to sell is related to the so-called *beta-coefficient*, which measures the volatility of the stock relative to the overall market. If, on average, the price of a given stock changes by the same percentage as the overall market over a substantial period of time (five years), then it has a beta-coefficient of unity. If it fluctuates only half as much, the coefficient is 0.5, and if it fluctuates twice as much, the coefficient is 2.0. Most betas are between 0.5 and 1.5; it's very rare for a stock to have a beta of more than 2.5.

The Evans rule: When a stock declines 5 percent times its beta—the use of the beta-coefficient allows greater flexibility for more volatile stocks— it's time to stop, look, and listen. Has something happened to make the stock go down? The short checklist is:

1. Recent decline in earnings growth
2. In an industry that's being hard hit by economic factors (as, for example, high interest rates hurt the housing industry)
3. Widely announced piece of bad news (chairman was cooking the books)

4. Part of a general market slide. When I think the market is poised to decline 10 percent or more, I generally sell out my entire portfolio

If none of these factors seems to be occurring, the drop may simply be due to a short-term technical correction. I would hold the stock until the price declines 10 percent times beta, at which time I would get out with no exceptions.

Of course, you may be whipsawed; the stock could go back up after you sell. That's not necessarily disastrous, though. There is nothing wrong with reexamining the situation and buying back in, just as if you were purchasing the stock for the first time. However, selling it at least forces you to go through the discipline of examining precisely why you are still holding that stock in the first place. Besides, many stocks don't bounce back after a 10 percent loss for months or even years. This way, you don't ride stocks that lose 80 or 90 percent of their value. If you bought MCI at the peak of 28, swallow your pride and get out at 25. If you still like the company just before it started to head down, you could have bought it back later at 5 or 6.

Sometimes it may pay to get out of stocks before they have declined 5 percent times beta. If you have reason to believe that earnings will decline next quarter, or it's obvious that some strong competitor is starting to gobble up market share, or changes in the tax laws will decimate the company's earnings, you don't have to wait for a technical signal to sell. This set of rules is designed to get you out of stocks that start to plunge but you don't know why because the bad news hasn't been announced yet.

I have said you shouldn't buy stocks in a declining market, but the rules for selling are not symmetrical. If a stock starts to stagnate or decline while the market is still improving, it's definitely time to sell. Indeed, that's a surer sell signal than if the stock declines proportionately with the market but seems likely to hold its own once the overall market snaps back.

Evans Investment Advisors offers a computerized ranking service that ranks all NYSE and major OTC stocks every day; so do other companies. None of these will identify hidden long-term values; you have to do your homework. But once you've identified these winning stocks, technical analysis will help tell you when to buy and when to wait; whether the stock is about to start on a substantial climb or whether it has just about reached its peak; when to sell. No system is infallible, and for those who don't think they can afford such a service, you can get much of the same information just by looking at the daily chart patterns. But picking stocks on the basis of fundamentals and ignoring the technical factors is just as silly as doing all your research on what car to buy and then not shopping around to get the best deal.

Chapter 19

Should You Do Your
Own Investing?

CAN INDIVIDUAL INVESTORS BEAT THE MARKET?

Before answering this question, consider one salient fact. Over the past decade, 9 out of 10 professional money managers have been unable to beat the market averages consistently. This statement, however, could lead to one of three completely different conclusions.

1. If professional money managers, who devote most of their waking hours to studying the stock market, can't beat the averages, why should I, an amateur with little knowledge of the market and a full-time job to occupy my time, have the chutzpah to think I can do better?
2. Since I could do just about as well with a dart board, why not keep the funds under my own control? No point in paying fees and expenses to someone who can't even beat the market. Besides—who knows—I might get lucky and pick a few big winners.
3. Never mind the averages. Just find me a money manager who consistently outperforms the averages in both bull and bear markets, and has a long enough track record to establish consistency—if such an individual exists.

Before you come to your own conclusion, a few explanatory comments on the opening sentence.

Over the 1980–90 decade, the average annual rate of return in the S&P 500—capital gains plus dividends—was 16 percent. The *Forbes* 1989–90 Mutual Fund Survey lists 292 mutual funds that met minimum-size requirements, invested entirely in common stocks—no bonds, preferred stocks, balanced funds, or money market instruments—and had been in business continuously over that period. In defining the market "average," I have allowed a 1 percent deviation on either side of the 16 percent figure as being not significantly different from the average, since that represents sales fees and management costs over and above what an individual investor would probably pay on his own. The percentage distribution of performance over that period is:

Below Average

Less than 10% per year	19%
10–13% per year	33%
13–15% per year	22%
Total Below Average	74%

Average

15–17% per year	19%

Above Average

17–18% per year	3%
18–19% per year	2½%
19–20% per year	1%
23.1%	0.3% (i.e., 1 of 292)
Total Above Average	7%

THE UNIMPRESSIVE RECORD OF MUTUAL FUNDS

By now you may be asking yourself not only why less than 10 percent of mutual fund managers can beat the averages, but who is this mystery guru, the only one over 23 percent per year? If you've read this far, it's not much of a secret; you have probably guessed it is none other than Peter Lynch, who runs the Fidelity Magellan Fund. So the miracle man really does exist. Or, more accurately, did exist. For on May 31, 1990, Peter Lynch resigned from Fidelity, leaving the Magellan Fund in uncertain hands.

I'm not the only one who was impressed with Peter Lynch's record and thinks it may never be duplicated again. The usually hard-nosed *Barron's*, in an unusually laudatory article entitled "Peter Lynch: Goodbye, Babe Ruth," called him "without question, the best portfolio manager to grace the mutual-fund business," called his record "truly amazing," and referred to his "remarkable" performance even after the fund had reached "gargantuan" size. Unlike other successful funds that ultimately grew large, Fidelity Magellan never closed its book to new investors.

For several years, I invested the majority of my own retirement funds in the Magellan Fund, always with superior results. But after Peter Lynch left, I pulled my money out of that fund—and although a few months isn't a fair test, it hasn't done very well recently. So what used to be one of my few invariant rules in investing—put some of your money in Magellan—has gone by the boards.

How about the other 19 funds that beat the averages? Three of them have excellent track records, but they don't take any new investors—and the newer funds they have opened up haven't done that well. That leaves 16 funds.

Of those, 12 failed to match the S&P average over the past year, even excluding sales and administrative costs. Maybe they just had a bad year—but maybe the above-average gains were racked up in earlier years and the fund managers are finally running out of new ideas.

That leaves four funds, which are Bergstrom Capital, Fidelity Congress Street, Janus, and New England Growth. I don't know how these funds will do in the coming years, but these are currently the ones with the best short- and long-term track records. My guess is they will continue to do well in the future, although better in up markets than down—since all four fell at least 15 percent during the second half of 1990.

CHOOSING THE BEST MUTUAL FUNDS

If you decide to go the mutual fund route, here's what I would look for besides an above-average long-term track record.

1. Volatility relative to the market. If the volatility is greater than the market averages, the return should also be greater, or it isn't worth the additional risk.
2. The performance of the fund should be above average in both up and down markets. (*Forbes* ranks the funds this way.) Ideally, the fund would still make money in down markets, but under this criterion virtually all stock funds are eliminated. A somewhat less

stringent and more realistic criterion is that the value of the fund falls less than the market in declining markets. Of course, you would like to be on the sidelines in a down market, but these behemoths simply don't have that flexibility. Those who see a major decline coming always have the option of selling their shares, putting the proceeds in the money market fund, and waiting for the next upturn.

3. Load or no-load. Much ado about nothing, especially for the longer-term investor. The standard argument is that several studies have shown that the average rate of return on load funds is no greater than the average rate of return on no-load funds, so why pay that extra fee up front? But I have a much more relevant question: Why buy an average fund? The key is whether the fund outperforms the market, not whether it charges you something to get in.

   Fidelity Magellan now charges a 3 percent fee; when it started, it was a no-load fund. For the other top four funds, the sales commission fee ranges from 0 to 6½ percent. For the longer-term investor, however, performance is almost everything; load almost nothing. Over a 10-year period, a fund that averages 20 percent a year with the maximum load of 8.5 percent will do just as well as one that averages 19 percent a year with no load.

4. Sector funds aren't very good either, unless you make your own investment decisions. Unlike Magellan, the performance of Fidelity sector funds is absolutely nothing to write home about. Because they have so many funds, one or the other is always near the top of the list. But taken together, they're below average. Most of these funds haven't been around long enough to have established a complete track record, but according to the calculations given in *Forbes*, as an aggregate they underperformed the market by 1 percent in 1988 and almost 2 percent in 1989. In order to beat the market in sector funds, you have to be adept at cyclical rotation, which in my opinion is actually much harder than picking individual stocks or calling market turns.

5. Track record is obviously of some importance, but it can be misleading. Obviously I wouldn't feel very secure with a fund that has compiled an average or worse track record over several years, and you probably wouldn't invest in one either. But what about someone who has an excellent one- or two-year track record: Is he the next Peter Lynch—or just a flash in the pan?

   This is a difficult area in which to give hard-and-fast guidelines, so you won't find any definitive rules here. The best tactic I know is to call up the funds and get some direct information on how they operate. If it's a small fund, you may even get some of the principals on the phone, but even if you don't, the company will presumably have brochures explaining its strategy and its recent picks. If it can't even afford that, you have your answer.

6. Try to avoid fads and scams. By fads I mean a big increase that won't last. If gold, oil, or real estate prices soar one year, then a fund that concentrates heavily in those stocks is almost sure to outperform the market averages by a wide margin. If the fund manager claims to have picked those stocks because of unusual circumstances and plans to switch into other types of stocks as soon as the economic environment changes, that's fine. But if you run into a demented goldbug who thinks gold prices will rise every year, thank him politely, hang up the phone, and move on to the next fund on the list.

Scams are more serious, and here's how they work. A brokerage house that floats a fair number of new issues each year puts together a fund that specializes in these issues. The fund posts remarkable gains the first year. This brokerage house just might be unusually adept at picking future winners to bring public, which would be fine. But often this isn't what really happens. Instead, the underwriter has permitted its own in-house fund to purchase some of the new issues at bargain prices shortly before the public offering so it will appear that the fund has an outstanding track record. After perpetrating this scam for a year or two, the brokerage firm then announces that this very exclusive fund, which previously accepted accounts only from the cognoscenti, is now open to the general public. Perhaps they will lower the minimum from $25,000 to $1,000. At the same time, they also stop buying new-issue stock at below-market prices, so the performance level sinks to average or worse.

Thus if any fund has based its tremendous short-term track record on new issues, be wary. Check the prospectus to find out whether the profit it shows is based on the price at which the public could have purchased the new issues or on some lower price.

I don't know who the next hot young money manager will be. However, it is unlikely that, as opposed to those great computer geniuses who start in their own garages, this one will work out of his own study or small office. Top talent in the money-management field is highly coveted in the canyons of Wall Street, and those with above-average talent are usually given the chance to manage modest amounts of money before moving up to the big time. Thus the fact that a fund has a new manager isn't necessarily a minus, provided he has a good track record in his previous job. But when a friend of a friend tells you about some whiz kid who has a fantastic ability to pick stocks and manage money but no track record as yet, I'd give him a couple of years to prove himself. If he's as good as this acquaintance says, there will be plenty of time to ingratiate yourself later on. If he isn't, you've saved yourself a bundle.

To summarize, investing funds with Fidelity Magellan or some of the other big winners (if they will take your money) is a sound strategy, although it is riskier than it used to be. Avoid funds with below-average records. Don't necessarily avoid those with short track records, but be careful of fads and scams. It's hard to see the advantage of entrusting your funds to someone who has no demonstrable track record at all. Finally, unless you have a marked aversion to making your own investment decisions, I suggest that you keep some of your money under your own management. If you do, here are a few hints to follow.

THE MYTH OF THE ONE-DECISION STOCK

Life would be much simpler if, after doing our research carefully, we could all find a stock that was immune to the vicissitudes of business cycles and competition, whose earnings always grew steadily, and whose price rose at above-average rates each year.

I assume you know there are no such stocks. However, many brokerage houses and money managers apparently don't, because they continue to search for what are known as one-decision stocks. Once you buy them, you never have to sell them. I suppose these gurus figure that after discovering these stocks they'll be able to play golf or drink martinis all day. Yet the performance of these stocks, once they have been identified, is not just mediocre but downright terrible. In late 1972, just before the stock market declined 45 percent over the next two years, there were indeed such a group of stocks, generally known as the Nifty Fifty. They were the quintessential one-decision stocks.

If you had put your money in the bank in 1972, it would roughly have doubled by 1982. Only six of the Nifty Fifty—12 percent of the total—did as well as the bank account. Furthermore, 70 percent of them actually fell in price over the decade. Investing in the Nifty Fifty at the end of 1972 would have been an unmitigated horror show. Your total portfolio would have declined 17 percent, compared with doubling the money left in the bank. And we're not talking no-name stocks; they included Automatic Data Processing, Coca-Cola, Eastman Kodak, Johnson and Johnson, Polaroid, and Xerox.

However, the 1972–82 decade wasn't a very good one for stocks in general; the S&P 500 didn't show any gains over that period either.

Furthermore, maybe it didn't take a genius to realize that stocks with P/E ratios of 50 to 60 that had already started to slow down were over-priced, although many so-called geniuses missed precisely that.

So let's give them another chance and see how the once-nifty fifty did from 1982 to the peak in 1987, the greatest bull market of our time. Once again, they far underperformed the market. Of the six winners from the previous decade, three showed no gains at all, one rose about half as fast as the market, and one flitted out after the 1987 crash (Digital Equipment, which went from 199 to 50 and never fully recovered).

That leaves one glorious stock—Wal-Mart—which rose another 8-fold in the bull market and hence retained its original tag as a one-decision stock. It has indeed risen almost 400 times since 1972, and it's no coin-cidence that the man who started the company, Sam Walton, is the richest man in America, worth (together with his family) about $9 billion. But this means that of all the *thousands* of stocks traded on the various exchanges, only one—Wal-Mart—has qualified as a one-decision stock for the past 17 years. And the odds of you or me discovering this stock on our own and investing all our assets in it are too small even to be worth discussing.

With the exception of Wal-Mart, what did all the Nifty Fifty have in common?

They were the darlings of Wall Street analysts.

They were selling at P/E multiples that were well above both the market average and their own growth rates. Note that this applies to steady earnings trends, not to turnaround situations where earnings might be close to zero for a brief period before rebounding.

With the one exception (Wal-Mart), their best growth years were behind them by the time they were discovered by the hordes of Wall Street analysts. This almost always happens. Wall Street doesn't usually discover such stocks until their days of glory are history.

If you happen to run across any of these stocks—which you'll recognize because the P/E is well above the growth rate—skip to the next selection. Don't be tempted by an obviously overvalued stock.

Wal-Mart peaked at 42⅞ when the market peaked in August 1987. When the market reached its old peak in August 1989, Wal-Mart was 43¼. In other words, Wal-Mart kept pace with the overall market. Maybe that's an impressive performance for a stock that has grown so fast for so long, but I wouldn't buy any more of it now. The current P/E reflects past growth rates, which probably won't be replicated in the future.

All right. So I've convinced you not to buy overpriced stocks with stratospheric P/E ratios that have already stopped growing. But what about picking some rising stars in the high-tech field and holding on to them for a few years through a bull market? Surely that would work better.

It just so happens that there was a book written on this very subject in 1982. It's called *Future Stocks*, by someone named Robert Metz, who was then a financial reporter for *The New York Times*. The book was highly praised by Alan Abelson, the editor of *Barron's*, and by Jane Bryant Quinn, noted financial columnist. Metz selected 27 stocks, all of which, he claimed, had "prospects for providing gains large enough to result in 10-for-one rewards over the next 10 years." He concluded by saying, "At the Dawning of the Millennium, I paraphrase the prophet: go forth and multiply."

You probably know what to expect by now. During a period when the overall market tripled, these stocks somehow managed to *decline* on average.

Furthermore, this wasn't the only book to lay an ostrich-size egg. Another book, called *High-Tech—How to Find and Profit from Today's New Super Stocks*, was coauthored by Albert Toney, a general partner at the stock market firm of Hambrecht & Quist, which specializes in bringing new high-tech companies to market and has actually done quite well in choosing winners. But an average selection of the stocks featured in the book managed to decline more than 26 percent from 1983 to 1988.

If I manage to leave you with one investment tip, let it be that there are no one-decision stocks. Repeat to yourself every time you buy a stock, "There are no good stocks that last forever. There are only good times to buy those stocks."

HOW MUCH TURNOVER IN YOUR PORTFOLIO?

Since you won't find any stocks you can hold forever, what sort of turnover is optimal? To start, you should always make more on your portfolio than your broker does. If your commissions are more than your profits, you are clearly churning your portfolio too much. However, this probably applies to only a small percentage of hyperactive traders. For less frenetic traders, remember that the average length of a stock market upswing is about 18 months. Relatively few stocks are worth holding longer than that. If you think they are, at least reevaluate the situation just as if you were buying the stock for the first time to see whether you would still purchase it.

At the other end of the scale, assuming that you follow the market timing strategies outlined in earlier chapters, it generally makes sense to hold a stock for at least six months in order to give the fundamental factors that made it attractive in the first place time to develop. Of course, this doesn't apply to takeover situations where a successful tender offer has been made and there's nothing to do but wait until the deal is finalized. Also, as throughout this book, I've assumed this investment is being done in tax-deferred accounts so you don't have to pay capital gains every time you sell the stock.

This suggests on average that you turn your portfolio over about once a year. This is not a hard-and-fast rule. If you discover the next Masco at 1, on its way to 1,000 (before splits), you needn't sell at 50. However, such glamour stories are clearly few and far between. Far too many investors—professional as well as amateur—tend to ascribe anthropomorphic qualities to stock: "It's been good to me, so I'll hold on to it for a while longer." Stocks are not relatives, not even business acquaintances. They won't take it personally if you sell them.

As each bull market draws to a close, you owe it to yourself to examine the stocks in your portfolio that remain from the beginning of the upturn and refresh your research. Even if they remain top-notch long-term picks, it may be better to sell them before the next downturn.

These comments represent guidelines, not commandments. Following them will help to ensure that you continue to follow a disciplined approach after making the initial selection of a solid stock. The last thing most investors want to do is take a round-trip—watch those substantial gains melt away as the stock sinks back to the level at which it was originally purchased. Of course, that's what invariably happens with so-called one-decision stocks.

THE OPTIMAL LEVEL OF DIVERSIFICATION

If you'd picked Masco in 1959, S. S. Kresge in 1963, Boeing in 1975, Chrysler in 1982, or Compaq in 1984, you wouldn't have had to diversify at all, because you would have earned about 100 percent per year on your investment. So after 30 years, an original $10,000 would have been worth $10,737,418,240,000—that's more than $10 trillion. Obviously no one is that smart. More often, the stock of your dreams turns out to be a nightmare. No prudent investor ever puts all his eggs into one basket, unless he has inside information that would now be considered illegal to use for trading purposes.

On the other hand, diversification just for its own sake makes no sense either. There is no point in buying a stock you don't feel comfortable with just to pad out the list. From a statistical point of view, your risk will be adequately spread if you hold between 8 and 12 stocks. If you find an additional can't-miss stock, naturally this doesn't preclude you from buying it. However, most portfolios with more than 20 stocks suffer from needless diversification. Unless you like to spend most of your day following the market, it's hard to keep track of that many stocks anyhow.

There are also some economies of scale involved here. Transactions costs per share are much higher if you buy 100 shares than if you buy 1,000 or more shares, whether you use a full-service or discount broker. Also, it generally takes some time and effort to track down winning stocks. If you have only a modest amount to invest, the cost of obtaining the information may be greater than the expected gain. So if you have a portfolio of under $25,000, it probably makes sense to hold 6 to 10 stocks, while if it is over $250,000, 15 to 20 stocks would not be out of line.

Never buy a stock, though, just to reach some preassigned number of issues. Diversification has very limited charm if it causes you to buy losers. In fact, if you have good reason to believe that a stock will soar in the near future, I see nothing wrong with investing heavily in that stock and watching it very carefully—*which* means monitoring it every day, and no vacations unless your broker can reach you or has standing orders about what to do in case of a market correction.

CONTRARIANISM

By nature I am something of a skeptic. When some broker calls me up with a "must-buy" proposition, my first thought is that he's getting paid to push that stock, and I almost always ignore the hot tip. Over the long run, brokerage-house recommendations, even from the biggest firms, seldom if ever outperform the dart board.

Having admitted my biases on this matter, let me say that I have not made most of my money in the stock market by being a contrarian either. Going short on a stock just because all major analysts recommend it isn't a surefire road to success—although in one well-publicized example, buying into the market just after *Business Week* had "The Death of Equities" as its cover story in mid-1982 turned out to be perfect timing.

Some of those marvelous success stories mentioned in the previous chapter—Boeing, Chrysler, International Harvester—were in a sense contrarian success stories. But in each case, profits had already turned up about a year earlier. That wasn't so much marching against the crowd as it was moving in front of a crowd that was still milling aimlessly.

The important fact to remember about being a contrarian is that informed opinion is *not* wrong most of the time. It's random. That means it's right about 50 percent of the time, and wrong about 50 percent of the time. The consensus is not always wrong at turning points. In fact, many investors had turned bearish before the October 19, 1987, crash, although few of them anticipated the full magnitude of the decline. A true contrarian would have bought the market on Friday, October 16, when informed opinion had overwhelmingly turned bearish. He would have lost not only his shirt but his complete wardrobe the following Monday.

A jaundiced eye for hype is a necessary adjunct for successful investment performance. An intelligent skepticism is a necessity. However, indexes of investor sentiment are *not* reliable contrarian predictors of the market; they turned bearish before the crashes in both October 1987 and 1989.

Thus I wouldn't so much go against the consensus wisdom as ignore it. If the vast majority of analysts think a stock is a great buy, and you happen to agree, it would be silly to stay away. And as I pointed out before, you can't fight the tape. If a stock keeps making new highs daily and you are convinced there's something phony about it, fine. Don't buy it. But don't short it either, not until it starts to turn down.

So in this regard I vote skepticism, yes; contrarianism, no.

PHASES OF UNIFORMED OPINION

Professional money managers and stock-market analysts, as I have said before, are right just about 50 percent of the time. But that isn't true for the man and woman in the street. They *are* wrong more than half of the time.

The cycle of uninformed public opinion—as opposed to the opinions of professional money managers—works approximately like this.

Phase 1. The market has just crashed. Small investors want nothing to do with stocks. If they do have money in the market, they are probably too embarrassed to mention it to anyone except their families and their psychiatrists. If you happen to mention at a cocktail party that you are in money management, the crowd quickly moves to another part of the room. You're lucky if someone doesn't spill his drink on you.

Phase 2. The market has started to pick up, as it always does if we are not in the midst of a worldwide depression. Small investors still have no interest in the market, but they are no longer so embarrassed to mention the words *stock market* in public. Now if they encounter a money manager at a cocktail party, they'll greet him with the same amount of interest they'd grant a fellow who admitted to being a turkey farmer. They'll ignore him, but they won't spin on their heels in mid-sentence.

Phase 3. The market is in full stride. Over time, small investors forget about their past losses and start to dabble in a few stocks again. In this phase, they nod attentively when introduced to the money manager and ask his advice on a number of stocks.

Phase 4. The market is roiling, just about to peak. Now is the time for the man in the street to give the investment manager hot tips. He hears them from everyone—the cab driver, the sales clerk, the parking lot attendant. Once that happens, the market is just about ready to crash.

I had heard similar cynical tales of this occurring in 1962, 1968, and 1973, but I assumed they were overblown. However, precisely the same pattern occurred in the summer of 1987. I am interviewed on TV fairly often, and the crews usually come into my office for the interviews. When the cameramen start telling me which stocks to buy, I know it's time to get out completely. Maybe I'll publish an index on it someday.

ADVISERS AND NEWSLETTERS

Let's assume you've decided to manage at least some of your own portfolio and you now know the criteria for picking good stocks and good markets. Should you do this all on your own, or does it help to rely on investment newsletters and advisers?

Since I publish *The Evans Report* and manage money, you might well have some grounds for claiming that my advice is not unbiased. All right, given these biases, here's my advice.

First, recommending stocks and actually trading them are not the same thing. Someone may make above-average picks consistently and yet turn in below-average performance when actually managing money. So let me discuss the Newsletter Biz first.

Paul Samuelson, who wrote the all-time best-selling economics textbook and also made millions in the commodities markets, once said that he looked for "one *net* good idea" in any newsletter to which he subscribed. That's a good rule to remember. Even the best newsletter will have its share of clunkers, and even the worst one will occasionally hit on a certifiable gold mine. As Peter Lynch puts it, if your adviser can pick good stocks 60 percent of the time, in the long run that will put him near the top of the list. No newsletter is going to recommend only successful stocks in every issue—and don't believe anyone who claims they can do that. And, of course, avoid hucksters who "guarantee" anything.

You also need to get some feel for the style of the newsletter. Does it lean toward blue chips or small OTC stocks? Does it rely on short-term technical indicators, thus missing the big upward swing in bull markets, or is it overly cautious and recommends too many stodgy stocks? Does it recommend going short on occasion, or is the adviser always fully invested? Is the writer by nature an optimist, a pessimist, or a contrarian? Once you've ascertained some of these biases, you will be better able to judge the latest picks.

Most important, the newsletter writer must have a disciplined approach. It could be strictly technical, primarily fundamental, or some particular blend. But the same criteria must be applied on a consistent basis. Newsletter writers who chase after the latest fad are never going to make a dime for their subscribers. Your newsletter adviser will be pleased to explain his system to you—or you shouldn't be giving him the subscription order.

Track records are a murky area in this regard, because a recommendation is different from an actual purchase. Obviously a bad track record is a danger signal, but a good track record may mean very little. I'd suggest instead a short trial subscription that will give you a chance to track the recommendations yourself and see how well they work out.

Part of the problem could be the timing. Between the time the recommendation is made, the newsletter is printed, and the U.S. mail does its usual superb job of delivery, over a week could elapse and the outlook for that stock or even the entire market might have shifted. In this technological age, every competent newsletter ought to have a hot line—although not necessarily a free one. That way you can listen in and find out whether the daily updates sound as if someone really is following the market closely all the time or the newsletter effort is just something the editor does for a hobby.

If the newsletter appears to be based on a consistent strategy that makes sense to you, if the hot line has intelligent comments, and if the track record during the trial subscription appears reasonable, it's probably worth subscribing to two or three of the better newsletters. If they haven't paid for themselves by the end of the year, try another brand. That's a fairly low-risk strategy.

Entrusting your funds to an investment adviser, on the other hand, can be a very high-risk strategy. With the larger mutual funds, there is at least no chance of fraud. Fidelity, Vanguard, or for that matter Shearson or Merrill Lynch, may or may not outperform the market in the future, but at least you know they aren't going to abscond with your money. If a polished, charming individual is working solo, you might never see your money again. In one highly publicized case, J. David Dominelli, a charlatan and superbly effective salesman operating in the San Diego area, took $40 million of his clients' money and absconded. How could they have been so gullible? Simple. By operating one of those Ponzi schemes, he apparently produced magnificent profits for his first few clients, thereby attracting hordes of the unwary. His track record meant nothing at all.

Checking out the adviser with personal references is far from foolproof; it might be his brother-in-law on the other end of the line. Maybe I sound paranoid, but I know some intelligent professionals who have been bilked by these scams. Furthermore, it's easy to avoid such traumas. If you do business with someone you don't know personally, insist that the funds remain in your name, that a separate brokerage account be started in your name, and that while the investment adviser has the full authority to trade the account—otherwise, don't bother with one—you get duplicate slips of all the trades. That way, money can't be siphoned off without your knowing about it immediately. This is a low-risk step to take, and any honest adviser should accept it immediately.

Picking an adviser really boils down to common sense. Hire someone who has a good track record of picking stocks, an investment philosophy that sounds believable to you, a reasonable number of satisfied clients, a sound record of investment under fire—in bad markets as well as good—and who is willing to segregate your accounts under your own name. It also helps if he has a newsletter, because from past issues you can get an idea of his thinking at different points in the stock market cycle. But then again, some of the best advisers don't need that marketing tool, so they don't bother.

In spite of the fact that I do manage money, I'm far from convinced that an investment adviser is right for everyone. But if you think it's a good idea, here's my final suggestion on the subject. Split your investment pool into three parts—give one-third to each of two investment advisers you've interviewed and keep the remaining third for yourself. At the end of the first year, drop the manager with the worst record—which could be you—and split the difference between the two remaining managers. At the end of the second year, assuming there is a sufficient difference, reward the one who did best. This doesn't guarantee anything, but at least you'll have your funds invested with someone who has a good two-year track record.

Some investment advisers will try to tell you that even though they have done poorly during the past several years, the types of stocks they have invested in and follow most closely are just about to turn around and outperform the market. If investment performance were truly random, they might be right. But over the long run, advisers with worse than average records usually stay at the bottom of the heap. I'd show any such would-be adviser the door.

Chapter 20

Bonds Are for Losers

You will never get rich investing your money in bonds.

And if you're already rich, the real value of your wealth will diminish over time if you invest it in bonds.

The reason is very simple. We live in an inflationary era. In some years, prices rise less than others, but in every year since 1955 they have risen. Thus the real value of your bond decreases as prices rise. Even at a relatively mild 5 percent annual rate of inflation, the real value of a dollar declines to 61 cents in 10 years, 38 cents in 20 years, and a measly 14 cents in 40 years.

While interest rates are usually slightly higher than the rate of inflation, the tax on the interest income more than eats up the difference. Yes, tax-free municipal bonds are available, but over the past 30 years the rate of interest they pay has averaged only 1.3 percent higher than the rate of inflation.

In that case, why a chapter on bonds?

1. Many people still waste their money by investing in bonds. I want to show you why this is a mistake, especially in the long run.
2. For one five-year period—1982 through 1986—bonds were a superior investment. Those who aren't long-time investors might assume that the economics of those years were normal, or at least likely to continue. Bond salesmen will encourage that misconception. However, I'll show you why that set of circumstances will

probably never arise again. Furthermore, although bonds had a phenomenal record during that period, stocks did even better.

3. Some people like bonds because, they claim, they aren't risky. It's true that if you buy a Treasury bond and hold it to maturity, the risk of default is zero. But if you buy a 30-year bond and have to sell it after, say five years, you might find that it was worth only 50 cents on the dollar. That actually happened from 1977 to 1982.

4. Junk bonds carry enticingly high rates of return but also have such a high risk of default that over the long haul, they have a lower rate of return than Treasury securities, in spite of some outdated academic studies to the contrary. Even high-grade corporate bonds are no longer immune to substantial risk.

5. If after all this, you are still unwilling to invest in stocks because of the perceived risk, I'll show you that over the past 24 years, the rate of return on insured bank deposits and Treasury bills would have been just as high as on Treasury bonds—without any of the market risk.

For those who are truly gifted at trading, it is possible to make a fortune by trading bonds with split-second accuracy—just as it is with stocks or any other asset. If you know precisely when major upswings and downswings in interest rates are about to start, I congratulate you. You don't need the advice in this book because you are already extremely wealthy.

I have not included a section on market timing in bond trading for two reasons. First, most people who decide to invest in bonds do so because they want less risk, not more. Second, trading bonds on a short-term basis is extremely difficult because only professionals do so, and they don't take any prisoners. There are enough amateurs in the stock market that someone who follows the technical and fundamental indicators closely can stay ahead of the game. But that simply isn't so for bonds, so you won't find any hints in this book on technical analysis for them. If you like high-risk situations, there are plenty in the stock market.

Glance at Table 22, particularly the last two lines. It tells you all you need to know about the value of investing in bonds in the long run. To review briefly, over the past 50 years:

1. The average rate of return on bonds has been only one-third that on stocks.

2. The rate of return on bonds has been only 0.5 percent more than on Treasury bills.

3. The rate of return on bonds has been only 0.3 percent higher than the rate of inflation.

Table 22
Percentage Change in Total Return for Stocks, Bonds, and Bills
Compared with the Rate of Inflation

	Stocks	Bonds	Bills	Inflation
1941–42	8.7	2.0	0.2	8.0
1943–44	22.9	2.5	0.3	3.9
1945–46	14.2	5.3	0.3	5.3
1947–48	5.6	0.4	0.7	11.3
1949–50	25.2	3.3	1.2	0.0
1951–52	21.2	− 1.3	1.6	4.9
1953–54	25.8	5.4	1.3	0.8
1955–56	19.1	− 3.3	2.0	0.5
1957–58	16.3	0.7	2.3	3.0
1959–60	6.3	5.8	2.9	1.2
1961–62	9.1	4.0	2.4	1.0
1963–64	19.7	2.4	3.3	1.3
1965–66	1.2	2.2	4.4	2.3
1967–68	17.5	− 4.8	4.7	3.6
1969–70	− 2.3	3.5	6.5	5.6
1971–72	16.7	9.5	4.1	3.8
1973–74	− 20.6	1.7	7.4	8.6
1975–76	30.5	13.0	5.4	7.5
1977–78	− 0.3	− 1.0	6.2	7.0
1979–80	25.4	− 2.6	10.8	12.2
1981–82	8.2	21.1	12.6	8.3
1983–84	14.4	8.1	9.3	3.8
1985–86	24.1	28.8	6.3	2.8
1987–88	10.9	3.2	7.0	3.9
1989–90	14.1	12.3	8.0	5.1
50-year average	13.3	4.9	4.4	4.6
Last 24 years	11.6	7.7	7.4	6.1

Some people would say that this comparison is biased, because during World War II and until 1966 monetary policy was designed to keep the economy at full employment by reducing interest rates and didn't really have any teeth. Yet the comparison from 1966 to the present still paints the same broad picture. It shows that:

1. The average rate of return on bonds has been 4 percent less than on stocks.
2. The rate of return on bonds has been only 0.3 percent higher than on Treasury bills.
3. The rate of return on bonds has been only 1.6 percent higher than the rate of inflation.

Yet in spite of these facts, enough people are enamored of investing in bonds that I'll discuss the pluses (if any) and minuses of investing in each type of bond.

TREASURY BONDS: NO RISK OF DEFAULT, GREAT RISK OF INFLATION

In early 1991, the yield on 30-year Treasury bonds was approximately 8 percent. The rate of inflation was about 5 percent. And the marginal tax rate for investors was anywhere between 31 and 40 percent, depending on your income level and the rate of state and local income taxes; to make the calculations simple, assume it was 37.5 percent.

Thirty years from now, that bond will be redeemed at its face value; let's say $1,000. However, because of inflation, the real purchasing power of that $1,000 will be worth only $231, assuming an average 5 percent rate of inflation.

Now suppose you took the $80 in interest each year, paid your taxes at the 37.5 percent marginal tax rate—leaving you with $50—and invested *that* amount each year, too. After 30 years, the total amount of these $50 investments, invested at an after-tax rate of 5 percent, would be $3,488—but that's before adjusting for inflation. After inflation, it would be worth only $769. When added to your principal of $231, that adds up to precisely $1,000—which should be no surprise. Since the after-tax return is the same as the rate of inflation, your real after-tax rate of return must be zero.

Of course, each year you could have spent the $50 in after-tax income instead of reinvesting it. However, that $50 would have bought progressively less every year, until in 30 years' time it would have been worth less than one-fourth of its original value. Thus the allegedly attractive rate of return on the bond makes sense only if you are not planning to live much longer and don't care about the size of the estate you pass along to the next generation.

Some will argue that bonds can be a superior investment if the rate of inflation declines in the future. That's true, and it is valuable information—providing you know it will happen. Here's what to look for.

Over the long run, in *nonrecession* years, the Treasury bond yield averages about 3 percent above the rate of inflation. If that spread narrows appreciably—and particularly if it turns negative—bonds will be a very poor investment over the next few years. When interest rates are below the rate of inflation, that is essentially a license to borrow money at a negative spread; borrowing skyrockets, and inflation follows suit. Eventually the Fed has to clamp down by tightening policy and boosting interest rates. When that happens, bond prices plummet.

On the other hand, when the spread between bond yields and the inflation rate is 5 percent or more bonds will be a very good investment over the next few years. High real interest rates depress economic activity and cause recessions; when that happens, the Fed then eases, interest rates plummet, and bond prices soar.

These major divergences don't happen very often because interest rates usually follow inflation fairly closely. In fact, the only major instance occurred during the 1982–84 period, when the spread reached almost 10 percent. It was precisely this spread between bond yields and inflation that caused the one great bull market in bonds of the past 50 years.

That period is likely to be unique for many decades. The economy had just finished two bouts of double-digit inflation, each of which contained a major energy shock. For a while, the government seemed powerless to stop the upward drift of inflation. Then no-nonsense Paul Volcker appeared on the scene and drove the economy into the deepest slump since the 1930s in order to end inflation. Yet interest rates remained high for several years because the investment community didn't believe he could finish the job.

On August 2, 1990, Iraq invaded Kuwait, sending crude oil prices skyrocketing once again from $17 to over $40 a barrel. This development knocked an already fragile economy into recession and sent the stock market reeling—but had a far smaller effect on bond yields or prices than previous oil shocks, because this one was perceived to be temporary. Thus when oil prices returned to normal, bond prices rallied only moderately.

Since I don't expect another bout of 13 percent inflation and 14 percent bond yields, the price of any Treasury bonds you happen to purchase now won't be cut in half over the next five years. On the other hand, fluctuations in bond prices of 10 to 20 percent will remain commonplace, as was the case in 1989 and 1990. For that kind of risk, you may as well invest in stocks.

If Fed policy and the economy remain stable, the spread between interest rates and inflation will remain near 3 percent, as was the case from 1983 through the first half of 1988. If the spread between interest rates and inflation ever rises above 5 percent again, bonds could once again become a superior investment for a few years. It's likely, however, that while you are spending years waiting for this to happen, the money could be more profitably invested in the stock market.

To summarize: Treasury bonds have zero risk of default, but their prices are likely to fluctuate 10 to 20 percent in the intervening years before maturity. Their real after-tax rate of return is usually close to zero. The only time this was not true was during the 1982–86 period, thanks to a unique set of circumstances that I don't think will be repeated.

CORPORATE BONDS: INSTANT JUNK?

Suppose you had a choice of purchasing two corporate bonds. One had a 9 percent rate of return and the other had a 30 percent rate. Which would you choose?

Obviously the bond with the 30 percent yield carried a much greater risk of default. In fact, if the market were pricing the bonds properly and the first bond was a Aaa corporate bond with a risk of default of about 1 percent, the risk of default on the other bond would be about 22 percent. Both would have an estimated risk-free yield of 8 percent, the same as the Treasury bond. Theoretically, therefore, it would make no difference which bond you purchased.

In the real world, however, several factors could intervene to upset your carefully planned calculations of which bonds produce the highest yields.

1. Most corporate bonds are "callable," while Treasuries generally are not. This means that if interest rates decline and bond prices rise, you may not be able to share in the gains.
2. Ratings can change literally overnight. The credit rating of a company may deteriorate because its earnings decline or—more likely these days—because it suddenly becomes the victim of a hostile takeover.
3. A group of investors and brokerage firms may act fraudulently to conceal the true risk of the bonds, making them appear much less risky than is actually the case—until it's too late.

Callable Bonds: Heads They Win, Tails You Lose

Suppose you had purchased a corporate bond in early 1982, when long-term interest rates were at their peak. Assume this bond was Aaa-rated—issued by one of the corporate giants, such as Exxon, General Electric, AT&T, or IBM—so there was virtually no chance of default. The yield on such a bond would have been at least 15 percent.

Now fast forward to 1986, when the interest rate on newly issued bonds of the same high quality had declined to 9 percent. You might feel fairly smug at that point. You would be earning 15 percent interest while others, who didn't have the foresight to buy at the right time, would be receiving only 9 percent. Or if you chose to sell the bond, you would have a capital gain of over 50 percent.

Except you wouldn't because these companies retired those high-yield bonds from circulation when rates fell. After all, they see no reason to pay 15 percent interest when the going rate is 9 percent. The fine print on corporate bonds usually states that after five years the corporation can recall the bond at par. As a result, the price never rises much above 100, your capital gain never materializes, and after five years your high yield disappears, too.

Of course, it's only a one-way street. If you happened to buy a bond when interest rates were 9 percent and five years later they rose to 15 percent, your bond could be underwater as much as 50 percent, but no kindhearted corporation will come and bail you out. So heads they win, tails you lose.

Most Treasury bonds are not callable, and thus make much better vehicles for long-term investments. Considering the fact that the spread on Aaa corporate bonds is usually only ½ to 1 percent higher than on Treasury securities, plus the fact that they carry a slightly higher risk and are callable, it's not clear why anyone would want to buy them as an investment—assuming they wanted bonds in the first place.

LBOs, Takeovers, and Other Manias

Having your bond called at par is far from the biggest problem you face with corporate bonds these days. The much greater risk is seeing your high-quality bond disintegrate into junk almost overnight. Investors who had purchased RJR Nabisco bonds before the buyout saw their value plummet 20 percent before they even had a chance to sell them.

The bondholders who purchased RJR Nabisco or other similar high-quality bonds cannot really be faulted for having made a bad investment decision; instead, "they wuz robbed." In fact, several large pension funds and insurance companies felt just that way about it and went to court, arguing that their rights as bondholders had been trampled in the financial restructuring. However, at press time, none of these suits had been successful.

Transforming high-quality bonds into junk overnight is capitalism run amok. Yet, for the most part—excluding insider trading—these transactions are all legal under existing laws. The only thing you can do about it is not buy high-quality corporate bonds in the first place, because that term is fast turning into an oxymoron.

JUNK BONDS: WORTH THE RISK?

It is one thing to be sandbagged after buying an Aaa-rated security only to find out the new owners have no intention of meeting their interest obligations. On the other hand, if the bond is initially presented as a high-risk, high-yield security, with all the caveats spelled out in advance, is that really so bad? Maybe some investors would prefer the trade-off of higher yield for higher risk. Before 1984, in fact, junk bonds weren't such a bad deal at all, and for many years their risk-adjusted yield was actually higher than on Treasury securities.

Old-time purveyors of junk bonds never pretended that there would be zero defaults. Their very name implies a less than sterling quality. If Treasury bond yields, which have zero risk of default, carried an 8 percent rate of interest, then junk bonds, with an estimated default risk of 4 percent, should have a yield of 12 percent to be equivalent. If in fact their yield was 15 percent, then even after adjustment for risk, the rate of return would be higher. Billions of dollars of junk bonds were sold on that basis.

There is nothing wrong with a sliding scale on bond yields relating risk and reward in a rational fashion. The giants of American industry, such as Exxon, IBM, GE, and AT&T, garnered the Aaa ratings, and hence offered the lowest yield. Further down the scale, well-managed but smaller companies paid a higher rate of return. And at the bottom of the heap were admittedly speculative ventures—Carl's Dynamic Random Access Memory Chips and Storm Door Company, Inc.—that did not purport to fool any would-be investors. If someone offers you a 20 percent rate of return, you know it's a risky proposition, and as long as the risks are clearly spelled out, it's a transaction that should benefit both parties.

Before 1983, bonds were usually secured by the assets of the corporation. Even if the company went belly-up, creditors could seize the rolling mills, railroad cars, or whatever, and collect most if not all of their money. Junk bonds differed in that they were backed not by any specific assets but by the expected future earnings of the corporations.

This wasn't necessarily bad. Before the banking system went haywire and banks started lending money for holes in the ground and Super Bowl bets—yes, that really did happen—many banks prospered by lending money to growing firms, backed by the expectation that debt could be repaid from future earnings. Just because a bond isn't backed by assets doesn't mean the company won't pay the interest and principal when due. After all, owners and executives of a company generally have a vested interest in keeping the company healthy—otherwise they would lose their jobs, stock options, and in many cases their reputations as astute managers. Of course, that was before the era of the golden parachute.

Even today, small, high-yield bonds issued by growing companies that have not yet risen to the point where they can obtain a Moody's or an S&P rating still represent a reasonable value. Some will default, but that risk can be adequately compensated for by higher yield. So buying high-yield bonds of rapidly growing companies used to be a respectable way of investing one's money. But that was before Michael Milken, working at Drexel Burnham, invented the multibillion-dollar junk bond scam. Essentially here's how it worked.

Company A needs to obtain financing but is unable to raise funds in the capital markets through normal channels. It turns to Drexel Burnham, which raises the money through a junk-bond issue. To sell this issue, Drexel then calls on Companies B and C, which would also like to raise money, and informs them that the deal is they must use part of the proceeds to buy some of Company A's bonds. Company A in turn must use some of its proceeds to buy bonds of Companies B and C, and the system cycles around indefinitely.

Anyone who has had the misfortune to sit in on a poker game where the house takes a cut out of each pot knows that eventually, no matter how good a player you are, the house ends up with all the money. That is what Drexel Burnham did; by taking its cut out of the same funds that had been recirculating through many different companies, it eventually ended up with billions of dollars, and left bondholders with essentially worthless securities. If Ivan Boesky had never existed, Drexel and Milken would eventually have headed into trouble anyway.

Many investors, realizing that individual junk bonds might fail, have opted for the relative safety of a junk-bond mutual fund. But because of the Drexel scam, even that won't work. Indeed, the single most important fact to realize about junk-bond mutual funds is that increased diversification won't protect you. In an updated version of Gresham's Law, the bad junk bonds drive out the good.

Suppose that for whatever reason—negative publicity on junk bonds, higher interest rates, an ensuing recession, war in the Middle East—investors get nervous and start to cash in their junk-bond funds, switching their assets into Treasury securities or money market funds backed by government-insured CDs. Unless the junk-bond fund in question is holding an unusually large amount of Treasury securities itself—which significantly dilutes the yield and essentially defeats the purpose—it will have to sell some of those bonds in order to fund the redemptions.

Now ask yourself: Is it going to sell those bonds that are already way underwater, selling at perhaps 25 cents or less on the dollar—and have to admit to the remaining investors that they took a huge loss—or is it going to sell those bonds that are the best performers in the portfolio, the ones that are trading at near par value?

The answer to this one is obvious. The funds sell off their best-performing assets to meet the redemptions, and the remaining investors are left with assets of lower and lower quality. If this charade proceeds long enough, the mutual funds are eventually left *exclusively with nonperforming assets*. In other words, it's not a question of whether you earn 14, 9, or even 0 percent. Your total return will end up being − 100 percent, which means you will lose not only all the interest but all the principal as well.

That is the real secret to junk-bond funds, and it explains why contrarian logic doesn't work for this particular class of assets. It isn't even an issue of whether 3, 5, or 10 percent of the junk bonds will default over the next few years. As redemptions increase, selective pruning of the portfolios will mean that only the worst junk of all will remain in the mutual fund.

In that case, what about abandoning the mutual fund route and, after doing some study, buying those relatively high-quality issues that aren't likely to default? You may succeed. But I'll warn you in advance that even many of the big players in this league are wearing blinders.

In fact, my nomination for the biggest ripoff of all time—and a deal that is headed toward ignominy—is the RJR Nabisco buyout.

RJR Nabisco has two major types of debt securities outstanding. One of them is the normal, garden-variety bond that pays cash interest payments at normal intervals. All those payments are being met on a timely basis and, at least to date, servicing of that debt is not in arrears. In fact, after the U.S. entered the Persian Gulf War, many of these bonds significantly appreciated in price.

The ticking time bomb, however, is a particularly nasty invention known as PIK bonds, meaning payment in kind. For these securities, the interest is paid not in cash but in more bonds. That way, RJR Nabisco doesn't have to shell out any actual money to service these debts. Of course, that game can't continue forever. Starting in 1993, RJR Nabisco must begin paying cash interest on the barrelhead to meet their obligations on these PIK securities.

If it's only play money until 1993, what difference does that make? Even if RJR Nabisco doesn't pay out the interest, it must accrue it on the books as an expense. If that expense rises too much, that could trigger debt-restriction covenants requiring it to sell more of its valuable assets at fire-sale prices. This quickly becomes a vicious circle, and when the game is completed, the total value of the assets is likely to be less than the $25 billion at which the deal was originally structured. That would lead to a total meltdown, with none of the RJR bonds worth anything more than the paper on which they are printed.

I'm not necessarily dead set against all junk bonds. Many of the "old style" bonds—those high-yield instruments floated by small but growing companies—are still reasonable investments, and since virtually all junk bonds were tarred and feathered in 1990, there may be some relative bargains available. But stay far away from any junk bond that was floated to finance a corporative takeover—and even farther away from any junk bond that pays you in even more junk instead of cold cash.

MUNICIPAL BONDS: BEATING THE TAXMAN?

All right. I'll admit you can't lose your money in a municipal bond (muni) through a takeover. I'll also concede that the interest is tax-free—at least most of the time. Furthermore, you can buy "insured" municipal bonds, so even if the municipality or other issuing agency fails to collect enough tax revenues to meet the interest payments, the bondholder will be paid the interest in full. If held until maturity, the bonds will also be redeemable at their original purchase price, even if the issuing agency is six feet under.

So in fairness to munis, if you buy high-quality bonds and hold them to maturity—that is, you won't need to cash them out in midstream—the after-tax rate of return will be considerably higher than on Treasury or corporate bonds. Over the past 20 years, the average yield on high-quality munis has been about 78 percent of that for Treasury bonds—and with the marginal tax rate at 31 percent and in some cases as high as 40 percent, the difference is substantial. In early 1991, the spread was even more favorable: The interest rate on munis averaged 86% of the Treasury bond yield and 80% of the Aaa Corporate bond yield. However, I still have a few caveats about what type of muni bond you should buy. With careful research, or by buying shares in a reputable municipal bond fund, you should be able to heed them.

Since there are literally thousands of state and local governments and taxing subdivisions that issue securities, it would be extremely difficult for an individual investor—or even a relatively sophisticated brokerage house—to keep track of the credit ratings of all these cities and towns. That's why most investors rely on the municipal-bond ratings prepared by Standard & Poor's and Moody's. These are generally considered the Bibles of municipal-bond ratings.

Occasionally, however, they come under heavy criticism for failing to keep up with changing economic conditions. The *Wall Street Journal*, in a blistering editorial entitled "The Last to Know," accused S&P and Moody's raters of pandering to the more liberal domains of the country, claiming that "many bond analysts are prejudiced in favor of liberal, big-spending governments." Referring to the over-rating of Massachusetts state bonds, the paper charged that "politics and cowardice intruded . . . the agencies did not avoid politics but immersed themselves in it. Those supposed guardians of financial probity, Standard & Poor's and Moody's, were the last to know. . . . The lesson is: When it comes to opinions of rating agencies, let the buyer beware." Eventually, S&P had to drop the Massachusetts ratings three separate times as revenue collections consistently fell short of expectations. Anyone who had bought Massachusetts bonds based on the Aa-plus rating would have found the prices far underwater once the rating readjustment was completed. According to the *Wall Street Journal*, you can't trust the rating services. I have no reason to disagree.

Another possible problem with munis is that the tax advantage is granted courtesy of Congress and could be revoked at any time. Before 1986, many muni bond salespeople claimed the Constitution said the federal government could not tax the obligations of the state and local governments. After the Tax Reform Act of 1986, that interpretation was indeed tested in the courts, and lo and behold, it turned out the muni bond salesmen were deficient in constitutional law. Congress can tax interest on municipal bonds at any rate it chooses.

This threw the muni markets into catatonic shock, with the result that from May through August 1986, the yields on muni bonds were actually higher than those on taxable Treasury securities. That was clearly an overreaction and soon dissipated. However, the price of munis dropped over 20 percent during that period; if you needed to sell those bonds in 1986, you would have taken a tremendous bath on what is supposed to be a "riskless" investment.

Congress was trying to end what it viewed as abusive use of muni bonds for corporate purposes. Many states and municipalities try to attract new industry by raising money for new plants at tax-free rates and passing the savings on to private corporations. These types of bonds had their tax exemptions terminated; interest on muni bonds for public purposes, such as schools, roads, waterworks, airports, etc., remained tax-free.

Nonetheless, I wouldn't be surprised if the tax advantages of municipal securities were further curtailed. For example, all municipal bond interest could be subject to the 21 percent alternative minimum tax. If that were to happen, bondholders would be locked into low yields that then became taxable, and couldn't sell the securities without taking a substantial capital loss.

Don't say it can't happen—that existing bondholders would be "grand-fathered" so the additional tax would not apply to them. We all thought that would be the case with the tax shelters purchased in the 1980s; even if tax reform were passed, deductions would not be denied to those who had invested in shelters several years earlier. However, when the Tax Reform Act of 1986 was signed into law, many would-be tax avoiders not only had to pay those hefty fees to the tax-shelter syndicates, but also had to pay taxes on the income they had previously sheltered—occasionally leading to a total penalty of over 50 percent of the allegedly sheltered income.

To many investors, municipal bonds suggest a security whose interest payments are backed by the general tax revenues of that municipality. While this is true in many cases, it certainly isn't true for most of them. Here's what to check.

The safest type of municipal bonds are those that are backed by the "full faith and credit" of the state or municipality in question. Naturally they carry somewhat lower interest rates. Most munis don't fall into this category, however, but are bonds issued by some particular agency, such as a housing authority, water district, or airport.

Airport-backed bonds are fairly popular these days, but even among them there are several differences. Some are backed by revenues collected from the entire airport. Others, however, are based only on a lease with a *specific* airline. So when Braniff went bankrupt in Kansas City, the bonds that were secured by the Braniff lease fell off the table. An unusual circumstance, perhaps—but you have to read the fine print on muni agency bonds.

Some muni bonds that are known to be funded by a shaky revenue basis have a secondary fallback in which the principal and interest are "guaranteed" by some bank or savings and loan. That's turned out to be a bad joke; many of those estimable financial institutions are now bankrupt themselves, so their guarantee is completely worthless.

Admittedly, only a small percentage of municipal bonds fall into these doubtful categories. But if you are looking for the maximum return, and your friendly broker points out one particular bond that has an exceptionally generous yield, I hope you'll take the time to find out precisely why. Most of the time, you'll uncover a can of worms.

Which brings us to the so-called municipal-bond insurance that some of the investment houses are currently pushing. Again, just so you won't think I'm deliberately painting a worst-case scenario, let's go back and see what happened to mortgage guaranty insurance several years ago.

Starting in 1957, a company called the Mortgage Guaranty Insurance Corporation, or MGIC for short, began to insure home mortgages. Many first-time homeowners who were short of liquidity wanted to buy a home with only 10 percent down instead of the usual 20 to 25 percent that banks usually require. They paid an extra ¼ percent on the interest rate for the mortgage—say, 6¼ instead of 6 percent (rates were lower then). MGIC would then insure the mortgage, meaning that it would pay the bank in case you defaulted and the value of the home was less than the remaining mortgage. For many years, real estate prices grew steadily, default rates were extraordinarily low, and MGIC was a very profitable cash cow.

However, real estate prices hyperventilated during the late 1970s, and when they came back to normal in the 1980s, many banks in Texas, Louisiana, Colorado, Arizona, and other former boomtime areas found that many homeowners were simply mailing in the key and walking away from the mortgage. So the banks went to MGIC to collect, and guess what? MGIC had by that time been bought out by Baldwin United, which had declared bankruptcy.

Fast forward to 1991, and there is your friendly smiling broker or bond salesperson who claims he has never given you a bad tip in your life, telling you that insured munis are the wave of the future. I'm not even hinting that the financial giants of the brokerage world are about to go bankrupt, but I certainly am suggesting you read the fine print very carefully. Because the prospectus is likely to reveal that in fact it isn't Merrill Lynch or Dean Witter or Prudential Bache that is insuring these munis, but a subsidiary of the firm that has *no assets*. In other words, if the bonds really do bomb out, the guarantee is worthless.

But just let's suppose, for purposes of argument, that these financial stalwarts are as honest as they say they are, and they really will stand behind each and every municipal bond they insure. While that would insure you against loss of interest payments or principal at maturity, no financial organization in its right mind will insure you against market risk. So if word gets around that the municipal agency of your choice is lagging behind in its revenue collection and its interest payments, the market price will drop suddenly, once again saddling you with a substantial capital loss—even if the insurance does kick in and the interest checks continue to flow on a regular basis.

Not all municipal bonds are risk-prone. However, except for Treasury securities, there are no financial guarantees in life. If municipal bonds appeal to you, at least take time to read the fine print and assess how solid the underlying revenue base really is. Because even the rating houses and major brokerage firms don't keep up with all the municipal bond issues.

MORTGAGE-BACKED SECURITIES: HIGHER YIELD, NO ADDITIONAL RISK

On a slightly more positive note, mortgage-backed securities (MBS) offer the full security of Treasury securities, but with a higher yield. Their only drawback is that they can be callable, depending on how fast individual homeowners pay off their mortgages.

MBS are one of a class of debt instruments that are formed by bundling individual mortgages or loans into a single security. This reduces the risk of default. In addition, MBSs have the following characteristics.

1. These are pass-through securities, which means investors receive their pro-rated portion from payment of both interest and principal.
2. These securities are guaranteed by a government agency; usually a federal agency, although some states have set up their own mortgage associations.

In addition to mortgages, similar securities exist for auto loans, student educational loans, and personal loans, but since these aren't traded as widely and involve somewhat greater risks, I'll stick to the mortgage-backed variety here.

The biggest player in this league is the Government National Mortgage Association, ubiquitously known as Ginnie Mae. Other important organizations are the Federal Housing Administration (FHA), the Federal National Mortgage Association (Fannie Mae) the Federal Home Loan Mortgage Association (Freddie Mae), and the Student Loan Marketing Association (Sallie Mae); income from the latter is also exempt from state and local taxes. However, only GNMA and FHA bonds carry a federal government guarantee, while the others have minimal risk of default, they are no longer unconditionally guaranteed federal government, although the risk on the other agencies is extremely low.

Ginnie Mae and Fannie Mae bundle many FHA and VA mortgages into a single mortgage-backed security. This security is then sold on the market and traded like any other bond. The original coupon rate is based on the average interest rate on all the mortgages that comprise the security. Its price then moves with market forces; if interest rates decline, the price of the bond appreciates, and if rates rise, the price declines.

Because mortgage rates are higher than Treasury bond rates, these instruments yield a substantially higher rate of return; yet they are government-guaranteed. The spread isn't equal to the entire difference, since the issuing agency takes its cut, but ordinarily Ginnie Mae and Fannie Mae securities carry an interest rate about 1 percent above Treasury bonds.

Since these are pass-through securities, investors receive a proportion of the actual monthly mortgage payment, which includes principal as well as interest. This generally boosts the near-term yield even more, usually by ¼ to ½ percent. Since Ginnie Maes are often based on relatively few mortgages—40 to 50—the cash flow can be much more uneven if a few large mortgage holders decide to prepay. Fannie Mae securities, on the other hand, are generally backed by thousands of individual mortgages, and hence generally provide a more stable cash flow.

It sounds as if these bonds carry a government guarantee against default and have a rate of return 1½ percent above Treasury securities. What's the catch?

Somewhat surprisingly, there isn't a very big one. The only drawback is that holders of the individual mortgages that comprise this security usually prepay their loans. While the stated contract length of most mortgages is 25 to 30 years, the average actual length of a mortgage is 8 years, because people move often or prepay when interest rates decline. If the latter occurs, the funds must be reinvested in other assets carrying a lower rate of return. This is very similar to the "callable" aspect of corporate bonds and is the major difference between MBS and Treasury securities.

If interest rates rise, however, the interest payments will remain at the same level even if individual mortgage holders default. In that case, the profits of Fannie Mae and Ginnie Mae will decline and you might not want to hold their stocks. But MBS holders don't share this risk. As a result, mortgage-backed securities have increased rapidly in popularity in recent years. If you do favor bonds, this is one of the better instruments.

Finally, it is possible to get a tax-free mortgage-backed security based on housing loans made by the states. The State of New York Mortgage Authority is known, not too surprisingly, as Sonny Mae; other states have less colorful acronyms. The interest is tax-free and is generally well above other tax-free muni rates because it is a pass-through rate from mortgages for low-income housing. However, these are definitely *not* guaranteed by the federal government, only by the state governments. The risk is somewhat greater, because a drop in the credit rating of the state will depress the price of securities. If you're willing to hold to maturity, though, they're your best tax-free yield.

CONVERTIBLE BONDS:
THE BEST OF BOTH WORLDS?

Convertible bonds act like a stock when the stock market goes up and like a bond when the stock market goes down. At first glance, this sounds like the best of all possible worlds. However, unlike mortgage-backed securities, convertible bonds are risky because of the problems with all corporate bonds. In other words, the advantages of convertible bonds apply only if the company doesn't get taken over or gobbled up by LBO raiders.

The convertible bond field is rather thinly traded, and the exact yield obviously depends on the convertibility provisions, but usually the yield on these bonds is only slightly less than the yield on a straight corporate bond of similar risk. Plus, you have the opportunity to cash in on substantial gains if the stock of that company rises significantly.

The major problem with convertible bonds is the same one that occurs with any corporate bond—it could transmogrify into junk before your very eyes. In that case, of course, the convertibility option is worthless, since the value of the stock has slumped precipitously as well. You could protect yourself against this eventuality by buying a put option or selling the stock short, but then you are defeating the major purposes—low risk and simplicity—of holding a bond.

The main reason firms issue convertible bonds is that their credit ranking is far from Aaa; if it were good enough, they would simply issue straight debt. Considering the equity kicker, the cost to the issuer of convertible bonds is significantly more expensive than that for a regular bond, and hence companies will choose this route only if other, more well-trodden paths aren't available to them.

As I noted above, the greatest risk to corporate bondholders occurs when mature companies are taken over and stripped of their assets. This ploy doesn't work for raiders unless the value of the assets is substantially greater than the current value placed on them by the stock market. Thus raiders are usually attracted to companies with low stock-price to book-value ratios. A rapidly growing company whose stock price is well above book value has only a minuscule chance of a recapitalization and down-grading of its bonds. Furthermore, stocks of rapidly growing companies should have a better chance of appreciating enough so that the convert-ibility option is actually exercised. Thus their convertible bonds could turn out to yield a high total return. However, most of these companies don't need to issue convertible bonds; they can raise money through stocks. Besides, the obvious question then becomes: If you can identify these nifty high-growth companies, why not buy the stock?

PUT BONDS: HEDGING AGAINST HIGHER INTEREST RATES

The major risk of bonds, excluding default, is that interest rates will rise in the near future and the value of the bonds will then be far underwater, so those who sell before maturity will be saddled with a substantial capital loss. However, one type of security enables you to offset this risk, which is known as a put bond.

Suppose interest rates were to rise from 9 to 12 percent over the next few years. The value of a 15-year bond with a 9 percent coupon rate would fall from $1,000 to about $800—precisely the type of situation most investors want to avoid. However, put bonds permit the investor, on certain specified dates known as *put dates*, to sell the bonds back to the original issuers at the full $1,000 face value. These bonds aren't just issued by desperate companies that have no other means of raising capital either.

In a typical year, over $10 billion worth of put bonds are issued by reputable firms, including such financial giants as Citicorp, Chase Manhattan Bank, and Ford Motor Credit.

From time to time many of us have our doubts about the financial acumen of many of these mammoth financial institutions, but those questions usually arise in the areas of making multimillion-dollar loans to borrowers with less than sterling credit references. Why would any rational financial institution offer you this guarantee to buy back an $800 bond for $1,000?

First and most obvious, you earn a lower interest rate in the meantime. The trade-off for this guarantee is usually a ½ or even a 1 percent reduction in the interest rate.

Second, the companies are gambling that rates won't go up very much. As a result, put option bonds are much more popular in years when financial forecasters think interest rates are likely to decline than when they are expected to rise.

Third, and perhaps most important, these financial institutions assume that not everyone will exercise their options, but will be content to wait until the bonds mature. Not everyone needs to cash out their bonds well before the maturity dates. If you plan to hold to maturity, you would be better off simply buying a higher-yield bond in the first place—but people do like to buy insurance, and this particular brand isn't that expensive.

Two cautionary notes and one unexpected bonus feature of put bonds:

If you decide to buy put bonds, make sure they aren't callable. No, this isn't another comedy routine. Some of these put bonds can be redeemed at par if interest rates fall, just as is the case for other bonds. Thus you not only end up losing your capital gain, but in the meantime you've been earning a below-market rate of interest. Avoid these.

Be sure you observe the put dates, and let the issuer know whether or not you will be exercising your option. The bonds can be returned only on certain specified dates; it isn't like calling up your broker and placing your order to sell 100 shares of Exxon. Those who miss the option date must wait for the next turn at bat; in the meantime, of course, the value of the bonds could fall substantially.

Muni Puts: The Only Free Lunch in Town

The bonus feature: Put bonds exist for munis as well as corporate bonds, but the difference here is that for certain issues, a municipal bond with a put option actually carries a higher yield than one with similar risk and maturity without the option. You not only get protection against capital loss, but a higher yield to boot. That sounds like a violation of the no free lunch code—so what's the catch?

Believe it or not, there isn't any. And it's not that financial officers of municipalities are dunderheads either. Municipalities are permitted to issue put option bonds to replace short-term debt issues, thereby saving on the cost of floating new issues frequently. Those costs, which include underwriting and legal fees for each new issue, are often substantial. So your savings come out of the fees that the brokers and lawyers would otherwise receive. You can earn a higher rate of return at their expense. So let's hear it for the muni puts!

Before cheering this turn of events too lustily, I should point out that this option is usually offered only on short-term municipal debt, which tends to carry a substantially lower interest rate than long-term debt. So your savings won't be enormous. It is, however, a pleasant little cul-de-sac in a world where most returns are diluted by the financial establishment.

ZERO COUPON BONDS: THE FINANCIAL ZOO

The general concept of a zero coupon bond can apply to any Treasury, corporate, or municipal debt instrument. The idea is quite straightforward. Ordinarily, when you purchase a bond it comes with a set of coupons which you send in to receive the quarterly interest payments. In the old days rich old dowagers actually used to sit and clip coupons; now all this is done by computer, but the idea is exactly the same. When the bond has reached its maturity date, all the coupons have been used up, and only the face amount of the bond is left, which is then remitted for its original value.

The value of the interest coupon will never change, regardless of market conditions. If the bond has a face value of $1,000 and a coupon rate of 12 percent per year, the bondholder will receive $30 each quarter regardless of what happens to market interest rates in the interim. However, as I've pointed out several times, the value of the bond itself will decline if interest rates rise.

To separate the stable coupon payments from the fluctuating capital value, you could strip off the coupons and sell them separately, leaving the bond without any of its coupons at all. For fairly obvious reasons, this became known as a zero coupon bond. The big brokerage houses jazzed up the concept with feline names—CATS, TIGRS, and LIONS, for example—but the concept is the same. You buy a bond without any coupons. Naturally you pay a lot less for it. But how much less?

When zero coupon bonds were first introduced, long-term interest rates were very high, with many of them near 14 percent. Suppose you had bought a zero coupon 30-year Treasury bond when interest rates were at their peak. The present value of the bond would be a figure low enough that, when compounded at 14 percent for 30 years, it would come out to exactly $1,000. That means you could purchase a $1,000 bond for only $19.63. Now is that a bargain or is that a bargain?

If you've followed my logic throughout the book, by now you'll recognize this as just one more example of the miracle of compound interest. But a huge number of investors were sufficiently inveigled by the pitch to buy in at that price—and the good news is that, for once, they weren't wrong. The bad news, however, is that since interest rates were near an all-time peak then, this opportunity won't be repeated.

Originally it was hoped that the gains in zero coupon bonds might be tax-deferred, just as you don't pay gains on the increase in the price of your favorite stock until you sell it. But the IRS vetoed that idea immediately. You have to pay income tax each year on the gain in the value of the bond—even though you don't receive any money. For that reason, zeros make sense only for IRAs, Keoghs, or similar tax-deferred retirement plans—unless it's a zero-coupon municipal bond. Obviously these are not for current income, because there isn't any.

Just like other bonds, zeros can be callable. If you choose this investment vehicle, make sure you don't fall into that trap.

You can even buy zero coupon junk bonds. Personally, I'd rather head for the track. You're betting that some highly leveraged, underfinanced company will be in business and healthy in 20 or 30 years—and you won't have received a penny in the meantime. At least with ordinary junk bonds you usually get some interest payments before they go belly-up.

Finally—and most important—zero coupon bonds were a great idea when interest rates were near their all-time highs. Now that interest rates have declined to normal, zeros have lost most of their charm. Their major advantage was that investors could lock in high rates of return when interest rates fell. That was indeed the case, and I enthusiastically recommended zeros in 1984 and 1985. Now that rates have returned to normal levels and are just as likely to go up as down in the next few years, they have no special advantages left.

To summarize zeros:

1. You don't get any income until the security matures.
2. Unless the funds are in a tax-deferred account, or unless it's a muni

zero, you will have to pay taxes on income you haven't received.
3. If interest rates decline, the price of zeros *rises faster* than other bonds.
4. If interest rates rise, the price of zeros *falls faster* than other bonds.

Thus what zeros boil down to is a guess on what interest rates will do in the future. To paraphrase my earlier comment, if you know that, you don't need zeros at all.

EXCUSES FOR BUYING BONDS

In spite of these acerbic comments, I realize lots of individuals invest in bonds or bond funds. The usual reasons given are:

1. I can't stand the fluctuations in the stock market; it upsets my stomach. Besides, I always pick the wrong stocks or buy in and cash out at the wrong time.

   This is all too true for many of us. But if that's your problem, buy an index fund—one that exactly mirrors the S&P 500—and follow a buy-and-hold strategy. In the long run, you're virtually guaranteed to come out ahead of bonds.

   You're skeptical? I'll make you a deal. This is a bona fide offer. My attorney has approved it. I'll invest your money for you for 10 years, and I *guarantee* that it will earn at least as high a rate of return as could have been obtained from a 10-year U.S. Treasury note—and I'll make up any shortfall at the end of 10 years. However, in return for that guarantee, I'll split the profits with you— the return of the stocks I do pick over and above the return on bonds—50–50. Still interested? Then give me a call.

2. Yields on bonds are unusually high by historical standards. When they return to normal, I'll get capital gains as well as a generous rate of interest.

   This was true from 1982 through 1985, but it's no longer true. Furthermore, if you buy the bond as an original issue and hold it to maturity, there will never be a capital gain.

3. I need the income now and don't care about capital gains in the future. Either I have no heirs or I don't believe in spoiling them.

   If for some reason you have good reason to believe you won't live much longer, and the coupon payment from the bonds is the principal or entire source of your income, then yes, you have a point. In that case, however, you can do even better with an annuity—you won't have any principal left when you die, but under these assumptions that doesn't matter. Either way, bonds come in no better than second.

Just remember that inflation does miserable things to the purchasing power of your capital. Suppose you retire at 65 and are fortunate enough to live another 25 years. Also, assume that inflation is 6 percent per year and real growth is 3 percent per year. Because you need income, you pick some conservative stocks that pay a 5 percent dividend and grow only 6 percent per year, instead of the average growth rate of 8 percent. Several utilities, oil companies, and banks fit that criterion.

Let's say you have $500,000 set aside for investment. The first year your income is $40,000 from bonds, and only $30,000 from stocks. But 25 years from now, the situation is entirely reversed. Your $40,000 annual income from the bonds has shrunk in purchasing power to only $8,465. On the other hand, your stock portfolio has increased in value from $500,000 to $2.15 million, assuming a 6 percent growth rate. With a 6 percent dividend, your nominal income is $129,000 per year, compared with $40,000 from the bonds. Thus your purchasing power rises as you get older. Also, if such things matter to you, you can leave a much more valuable estate to your heirs, favorite charity, or other beneficiary.

. . . AND GUIDELINES IF YOU DO

By now it's presumably obvious that I've never owned any bonds, and I probably never will. But if you do buy bonds because you need the current income, my principal guidelines are as follows.

1. High-yield bonds are all right if they're issued by legitimate companies, but don't be tempted by junk bonds generated in an LBO scam. There's not only a greater chance of default, but it's a rigged game.
2. If you have a substantial amount of income, municipal bonds will provide a higher after-tax rate of return, providing the tax rules aren't changed again. The best bet is general-obligation bonds— the ones that are backed by tax revenues of the entire political subdivision, not just one small segment. Try to buy bonds issued by districts that you know something about, or in areas that are fiscally stable—and don't invest too heavily in areas where economic prosperity depends on natural resource prices that could fluctuate wildly.
3. If tax considerations aren't a problem, government-backed mortgage securities are usually the best buy. The principal is guaranteed by the federal government, and the interest rate is usually about 1 percent higher than Treasury securities, plus a slight additional

increment from the repayment of principal. The only problem is the underlying mortgages may be paid ahead of time if interest rates decline further.

4. If the spread between long-term interest rates and inflation is "normal," which I would define as between 2 and 4 percent, don't lock in unnecessarily long maturities. The interest rate on a 5- to 7-year security is usually just about the same as one for 30 years. Give yourself added flexibility. If, on the other hand, the spread between interest rates and inflation is unusually high, by which I mean above 5 percent, take advantage and lock in the yields for as long as possible. However, this has happened only once in the past century, and I doubt it will happen again.

5. Finally, if you are truly risk-averse, invest your money in $100,000 CDs at federally insured banks. Your principal is 100 percent guaranteed, they can't call your deposit, it won't diminish in value if interest rates rise—and over the long run, it pays the same rate of interest as Treasury bonds.

However, you will never get rich by buying bonds or CDs—which brings us full circle to my opening comments. If you want to beat inflation and taxes, don't invest in any fixed-income asset. It's better to take some risk in your investment portfolio—and reach your lifetime goal of becoming a multimillionaire.

Epilogue

When I first started planning this book, the stock market had just tripled over the past five years, Michael Milken was about to earn over $500 million for one year's work, and Donald Trump was—he said—on his way to becoming the country's wealthiest man.

Few tears will be shed for Milken, Trump, or other high-stakes players who Lost It All in the various market declines from 1987 through 1990. Those reversals restored a long-overdue sense of balance in financial markets. But they also fell on those who had not speculated wildly but had simply tried to accumulate wealth in the time-honored way of leveraging real estate, seeking the highest yield on fixed-income securities, and investing their money with the fund managers who seemed to have the best track records. Even less fortunate were those who lost their life savings at non-federally insured banks or credit unions, and those whose contractual pension benefits were not honored.

As these words are being written in April, 1991, the Persian Gulf War has ended, oil prices and interest rates have returned to normal, the stock market has rebounded sharply, and recovery seems to be right around the corner. Nonetheless, the weaknesses of the economy still overwhelm its strengths. The budget deficit is enormous and shows no signs of decreasing, profit margins are at record lows, tax rates are being boosted again after a decade of stability, and inflation continues to rise faster than the average paycheck. Accumulating wealth in the 1990s will not be nearly as easy as it was in the 1980s.

If you were to use Evans Investment Advisors to guide you through the shoals of investing in the 1990s, of course I'd be pleased. But if I've been able to open your eyes to the basic investment relationship that should be the most profitable in the future, and shown you how to avoid the most common errors and scams that plague investors, I'll be delighted. And if I can help you to achieve financial independence and security on your own, this book will have accomplished its primary goal.

May you enjoy financial success in the 1990s—and far beyond.

—Michael K. Evans

Index

About the Author

MICHAEL K. EVANS is chairman and president of Evans Economics, Inc., which he founded in 1979, and Evans Investment Advisors, Inc., which he started in 1984. One of the nation's foremost econometricians, he was previously president of Chase Econometric Associates, Inc., which was later sold to the Chase Manhattan Bank. Before that, Evans was assistant and associate professor of economics at the Wharton School, where he and Nobel Laureate Lawrence R. Klein developed the Wharton Model.

Now a resident of Boca Raton, Florida, Evans divides his time between Florida, Washington, D.C., and Cape Cod. Author of five other books and over fifty articles, he appears frequently on major network news programs and morning talk shows, and is regularly quoted in *The Wall Street Journal, The New York Times*, and other leading publications.

Evans is a contributing writer to *GQ* magazine, where he writes the "Money" column and a contributing editor at *Investment Vision,* where he writes the "Market Letter." He has written a syndicated column for UPI, "Dollars and Trends," and is also a contributing editor at *Industry Week,* where he has written a regular column since 1980.

In 1975, Evans pioneered the concept of the Monthly Tracking Model, which linked the short-term relationship between economic variables and financial markets. This work was later expanded to become the Electronic News Service (ENS), which provides a continuously updated flow of information to thousands of institutional and individual clients, enabling them to make more timely and intelligent financial planning decisions.

To receive more information about ENS, the various newsletters offered by Evans Investment Advisors, Inc., and your *free* update of the information contained in this book, or to learn more about other financial planning services offered by the Evans group, please call 1-800-833-4437 or write to Evans Investment Advisors, Inc., P.O. Box 25303, Washington, D.C. 20007.